INCOME TO
IMPACT

The Financial Stewardship
of Not-for-Profit and Public
Sector Organisations

2nd edition

Adrian Poffley

DIRECTORY OF SOCIAL CHANGE

'Every organisation – whether a national Government or a local NGO – is under pressure to deliver results with limited resources. **Income to Impact** shows what it takes to succeed. Leaders should read it carefully if they are serious about improving performance and productivity.'
Sir Michael Barber, former Head of the UK Prime Minister's Delivery Unit

'In these tough economic times those of us who work in the voluntary and public sectors must make every penny count for those we exist to serve. **Income to Impact** shows what financial management with the beneficiary in mind means. Adrian Poffley writes with the authority that comes from an impressive track record of designing and implementing innovative, robust and high impact management practices in organisations as diverse as The Refugee Council and The World Bank.'
Naaz Coker, Chair of St George's Healthcare NHS Trust, UK

'Most public sector and nonprofit managers spend their time managing budgets and people rather than meeting the purpose of the organization and designing systems that help them to achieve this purpose. The result is that many managers are dissatisfied and demoralized. In this excellent book Adrian Poffley not only explores these problems but also provides a roadmap for change based on leading-edge thinking and practice. This book should be mandatory reading for all CFOs (and even CEOs) of public sector and other nonprofit organizations who really want to improve their management practices and transform the performance of their organizations.'
Jeremy Hope, co-founder of Beyond Budgeting Round Table and author of *Reinventing the CFO*

'An insightful book that challenges conventional wisdom and sets out new ways of stewarding financial resources more rigorously.'
Mike Hudson, founder and Director of Compass Partnership and author of *Managing Without Profit*

'Adrian Poffley argues persuasively for the need to weave process-oriented systems thinking into the management of financial resources in public sector and nonprofit organizations. His concept of "Income to Impact" replaces the traditional "ends justify the means" logic taught in business schools with a "means are the ends-in-the-making" logic once taught by W. Edwards Deming and followed for years by management in Toyota. **Income to Impact** opens a door to new thinking that will be indispensable to managers of public sector and nonprofit organizations around the world.'
Professor H. Thomas Johnson, Portland State University, USA

'This insightful and well-written book covers all the important topics thoroughly, drawing on many sources to provide a systematic guide that acknowledges and tackles the tricky realities of organizational life. It will be invaluable to anyone who manages the finances and performance of not-for-profit and public sector organisations. I soon found I had made many notes as I read and I think readers are almost guaranteed to learn something important they didn't know before.'
Matthew Leitch, author of *Intelligent Internal Control & Risk Management*

Published by
Directory of Social Change
24 Stephenson Way
London NW1 2DP
Tel: 08450 77 77 07; Fax: 020 7391 4804
email: publications@dsc.org.uk
www.dsc.org.uk
from whom further copies and a full publications catalogue are available.

Directory of Social Change Northern Office
Federation House, Hope Street, Liverpool L1 9BW
Policy & Research 0151 708 0136; email: research@dsc.org.uk

Directory of Social Change is a Registered Charity no. 800517

First published 2002
Reprinted 2009
Second edition 2010

ISBN 978 1 906294 45 8

British Library Cataloguing in Publication Data
A catalogue record for this book is available from the British Library

Cover design by Kate Bass
Text designed by Kate Bass and Richard Poffley
Typeset by Marlinzo Services, Frome
Printed and bound in the United Kingdom by CPI Antony Rowe, Chippenham

Contents

Preface   vii

About the author   x

Foreword   xi

Acknowledgements   xii

1 Introduction   1

Part 1 **Clear strategic direction**   15

2 Setting direction   17

3 Setting and implementing strategy   39

4 Case studies in setting direction and strategy   57

Part 2 **Robust financial framework**   73

5 The overall financial framework   75

6 The level, type and source of income   83

7 The level, form and matching of funds   99

8 Managing assets for financial health   115

9 The level, distribution and effectiveness of expenditure   127

10 Establishing effective risk-control practices   139

Part 3 **Aligned resources**   159

11 The allocation traps   161

12 Allocation aids   173

Part 4 **Dynamic financial management**   187

13 A new financial stewardship   189

14 Step 1: monitor   201

15 Step 2: forecast   223

16 Step 3: aim   243

17 Step 4: plan   257

18 Step 5: act   279

Part 5 **Enabling environment**   293

19 Roles: determining the spread of responsibility   295

20 Capabilities: employing the requisite financial skills   313

21 Managing information with technology   335

Bibliography   351

Index   359

v

For Mariela, Jonathan and Alison

Preface

It is eight years since *Financial Stewardship of Charities* was published in early 2002. As the title implies its focus was exclusively on charities – UK ones – reflecting my own experience as an honorary treasurer and finance executive based in the middle of such organisations. It sought to present a new financial management model for voluntary organisations; one based on nimble, responsive practices in the face of operating uncertainty. It aimed to provide a complete, yet straightforward guide on how to use a charity's financial resources to maximum effect *despite* uncertainty, grounded in particular in the experiences of Sightsavers International, where I held the position of Finance & Support Services Director and the Refugee Council on whose board I served.

Just as *Financial Stewardship* was published, the story of Sightsavers International's experience with an innovative approach to financial management began to attract wider attention. The charity became one of the first not-for-profit participants of the Beyond Budgeting Round Table (BBRT), a global consortium of mainly international commercial organisations funding research into performance management practices in the age of uncertainty and discontinuous change, where it was recognised as one of the 'barrier breakers' (www.bbrt.org). It was nominated for charity awards and received public commendation for having 'pioneered dynamic decision making suitable for an uncertain operating environment' (UK Charity Awards, 2001); UK national press coverage headlined the potential of its approach to 'revolutionise financial management' (Caulkin, 2003); and an academic case study on the organisation's approach to financial management was written for teaching use at a leading Canadian Business School (Lindsay and Mark, 2005). Early reaction outside the UK to *Financial Stewardship* confirmed the book's international relevance. Further, Sightsavers' participation in the BBRT quickly confirmed that the adaptive management principles promoted by the BBRT and its members, and the management methodology implemented by the charity, had wide applicability across sectors and national borders.

My recruitment by the World Bank in Washington, DC in 2003 – specifically to contribute to the design and implementation of reforms to the institution's corporate performance management practices – provided an opportunity to test the truth of this supposition from within one of the most extraordinarily complex, diverse organisations imaginable. It quickly became apparent that the performance management challenges applicable to an NGO with an annual turnover of £32 million (Sightsavers International, 2008) and an International Finance Institution lending US$47 billion a year (World Bank, 2009c) to developing countries are, in essence, the same: how best to use the money available to it in conditions of uncertainty given its development mandate, and how to assess the cost-effectiveness of its chosen actions. The scale of operations may be vastly different and the level of political and administrative complexity almost incomparable. Nevertheless, all not-for-profit and public sector organisations must grapple with setting objectives, defining direction, and aligning strategies, work programs, staffing and money. The symptoms of that struggle are prevalent everywhere: difficulties in measuring success; in prioritising and therefore in making trade-offs between competing demands on the organisation's focus and resources; and, most noticeable of all, flawed financial planning and monitoring processes, dominated by annual budgets and year-end targets that drive behaviour that significantly dilutes organisational effectiveness. Reform of management practices in the World Bank has proved a tough journey so far, but even in this most change-resistant of cultures some important progress has been made. The budget preparation process has been streamlined, planning ranges within a multi-year horizon have become the norm, and the quality of business reviews has improved significantly.

Above all, working in the World Bank and in the United States has assured me that the key themes and principles of the first edition are relevant to a much broader constituency of organisations, big and small, across the not-for-profit and public sectors worldwide. *Income to Impact* therefore builds on *Financial Stewardship*, complementing the UK charity case study material with illustrative practice from within the World Bank and the international public sector. New chapters offer insights on the huge challenges of setting clear direction and allocating resources effectively. Other chapters have been updated or extended to include new material. My aim throughout has been to embed the function of financial stewardship within the much broader responsibility of managing organisational performance. Extensive references to leading thinkers and practitioners in organisational performance management serve to point the reader to up-to-date concepts, practices and debates. They demonstrate how much of value there is to share across organisations of all types.

The roots of the first edition are not forgotten, however. The appeals from leaders and managers of organisations for clarity and guidance on how to manage the finances remain as vocal as ever. The economic crisis that has enveloped all organisations across the globe has placed unprecedented focus on the financial management responsibilities that must be discharged, even though many governing bodies of not-for-profit entities meet as a board for just a few hours each year. Ever greater accountability is expected. The controls industry has proliferated in recent years placing ever more stringent demands on leaders to justify their organisation's actions and demonstrate its results. Rapid globalisation is forcing organisations to collaborate, to find new ways of working. Chief executives, trustees and governors have no choice but to invest in understanding the financial fundamentals that underpin the capacity of the organisation to deliver its purpose. They have to understand the relationship between the income they generate and the impact they have and how to leverage the former in pursuit of the latter. The finance function is right at the heart of that challenge. The finance fraternity cannot hide in the back-office counting the numbers.

The title *Income to Impact* captures the essence of the real job facing leaders, operations and finance: how best to convert income into impact. Organisational success has to be measured in terms of the ability to deliver beneficial impact with the resources available.

Income to Impact reflects the ideas and experiences of many people. I would like to thank my colleagues at the World Bank, my fellow trustees on the board of the International Agency for the Prevention of Blindness (IAPB), and those with whom I worked at Voluntary Service Overseas (VSO), National Asthma Campaign, Sightsavers International and The Refugee Council. With humility and admiration I praise the guidance and leadership I have received over the years from Ken Caldwell, Naaz Coker, Christian Garms, David Green, Nick Hardwick, Achim von Heynitz, Andrew Hind, Martin Kyndt, Melinda Letts, Jennie Meadows, Dick Porter, Nag Rao, Kate Sayer, Hugh Taylor, Hasan Tuluy, Julia Unwin and John Wilton. Let me also acknowledge the continued pioneering work of the BBRT under the direction of Peter Bunce, Robin Fraser, Jeremy Hope and Steve Player. I would like to thank Caroline Harper, Chief Executive of Sightsavers International, for her willingness to allow me to share the charity's latest material and experiences with a wider audience. I am also grateful to my brother Richard Poffley for the many hours and ideas that he has invested in the book and acknowledge with gratitude the collaboration and guidance of Kate Bass, John Martin, Christopher Moore and Lucy Muir-Smith at DSC.

Finally, I thank my family. I salute the inspiring lives and lifelong support of my parents, Michael and Betty, my brothers Richard, Mark and Christopher and their families. In particular at this time, I pay tribute to my mother. Through her life of unconditional, dedicated love she has had more influence on this book than she will ever know. Above all, I thank the three people who have been immeasurably impacted by this book even before its publication. Completing *Income to Impact* has placed a heavy burden over many months on Mariela, my wife, and on Jonathan and Alison, our children. I dedicate this to them hopeful that, in their eyes, it will justify the sacrifices they have made. Their unwavering support, encouragement and total belief in the book has been extraordinary. Without their love and example *Income to Impact* would never have happened. I hope it encourages them to continue to be the wonderful people that they are, living meaningful lives, having beneficial impact on others.

Adrian Poffley
Washington DC
August 2010

About the author

Adrian Poffley joined the World Bank in Washington DC in 2003, where he is currently Chief Administrative Officer, Human Resources. Previously he was Senior Resource Management Officer, Corporate Finance & Risk Management. Before joining the Bank, Adrian spent 13 years in the UK voluntary sector including as Director of Finance & Support Services of Sightsavers International and Chief Accountant of Voluntary Service Overseas. He has been Honorary Treasurer of the International Agency for the Prevention of Blindness since 2004, and previously served for eight years on the board of the Refugee Council in the same role. He is a Fellow of The Chartered Institute of Management Accountants. The first edition of *Income to Impact*, called *Financial Stewardship of Charities* was published in 2002.

Adrian can be contacted at www.incometoimpact.com.

Foreword

The task of governing, managing and leading not-for-profit and public sector organisations is in itself an immense privilege. To be charged with the distribution of resource for the common good must be one of the greatest honours available to any of us. And yet, too often academic and managerial text books assume that skills, knowledge and experience from the private sector can simply be imported. Adrian Poffley's thoughtful, challenging and deeply committed book comes from a different impulse. With a clear unblinking focus on the need to maximise the impact of every pound or dollar spent, Adrian Poffley brings to this work wide experience, deep knowledge and abundant commitment to explain the very real, and very different priorities, pressures and purposes of the not-for-profit and public sectors.

It is easy for commentators to dismiss both sectors as fluffy, unfocused and insufficiently disciplined in the allocation of time, money and carbon. So too it is easy for those who lead organisations in these sectors to hide behind generalisations and to protest that measurement only detracts from our core purpose. In elegant and insightful analysis this book challenges both these stances.

Highlighting excellent practice from across both the not-for-profit and public sectors, this book demonstrates their capability and commitment, making the indisputable case that efficiency and economy can be the hallmarks of high performing not-for-profit and public organisations. But this book also makes the case that organisations which exist for the public benefit cannot avoid this obligation. Perhaps even more than companies with a single bottom line for which they need to account, not-for-profit and public sector organisations need to manage increasingly scarce resources brilliantly if any of us are to achieve any of our ambitions.

Practical as well as inspirational, this book serves as an urgent reminder to those of us seeking to lead such organisations through a very challenging external environment, that our greater purpose is only serviced by high-quality stewardship, innovative approaches, and most importantly a clear and unwavering focus on the needs of our beneficiaries. To do any less is to let down people in poverty everywhere. This book is an excellent guide to making sure that we all avoid squandering the resource that is so desperately needed.

Julia Unwin CBE
Chief Executive
Joseph Rowntree Foundation

Acknowledgements

We are grateful to the following people and organisations for their permission to reproduce their material(s).

ACEVO, London, for excerpts from: 'Full Cost Recovery', www.fullcostrecovery. org.uk; *Funding our Future: Core Costs Revisited* Julia Unwin, 2001; *Partners in Leadership* by Becky Blackmore, Richard Hardy and Christina Hogg, 1998.

John Argenti (author), for excerpts from *Your Organization: What is it for?*, London, McGraw Hill, 1993.

David Axson (author) for excerpts from 'Rolling Forecasts', www.davidaxson.com, n.d.

Bond for excerpts from *Statement of Principles*, London, January 2006.

Cengage Learning Inc. for excerpts from Herzlinger/Nitterhouse, *Financial Accounting and Managerial Control for Nonprofit Organizations*, 1E. © 1994 South-Western, a part of Cengage Learning, Inc. Reproduced by permission. www.cengage.com/permissions.

Charity Commission, London, HMSO, for excerpts from *Accounting and Reporting by Charities: Statement of Recommended Practice*, rev. 2005, HMSO; *Charities' Reserves*, CC19, 2008; *Charities and Reserves*, CC19, 2010; *The Essential Trustee: What You Need to Know*, CC03, 2008; 'Key Principles of Good Governance', www.charity-commission.gov.uk, 2010. Crown copyright material is reproduced with the permission of the Controller of HMSO and the Queen's Printer for Scotland.

Chartered Institute of Management Accountants for excerpts from: *Introduction to Managing Risk*, London, CIMAglobal.com, 2007, rev. 2008; 'Professional Qualification', www.CIMAglobal.com, n.d.

Jim Collins (author) for excerpts from *Good to Great*. Copyright © 2001 by Jim Collins. Reprinted with permission from Jim Collins.

Department for International Development for excerpts from 'International Aid Transparency Initiative', www.dfid.gov.uk, n.d. Crown copyright material is reproduced with the permission of the Controller of HMSO and the Queen's Printer for Scotland.

Bill Dorotinsky (author) for use of excerpts from 'Developing a Medium-Term Expenditure Framework' in *Reforming the Public Expenditure Management*

System, The World Bank and Korea Development Institute Conference Proceedings, chapter 1, pp. 37–52.

Elsevier for excerpts from 'Management Accounting Official Terminology', London, CIMA, 2000.

Elsevier Science Ltd for excerpts reprinted from *Long Range Planning*, vol. 26, no. 1, International Journal of Strategic Management, Ralph Stacey, 'Strategy as Order Emerging from Chaos', pp. 10–11, Copyright (1993), with permission from Elsevier.

Ernst & Young, London, for adapted excerpts from *Programmed for Control* by Amin Mawji, 2004.

Gower Publishing Limited, London, for excerpts from *Intelligent Internal Control and Risk Management*, by Matthew Leitch, © Gower Publishing Limited, 2008.

Stephan Haeckel for the excerpt on p. 50, 31 May 2010.

Harvard Business Publishing, for excerpts from *Adaptive Enterprise*, Haeckel, Stephan H., 1999; *Beyond Budgeting*, Jeremy Hope and Robin Fraser, 2001; *Hard Facts, Dangerous Half-Truths, and Total Nonsense: Profiting from Evidence-Based Management* by Jeffrey Pfeffer, Robert I. Sutton, 2006; *Reinventing the CFO*, Jeremy Hope, 2006; *The Strategy-Focused Organization* by Robert Kaplan and David Norton, 2001; 'What is Strategy?' by Michael Porter in *Harvard Business Review*, November/December, 1996. All published in Boston by Harvard Business School Press.

Harvard University Press, Cambridge, for excerpts from *Creating Public Value: Strategic Management in Government* by Mark H. Moore. Copyright © 1995 by the President and Fellows of Harvard College; All rights reserved; Printed in the United States of America; Seventh printing, 2002.

Andrew Hind (author) for excerpts from *The Governance and Management of Charities*, London, Voluntary Sector Press, 1995.

HMSO, London, for excerpts from: *Delivering Efficiently: Strengthening the Links in Public Service Delivery Chains*, London, National Audit Office/Audit Commission, 2006; *Joint Compact Action Plan 2008–2009* by the Commission for the Compact, Compact Voice, Local Government Association and the Office of the Third Sector, 2008. Crown copyright material is reproduced with the permission of the Controller of HMSO and the Queen's Printer for Scotland.

HM Treasury, London, for excerpts from: *2007 Pre-Budget Report and Comprehensive Spending Review*, 2007; *Compact on Relations between Government and the Third Sector in England*, 2009; *The Future Role of the Third Sector in*

Social and Economic Regeneration: Final Report, 2007; *Improving Financial Relationships with the Third Sector: Guidance to Funders and Purchasers,* 2006; 'Public Expenditure Planning and Control in the UK', *Spending Review,* www.hm-treasury.gov.uk, 2010; 'Spending Reviews', www.hm-treasury.gov.uk, 2008. Crown copyright material is reproduced with the permission of the Controller of HMSO and the Queen's Printer for Scotland.

Jeremy Hope and Robin Fraser (authors) for an excerpt reproduced on p. 34, and for excerpts from *The BBRT Guide to Managing Without Budgets,* release v3.01, n.d., Poole, CAM-I and a letter to *Financial Management* in September, CIMA, London, 2001.

Mike Hudson (author) for excerpts from *Managing Without Profit,* Directory of Social Change, London, 2009.

International Business Machines Corporation, Somers NY, for excerpts from *The New Voice of the CIO: Insights from the Global Chief Information Officer Study,* 2009.

International Monetary Fund, Washington, for an excerpt from *Revenue Forecasts as Performance Targets* by Stephan Danninger, 2005.

H. Thomas Johnson (author) for excerpts from *Profit Beyond Measure* by H. Thomas Johnson and Anders Bröms, New York, The Free Press, 2000.

John Wiley & Sons, Inc. for excerpts from: *Best Practices in Planning and Management Reporting* by David Axson, Wiley, Hoboken NJ, 2003; *Forces for Good* by Leslie R Crutchfield and Heather McLeod Grant, Jossey-Bass, San Francisco, 2008; *The Leader's Guide to Storytelling* by Stephen Denning, Jossey-Bass, San Francisco, 2005; *Strategic Planning for Public and Non-profit Organizations,* by John Bryson, Jossey-Bass, San Francisco, 2004.

McGraw-Hill Companies for an excerpt from *The Toyota Way* by Jeffrey Liker, McGraw Hill, New York, 2004.

Methuen for excerpts from *Instruction to Deliver* by Michael Barber, Politico's, London, 2007.

National Performance Review for an excerpt from 'Mission Driven, Results Oriented Budgeting', National Partnership for Reinventing Government, http://govinfo.library.unt.edu, 1993.

News International for an excerpt from 'Why Targets Miss the Point' by Libby Purves in *The Times,* London, 2 May 2006.

Nobel Foundation for excerpts from Friedrich August Hayek's lecture 'The Pretence of Knowledge', © The Nobel Foundation, Oslo, 1974.

ORC Worldwide for an excerpt from *World Bank: A Study of the HRS Recruitment Function*, The World Bank, Washington, 2006.

Organisation for European Economic Co-operation for excerpts from *Performance Budgeting in OECD Countries* edited by Teresa Curristine, OECD, Paris, 2007.

Organisation for European Economic Co-operation/Development Assistance Committee for excerpts from *Emerging Good Practice in Managing for Development Results*, 1st and 3rd edns, Managing for Development Results, www.mfdr.org, 2006 and 2008.

Osmosis Publications for excerpts from *The Genghis Khan Guide to Business* by Brian Warnes, London, 1984, copyright © 1984 by Osmosis Publications, reprinted with permission of the author, tel. 020 8852 6560; email business.dynamics@btinternet.com.

Oxfam: the material on page 133 from *Impact Assessment for Developing Agencies* by Chris Roche, Oxfam Publishing, 1999, is reproduced with the permission of Oxfam GB, Oxfam House, John Smith Drive, Cowley, Oxford OX4 2JY, UK www.oxfam.org.uk. Oxfam GB does not necessarily endorse any text or activities that accompany the materials.

Plaza Publishing for permission to use material of the author Adrian Poffley previously published in *NGO Finance* magazine.

Rennselaerville Institute for excerpts from *Outcome Funding: a New Approach to Targeted Grantmaking* (paper), by Harold S. Williams, Arthur Y. Webb and William J. Phillips, copyright 1996 by Rennselaerville Institute. Reproduced with permission of Rennselaerville Institute in the format Other book via Copyright Clearance Center.

Deborah Rosenberg (author) for an excerpt from 'Methods for Analyzing Trend Data' in *Analytic Methods in Maternal and Child Health*, Maternal and Child Health Bureau, HRSA, DHHS, 1998.

SAGE Publications: excerpts reproduced by permission of SAGE Publications, London, Los Angeles, New Delhi and Singapore, from Rob Paton, *Managing and Measuring Social Enterprises*, Copyright (© Sage Publications, 2003).

Sayer Vincent for excerpts from *Achieving a Balanced Framework of Controls*, March 2006, www.sayervincent.co.uk; *Adaptive Procurement*, unpublished draft discussion paper, July 2009.

Graham Scott (author) for excerpts from *Public Sector Management in New Zealand*, Centre for Law and Economics, Australia National University, 2001.

John Seddon (author) for excerpts from: *Open Letter to Ruth Kelly, MP, Minister of Communities and Local Government*, www.systemsthinking.co.uk, 2006; *Written Submission to Public Administration's Select Committee's Inquiry into Public Sector Performance Targets*, www.systemsthinking.co.uk, 2003.

Sightsavers International for excerpts from: *Overseas Programmes Department Manual*, Sightsavers International 2005; *Reward Policy*, Sightsavers International, 2006; *Sightsavers International Annual Report and Financial Statements 2008*, Sightsavers International 2008; *Strategic Framework 2009–2013: Making the Connections*, www.sightsavers.org, 2009.

Society for Organizational Learning for excerpts from 'Reflections of a Recovering Management Accountant', www.solonline.org, 2008.

Stanford Social Innovation Review for excerpts from 'The Nonprofit Starvation Cycle', *Stanford Social Innovation Review* by Ann Goggins Gregory and Don Howard, Stanford Graduate School of Business, Fall issue, 2009.

Taylor & Francis Group for excerpts from 'Improving Service Delivery Performance in the United Kingdom: Organization Theory Perspectives on Central Intervention Strategies' by Steven Kelman in *Journal of Comparative Policy Analysis*, 8(4), January 2006 working paper version, Taylor & Francis, reprinted by permission of the publisher (Taylor & Francis Group, http://www.informaworld.com).

Margaret Wheatley (author) for excerpts from 'What Do We Measure and Why? Questions about the Uses of Measurement' by Margaret Wheatley and Myron Kellner-Rogers in *Journal for Strategic Performance Measurement*, 1999, accessed from www.margaretwheatley.com.

Clyde Williams (author) for excerpts from *Computers can be Managed: A CEO's Guide*, Sho-Net Systems Ltd, London, 1999.

The World Bank, Washington, for excerpts from: *FY08 Trust Fund Portfolio Review: Raising Awareness of Trust Fund Complexities*, 2008; *HR Strategy Update*, 2009; *HRS FY09 Performance Memo*, 2009; IDA 15 Fact Sheet, www.worldbank.org, 2007; *A Vision for Excellence in Performance Management*, 2007.

1 Introduction

HOW WELL IS YOUR ORGANISATION DOING?

Is your organisation having as much beneficial impact on those it exists to serve as it should be, given the financial resources available to it? How do you know? These are not easy questions to answer, but you must answer them. You need to be able to explain what your organisation has achieved with the resources available to it.

All public and not-for-profit organisations face a common challenge, whether they are major government departments, small community-based charities, schools, or organisations such as the World Bank, which is structured as a cooperative where its member countries are shareholders. Finding themselves under increasing scrutiny to justify their *raison d'être*, they have to account for the results they achieve, for how they choose to operate, and for how they manage the financial resources placed in their trust by others (whether central or local government treasury departments, taxpayers, private donors, foundations or other types of funding agency).

In short, all public and not-for-profit organisations are on the hook to demonstrate how they add value. 'What do our donors get for their money?' is a question that should preoccupy board members, senior executives, managers and employees of all public and not-for-profit organisations across the world. It demands an assessment of organisational performance.

This book is about how such organisations convert income into intended impact – or rather, how they should convert income into impact (see fig. 1.1). Many fail to have the impact that they should have, even allowing for resource constraints and challenging environments. Many are trying to do something about it, often under ambitious reform banners. The book's key focus is the central role of financial stewardship – in other words, how public and not-for-profit organisations should steward the financial resources at their disposal in order to maximise the impact that they have over time – while operating in an environment of increasing uncertainty.

Coping with uncertainty is paramount, as the global economic crisis that erupted in 2008 demonstrates all too well. Organisations' capacity to anticipate the future

1

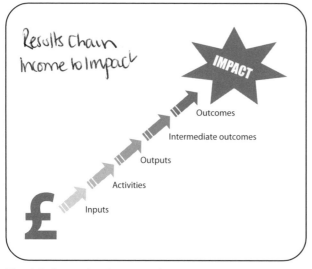

Results Chain
Income to Impact

Fig. 1.1 Converting income to impact

correctly is understandably difficult, given the number of interconnected factors at play. As a result, they must be organised to adapt and respond with agility.

DEFINING SUCCESS

The core proposition of this book is that the goal of any public or not-for-profit organisation is to maximise its impact over time for those it exists to serve. The impact must be beneficial rather than detrimental (whether intended or not), must be sustained over time, and must be enjoyed by the group of individuals targeted. Impact must not just be promised – it must be delivered. Successful organisations convert income into impact efficiently and effectively. Unsuccessful ones do not. Their conversion rate is low. But there is no place for complacency for any organisation: whatever the level of performance today, all organisations need to be on a journey of continuous improvement.

The task of converting income to impact can be helpfully depicted using a results chain (see box 1.1). This concept is frequently used to explain how inputs – including money – are used to generate impact. The task facing every organisation is to move along the chain as effectively and efficiently as possible. This book attempts to explain why many organisations struggle to do this well, to draw key lessons from the emerging practice being adopted by innovative organisations, and to offer its own contribution to what organisations can do to improve performance.

Box 1.1   The results chain

The objective of interventions is to improve the welfare **outcomes** *of the target group, based on the achievement of ...*

- **Intermediate outcomes**, *such as increased consumption of goods and services, as a result of ...*
- **Outputs**, *such as the goods produced or services delivered, as a result of ...*
- **Inputs**, *such as the financing, organizational capacities, and human capital provided by the intervention.*

The World Bank, 2005, p. 2

The logic of the results chain is straightforward. However, if it is used and interpreted effectively it can provide profound insights into how an organisation must operate, as follows.

- **The chain provides an explicit definition of performance** – of what organisational success actually looks like. Unless it has beneficial impact on its targeted beneficiaries, then an organisation has failed – however virtuous its intentions or industrious its efforts. Nothing is delivered unless the intended beneficiaries (real people) enjoy real benefit. The focus of an organisation, as manifested in its values, strategies, programmes, processes and incentives, must therefore be orientated towards outcomes and impact. It must be clear how all of the inputs and outputs contribute to the generation of outcomes and impact.
- **Yet many organisations focus predominantly on inputs and outputs** – on money, staffing and activities. Everyone's head is down, furiously busy, completing task after task. This raises the risk of non-alignment, meaning that the activities of the organisation are either inappropriate – the wrong work programme is carried out – or managed in a way that will fail to deliver the intended outcomes and impact.
- **Clarity about what success looks like also defines accountability** – in other words, what an organisation's people are accountable for. There is an obvious basis for establishing how the performance of individuals, units and teams need to link to organisational success. It becomes possible to provide a line of sight, so that everyone can see how their effort contributes to the organisation's outcomes and impact.
- **The chain highlights how to plan, and how to execute those plans** – given that the task of any organisation is to convert income to impact efficiently and effectively. Note in box 1.1 how the design of work undertaken can derive from outcomes backwards. Strategy and work programmes should be designed from intended outcomes backwards. Implementation of those plans takes place from inputs forwards. That's the message of the chain: plan from outcomes backwards; deliver from inputs forwards. By working from impact to inputs, the chain helps design strategy. By working from inputs to impact, the chain helps manage implementation.
- **The chain explicitly connects finance to the business of the organisation** – it shows that it is not possible to divorce the management of the organisation's financial resources from the management of its programmes and strategy. They sit on a single spectrum: a single results chain. So, those charged with financial stewardship of the organisation have to understand how the conversion of funds moves along the chain. This fundamentally influences how such stewardship is undertaken, and the roles that leaders (including for example the chief financial officer), need to play. Financial stewards must be judged, and judge others, in the same way as the organisation as a whole: on the extent

to which income is converted into impact. Those who can understand the whole chain, and maintain the line of sight from income to impact, must be instrumental in running the organisation.

THE TRACK RECORD

The results chain helps to explain why many public and not-for-profit organisations are not set up to enable success – to achieve impact efficiently and effectively. This is often true for one or more of the following reasons.

- There is a lack of focus on the top end of the chain, on outcomes and impact. Poorly performing organisations – and, therefore, their people – are not clear about what they are trying to achieve and how they intend to achieve it. This means that there is ambiguity about what individuals in the organisation are accountable for.
- There is not a clear financial framework within which organisations can ensure that they can have the desired impact today while also remaining financially viable to have impact tomorrow. To enjoy success over time means that organisations have to make crucial judgements between spending and saving, understand when to do which, and manage the competing demands of the two.
- In organisations that struggle to climb the results chain effectively there is a lack of alignment between the allocation of funds and the organisation's priorities. The most important activities of the organisation do not necessarily command the money. This is most evident in the issuing of one-year budget envelopes to spending units, despite the long-term nature of the welfare issues being addressed. This focus on short-term budgets is often accompanied by an implicit or explicit 'hit the budget' performance contract, which stimulates behaviour that is inconsistent with the objectives of the organisation.
- When the day-to-day processes and practices that are used in planning, and in executing those plans, are ineffective, they do not drive high performance. They do not focus sufficiently on delivery. They are slow and overly prescriptive, preventing organisations from being agile, adaptive and responsive enough in today's fast-moving, ever-changing business environment. They fail to ensure effective accountability for the actual level of performance delivered. Organisations that exhibit these features struggle to assess performance in a meaningful way, and their processes and practices reflect an absence of business-orientated culture and discipline.
- The internal environment of an underperforming organisation impedes, rather than enables, success. This is characterised by, for example, ambiguous roles, outdated and/or inadequate skills, misguided incentives and unsupportive systems.

> ## Box 1.2 Distortions created by the management system: New Zealand government in the 1980s
>
> - *The information system was based on inputs and largely useless for making effective decisions*
> - *The incentives affecting ministerial and departmental decision makers were not aligned with the government's need for a comprehensive grip on public expenditure*
> - *The system created incentives for managers to protect and expand their resource bases and the information available made effective external scrutiny of resource use and risks very difficult*
> - *Ministers saw the budget process as a game in which the winner extracted the biggest expenditure increases from the minister of finance*
> - *The input controls led to complaints from managers to their ministers that they could not use their discretion to raise efficiency and effectiveness in ways that could be demonstrated as practical common sense.*
>
> *Scott, 2001, p. 2*

These deficiencies are not new, as the example of the New Zealand government in the 1980s (see box 1.2) demonstrates, and solving them is not easy – particularly in the public and not-for-profit sectors. There are a number of characteristics of organisations in these sectors that can make moving up the chain extremely challenging.

Clarifying organisational goals can be complicated. There are often multiple stakeholders with conflicting views about what the organisation's principal purpose is, what goals it should have, and how it should best achieve them.

A lack of clarity around organisational goals often results in conflicting pressures for the organisation. For example, there can be as much pressure to increase spending as there is to constrain it. Meanwhile, measuring performance is complicated. It is very difficult to summarise succinctly how well a public sector or not-for-profit organisation is doing. This makes it difficult to maintain a clear line of sight from mission to individual staff objectives, so defining aligned staff objectives is difficult. This in turn means that accountability is not easy to define or to achieve. The governance of such organisations in this situation is often highly political, and beneficiaries, donors, trustees, governors and the public are not well placed to ensure that the organisation can demonstrate value for money.

FINANCIAL STEWARDSHIP AND THE ROLE OF THE FINANCIAL STEWARD

At its simplest, financial stewardship refers to the responsible use of financial resources. The quality of financial stewardship – the responsible use of the organisation's financial resources – is integral to the success of the organisation in moving from one end of the chain to the other. It relates to how organisations choose to use the financial resources available to them, and how they manage themselves to maximise the conversion of these resources into beneficial impact. It is about how organisations successfully climb the chain.

In the public sector, the central role played by finance is long established. The US government's Performance Results Act, enacted in 1993 (Office of Management and Budget n.d.), noted that '60 percent of all roll call votes in Congress are on budget-related issues' (p. 3). It goes on to note the overarching role played by the budget in the federal government, stressing the need for:

> ... *a fundamental shift in the federal government's accountability system from one orientated to accountability for processes and who get which "inputs" (in this case fiscal resources) to one focusing accountability on performance and results.*
>
> National Partnership for Reinventing Government, 1993, p. 6

Similarly, the Organisation for Economic Co-operation and Development (OECD) notes that 'in most OECD countries, the central agency with responsibility for performance budgeting initiatives tends to be the MOF [Ministry of Finance]' (OECD, 2007, p. 33).

This places those charged with managing the organisation's financial resources – the financial stewards – at the very centre of any organisation's leadership and management function. Organisations need new financial leadership that extends well beyond the domain of the traditional finance function. Financial stewardship has to be undertaken around the top table of the organisation, and must be fully integrated into the task of managing organisational performance. This increases the relevance of the finance function, but it also raises the bar. The financial steward needs to be able to understand the business and culture of the organisation, guide its management in planning how to apply its resources judiciously, and ensure that the organisation delivers the intended benefits to the targeted group. In this way, finance becomes a driver of organisational performance.

The more forward-thinking, innovative and successful organisations recognise this. As a result, many organisations find a need to integrate closely the tasks of strategy, resource management and performance management in their organisational design. The role of those positions responsible for financial stewardship is evolving accordingly.

Here are just two examples, published at the time of drafting this second edition. The first is from Scottish Enterprise's website (www.scottishenterprise.com), describing the role of the organisation's chief financial officer. The role, it states, includes responsibility for 'ensuring that strategic financial management and value for money are at the heart of the business and its decision-making processes'. The second comes from a job description posted in *The Economist*, on 25 October 2008. The organisation (Greenpeace) was seeking to recruit a director-level individual whose responsibilities would include: 'strategic direction and programme design, budgeting and financial control, international coordination and engagement.'

Both examples articulate clearly the broad role that the most senior financial executive in the organisation is expected to play in the organisation's management. They are expected to concern themselves all the way up the chain, driving performance.

Financial stewardship principles

Successful stewardship of the sort described here results from the application of five principles.

1. **Set clear strategic direction**. Successful organisations are clear about where they are trying to get to, and how they intend to get there. They are crystal clear, therefore, about what they are trying to achieve. Donors know what they can expect in return for their funds. Leaders are clear about how their organisation's strategies and work programmes take it in this intended direction.
2. **Maintain a robust financial framework**. Financial stewardship excellence means operating within clear financial parameters and controls, to ensure that the organisation can remain financially viable and effective over time.
3. **Align resources to results**. Organisations that convert income to impact effectively make resources available as needed over the medium term so that, for example, their strategies can be implemented while being underpinned by secure funding.
4. **Manage day-to-day finances dynamically, to ensure programme delivery**. Holding people accountable for actual performance delivery, using dynamic daily processes (including financial ones), is the norm and part of the culture in agile, accountable organisations that are focused on beneficiaries.
5. **Nurture an enabling environment**. Organisations that steward their resources well enable successful delivery of impact by creating appropriate structures, capabilities and systems.

All five principles are necessary. If applied together, they create the essential components of a successful organisation: one that has clear strategic direction, a robust financial framework, aligned resources and effective financial processes to ensure day-to-day delivery within an enabling environment. Each principle is dependent on, and supports, the other four. Implicit throughout this book is a recognition that successful application of the principles is crucially reliant on organisational culture. Tools and processes are not enough.

The book is divided into five parts – one for each principle, in order to build a financial stewardship 'map' step by step (see fig. 1.2). Each principle is made up of key building blocks. For example, the principle maintaining a 'robust financial framework' is made up of five blocks (income, funds, assets, expenditure and risk controls), while the principle nurturing an 'enabling environment' is made up of three (roles, capabilities and technology). A chapter is given to each block, and key stewardship questions that need to be addressed are listed at the end of each chapter.

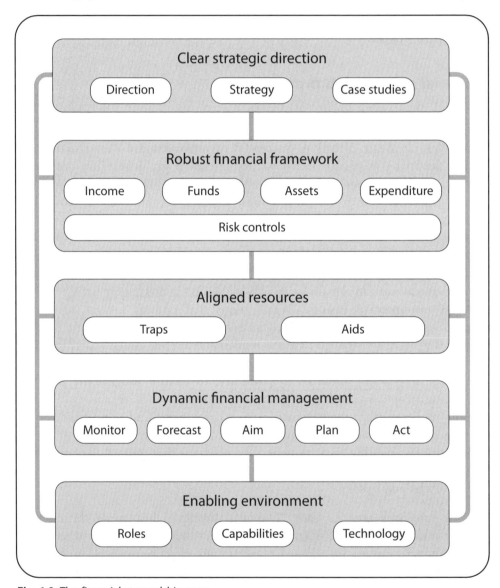

Fig. 1.2 The financial stewardship map

Part 1: Clear strategic direction

Part 1 focuses on what it means, and takes, to set clear strategic direction – and the risks associated with doing so.

Chapter 2 discusses the challenge of setting direction. It outlines the role of goals, and how they should be used. In doing so, it exposes the very active and public debate about the value of setting targets. The opinions are polarised, and the chapter illustrates the views both of the proponents of targets and of those who declare them as capable of destroying an organisation. What becomes evident is that using targets to motivate behaviour, and to measure performance, have the potential to lead to very different consequences. This has major implications for accountability, and the chapter assesses the extent to which it is feasible to hold organisations' leaders accountable for outcomes. The challenge of measurement is explored, and the chapter concludes with a definition of the performance contract that must be in place, introducing the concept of maximising the income to impact return.

Chapter 3 considers what benefits should result from the creation of a clear strategic direction, and what process might be used to develop a strategy. It also challenges the extent to which detailed, accurate planning is possible or sensible. So many factors influence performance, and many of these are not only out of the control of the organisation, but are entirely unpredictable. For example, for international organisations, factors such as natural disasters and political or economic crises in the countries of operation occur with depressing frequency, and yet are impossible to reflect accurately in operational or financial planning. The degree of uncertainty present in an organisation's operating environment emerges as being critical in determining an appropriate approach to corporate strategy, and thereby to financial stewardship.

The chapter introduces three approaches, considered along a spectrum of increasing operational uncertainty, ranging from rational planning to chaos management, with proponents of the latter questioning the whole value of traditional strategic planning. It exposes the challenge of ensuring that setting strategic direction provides the intended benefits to the organisation while avoiding two major risks: first, that preparation of a strategy and its subsequent implementation disables the organisation from sensing and responding to emerging priorities, and second, that the organisation over-invests in planning and underachieves in delivery. The factors influencing strategic choices are explored.

Chapter 4 draws on case study material from the public and not-for-profit sectors to illustrate how different organisations have chosen to develop, and to describe a clear strategic direction and manage corporate performance. It presents the strategic framework of the non-governmental organisation (NGO) Sightsavers

International, summarises the efforts of OECD country governments to establish performance-based accountability frameworks, and describes the framework adopted by the UK government in 2007.

Part 2: Robust financial framework

Part 2 is devoted to recognising that as well as focusing on delivering the intended beneficial impact, organisations have to maintain financial viability over time. They need to be organised and managed in such a way that they can deliver tomorrow as well as today. This requires critical financial choices to be made, using a financial framework that defines the parameters within which the organisation is expected to operate. Leaders need to be clear how much financial room they have, be able to define what financial success looks like, and have in place a finance strategy that explains how they will achieve that financial success.

Chapter 5 describes the framework that must exist alongside the clear *raison d'être* and strategic direction discussed in part 1. A ready-made framework is provided by the three primary statements of any organisation's published accounting information (the operating statement of income received and expenditure incurred, the balance sheet, and the cash flow statement), using the four perspectives of income, funds, assets and expenditure (see fig. 1.3).

The chapter also introduces the concept of fund accounting and the statement of financial activities (SOFA) adopted in the UK charity sector, in recognition of the distinct way that the financial position of not-for-profit organisations must be presented and assessed (see p. 78). Chapters 6 to 9 consider each of the four perspectives in turn, laying out the critical features of each that need to be considered.

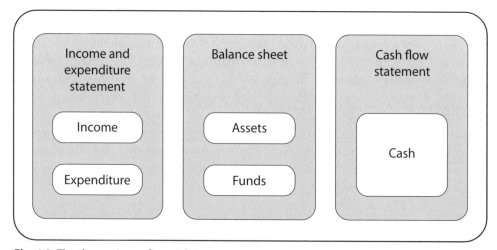

Fig. 1.3 The three primary financial statements

The final chapter of part 2 – chapter 10 – also addresses the overarching need for effective controls as part of the overall financial framework. It offers the proposition that effective internal controls and risk management processes must cater for uncertainty. Real control is about adjusting appropriately to the prevailing circumstances – whether or not these are anticipated or intended.

Part 3: Aligned resources

Part 3 considers how to ensure that financial resources are directed to where they are needed most over the medium term. The task of aligning resources to results is one of ensuring that the financial resources made available within the overall finance framework are put to best use, so that they are converted as efficiently and effectively as possible.

In most organisations this task is completed using an annual budget-setting process. Part 3 questions this approach, and argues the case for indicative medium-term expenditure directions, rather than precise one-year budget allocations. Spenders do need clarity about the direction in which spending should move over time – they must have clear signals about what is expected of them – but offering one-year envelopes, it is argued, is not the way. Intuitively, distributing one-year budgets to finance multi-year strategies creates an obvious risk of misalignment.

Chapter 11 explores in detail the inadequacy of allocating one-year budget envelopes to spenders, identifying five traps into which this traditional method of making resources available falls. The chapter discusses the contract that is established with the allocation of budgets and how to avoid those traps, and addresses the need to create room for emerging priorities. It argues that the allocation of budgets – intended to provide the means to deliver outputs, outcomes and impact – in fact leads to the creation of an alternative contract – 'hit the budget'. Allocations risk stimulating the wrong type of behaviour: a funding entitlement mentality that promotes either budget stockpiling or spending profligacy.

The chapter promotes the concept of medium-term expenditure directions which provide sufficient funding security over a multi-year timeframe but avoid the budget traps. Such security is essential for implementing complex beneficiary-orientated strategies which must be sustained over several years.

Chapter 12 explores how to avoid the allocation traps, presenting a menu of aids that can alleviate the consequences of the traps, and that better enable stewards to align the available financial resources to the work programme, strategies and objectives of the organisation. The chapter offers a definition of a budget expressed in terms of the results chain, together with a discussion on the implications for managerial accountability.

Part 4: Dynamic financial management

With a clear strategic direction set, a robust financial framework in place, and medium-term expenditure directions signalled, part 4 goes on to consider what day-to-day financial management practices and processes have to be in place to ensure delivery of intended benefits to the targeted group. It focuses on the daily processes by which the financial resources of the organisation should be managed – particularly within uncertain operating environments.

At the heart of the discussion is a detailed explanation of a financial management methodology that is appropriate for conditions of uncertainty. There is an explanation of the principles and processes by which organisations should make decisions about how they spend their funds within uncertain operating environments.

Chapter 13 describes a framework that is designed to be lightweight but highly effective in guiding decision makers' actions, following a simple five-step cycle of 'monitor, forecast, aim, plan, act'. Its philosophy is one of adaptability: of recognising that, whether planned or not, organisations have to respond to the circumstances in which they find themselves. This methodology promotes a rolling approach to financial management that mirrors the decision making of a traveller who has a destination in mind, but who has to respond to unexpected events.

Planning the journey, while crucial, can only help so much: unplanned events will inevitably arise. Similarly, in the case of financial management in conditions of uncertainty, an organisation needs to have a clear sense of where it is trying to get to (in other words, what the end of the results chain looks like) and how it intends to get there, but it cannot know the unknown. It has to be ready to react to the unexpected and uncontrollable events – good and bad – that it experiences along the way.

Guided by the clear sense of intended direction established in part 3, chapters 14 to 18 detail five ongoing financial management practices that should be followed as organisations move forward.

1. **Understand the current financial position:** The organisation needs to know where it is, irrespective of whether this position is considered intentional or desirable. The organisation needs fast, accurate information about its financial circumstance in order to appreciate its current financial condition and recent business performance. Monitoring actual results is the focus of chapter 14.

2. **Look forward and see what is ahead:** A forward-looking perspective is crucial if an organisation is to navigate its future environment successfully. Since no organisation can react instantaneously, a high premium is attached to maintaining a constant outlook and converting early warning signals into quality forecasts that can guide decision making. Chapter 15 discusses the role of forecasts, and the importance of understanding what financial commitments have already been made, in order to determine how much is now available.

3. **Decide where to aim for:** Informed by a clear understanding of the organisation's recent record and its current state and outlook, stewards are able sensibly to set the direction forward. Chapter 16 discusses what financial parameters and targets are needed, and how to govern them. It also addresses the need to integrate financial measures with other, non-financial, perspectives.

4. **Decide how to get there:** The organisation now has to plan ahead. It has to make resources available, and make operational commitments. Medium-term allocations define the road for the journey. It then needs to take steps forward, one by one, from one day to the next, along that road. It has to make choices about alternative activities and programmes, competing for finite resources. This requires resource-allocation decision-making processes, both strategic and tactical, and these are the subject of chapter 17.

5. **Set off in the intended direction, maintaining continuous review of progress:** Once decisions are made and actions taken, a review is needed to ensure that the intended results materialise. Leaders, managers and staff all have to address the question of whether the action taken has moved the organisation along the chain satisfactorily – in short, whether it has delivered. The organisation needs a review process through which it can understand its current state of play, make performance assessments, consider short-term outlooks, and take decisions. Meanwhile, managers have to be accountable for the decisions that have been made. Chapter 18 outlines a possible review process, and proposes how to structure reviews that will ensure genuine accountability.

The less certain the environment, the more frequently these practices must be undertaken. The chapters recognise the need to establish broad financial parameters that are relevant over the medium term, and to maintain day-to-day financial disciplines within those parameters. Organisations typically observe a monthly or quarterly cycle, but in fact the tasks must be completed whenever the need arises within the organisation's operational cycle.

Part 5: Enabling environment

The four principles outlined in parts 1 to 4 are all necessary for good financial stewardship to be demonstrated, but they are not sufficient. Nothing will happen unless the appropriate environment has been provided by an appropriately designed and maintained set of enablers. These enablers provide the foundations for excellence. So, part 5 focuses on three prerequisites – or inputs – that must be in place. *where CEO??*

- **Organisational roles:** Crucially, this is about who does what. Who should play the respective financial stewardship roles of trustees, the honorary treasurer, the finance director, finance specialists and operational management as they seek to lead and guide the organisation along the results chain? There are important lines in the sand to be drawn between these players, and chapter 19 endeavours to do this.

- **Capabilities:** Even with the right structure in place, the organisation has to recruit and retain staff with the appropriate financial capability. This poses challenges for any organisation's reward, performance management and professional development strategies, requiring it to compete in an open marketplace against employers in all sectors searching for the same skills, while honouring values as an organisation created for public, not private, benefit. Chapter 20 asks what it takes to attract, retain and develop high-quality financial stewards, considering what competencies are needed, how to create a coherent reward strategy, and the critical human resources (HR) processes of recruitment, performance management and professional development.

- **Information:** This is an enabler now critically influenced by technology. Effective and reliable information systems underpin the whole financial stewardship model. Chapter 21 outlines how technology is transforming the information generation and communication capabilities of organisations. Recognising the challenge of using technology well, the chapter highlights the critical success factors that will determine whether the investment in technology adds the intended value. With investment in technology in mind, the chapter identifies the risks associated with the typical procurement process, and discusses how to manage the overall information technology (IT)-related costs facing the organisation.

Part 1:
Clear strategic direction

2 Setting direction

THE ROLES OF GOALS

'Be clear where you are trying to get to', counselled chapter 1, which defined organisational success in terms of progressing to the top of the results chain, and argued that this was reached when the intended beneficiaries enjoy real benefit. This forces an immediate question: how should organisations define the intended destination? It is a question that provokes debate about the pros and cons of goals or targets.

Goals potentially play two crucial roles. The first is to answer the question 'What does success look like?' They establish direction and thereby help organisations to set priorities that reflect the hard choices that have to be made

How goals are used
1. To set direction by defining aspirations and characterising vision.
2. To establish targets against which the performance of organisations and their people can be judged.

between competing demands at all levels. To this extent, they guide strategic planning and decision making by defining aspirations and characterising the vision of where the organisation is trying to reach.

The second is to support performance management and improvement by providing a future context against which to review actual performance. In this regard, goals set the context for accountability by providing targets to aim for and against which to be judged. Organisations, and their people, become accountable for achieving the agreed goals.

TARGETS

In recent years there has been a significant increase in organisations' use of targets – defining desired results in relation to specific metrics, progress towards which can be measured and tracked over time – to set direction and assess performance.

A particularly well-documented case is that of the UK government – particularly since 2001, when then Prime Minister Tony Blair established the Delivery Unit, which was responsible for ensuring the delivery of public sector priorities in the departments of health, education, crime and transport. Specific targets were defined in relation to 14 priorities which, according to the former unit head, Michael Barber, 'translated airy aspirations into specific measurable commitments' (Barber, 2007, p. 50).

In Barber's eyes, at least, the UK experience makes a compelling case both for the use of targets, and for their public adoption:

> *Any government with energy and aspiration has to be able to explain what it is planning to do and how people will know when it has succeeded ... in each key area, government has to be able to answer the question: 'what would success look like?' Once that question has been answered properly, you have a target in all but name. By stating the target or goal publicly, you create pressure on the system to deliver it and a timetable which drives the urgency ... Targets in one form or another, are therefore both necessary and beneficial.*
>
> Barber, 2007, p. 80

> *Whether or not to publish targets ... is a matter of choice. Any credible government, though, must have clear objectives and must have the means of knowing at any given moment whether it is on track – or not – to achieving its objectives. Making those objectives public ... requires greater political courage but it is also more transparent and makes it more likely that progress will be made.*
>
> Barber, 2007, p. 82

However, there are certain risks associated with targets, as described below.

The risks of targets

The use of targets has sparked an active debate about their effect on organisational behaviour, and there is universal recognition – even from their supporters – of the associated risks. It is clear that any steward intending to adopt targets should do so with their eyes wide open – otherwise the unintended consequences may obviate all the potential benefits. The 20th-century management thinker Dr W. Edwards Deming is often cited by critics of targets such as Professor Tom Johnson: 'W. Edwards Deming used to say that, if management sets quantitative targets and makes people's jobs depend on meeting them, "they will likely meet the targets – even if they have to destroy the enterprise to do it"' (Johnson and Bröms, 2000, p. xiii). Meanwhile, others make the accusation that 'targets actually undermine achievement of purpose' (Seddon, 2003, n.p.).

The case against targets focuses on the incentives they create, the focus they stimulate and the burden associated with their administration. Consider the following assertions, adapted from Seddon (2003, 2006).

> *The managerialist culture of 'target-setting' … sounds dynamic, but hardly ever does more than make the targetees fiddle their results and distort their priorities.*
>
> *Targetism is a footling displacement activity. And it can lead to worse: distortion, cheating, danger.*
>
> *Purves, 2006, n.p.*

- Targets focus people on the wrong things. They focus people's ingenuity on survival, rather than improvement. They focus people on what is auditable, not what is important.
- Targets distort systems. Organisations focus not on the customer but on the paymaster. Meeting the target becomes the organisation's *raison d'être*. Managers focus on meeting the regulatory requirements, and unknowingly distort and diminish their organisation's ability to serve customers.
- Targets have no value in understanding or improving performance.
- There is no reliable method of setting targets: they are arbitrary.
- Targets demotivate, by evaluating organisations and their people on measures that are not relevant to the work being undertaken, and by burdening them with reporting and administrative procedures that add no value to their work.
- Targets offer no help with method. Organisations meet targets and create losses elsewhere: optimising part of the system sub-optimises the system as a whole.
- Targets drive the wrong behaviour, encouraging game playing and manipulation.
- Targets breed more targets. The fewer the targets, the broader they have to be. The broader they are, the cruder the results and the more gross the distortions.

Johnson and Bröms, in their seminal text *Profit Beyond Measure* (2000), couple their diagnosis of the problems associated with centralised control and quantified targets with promotion of 'management by

> *The unacknowledged assumption in support of aiming at targets is that a business is a mechanistic system not a natural living system. Managers attempt to drive work with quantitative targets, blissfully unaware that a business is a living system and therefore any changes in any of its parts will reverberate throughout it in what Dr. Deming called 'unknown and unknowable ways'. These ways will lead to unexpected and even counter-intuitive overall results. Unconsciously locked into a mechanistic thought pattern, frustrated managers react to their evident failure to 'control' results by expanding and sharpening their use of measurement tools, unconsciously making things worse in the long run.*
>
> *Johnson and Bröms, 2000, p. 69*

means' in place of target-driven 'management by results'. Operate brilliant processes, they argue, and the results will look after themselves. They advise that organisations need to think systemically, to understand the detailed processes by which clients are served, and to be managed using principles that apply to natural living conditions. Their belief is that 'the key to superior performance and to continual innovation lives in the "minute particulars" of how local work is done, not in sacrificing those particulars to the pursuit of management-imposed metrics' (Johnson and Bröms, 2000, p. xiii). They stress the importance of learning, and the network of relationships within any organisation. Significantly, they describe how management by means 'nurtures aspirations' (Johnson and Bröms 2000, p. xv).

John Seddon's application of these principles to local authorities in the UK have led him to call for the abandonment of the 'specification and inspection regime altogether' (Seddon, 2006, n.p.). Pre-empting the often-asked question 'How can we tell if local authorities are improving?', Seddon has a cogent response, which is telling and worth reproducing in full (see box 2.1). It is a case for customer-focused measurement that informs dialogue and judgement in place of targets.

Box 2.1   How can we tell if local authorities are improving?

How can we ensure that they are held accountable for what they are doing with public money? To which there is a very simple answer. You can replace the entire current regulation regime with one question: what measures are you using to understand and improve each service? Note the word 'understand'; it begs managers to actually study the work and determine measures that might illuminate what is going on. There are no current performance indicators that lead to understanding, as they are all arbitrary and/or 'rear view mirror' measures. To declare a requirement for understanding would be a significant change.

*An authority that is systematically measuring demand and its capability to meet it – so it can tell you how long it takes **end-to-end** (i.e. from a customer's point of view) to complete a housing repair, pay a benefit or install a walk-in shower for someone in need of social care – is by definition taking a systems view. Its frontline workers and managers will be learning **from customers** how to give them more of what they want with less fuss. It will be a simple matter to show performance (real performance) changes year on year. The goal is improvement. Those who already use such measures will have their position strengthened vis-à-vis a much reduced inspection regime. Others – and there are many as they are products of the current regime – whose measures are to do with activities, such as transaction costs or time to make an appointment, or arbitrary targets and standards will find themselves engaged in a debate that needs to be had.*

Seddon, 2006, n.p.

Behind much of the criticism of target setting lies a challenge to organisational leaders to consider the role they play in defining the pervading performance culture. Steven Kelman's study (2006) of the Blair government's actual performance management activities – including the use of targets – focuses on the role that central government can play in improving the performance of frontline service-delivering organisations. Using the UK experience to assess the role of one central unit versus several decentralised ones, Kelman highlights two risks (insufficient visioning and excessive decision making), which refer to the two roles of goals that were defined at the start of the chapter – to set direction, and to establish performance targets. His observations offer valuable guidance to those charged with designing and overseeing organisational performance management who might be tempted to introduce statistical targets.

On insufficient visioning, Kelman argues that the visioning role of leaders and of central units is uncontroversial, and endorses the legitimacy of the first role of targets defined at the start of this chapter ('describing direction and characterising vision'). He says: 'The more leaders can associate targets with an appealing vision of public-service motivation and mission-attainment, the greater their motivating force is likely to be' (Kelman, 2006, n.p.). From his study of the UK government, Kelman reports a 'lack of attention to visioning'. He cites interviewees acknowledging the lack of connection between the targets and the mission, resulting in the risk of what he calls 'goal displacement – where people orient themselves to attaining the target rather than to the underlying mission goal' (Kelman, 2006, n.p.).

On the issue of excessive decision making, Kelman argues that central units may not be best placed to approve or make decisions about how frontline units can improve performance, including through setting or imposing targets. This is because the centre may not have the capacity to absorb all the information necessary to make such decisions, he says. Client-facing units may better understand how to address local problems and maximise opportunities that arise. Further, centralised decision making may well reduce morale of local units whose autonomy is reduced, he argues. Kelman reports some 'skepticism about lower-level willingness voluntarily to embrace performance improvement using targets', and warns of 'an itch to impose decisions centrally' (Kelman, 2006, n.p.).

Reflections

What lessons can be learnt from these insights and opinions about targets? The importance of being able to provide the line of sight for everyone associated with an organisation is apparent. Individuals must be able to connect to the purpose for which the organisation exists, and targets can provide a valuable means of making the organisation's purpose, mission and vision become meaningful. There appears to be little controversy about the value that targets can bring in terms of defining aspirations and characterising vision: they can be aspirational, in the sense of being defined as destinations that are highly ambitious, that

[handwritten: predetermine what good look like]
[handwritten: discuss re SIB] ← *[handwritten: assume controlover target]*

> *Simply setting specific, measurable, challenging goals and then measuring progress is highly motivating.*
>
> Liker, 2004, p. 262[1]

represent a significant improvement on current state, and that are likely to take several years to achieve.

However, in relation to performance management, setting quantitative targets runs a risk – potentially a high one – of having unintended consequences. The adage 'Be careful what you wish for – you may get it' springs to mind. People tend to be highly responsive to the incentives that targets signal: they will do what they can to meet them, and may do so despite being conscious of negative implications elsewhere. Even Barber tells of Blair's worries that 'the system would take [the targets] too literally and hit the target but miss the point' (Barber, 2007, p. 82).

Setting targets for performance measurement purposes involves at least two crucial assumptions: first, that it is possible to predetermine what good performance looks like, and second, that it is possible to focus the target on work over which the entity or individual being reviewed has control. The first assumption implies an ability to anticipate the future accurately, while the second requires an ability to distinguish the effort and results achieved from those of other individuals or entities, so as to measure performance accurately. Both assumptions hardly seem realistic other than in extraordinary, atypical circumstances.

So, in terms of performance assessment, goals are best used to help organisations decide on the speed and direction of future action, rather than providing a precise definition of success. Goals do not serve well as hard targets against which performance can be measured. So, an organisation's aim should be perhaps less about reaching the goals than about demonstrating continuous improvement. Indeed, for motivational purposes it may well be appropriate to reset goals once their achievement is imminent.

The delicate task that emerges from this conclusion is the need to divorce target setting from performance management. This is essential to avoid a scenario in which targets are set solely for the purpose of motivating individuals to obtain results for their beneficiaries that they previously thought were unattainable.

THE IMPLICATIONS FOR ACCOUNTABILITY

The discussion so far in this chapter has significant implications for accountability. Again, the results chain offers a useful taxonomy to illustrate the point. Goals can be set for any stage of the chain: to guide how inputs are used,

---

[1] Jeffrey Liker, The Toyota Way, McGraw Hill, 2004, reproduced with permission of The McGraw-Hill Companies

targets useful for setting direction but not an end in themselves.

to encourage process improvement, and to define required outputs or desired outcomes. However, their use – and consequent effectiveness – will be significantly influenced by the factors of causality and measurement. For performance management purposes, results must be measurable and attributable.

Motivational goals that define purpose, aspirations and vision most readily relate to the top of the results chain (defining the intended impact or outcomes). The Millennium Development Goals (MDGs) fall into this category. These goals 'have galvanised unprecedented efforts to meet the needs of the world's poorest,' says the United Nations MDG website, in suitably rousing language.

Note the language used by United Nations Secretary-General Ban Ki-Moon in box 2.2 – he talks of 'time-bound targets', of measuring progress, of 'ambitious but feasible'

> **Box 2.2   Millennium Development Goals**
>
> *The Millennium Development Goals set time-bound targets, by which progress in reducing income poverty, hunger, disease, lack of adequate shelter and exclusion — while promoting gender equality, health, education and environmental sustainability — can be measured. They also embody basic human rights — the rights of each person on the planet to health, education, shelter and security. The Goals are ambitious but feasible and, together with the comprehensive United Nations development agenda, set the course for the world's efforts to alleviate extreme poverty by 2015.*
>
> *United Nations, n.d., n.p.*

goals, and of setting the course – in other words, of setting direction. There is a clear aim to develop a sense of urgency, in order to create a sustainable sense of momentum towards the ultimate objective.

Outcome-orientated goals such as the MDGs represent high-level aspirations expressed in relation to factors that define an organisation's *raison d'être*. They focus on the desired future state, on the impact that the organisation wishes to have. They are goals that can explain the organisation's purpose but not ones against which the organisation or its people can be held accountable. For example, the capacity of any single institution to influence the global prevalence of HIV and AIDS is modest: no meaningful cause and effect can be established between an enterprise's action and movements in HIV and AIDS prevalence. Nevertheless, understanding the degree of prevalence is crucial if the organisation is to set appropriate priorities, and is to harness the motivation of its people.

Accountability needs to focus on those stages of the results chain over which the entity or individual being held accountable has a high degree of influence, recognising that the degree of influence that an organisation has diminishes as it moves up the chain. At the bottom of the chain, it can be argued that an organisation has total discretion over use of funds. By the time the top of the chain is reached, the influence of the organisation might be minimal.

What is certain is that there must be an appropriate match between that part of the chain over which a constituency has influence and the performance contract for which that constituency is accountable. The more influence a constituency has on the overall impact of an organisation, the more the focus of attention – the accountability – should be concentrated on the 'outcomes' end of the chain. For example, an organisation's board should focus on the 'outcomes' end of the chain – on assessing the impact that the organisation is having. Meanwhile, management is more likely to be accountable for how resources are used to implement strategy. In terms of the chain, this means focusing on inputs, activities and outputs.

What is incontestable is that the stakeholders financing a not-for-profit organisation should be interested in outcomes. Funders should want to know what they will get for their money, and to be confident, up front when the agreement is signed, that the organisation has a realistic plan by which it will achieve the outcomes. They also want confidence that they could not earn a better return on their investment elsewhere. In fact, the Rensselaerville Institute provides an assessment of the degree to which funding decisions have lost touch with outcomes and begun focusing on activities instead. It claims that funding proposers often fail, 'to state in specific terms just what they are willing to be held accountable to achieve. When those fabled "measurable objectives" *are* stated, they often turn out to be inputs, not outcomes' (Williams *et al*, 1996, p. 13).

There would also appear to be much evidence to suggest that both funder and grantee invest more energy in preparing and assessing the funding proposal than in assessing whether the project or programme actually delivered the promised outcomes to the targeted beneficiaries. _Outcome Funding_ offers a thorough outcome-based approach to grant-making, which helpfully positions funders as investors 'charged with dealing with a given problem [who] employ funds to target investments to achieve specific benefits' (Williams *et al*, 1996, p. 45).

> *Used as the central accountability concept, the outcome focus creates a rich opportunity for plausible excuses*
>
> *Scott, 2001, pp. 175–76*

Scott makes four observations to explain why holding organisations and their leaders accountable for outcomes is difficult to enforce.

- *Outcomes are typically the result of a wide range of factors that are only partially within the control of an individual [organisation].*
- *The causal relationships between outputs and outcomes are frequently not well understood.*
- *There are problems in holding managers accountable when the timeframe is such that the outcome may not be visible for many years as, for example, with education.*
- *Many outcomes are difficult to measure.*

Scott, 2001, p. 175

He concludes that 'attempting to [hold organisations accountable only for outcomes] has great potential to descend into a debate about evidence, causality and degree of control' (Scott, 2001, p. 175).

Scott's assessment of the limitations of using outcomes highlights four criteria that need to apply if accountability is to be possible and meaningful.

1. Accountability should be focused as close to client outcomes – as far up the results chain – as possible. This reflects this book's core proposition that not-for-profit organisations exist to maximise beneficial impact for those individuals they serve. The further the accountability focuses away from outcomes (down the chain), the greater the risk of non-alignment between activity and outcome – in other words, the greater the chance that performance fails to deliver the intended benefits.
2. The desired results must be within the control of the constituency being held accountable, so that meaningful cause and effect can be established. It must be possible to determine that the actions of the constituency have caused the result.
3. It must be possible to assess whether the result has occurred or not. Having evidence of the result – particularly if supported with measurement – aids the assessment considerably, placing an onus on careful definition of the desired result.
4. Assessment must be timely, so that appropriate learning can be converted into follow-up action, such as reward, repetition or correction.

These four criteria help diagnose the inherent tension in enforcing accountability. True accountability needs to focus on outcomes – on the welfare of the targeted group. Yet measuring and assessing the state of outcomes will almost certainly be hard to do compared to components further down the chain. Leaders cannot run the organisation while waiting for outcome measures: they need to focus along the whole chain. So, the importance of focusing on outcomes to drive organisational purpose and design, strategy and work programme has to be balanced by a recognition that it may not be possible to influence or measure outcomes sufficiently to be able to hold the organisation accountable for them. Day-to-day accountability, perhaps, must move down the results chain and focus on the conversion of pounds to outputs.

Barber's UK experience (see p. 43) does challenge the conclusion that basing accountability on outcomes is unlikely to be successful. Armed with considerable political will, and a clear understanding of the delivery chain (see box 2.3), it would appear that the UK government was able to drive improvement in public services by focusing very clearly on outcomes from the public's point of view. The Rensselaerville Institute, too, makes an impressive case for targets in terms of enabling organisations to retain an outcomes focus, including adopting a customer-orientated approach to tracking progress past milestones. 'Are enough customers reaching each milestone of the programme to ensure that the final outcomes are satisfactory?' the Institute asks.

Box 2.3   Delivery chain
A 'delivery chain' refers to the complex networks of organisations, including central and local government, agencies, and bodies from the private and third sectors that need to work together to achieve or deliver an improved public sector outcome. National Audit Office/Audit Commission, 2006, p. 1

Scott's case for an output focus to performance is based on the scope that such a focus provides to concentrate on deliverables over which the constituency has control. This enables a contract to be established. Then, how the contract is implemented can be measured in a timely manner. With evidence, appropriate consequences can be applied judiciously. Using outputs appears to meet Scott's four criteria listed on p. 25, in that outputs are high up the results chain, within the control of management, measurable and without excessive time lags. However, in relation to the first criterion, note that while a focus on outputs rather than outcomes is sensible in many regards, it does expose the risk that the entity will deliver the desired outputs but fail to deliver the desired outcomes. The organisation may be complemented for its industry, but guilty of failure to deliver meaningful outcomes to beneficiaries.

What is clear is that using outputs does not avoid the need to focus on outcomes. Instead, leaders must track outcomes in order to define purpose, track outputs to define performance, and apply judgement to assure themselves of the link – the line of sight – between the two. They must have confidence that the outputs delivered represent the most impactful contribution that the organisation could make to the desired outcomes – however difficult it is to measure the cause and effect. The further the attention moves from outcomes, the greater the risk of non-alignment.

There is considerable temptation to define accountability in terms of the bottom sections of the chain, where influence and possible control is greatest. The financial steward, groomed on the accountant's predilection for numbers, is particularly susceptible to introducing input-orientated accountability, using controls that can easily become input targets. The attraction is easily understood. The 'input' end of the chain is where organisations have most control, results are most amenable to measurement, and measurement is available frequently and relatively easily. Three of the four criteria are met. The harder that leaders and managers find it to ensure accountability in terms of outputs and outcomes, the more they will tend to revert to the 'input' end of the chain, articulating accountability in terms of spending, staffing and other resources. The more this happens, the less latitude is given to the operating units, and the greater the risk of excessive centralised decision making.

The budget is particularly vulnerable to misuse. What is intended as no more than an allocation of resources, in order to enable activity to be undertaken, becomes instead a performance target to be hit. As chapter 11 details, the consequences can be dramatic, stimulating 'spend or lose' mindsets and other gaming behaviours. Paymasters can try to quickly exercise control by imposing input-based spending controls – for example, placing tight rules on certain types of expenditure, such as travel, IT equipment or consultants.

The risk of excessive decision making by the centre – highlighted by Kelman earlier in this chapter – is a real one. Ideally, the budget distributor would establish a contract that expresses return in terms of beneficiary outcomes. However, in practice, because of the difficulties of attribution, measurement and time-liness, outputs become the best surrogate for outcomes. However, outputs can also be subject to similar difficulties – albeit on a lesser scale. As a result, attention focuses – sometimes almost exclusively so – on

> **Box 2.4   How input-based controls can distort**
>
> Spenders are held accountable for limiting spending on, say, travel, to £x in the year, and typically this is what they will do! Travel expenditure is increasingly actively 'managed' as the year progresses, with journeys and payments being scheduled to fall whichever side of the year end serves the short-term purpose of spending to target. At the end of the year, the budget distributor announces success in controlling costs; the spender, success in hitting spending targets. The consequences on outputs and outcomes are unknown and unproclaimed.

inputs. Energy is spent enforcing control over input spending, but with potentially perverse consequences if this is done in a crude, target-based, measurement-driven way (see box 2.4). Basing accountability on inputs can be as sub-optimal as basing it on outcomes can be forlorn.

EVIDENCE-BASED MANAGEMENT AND THE CHALLENGE OF MEASUREMENT

The challenges of applying targets to metrics are illustrated earlier in this chapter. However, what about the use of metrics themselves, even if without targets? How valuable is measurement in establishing and maintaining accountability within an organisation? Intuitively, the value of measurement would seem to be high, facilitating evidence-based management. Jim Collins, author of the much-heralded *Good to Great* (2001), is in no doubt of its value in any organisation, including those in the public and social sectors (see box 2.5). He has no sympathy with those who sigh at the challenge of measurement without profit.

Box 2.5   The importance of evidence

It doesn't really matter whether you can quantify your results. What matters is that you rigorously assemble **evidence** *– quantitative or qualitative – to track your progress ...*

To throw our hands up and say 'but we cannot measure performance in the social sectors the way you can in a business' is simply lack of discipline. All indicators are flawed, whether qualitative or quantitative ... What matters is not finding the perfect indicator, but settling upon a **consistent and intelligent** *method of assessing your output results, and then tracking your trajectory with rigor. What do you mean by great performance? Have you established a baseline? Are you improving? If not, why not? How can you improve even faster towards your audacious goals?*

Collins, 2005, pp. 7–8[2]

Much store is (rightly) placed on being able to state not only what you plan to achieve, how you intend to achieve it, and who will be accountable for what – but also how you will know if you have succeeded. However, to add value, measurement must contribute to decision making. If the information collected and shared does not inform decisions, then its value is minimal. Collecting the data bears an opportunity cost – the resources could have been used for other activities that add more value.

Converting income to impact – climbing the chain – incontrovertibly benefits from the discipline of using facts to inform decision making. Returning to our earlier example, without the facts (established through the sometimes laborious and expensive process of data collection), it is impossible to imagine assessing whether the prevalence of HIV and AIDS has declined. It is also easy to understand how important it is to maintain a constant watch on outcomes – if only to drive an incessant questioning of the organisation's strategy, of how the organisation is contributing to the desired outcome, and of how it intends to contribute in the future.

Similarly, organisations rely on operational measurement. They must know how much they are spending. They can benefit considerably from measuring the efficacy of processes, and from undertaking pilot studies to learn the likely implications of introducing a particular change, a new process or policy. Data mining and analytical capabilities and processes can be among the most valuable, and undervalued, skills in an organisation.

Pfeffer and Sutton (2006) have devoted an entire book to extolling the virtues of evidence-based management (see box 2.6). Their very title – *Hard Facts, Dangerous Half-Truths and Total Nonsense* – indicates what the authors believe organisations often use in place of evidence to make decisions – hope or fear,

---

[2] *Good to Great,* Copyright © 2001 by Jim Collins. Reprinted with permission from Jim Collins

practice that is commonly accepted elsewhere, past practice in-house, and ideologies – and the likely consequences of doing so.

By 'evidence-base', Pfeffer and Sutton are referring to evidence gathered through both quantitative and qualitative measurement:

> *Although quantitative data are important, it is crucial to also learn from clinical practice and observation, and to understand that management, like medicine, is both an art and a science … By focusing only on what can be quantified, we can lose sight of what matters most.*
>
> Pfeffer and Sutton, 2006, p. 40

Box 2.6   Evidence-based management

Evidence-based management proceeds from the premise that using better, deeper logic and employing facts to the extent possible permits leaders to do their jobs better. Evidence-based management is based on the belief that facing the hard facts about what works and what doesn't, understanding the dangerous half-truths that constitute so much conventional wisdom about management, and rejecting the total nonsense that too often passes for sound advice will help organizations perform better.

Pfeffer and Sutton, 2006, p. 13

Pfeffer and Sutton promote vigorously the value of experimentation followed by analysis of the results. They urge readers to replace endless debating with experimentation, and to learn by doing and seeing what works.

Of course, often the necessary data is not to hand. It can be complicated and time-consuming to collect, and difficult to interpret. As a result, it can often be unavailable at the moment that decisions have to be made. Suggesting that 'qualitative data, especially field trips to test existing assumptions, can be powerful tools for gathering useful evidence quickly' (Pfeffer and Sutton, 2006, p. 21), Pfeffer and Sutton offer a set of diagnostic questions that can be asked up front, before any data collection is attempted. The questions are perceptive and, if answered honestly, can be profound, offering organisations the potential to avoid costly, erroneous decisions. For example:

- *What assumptions does the idea or practice make about people and organizations? What would have to be true about people and organizations for the idea or practice to be effective?*
- *Which of these assumptions seem reasonable and correct to you and your colleagues? Which seem wrong or suspect?*
- *Could this idea or practice still succeed if the assumptions turned out to be wrong?*

- *How might you and your colleagues quickly and inexpensively gather some data to test the reasonableness of the underlying assumptions?*
- *What other ideas or management practices can you think of that would address the same problem or issue **and** be more consistent with what you believe to be true about people and organizations?*

Pfeffer and Sutton, 2006, p. 22

Pfeffer and Sutton's rejection of the notion that only quantitative data is relevant to evidence-based management – the 'what gets measured gets done' school – begins to move the discussion towards the Deming philosophy. Deming is attributed with the observation that:

97 percent of what matters in an organization can't be measured. Only maybe 3 per cent can be measured. But when you go into most organizations and look at what people are doing, they're spending all their time focusing on what they can measure and none of their time on what really matters – what they can't measure.

Johnson, 1998, n.p.

> *In the study of complex phenomena … which depend on the actions of many individuals, all the circumstances which will determine the outcome of a process … will hardly ever be fully known or measurable.*
>
> *Hayek, 1974, n.p.*

Economic Sciences Nobel Prizewinner Friedrich August Hayek (1974), Wheatley and Kellner-Rogers (1999), Johnson and Bröms (2000) and Seddon (2006) all argue that measurement is not the panacea for performance management (see box 2.7 for an example), and that there are crucial lessons to be learned from nature. All refer to the evidence of living systems to adapt and thrive. 'Measurement is crucial,' pronounces Wheatley and Kellner-Rogers (1999, n.p.) – but only if it provides feedback that is self-generated, context-specific and permeates new and surprising information. 'The recognition of the insuperable limits to his knowledge ought to teach the student of society a lesson of humility which should guard him against becoming an accomplice in men's fatal striving to control society,' warns Hayek (1974, n.p.). In fact, Hayek uses the analogy of sport to illustrate his point that many of the factors that contribute to the final result defy measurement, not least the people-orientated factors, such as motivation and psychology.

Consider Seddon's appeal for measurement to enable learning and understanding rather than to support performance management (see box 2.1). It is the cry of all Deming supporters: 'Don't let the urge to control performance suffocate the learning inherent in measurement!' Arguably, there is an inherent tension between measuring for the purpose of learning and measuring for the purpose of performance management. Seddon advocates a single test of the value of a measure by asking: 'Can this help us understand and improve performance?' He promotes capability measures (defined as the measurement of end-to-end process elapsed time to deliver the purpose of the process to the customer). It is an approach consistent with Johnson and Bröms's 'management by means', with the manager's task being to improve the system's capability to serve the needs of customers.

Box 2.7   What do we measure and why?
Assumedly, most managers want reliable, high quality work. They want commitment, focus, teamwork, learning and quality. They want people to pay attention to those things that contribute to performance.
If you agree that these are the general attributes and behaviors you're seeking, we'd like to ask whether, in your experience, you have been able to find measures that **sustain** these strong and important behaviors over time. Or if you haven't succeeded at finding them yet, are you still hopeful that you **will** find the right measures? Do you still believe in the power of measures to elicit these performance qualities?
The longer we try to garner these behaviors through measurement and reward, the more damage we do to the quality of our relationships, and the more we trivialize the meaning of work.
Wheatley and Kellner-Rogers, 1999, n.p.

KEY PERFORMANCE INDICATORS

Key performance indicators (KPIs) are among the crop of management terms currently in vogue. Led by performance management models such as the Balanced Scorecard (Kaplan and Norton, 1996), KPIs are now being used to measure organisational performance from many perspectives, of which finance is just one. It is through comparison of actual and forecast results with the KPIs that corrective or reinforcing action is stimulated, with the aim of ensuring that the organisational objectives are achieved at all times. If KPIs are well defined, they will reassure when all is well and raise a flag when corrective action is needed. When used as targets, the KPIs reflect the aspirations of the organisation, while as parameters they identify the boundaries within which performance is expected.

As their very name, and the definitions in box 2.8 imply, KPIs are typically regarded as being measures by which performance can be judged. They comprise a small number of measures that track critical elements of performance over time. They help managers to review actual performance and often can also be used to look forward, to provide the short- and long-term outlook. Their primary purpose is to inform decision making. Organisations can set performance target levels by defining the standards that should be reached in relation to each KPI within a defined time period. Through comparing the actual and forecast results with the KPIs, corrective or reinforcing action can be stimulated, with the aim of ensuring that the organisational objectives are achieved at all times.

So, good KPIs do the following:

- focus attention, requiring the discipline to focus on just a few indicators
- look at trends over time and invite discussion about whether the trend is satisfactory, the root causes driving the trend, and therefore the likely future outlook
- provide comparisons across units, or across organisations. Bringing peers from different units or organisations together with common indicators can be extremely powerful. Such benchmarking, or peer review, is intended to stimulate learning through highlighting best practice, by provoking understanding about the reasons for differences and debate about the reasonableness of those differences.
- inform decision making and action planning on important issues – this is their most important function.

Box 2.8   Definitions of KPIs

Performance measures track key elements of the input, process and output chain that need to be managed. They measure 'whether' objectives are being achieved.

Hudson, 2009, p. 139

Key success factors or critical success factors. *These are the things the organization must do, the criteria it must meet, or the performance indicators it must do well against (because they matter to key stakeholders) in order to survive and prosper.*

Bryson, 2004, p. 126

Nevertheless, it is easy to misuse KPIs as a control tool that drives staff to do whatever is necessary to hit inappropriate targets. They should not be used in isolation. Instead, they must form part of an overall approach to managing units, integrating strategy and performance management with high-quality HR practices. In other words, KPIs are a vital support tool to help organisations run themselves effectively. To this end, the indicators play a valuable role in supporting dialogue, but they can do no more than that. They are no substitute for open, critical management discussion and judgement, and it is important to understand their limitations.

It is comparatively easy for the collection and publication of KPIs to become a measurement industry. The collection and publication process must not crowd out scope for interpretation and dialogue, and it is important that the focus of discussion centres on the business implications, rather than the calculation methodology. It is equally easy to fall into the trap of endlessly refining metrics in pursuit of the 'perfect indicator'. It is much better to table the available data and seek to improve it over time, through use, rather than to operate in a vacuum without any indicators at all.

> KPIs must *inform* the topics of discussion – not *become* the topics of discussion.

A further risk is that discussions may focus on metrics rather than outcomes. Business reviews (the subject of chapter 18) have to focus on what needs to be done in order to achieve the desired impact. Metrics should provide answers to questions raised by participants, but too often the metric becomes the subject – in other words, the question itself – rather than providing supportive evidence to a discussion on outcomes and impact.

It is clearly difficult for a set of indicators to be both comprehensive and focused, and be simple to understand without being over-simplistic. Perhaps most fundamentally of all, organisations must resist the temptation to believe that the standard of performance will become self-evident, simply through publishing data in relation to a set of indicators. Rarely can a KPI adequately describe the context in which performance was achieved, or overcome the challenges of attribution.

Instead, the way forward must be to engage actively in dialogue within and across organisations, using the indicators realistically, acknowledging their value and their limitations (see box 2.9). Then, users can focus on what the indicators tell them about performance, whether performance is improving over time, and how the unit compares to others. Indicators should provoke leaders to reflect on how good performance should have been, given the circumstances that actually prevailed, rather than on being preoccupied with whether the planned number was hit. Most importantly of all, indicators

Box 2.9   A more measured management?

The performance agenda, like all the other important aspects of management, has to be pursued with and through people – or else it falters. Measurement and other techniques are at their best when they support and inform dialogue around different concerns and conceptions of performance. They are least helpful when they are seen as an alternative to dialogue (e.g. with reports being used as the basis for 'management by exception').

Paton, 2003, p. 167

should help organisations to look forward, by helping to inform decisions about long-term direction and short-term action.

However, as discussed earlier in the chapter, conditions of uncertainty raise questions about the value of using targets as performance measures – whether expressed in relation to KPIs or in more traditional forms, such as budgets. The less certain the future, the less easily an organisation can predetermine what success will look like, and therefore the less validity any such predetermined definitions of success have when analysing actual results.

Hope and Fraser (2001a) argue that it must make sense to decide what acceptable performance is retrospectively. This means judging the level of performance once the actual circumstances in which the performance was delivered can be considered, and once it has been possible to compare against others in a similar position. What is the sense in deciding now what will be an acceptable performance in, say, 12 months' time? What is now expected to be excellent or poor performance may, in hindsight, prove to have been quite the reverse. Ten per cent income growth may sound fine until it is compared with what everyone else has achieved. Five per cent growth might actually have been fantastic performance given the conditions under which it was achieved.

The more this argument is accepted, the more that KPI targets need to be regarded not as predetermined measures of performance but as intended outcomes made at a certain point in time, and which can change as time moves forward. Human nature responds very positively to targets, to setting and reaching goals: ask any fundraiser. The Beyond Budgeting model promoted by Hope and Fraser (2001a) strongly advocates setting relative, rather than absolute, measures of performance. Good performance, it persuasively argues, is reflected by doing better than others rather than by passing absolute milestones. This approach ensures that targets provide continuous stretch, thereby driving incremental, continuous improvement (see box 2.10).

Box 2.10 Adaptive performance management

Specific targets are constantly reset at a level that, if reached, will improve the relative position of the organisation unit (or whole company) against some relative benchmark. This can be an external or internal competitor, last quarter or year, or simply a self-imposed stretch target based, perhaps, on some world-class benchmark or group aspiration.

Jeremy Hope and Robin Fraser (personal communication, 13 March 2001)

ADOPTING A REFLECTIVE APPROACH TO THE PERFORMANCE AGENDA

This brief discussion about targets and accountability highlights the challenge that leaders face if they wish to ensure that everyone is appropriately aligned with the organisational purpose. It is all too easy to impose or encourage inappropriate practices and give unintended signals that dilute the effectiveness of effort. The risk of what Paton (2003) labels 'disconnected managerialism' is high (see box 2.11). His solution is to advocate realism by, for example, being aware of the difference between the necessary simplicities of measures and the ambiguities and inconsistencies of real organisational performance:

> **Box 2.11   Disconnected managerialism**
>
> *Where modern discourse and methods are conspicuous (and may even play well externally) but they do not impact the main work, except as noise and a burden. This may happen because they are handed down unilaterally, or because they change too frequently, or because they are overlayed upon unresolved difficulties and divisions.*
>
> *Paton, 2003, p. 161*

> *Additional performance information will often be warranted, but more realism and less rhetoric regarding its value, and especially regarding the costs, difficulties and pitfalls of obtaining it, are badly needed.*
>
> Paton, 2003 p. 162

Paton advocates that such realism should come from adopting a reflective approach to performance measurement and performance improvement as opposed to either a committed or cynical one (see fig. 2.1).

ESTABLISHING THE PERFORMANCE CONTRACT

This book started by laying out the core proposition – that organisations are accountable for maximising impact over time for those that they exist to serve. This means converting funds received into impact (climbing the results chain) as effectively and efficiently as possible. Think of it as a ratio: the rate of conversion of income into impact over time.

$$\frac{\text{Impact}}{\text{Income}} = \text{Return}$$

The higher the numerator (impact) and/or the lower the denominator (income), the greater the return will be. It is not sufficient to maximise impact without reference to the income received that enabled the organisation to function, as overspending can lead, ultimately, to bankruptcy. Equally, if an organisation fails to focus on impact while preoccupying itself with income, expenditure and other internal matters, this will leave it impotent.

	Committed	Cynical	Reflective
Philosophical position	Positivist, rationalist	Sceptic	Constructivist
Attitude to measurement	Generally positive	Generally negative	Interested but cautious
Where measures come from	Goals	Someone's agenda	Problems and issues
Expected use of measurement	For learning and accountability	For control	Various — for dialogue, to clarify expectations; for 'challenge, check and conformity'
What matters in performance reporting	The facts	Creative accounting	A grounded narrative and analysis tailored to the concerns of the stakeholder(s) in question
Proper relationship between institutional, managerial and professional levels	Close alignment	Close alignment with own view — failing which, decoupling	Loose coupling (to accommodate differences, and change, in concepts of performance)
Attitude to new improvement methods	Useful tools	Fads, waste of time	Depends on use and context
Ways of applying new methods	Follow the rules, do it properly	Tactically, perhaps collusively, with a view to appearances	Open-minded, willing to improvise, adapt, collude, depending on context
Internal/external orientation	Internal orientation ('integration' or 'emulation')	External orientation ('bearing' or 'badging')	If possible, a dual orientation ('creative integration')
Benefits sought	Improved performance	Maintain confidence of external bodies; preserve autonomy	Develop relationship with external bodies and make some improvements (while accepting that one or the other may not be achievable)

Fig. 2.1 Approaches to methods of performance measurement and improvement (Paton, 2003, p. 166)

A helpful adage is 'Until your customer is satisfied, you are just cost'. In other words, until the targeted beneficiary benefits, the organisation has achieved nothing. Its task is to maximise return over time, and this requires financial viability. In practice, the task facing organisations is to demonstrate continuous improvement in the ratio – to get better and better at addressing the target group's welfare effectively and efficiently. This simple concept applies throughout the chain, and is valid in relation to the work of any individual or unit associated with the organisation. Maximise customer impact (whoever the customer is) for minimal cost (expenditure of income). It's an extremely helpful directive.

What becomes critical is to bestow on organisations, and the units within them, the responsibility and incentive to maximise the effectiveness and efficiency of resource utilisation, as part of a broader set of objectives focused on 'doing the right thing' for the client. Units must be judged on how well they have used resources, including the level used, rather than exclusively on whether they spend what is allocated to them.

Key stewardship questions

1. Is the organisation clear on where it is trying to reach?

2. Is the organisation using targets? If so, why?

3. How does the organisation know how well it is performing?

4. What are the organisation and its leaders accountable for?

5. What approach does the organisation adopt to measuring and improving performance?

6. What is the implicit or explicit performance contract?

7. How does the organisation intend to obtain clarity and support on these issues?

3 Setting and implementing strategy

HOW STRATEGY ADDS VALUE

Strategy answers the question 'how?'. A corporate strategy is nothing more than a description of how an organisation intends to get where it wants to be. There are many definitions to choose from, each placing a distinct slant on what distinguishes strategy from other management activities and tools (see box 3.1). However, they all address the question 'how?'.

Box 3.1　Definitions of strategy

The essence of strategy is in the activities – choosing to perform activities differently or to perform different activities than rivals ...

Strategy renders choices about what not to do as important as choices about what to do.

Porter, 1996, pp. 64 and 77

A pattern of purposes, policies, programs, actions, decisions, or resource allocations that define what an organization is, what it does, and why it does it.

Bryson, 2004, p. 46

*Strategies are means not ends. Strategies are actions, they are what an organization **does**, not what it is **for**. The **sole** justification for a strategy is its effect on achieving the purpose or conduct.*

Argenti, 1993, p. 41

Strategy is one step in a logical continuum that moves an organization from a high-level mission statement to the work performed by frontline and back-office employees.

Kaplan and Norton, 2001, p. 72

Doing the right thing is important ... And having a clear strategy is essential for producing focus and facilitating communication and coordinated action inside companies.

Pfeffer and Sutton, 2006, p. 143–4

There is one powerful lesson from the strategy literature and that is the importance of having people understand what they are supposed to be doing and develop some consensus about where, in their view, business success comes from. In simple terms, you aren't likely to get anywhere if you don't know where you are going.

Pfeffer and Sutton, 2006, p. 153

Does your organisation need to prepare a corporate strategy? The answer is, unequivocally, 'Yes!'. Periodically it is vital to carry out high-level thinking about the *raison d'être* of the organisation and to consider how, in broad terms, the organisation intends to meet its mandate, whether or not this thinking ends up being pulled together in the form of a strategic plan. Otherwise, there will be no coherence or rationale to the activities undertaken. The common theme of all the definitions in box 3.1 is focus: on enabling everyone associated with the organisation to be clear about what the objectives of the organisation are, and on how it intends to achieve those objectives.

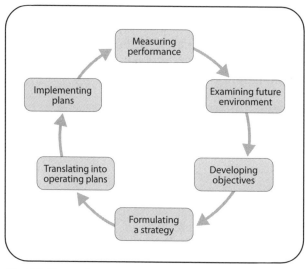

Fig. 3.1 The performance management cycle

To a lesser or greater extent, all planning (including determining corporate strategies) can be described in some form of the basic performance management cycle (see fig. 3.1). The organisation sets goals in order to confirm what it is trying to achieve in the context of where it is now. A plan of action is agreed that is intended to help achieve the goals. Then, the plan is implemented, results are monitored, and goals and plans are either revised or confirmed. There is a continuous process of looking ahead, establishing a destination and a plan of how to get there, setting off – and finally, monitoring one's progress, in the light of which goals or plans might need to be changed.

WHAT SHOULD A CORPORATE STRATEGY DESCRIBE?

Just a few minutes' research will quickly confirm that there is a whole myriad of theories and models on offer to guide the budding strategist. There is no 'right' way to prepare or write a strategy, and there is a real risk of trying to shoehorn the organisation and its unique circumstances into one particular theory. No two organisations' management systems look the same, and neither does any system mirror perfectly any of the theoretical models expounded by the academics, consultants, advisers or theorists. In practice, most organisations mix and match elements of different models, tailoring them to be effective in their particular environment.

Crucially, whatever strategy tools are used, they must enable the organisation to:

- understand why it exists, and how it intends to meet its purpose
- define what success looks like
- share that understanding with others – for example, employees, donors, beneficiaries and partners
- monitor how the organisation is getting on within a framework.

It does not matter what the corporate strategy looks like, or how it is prepared, as long as its implementation enables the organisation to meet its purpose. According to some research, the track record of organisations in implementing strategy may not be good. Kaplan and Norton, for example, refer to research that puts strategy implementation failure rates in the '70 percent to 90 percent range' (Kaplan and Norton, 2001, p. 1). Pfeffer and Sutton state that 'the empirical evidence shows a surprisingly weak link between the activity of strategic planning and company performance' (Pfeffer and Sutton, 2006, p. 136). However, to the extent that they do succeed, one could ask whether this success is in spite of their strategic planning or because of it. Before engaging in the exercise of strategic planning – which can achieve much, but can also prove to be a major distraction – it is worth being absolutely clear about the purpose of the exercise. By the end of a strategic planning process, the organisation should have:

- a clear sense of direction
- some defined organisational priorities
- an understanding of what it intends to do about the key issues facing it
- a sense of the internal and external environment in which it is operating
- clarity about responsibilities.

Bryson (2004, pp. 11–12) defines five overriding benefits that should result from engaging in strategic planning:

1. **The promotion of strategic thought, action and learning:** This leads the organisation to clarify its future direction and establish organisational priorities for action: 'Strategic planning can be used to help organize and manage effective organizational change processes in which the organization figures out what to change but also keeps the best' (p. 11).
2. **Improved decision making:** Strategic planning focuses attention on the crucial issues and challenges that an organisation faces, and helps key decision makers to plan how to cope with them.
3. **Enhanced organisational effectiveness:** Organisations engaging in strategic planning will be better placed to address major organisational issues, respond wisely to internal and external demands and pressures, and deal effectively with rapidly changing circumstances.
4. **Enhanced effectiveness of broader societal systems:** Most of the public problems that societies face stretch beyond the boundaries of any one

organisation. Strategic planning helps organisations to take the broader environment into account, helping them figure out how best to partner with other organisations so that they can jointly create better environments.

5. **Effective fulfilment of roles and responsibilities:** by those policy makers and key decision makers directly involved in the strategic planning process. This is likely to strengthen teamwork and expertise. What is more, public and not-for-profit organisations that provide real service, and continue to find ways to do so as circumstances change, are most likely to continue to exist.

Similarly, Hind (1995, pp. 85–86, text adapted) highlights three benefits, among others, that should come from strategic planning:

1. a set of objectives that provide focus for an organisation's activities and increase the commitment of its donors, staff, volunteers and trustees
2. a basis on which resource decisions can be made, by prioritising the organisation's proposed activities
3. a benchmark against which progress can be subsequently measured, by clearly setting out the organisation's objectives.

THE RISK OF STRATEGY

The benefits described above entice most organisations to invest huge efforts in strategic planning, typically led by the most senior individuals, often coordinated by a dedicated strategy function. Strategy is a common preoccupation of incoming chief executives.

However, there are two major risks to be aware of, and to manage. The first is that preparing and implementing a strategy disables the organisation from sensing and responding to priorities that emerge subsequently. This risk increases with uncertainty. Any strategy must cater for uncertainty, and the organisation must maintain a capability both to identify future opportunities and challenges, and to react appropriately to circumstances that were not anticipated at the time that the strategy was agreed. This means maintaining an inherent comfort with uncertainty and ambiguity, and being willing to shift direction if necessary.

The second is that the investment in planning comes at the expense of delivery. The management literature is full of stories of strategy implementation failures, with chief executive officers acknowledging that the secret of organisational success lies much more in an ability to execute effectively than in developing a strategic masterplan.

So, why is so much attention devoted to strategic planning, rather than to execution? Pfeffer (2006, p. 147) asserts that strategy is 'intellectually more engaging and analytically tractable' than operational matters. Similarly, Williams *et al*, commenting on the motivations of both funder and grantee in any grant application process, report that:

for both sides, there is higher status in the act of giving and getting than in spending and supporting over the long haul ... the top talent can now move to the next grant opportunity as the newly-funded project moves to line staff for implementation.

Williams et al, p. 28, 1996

'Implementation', 'delivery', 'execution' – call it what you will, it isn't as exciting as the diagnosis. Barber (2007) confirms this tendency from his UK government experience:

When [the prime minister's key advisers] spoke to me about education policy, it was usually to press me for new and bolder ideas. No harm in that, of course, but I used to say to them, 'Why don't you also ask me whether we have implemented existing policy effectively and whether it is making a real difference on the ground?' (pp. 44–45)

Well-established routines are as important to the ... delivery of results as major decisions on strategy or people. (p. 112)

Successful delivery often lay not in the big decisions, but in the everyday routine; the endless micro-decisions and interactions with officials, partners and stakeholders. (p. 124)

As the quotations in box 3.2 illustrate, these risks have led to the articulation of alternative theories of the benefits of strategy – for example, Haeckel describes strategy as though it is a state of being rather than the implementation of one predetermined plan of action – and to the emergence of schools of thought that question the whole value of traditional strategic planning.

Box 3.2   Strategy: the risks

Too much attention to strategic planning and reverence for strategic plans can blind organizations to unplanned and unexpected – yet incredibly useful – sources of information, insight, and action.

Bryson, 2004, p. 16

A fixation on strategy can obscure as much as it illuminates.

Pfeffer, 2006, p. 136

It is impossible for managers to plan or envision the long-term future of an innovative organization. Instead, they must create and discover an unfolding future, using their ability to learn together in groups and to interact politically in a spontaneous, self-organizing manner.

Stacey, 1993, p. 10

THE PROCESS OF DEVELOPING A STRATEGIC PLAN

There are many sources of material available to the reader to guide their thinking about how to design and manage a strategic planning process. It can be very helpful to try to determine where the organisation fits on an unpredictability spectrum, since the type of strategic planning that would be appropriate is crucially influenced by the extent to which the organisation is looking forward in an environment of certainty or uncertainty. The more certain the organisation's future, the more it can plan with confidence, adopting a rational, logical approach. The greater the uncertainty, the more important it is that the plan (and the process by which that plan is written and agreed) adopts flexible characteristics. The spectrum can be illustrated by reference to three types of strategic planning model: rational, political and chaotic (see fig. 3.2).

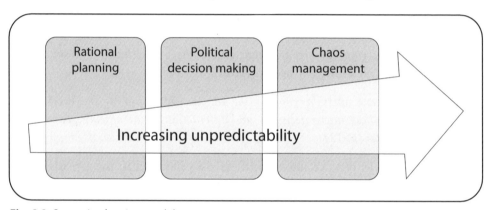

Fig. 3.2 Strategic planning models

The rational planning model

In this model, objectives are determined sequentially from goals, plans from objectives, and actions from plans. Goals are determined first – and from them, objectives are established over a defined period to meet those goals. With clear objectives in place, plans are then written outlining how the objectives will be met. This is all very neat, tidy and logical, but is heavily dependent on there being consensus among the parties on each of these steps. In practice, the steps can be reiterative, involving several refinements of thought before being agreed. This model reflects the basic performance management model presented in figure 3.1.

Hind lays out a very logical, easy-to-follow set of chronological steps by which to build a corporate strategy, which essentially follows the rational approach (see fig. 3.3):

1. the vision
2. the direction or mission statement
3. environmental analysis leading to corporate strategies

4. financial policies leading to a financial plan
5. key tasks
6. specific actions.

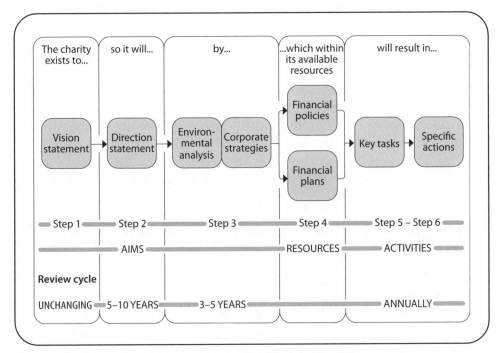

Fig. 3.3 The six steps in charity strategic planning (Hind, 1995, p. 88)

The political decision-making model

Recognising that in most organisations there is not such consensus, Bryson (2004) promotes an alternative model for determining strategy: the political decision-making model (see box 3.3).

Box 3.3   The political decision-making model

It begins with issues, which almost by definition involve conflict, not consensus. The conflicts may be over ends, means, timing, location, political advantage, reasons for change, or philosophy and values – and the conflicts may be severe. As efforts proceed to resolve these conflicts and learn how to move ahead, policies and programs emerge that address the issues and that are politically rational; that is, they are politically acceptable to involved or affected parties. Over time, more general policies may be formulated to capture, frame, shape, guide, or interpret the policies, programs and learning developed to deal with the issues. These various policies and programs are, in effect, treaties among the various stakeholder groups, and even though they may not record a true consensus, they do represent a reasonable level of agreement among stakeholders.

Bryson, 2004, p. 18

The political dimension of planning in public and not-for-profit organisations must be recognised head on. One of great strengths of these organisations is the commitment of its employees, volunteers, supporters and donors not only to their job, but to the cause: to 'making a difference'. Stakeholders are precisely that: they have a stake in the outcome, and very often their commitment is fuelled by deep-rooted ideology or conscience. With that commitment comes passion, intellect, but rarely consensus. Issues have to be put on the table and discussed.

Bryson (2004) takes readers through a 10-step strategic planning process (box 3.4) that reflects the political reality of establishing direction when multiple stakeholders must be engaged. He asserts that any not-for-profit organisation can follow this process if there is a 'dominant coalition' where a majority of participants support the process – or at least a 'coalition of the willing' – and if there is an individual willing and able to lead the organisation through it ('the process champion').

Box 3.4   The 10-step strategic planning process

1. *Initiate and agree on a strategic planning process.*
2. *Identify organizational mandates.*
3. *Clarify organizational mission and values.*
4. *Assess the external and internal environments to identify strengths, weaknesses, opportunities, and threats.*
5. *Identify the strategic issues facing the organization.*
6. *Formulate strategies to manage the issues.*
7. *Review and adopt the strategies or strategic plan.*
8. *Establish an effective organizational vision.*
9. *Develop an effective implementation process.*
10. *Reassess the strategies and the strategic planning process.*

Bryson, 2004, pp. 32–34

Hence step one of the 10 steps is the 'planning to plan' stage. Most of the steps are self-explanatory from the descriptions in box 3.4 but step two, 'identify organizational mandates', might not be. This refers simply to the need to identify early in the process what obligations the organisation has (whether legal or informal), and to understand clearly what area is not legitimate territory for it to enter. Bryson (2004, p. 37) makes a salutary observation in defence of this step, which ought to encourage all organisations to pause and reflect on what mandates they accept:

> *Most organizations make one or more of three fundamental mistakes. First, by not articulating or knowing what they must do, they are unlikely to do it. Second, they may believe they are more tightly constrained in their actions than they actually are. And third, they may assume that if they are not explicitly told to do something, they are not allowed to do it.*

One other question may stand out in considering the 10 steps – certainly when compared to the rational planning model: why is 'establish an effective organizational vision' positioned as late in the 10-step process as step eight? Bryson has a very pragmatic answer. If the organisation is able to define a generally accepted vision of success earlier in the process, then all well and good. Some organisations may indeed be able to kick off the whole process by agreeing its vision. Yet many others will not. This will only come when participants in the process have sorted out the difference between what they want and what they can have.

Helpfully, Bryson (2004) also defines 'two compelling reasons for holding off on a formal strategic planning effort'. The first is for 'an organization whose roof has fallen in' (p. 13) such as in a cash crisis, or where key leadership positions are vacant. The second reason is 'when the organization's key decision makers lack the skills, resources, or commitment to produce a good plan or when implementation is extremely unlikely' (p. 14). In such circumstances 'strategic planning will be a waste of time' says Bryson.

Acknowledging the political dimension to strategic management in the public sector, Michael Moore from the Kennedy School of Government at Harvard University defines three broad tests that organisational strategy (defined in box 3.5) must meet, the first of which describes the task of climbing the results chain.

Box 3.5 Organisational strategy for the public sector

Organizational strategy is a concept that simultaneously:
1. *declares the overall mission or purpose of an organization (cast in terms of important public values);*
2. *offers an account of the sources of support and legitimacy that will be tapped to sustain society's commitment to the enterprise; and*
3. *explains how the enterprise will have to be organized and operated to achieve the declared objectives.*

Moore, 1995, p. 71

These tests can be explained as follows (Moore, p. 71, 1995):

*First, the strategy must be **substantively valuable** in the sense that the organization produces things of value to overseers, clients and beneficiaries at low cost in terms of money and authority.*

*Second, it must be **legitimate and politically sustainable**. That is, the enterprise must be able to continually attract both authority and money from the political authorizing environment to which it is ultimately accountable.*

*Third, it must be **operationally and administratively feasible** in that the authorized, valuable activities can actually be accomplished by the existing* *organization with help from others who can be induced to contribute to the organization's goal.*

The chaos management model

In the political decision-making model, organisational leaders are responsible for meeting the three tests described above. The chaos management model, articulated by Stacey (1993), argues that management's task is to create unstable conditions from which the learning will take place (see box 3.6). In the Stacey model, strategy emerges spontaneously 'from the chaos of challenge and contradiction through a process of real time learning and politics' (Stacey 1993, p. 12). Stacey makes a coherent case, arguing that there is plenty of evidence that the strategic change introduced by organisations reflects their reaction to the uncertainty that they faced (in other words, the learning that they experienced) rather than the implementation of predetermined plans.

Box 3.6   Questioning causality

*As soon as we claim that we can envision and plan, that is, determine the long-term future of an organisation, we make the unquestioned assumption that there are identifiable links in organisational life, at least in principle, between a cause and an effect, between an action and an outcome. We could not possibly believe that a plan of action (for example, action A now, followed by action B next year and action C the year after) could lead to, say, a dominant market share, unless we were confident that there were causal links between an action now and a market share in five years' time. **It is no longer possible to avoid questioning that assumption about causality and when we do, we have to revise our views on how organisations develop strategically**.*

The new frame of reference exposes much of the received wisdom on strategic management to be a fantasy defence against anxiety, and points instead to the essential role of managers, in creating the necessary unstable conditions required for that effective learning and political interaction from which new strategic directions may or may not emerge.

Stacey, 1993, p. 11

Stacey (1993) gives an illuminating insight in how organisations will have to behave if they are to succeed in the uncertain future. He summarises this by contrasting two frames of reference – the current and the new (see fig. 3.4). The new frame challenges many of the deep-rooted conventions of how organisations should be run – particularly in values-driven, not-for-profit organisations that are stewarded on a culture of participation and reaching consensus. Stacey is challenging leaders to think about whether a single shared vision throughout the organisation is necessary, whether a strongly shared culture is desirable, and whether it is better to steward the organisation on the basis of self-policing learning rather than management by objectives.

Today's frame of reference	A new frame of reference
Long-term future is predictable to some extent	Long-term future is unknowable
Visions and plans are central to strategic management	Dynamic agendas of strategic issues are central to effective strategic management
Vision: single shared organisation-wide intention. A picture of a future state	Challenge: multiple aspirations, stretching and ambiguous. Arising out of current ill-structured and conflicting issues with long-term consequences
Strongly shared cultures	Contradictory counter cultures
Cohesive teams of managers operating in a state of consensus	Learning groups of managers, surfacing conflict, engaging in dialogue, publicly testing assertions
Decision making as purely logical, analytical process	Decision making as an exploratory, experimental process based on intuition and reasoning by analogy
Long-term control and development as the monitoring of progress against plan milestones. Constraints provided by rules, systems and rational argument	Control and development in open-ended situations as a political process. Constraints provided by need to build and sustain support. Control as a self-policing learning
Strategy as the realisation of prior intent	Strategy as spontaneously emerging from the chaos of challenge and contradiction, through a process of real-time learning and politics
Top management drives and controls strategic direction	Top management creates favourable conditions for complex learning and politics
General mental models and prescriptions for many specific situations	New mental models required for each new strategic situation
Adaptive equilibrium with the environment	Non-equilibrium, creative interaction with the environment

Fig. 3.4 Two frames of reference, Stacey, 1993, p. 12

However, what would the chaos management approach to running an organisation look like in practice? How does the Stacey model translate into action? What processes would be in place? Stacey offers an eight-step guide to help create the internal environment that will enable new strategic direction to emerge.

1. Develop new perspectives on the meaning of control by accepting learning as a form of control so that a sequence of actions will only continue in a particular direction while those espousing that direction continue to enjoy sufficient support.
2. Design the use of power to encourage open questioning and public testing of assertions, rather than competitive win/lose solutions.
3. Encourage self-organising groups, avoiding the temptation to set objectives, terms of reference, or promoting a particular predetermined outcome.
4. Provoke multiple cultures, by rotating people between functions or hiring experienced staff from other organisations.
5. Present ambiguous challenges instead of clear long-term objectives or visions, so that the emotion and conflict needed to encourage an active search for new ways of doing things is provoked.
6. Expose the business to challenging situations rather than running for cover.
7. Devote explicit attention to improving group learning skills, so that personal anxieties associated with uncomfortable learning experiences are overcome.
8. Create resource slack, so that learning and political interactions have time to take place properly.

Adapted from Stacey, 1993, pp. 16–17

It is not necessary to subscribe wholesale to the chaos management model in order to appreciate the potential value that could be gained from adopting some of the practices listed above. What is increasingly recognised by organisations in all sectors is that any strategic plan must be flexible so that unexpected circumstances (including opportunities and obstacles) can be managed appropriately at the time.

The challenge is to design a corporate strategy with enough clarity of thought about the vision of the future – and how that vision will be turned into reality – to guide decision making effectively, rather than simply creating a straitjacket that forces inappropriate decisions, or a document that is simply irrelevant. More and more organisations are looking to adapt strategy continuously but within the context, and with the guidance, of some principles, beliefs or values that critically define the organisation, what it is about and what it stands for. Haeckel proposes, as a result, that 'strategy should be expressed as a structure for action – an organizational system design of modular roles and accountabilities – when change is rapid and unpredictable' (personal communication, 31 May 2010).

DECIDING WHAT TO DO: DETERMINING PRIORITIES

The presentation of contrasting approaches to strategic planning aims to encourage stewards of every not-for-profit organisation to think carefully and creatively about the best method of developing and implementing a corporate strategy, given the unique circumstances that it faces. The result will almost certainly be a composite of the various theories and models. If this enables the organisation to climb the results chain with maximum effectiveness, then that is fine.

Bryson, Hind and others recognise the value that strategic planning can serve in establishing organisational priorities. In reality, organisations often face a bewildering choice of programmes, each of which in themselves are compelling, and which can be dissimilar to the extent of preventing easy comparison. Leaders need mechanisms for making choices. There are many factors that contribute to the decision. These include a mix of 'bottom-up' and 'top-down' internal influences, and a variety of external factors. Figure 3.5 identifies 13 factors. This list is not exhaustive, but it demonstrates the complexity of the selection task.

	Questions
Strategic importance	How critical is the programme in order to meet agreed institutional goals?
Strategic fit	How well does the programme fit with other priorities?
Client absorptive capacity	How able is the client to handle the intervention effectively?
Capacity	What else is the organisation already committed to? Does it have operational or financial capacity to carry out this programme?
Risk	How risky is the programme?
Track record	How successful has this sort of programme been in the past?
Potential	What impact can realistically be expected from the programme? What would be the cost–benefit?
Delivery competency	How competent is the organisation at handling this sort of programme?
Political importance	How much political support does the programme have?
Stakeholder requirements	Are stakeholders (such as donors and beneficiaries) expecting the organisation to run the programme?
Regulatory obligations	Is there a regulatory requirement to implement the programme?
Opportunity cost	What else could be done with the funds?
Values	How well does the programme fit with the organisation's values as an institution?

Fig. 3.5 The factors influencing strategic choices

In practice, it is clear that the ultimate decisions are highly judgemental and very difficult to rationalise in a scientific manner. For example, the World Bank has country assistance strategies that offer vital bottom-up insight into how it can best support its client countries individually. Shareholders and other donors apply top-down pressure on the institution. Further external pressure comes from the development community worldwide – both governmental and from the NGOs and other international institutions.

It can be difficult to pare down the potential programmes to a sensible list that can be successfully implemented. This is particularly true in organisations with strong political cultures where competing forces, backed by strong lobbying and weak decision-making capacity, rally behind any programme or initiative that looks at risk of being stopped or denied support. It is particularly important to consider how much change can be implemented simultaneously. While budget is often cited as a constraining factor, it may well be other factors, such as capacity to lead or to absorb implementation, that truly determine the pace of possible transformation.

Pfeffer and Sutton's diagnostic questions (see p. 29) provide one basis for assessing and comparing competing priorities. Another useful technique is to assess competing initiatives or programmes across two dimensions, representing two factors relevant to the selection decision. Figure 3.6 shows one example, making an assessment in relation to political obligation and likelihood of success. For each combination, an alternative course of action is appropriate.

		Likelihood of success	
		Low	High
Political obligation	Low	Ignore	Implement later
	High	Renegotiate	Implement now

Fig. 3.6 Assessing and comparing competing priorities

Particularly tricky can be those initiatives that have a high level of political support but which are unlikely to generate a high level of welfare impact. These programmes cannot be ignored, but will drain energy, resources and political capital if their implementation proceeds. In these cases it is critical that the agenda is renegotiated – at the very least in terms of timing the implementation. Implementation must focus on those programmes that have a high likelihood of success, with the sequencing influenced by factors such as political obligation.

Barber (2007, pp. 97–99) shares a framework that the Blair government used to assess the likelihood of successful delivery of any defined outcome. The framework uses four elements to establish an overall 'likelihood of delivery' assessment:

1. difficulty of the desired outcome (the degree of challenge)
2. quality of planning, implementation and performance management
3. capacity to drive progress – in other words, the political conduciveness and internal capacity to effect the desired change
4. the stage of delivery reached.

Barber's team used a four-point scale – 'policy development', 'early implementation', 'embedding change', with 'irreversible progress' being the most advanced of the four stages.

The Delivery Unit judged competing priorities in relation to each of the four elements, using current performance assessments as a reality check, and then reached an overall judgement on likelihood of delivery. For this, a traffic light scheme was used:

- **Red** – highly problematic: requires urgent and decisive action
- **Amber/red** – requires substantial action, some aspects need urgent action
- **Amber/green** – aspect(s) require substantial attention, some good
- **Green** – requires refinement and systematic implementation.

As Barber explains, the value of the framework was in enabling dissimilar programmes to be compared. This was possible as long as the judgements made were broadly right. The importance of being able to make good judgements is highly evident – not least given the challenges of measurement discussed in chapter 2. However, measurement, facts and evidence will take the decision maker only so far: they cannot make the ultimate decision.

The importance of trade-offs

Typically, discussions about strategic intentions will converge on the issue of trade-offs. This is because it is through identifying trade-offs that organisations demonstrate selectivity and choice. This is how they are able to show clarity about optimal use of resources (to identify which courses of action will best contribute to achieving the desired impact), and to demonstrate that inefficiencies have been eliminated. A lack of trade-offs suggests that there is still fat in the system: no choices have to be made. This implies that there is capacity to do everything!

CONVERTING STRATEGY INTO DELIVERY

The value of strategy comes from delivering the intended impact. While the organisational strategy sets direction, it is unlikely to be specific enough to serve as a guide for daily operational management. So, strategy must be converted into plans that are shorter term and more operational. Leaders must be able to assure themselves that the organisation has concrete action plans that can be implemented successfully and which, if this is done, will achieve the organisation's mission. They must be satisfied that the myriad of activities that will be undertaken day-by-day in multiple units will, in aggregate and over time, deliver the organisational impact intended.

Box 3.7   How to focus unit-based plans
■ Identify the five most important outcomes that the unit intends to deliver. ■ Indicate which organisational goal is addressed by each outcome. ■ Identify the key deliverables that the unit will supply in order to achieve the outcome. ■ State when each deliverable will be supplied, or each critical milestone reached.

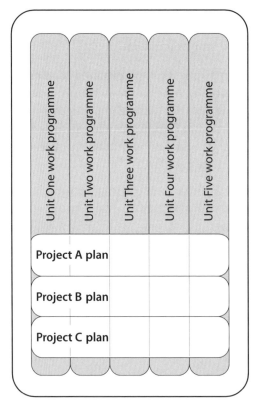

Fig. 3.7 Unit and project work programmes

Two types of plans will be useful: unit plans and programme-based plans. Both need to be succinct.

Unit-based plans

Mirroring the organisational structure, unit-based plans should outline what contribution each operational unit intends to make to the achievement of organisational objectives. Typically, units will supply deliverables – outputs, in the form of products, events and services. These plans should be driven from the top of the results chain down, enabling critical assessment of the plan. It must be apparent how the proposed activities do ultimately benefit the client (see box 3.7). A successful outcome is achieved through the uptake, adoption and use of the deliverable by the unit's client. The organisation can increase the delivery orientation and the onus of accountability for delivery by naming these plans 'unit results agreements'.

Programme-based plans

Programme-based plans straddle the organisational structure to look at programmes and processes end to end from the client perspective. These plans are particularly valuable in the case of time-limited projects that are in addition to the ongoing services that need to be provided. Such projects often span two or more years and require discrete multi-functional teams and specific financing. They don't neatly fit into the typical one-year unit-based work plans, and require explicit identification of accountabilities. They need to be managed using formal project management disciplines.

Organisations are rarely in a position of being able to choose just one of the two types of action plan. Typically they need both, as illustrated by fig. 3.7. This shows five discrete unit-based plans augmented by three cross-functional projects, each one of which might involve a different combination of units' involvement.

Key stewardship questions

1. Does the organisation have a strategy outlining how it intends to meet its purpose in the next x years?

2. What role does the strategy play in the overall management of the organisation?

3. Is the type of adopted strategy the most appropriate one, given the degree of uncertainty prevalent in the organisation's operating environment?

4. What strategic planning process best serves the organisation – rational, political or chaotic?

5. How is the organisation making strategic choices about what to do, and what not to do?

6. How does the organisation convert strategy into delivery?

4 Case studies in setting direction and strategy

Historically, strategic plans have been weighty tomes that set out in great detail what an organisation intends to achieve over a period of, typically, three to five years. However, after the great effort to produce such a plan, and the collective sigh of relief that greets its completion, the organisation often simply gets back to work, stopping only to refer to the plan in order to meet pre-arranged reporting deadlines. In fact, the very articulation in a quantifiable form of what the organisation aims to look like by the end of the plan period can become a millstone around the authors' necks, rather than an inspiration.

In hindsight, the plan can appear to have hardly influenced future actions. Chapter 3 highlighted the downside risk: that strategy can blinker an organisation. However, the upside of going public with organisations' intentions is real. Recall, for example, Barber's observation that 'making … objectives public … requires greater political courage but is also both more transparent and makes it more likely that progress will be made' (2007, p. 82).

Since the late 1990s, public sector and not-for-profit organisations have been writing different kinds of strategic plan. In fact, in many cases, these are not 'plans' as such. Rather, they are strategic frameworks that provide overall context, principles and direction, within which shorter-term plans and actions can be determined. They are typically short, easy-to-read documents that are inspiring, ambitious but increasingly honest about what can and can't be done, and what is needed.

This chapter introduces case studies to show how Sightsavers International (an NGO) and OECD member governments, particularly the UK government, have approached setting direction and strategy.

CASE STUDY 1: SIGHTSAVERS INTERNATIONAL

Sightsavers International has now developed its third strategic framework, covering the five-year period 2009 to 2013.[1] The framework includes a number of components, set out below. The last four of these – the vision, mission, values and change themes – collectively represent the organisation's strategic direction.

- **Context** – a summary of the external environment in which Sightsavers operates. For example, it refers to the latest research evidence of the link between blindness and poverty, the UN Convention on the Rights of Persons with Disabilities, and World Health Organization (WHO) statements on the future requirements of healthcare systems.
- **Lessons** – some headlines of achievements during the five-year period (from 2004 to 2008) of the previous framework and, more pertinently, acknowledgement of lessons learned. Demonstrating the candour exhibited by organisations that recognise their public accountability, Sightsavers draws lessons from its experience, performance and assessment of its operating environment. For example, it acknowledges the need to be less insular in its approach and to work more closely with community development programmes and the wider disability movement.
- **A vision statement** – an inspirational, concise statement of what the world could look like: 'a world where no one is blind from avoidable causes and where visually impaired people participate equally in society.'

> ### Box 4.1 Sightsavers International's mission statement
>
> *We are an international organisation working with partners in developing countries to eliminate avoidable blindness and promote equality of opportunity for disabled people.*

- **A mission statement** – a statement of how the organisation intends to contribute to advancement towards the vision (see box 4.1).
- **A statement of seven values** – those values that underpin all the work of the organisation and guide its decision makers.
- **Four change themes** – the key themes that drive the design of the organisation's strategy and work programme: health (see box 4.2), education, social inclusion, and community participation and development.

Against each of these themes Sightsavers identifies the external drivers that define why the theme needs to be addressed, the organisation's aims (both in the long term and over the five-year framework period), and the indicators that will be

---

[1] The first framework covered 2001 to 2003 and was featured in the first edition of this book (first edition entitled *Financial Stewardship*: Poffley, 2002). The second framework, originally covering 2004 to 2006, was extended to cover 2007 to 2008 while a major review of strategy was undertaken in preparation for the determination of a five-year strategy under a new chief executive.

used to help assess progress. Eye-catching potted case studies demonstrating how individuals' lives have been changed illustrate what is possible in each theme.

The statements incorporate what at first appear to be subtle changes from those in the previous framework. The vision statement recognises social inclusion more explicitly. Similarly, the mission statement refers to 'disabled' rather than 'blind' people, reflecting the organisation's view that the most effective way of helping people with, or threatened by, blindness is through the broader theme of disability. Both the vision and the mission statement have been simplified and shortened.

Box 4.2 Sightsavers change theme 1: health

External drivers: what led us to decide on our aims
- *Worldwide there are 314 million blind and visually impaired people, of whom 75% need not be (WHO, 2007 statistics).*
- *Avoidable blindness is best eliminated by aligning health systems with government policy. All health programmes should support and strengthen national health systems.*
- *Primary healthcare is the best means of reaching the greatest number of people. Eye health has not always been embedded in primary health care.*
- *There is a shortage of at least 1.5 million health workers in Africa.*

Aims: what we want to achieve

Ultimate aim: what we want to achieve in the long term
Governments will ensure that good quality eyecare is universally available to all people as an integral part of wider health systems.

Aim: what we want to achieve over this strategic framework period
Sightsavers will demonstrate approaches to eye health which are scalable, adaptable and cost-effective and which strengthen and support the overall health system.

Indicators: how we will measure our progress

Lead
% of Sightsavers supported eye health programmes that are embedded in national and local government health plans.

Lag
% of countries showing significant increase in public spending on eye health.

Sightsavers International, 2009, pp. 8–9

Meanwhile, the values have been redefined in terms of beliefs that are specifically relevant to Sightsavers:

- working with poor and marginalised communities
- collaborating with other organisations
- addressing avoidable blindness and promoting eye health

- working with disabled people to promote equal rights and opportunities
- enabling organisations and communities to find their own solutions
- ensuring learning and innovation
- embracing supporters to achieve the organisation's goals.

In the new framework, strategic priorities are replaced by change themes in an effort to introduce a greater sense of urgency, dynamism and to emphasise the fundamental need to inject change.

The changes to the statements resulted from extensive consultation and debate with beneficiaries, partners, supporters and staff, and are, in fact, substantive. It is not difficult to imagine how contentious the issue of referring to 'disabled' rather than 'blind' people was in revising the mission statement. The debate is important, and the words that ultimately appear in these statements are fundamental. The statements define who Sightsavers is, what it stands for, and how it behaves. The process by which the organisation makes these changes is a crucial part of establishing shared ownership of organisational performance. The process enables – but also requires – all participants to take collective responsibility for the organisation. The message is: 'We are all in this together, and we share the risks and the consequences of our decisions.'

The Sightsavers strategy map

The vision, mission and change themes look at the top of the results chain, and describe Sightsavers' desired outcomes from a beneficiary's point of view. They also provide crucial perspective on the sort of organisation that Sightsavers is, the type of work it undertakes, and the relationships it relies on.

To translate these directions into a strategy of action, Sightsavers describes its own results chain, developed as an application of the Kaplan and Norton strategy map (Kaplan and Norton, 2004) and innovatively marketed internally as a 'SIM card' ('SIM' referring to strategy, implementation and monitoring – see fig. 4.1). The Strategic Framework explains: 'This guides [the organisation's] work and measures progress, like a SIM card drives a mobile phone' (Sightsavers International, 2009, p. 19). The SIM card comes in two parts – a strategy map and a scoresheet, mirroring the Kaplan and Norton strategy map and Balanced Scorecard concepts.

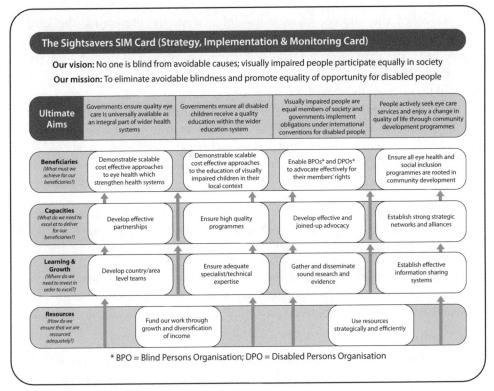

Fig. 4.1 Sightsavers SIM card

As with the generic results chain, the SIM card is designed top-down, aligning the organisation's ultimate aims at the top of the map (identified in the change themes) to resources at the bottom (see box 4.3). The SIM card explains what Sightsavers must achieve for its beneficiaries, what the organisation needs to excel at in order to do this, where it needs to invest in order to excel, and how it must ensure that it is adequately resourced. The card identifies the critical objectives sought by Sightsavers from these four perspectives, creating a set of 14 strategic objectives in total. For each objective, the key organisational initiatives that must be implemented are defined – 30 in total – along with the indicators of success that will be used to track progress.

Box 4.3   Sightsavers' alignment of outcomes to resources

- *We will achieve our strategy by delivering objectives for our beneficiaries, as identified in the change themes.*
- *We will deliver those objectives by developing key capacities.*
- *We will develop those capacities by making certain investments.*
- *We will make those investments by ensuring that we have adequate resources.*

Sightsavers International, 2009, p. 19

The power of the strategy map is twofold. First, by presenting the critical initiatives of a strategy in relation to the mission of the organisation graphically, on one page, the map offers a method of communicating and describing strategy in a digestible form to all stakeholders, including employees. This is more difficult for a narrative-based or numbers-dominated document, however well written it is. Second, the map requires the assumed causes and effects of the various initiatives to be defined. Crucially, this enables the links between the initiatives to be understood, and offers the scope for every stakeholder to understand where and how their contribution fits into the delivery of the overall organisational purpose.

Kaplan and Norton (2001, p. 76) acknowledge that strategy is a hypothesis of cause and effect, and argue that it should be constantly refined in the light of experiences and new ideas:

> The key for implementing strategy is to have everyone in the organization clearly understand the underlying hypotheses, to align resources with the hypotheses, to test the hypotheses continually, and to adapt as required in real time.

In the case of Sightsavers, the line of sight from the institutional-level SIM card to the contribution of each individual is developed through the preparation of unit-level SIM cards for the different operating units. Each departmental SIM card follows the same format as the organisational one, with two parts: a map and a scoresheet. The very process of requiring units to develop their own SIM cards has enabled the Sightsavers leadership to assess the degree of alignment, and to iron out – through debate if necessary – any misalignment.

These unit-level maps and scorecards provide the direction and context for developing and managing individual staff members' objectives and work programmes. If the process is well managed, as in the case of Sightsavers, the result is a hierarchy of aligned objectives, strategies and indicators that are owned by those within the organisation who are responsible for their achievement and implementation.

Lessons from the Sightsavers experience

There is no doubt that the latest strategic framework and the process by which it has been developed, have been crucial for Sightsavers. The key benefits have been as follows.

- The process of preparing the framework has forced the organisation's decision makers to reflect on the very issues that Bryson's definition of the political decision-making model highlights, and to look afresh and reaffirm or redefine what unique contribution the organisation can, and should, make.

- Through the framework, the charity has articulated its values: those inviolable principles that underpin everything it does. Strategies, plans, tactics, activities, decisions – all these have to be consistent with those values.

- The framework helps create the balance between providing, on the one hand, clear direction and parameters of operation and, on the other, flexibility to enable the organisation's decision makers to tailor solutions to beneficiaries, and to be able to react to emerging priorities. To these ends, the framework guides the determination of appropriate strategies and initiatives without imposing a potentially debilitating blueprint of a predetermined five-year plan. It becomes a constant reference document for the decision makers, continually reinforcing what the charity is about – and what it is not about.

- The framework is relevant irrespective of precise circumstances. External or internal events may change the organisation's operating environment unexpectedly, but the strategic direction of the organisation is unlikely to alter. The global financial crisis that emerged during 2008, affecting Sightsavers along with many other not-for-profit organisations, is a case in point. The 14 strategic objectives that are articulated on the institutional-level strategy map are not expected to change as a result of the crisis. However, implementation plans may well need to adjust in light of the financial implications for the organisation. So, the pace with which initiatives are implemented, and/or the sequence in which they are implemented, is indeed subject to change.

- By 2013 (the final year of the new five-year framework), Sightsavers will have being using this sort of methodology to run the organisation for 13 years. The essential elements of the organisation (the hereditary material – the organisational DNA, if you like) are becoming more and more deeply implanted and reinforced. This intangible 'glue' is priceless, enabling Sightsavers both to maintain its identity and evolve concurrently. Tellingly, it has done so while managing a complete turnover of membership of the board of trustees and senior executive management since the launch of the first framework in 2000. The process of developing the latest framework involved transferring to a new chair of the board of trustees mid-process.

- The framework is a flagship from which to lead major organisational change, including cultural change. For example, it has provided an opportunity to devolve greater decision-making authority to country representatives, and to redefine these roles with clearer accountability for directing the determination and implementation of country programmes. Consistent with this change, it has enabled the role of regional representatives to be repositioned as strategic advisers or mentors to the countries, with less of an operational role.

Six process lessons can be drawn from the approach that Sightsavers took in developing its new strategic framework.

1. It is a time-consuming process. Sightsavers began the process in 2007 – two years before the start of the time period to which the framework relates.
2. It requires leadership to drive the process, and benefits hugely from the personal investment and energy of the organisation's leaders – particularly its chief executive.
3. The process is a major activity that, inevitably, directs attention of the organisation away from implementation of the current work programme. Leaders have to balance running today's trains with improving and transforming those of tomorrow.
4. Developing a framework of this sort demands extensive participation by stakeholders of the organisation if it is to be adopted and used, and if it is to galvanise and direct performance throughout the organisation as intended. In the case of Sightsavers, the process included surveys, working groups, workshops, pilots and retreats.
5. As anticipated by Bryson, consultation is likely to expose conflicting views. Guiding the organisation through these discussions in order to arrive at a framework that all parties are willing to adopt requires active – sometimes forceful – management. Sightsavers had to work its way through major organisational issues, such as its commitment to disability and the importance of advocacy in addition to service delivery.
6. Reaching decisions about strategic directions must be supported by evidence: evidence about what works, and what doesn't. For example, in the case of Sightsavers, the organisation had to demonstrate that the tailored service delivery approaches that it supported in each country were, in each case, cost-effective, scalable and compatible with the overall national health system.

CASE STUDY 2: MEMBER GOVERNMENTS OF THE OECD

National governments have been extremely active in the past 20 years in efforts to improve performance management in the public sector and, in particular, to establish a better link between resources and outcomes. Pressures to reform – driven by financial crises, changes in political administrations, and requirements to reduce public expenditure – have focused attention on how effectively governments climb the results chain. Their experiences provide a rich seam of learning about the challenges of establishing meaningful strategic direction through 'performance contracts', which ensure value for money for beneficiaries and donors, and accountability from service providers.

A component of the overall reform efforts that is particularly relevant to financial stewardship of organisations is that of 'performance budgeting' – 'a form of budgeting that relates funds allocated to measurable results' (OECD, 2007, p. 20).

Reforms in this field reveal much about how governments are attempting to ensure the line of sight along the complete chain. In essence, performance budgeting is an attempt to define a performance contract that ties funds to results defined in terms of outputs and outcomes.

The OECD has published an excellent overview of the 'resurgence of efforts' in eight OECD countries – Australia, Canada, Denmark, Korea, the Netherlands, Sweden, United Kingdom and the United States – to establish explicit performance-based accountability frameworks. The central aim of these reforms is:

> ... to improve decision making by providing better quality and more concrete information on the performance of agencies and programmes. It is part of an ongoing process that seeks to move the focus of decision making in budgeting away from inputs (how much money can I get?) towards measurable results (what can I achieve with this money?).

OECD, 2007, p. 11

The governments recognise that focusing accountability at the top of the results chain provides the opportunity to afford discretion to managers on use of inputs (see box 4.4).

Noting that each country has developed its own distinct model of performance budgeting, and has adopted diverse approaches to implementation, the OECD draws two helpful sets of observations. The first acknowledges the differing extents to which outputs and/or outcomes are integrated in the resource allocation process. Recognising that performance information can be used to help plan future performance or to hold executives to account for

> **Box 4.4   OECD countries' reforms**
>
> *The introduction of performance budgeting has been linked to larger reform efforts to improve expenditure control and/or public sector efficiency and performance. Performance budgeting initiatives tend to go hand in hand with performance management or managing for results. These reforms can be combined with reductions in inputs controls and increased flexibility for managers – in return for stronger accountability for the results – so as to enable them to decide how to best deliver public services.*
>
> *OECD, 2007, p. 11*

actual performance results achieved, the OECD offers the following three broad classifications.

- **Presentational:** Performance information is presented in budget documents or other government documents. Information is included as background information for the purposes of accountability and dialogue with legislators and citizens on public policy issues and government direction. However, the information is outside the budget negotiation process: there is no expectation of a link between performance information and resource allocation.

- **Performance-informed budgeting:** Resources are indirectly related either to proposed future performance, or to performance results. Performance information is being used systematically to inform resource-allocation decisions, although it is only one factor in the decision-making process. There is no automatic linkage between performance (planned or actual) and funding.
- **Direct or formula performance budgeting:** Direct linkage involves allocating resources directly and explicitly to units of performance (generally, outputs). Funding is based directly on results achieved. The OECD observes that this type of performance management requires explicit output measures and information on unit costs, and these are not readily available in many government sectors. The research suggests that linking resources explicitly to results in this way is used only to a limited extent, and typically only for certain sectors.

OECD, 2007, p. 21 (text adapted)

The second set of observations that the OECD makes relates to the implementation strategies adopted by the countries studied. Again, the report offers three broad categories. It prefaces its analysis with the pertinent insight that, while ensuring some form of permanence, introducing reform through legislation 'is no guarantee that they will actually be implemented. Rather, implementation is more dependent on political and administrative support and the implementation strategy of the reformers' (OECD, 2007, p. 33). The message is clear: getting the in-house rules changed is not enough. The three categories are as follows.

1. **Top-down versus bottom-up:** Top-down implementation involves a centralised approach to developing performance measures and/or establishing performance targets. Bottom-up strategies typically allow individual ministries discretion and responsibility for implementation. There are risks with either approach, as set out in figure 4.2.
2. **Comprehensive versus partial:** Typically, countries that have adopted a centralised approach have also adopted a more comprehensive implementation, with performance information requirements for all ministries for planning and accountability purposes.
3. **Incremental versus 'big bang':** The 'big bang' approach involves 'introducing a number of sweeping reforms at the same time without a long lead time for implementation' (OECD, 2007, p. 36). Incremental implementation by contrast introduces reforms slowly, in phases, with opportunities included to learn from experience before each subsequent phase. The OECD illustrates the distinction between the two approaches, using Australia (incremental) and Korea ('big bang') as examples (see fig. 4.3). Critical to success with 'big bang'

is having strong drivers for change, such as economic crises or new political leadership. 'Without these drivers,' says the OECD, 'it can be too hard to develop the pressure to introduce sweeping reforms' (OECD, 2007, p. 37).

	Benefits	Risks
Top-down approach	■ Stronger pressure for reform ■ Uniformity in approach and framework across government ■ More information at the centre to make decisions ■ Better coordination and monitoring	■ Limiting flexibility to achieve results ■ Too rule-bound, and performance becomes mere compliance ■ Creating too many reporting requirements, and becoming an expensive paper exercise ■ Failing to gain the support of agencies ■ Creating perverse incentives and distorting behaviour
Bottom-up approach	■ Greater flexibility ■ Capacity to tailor reforms to agencies' needs ■ Enables greater responsiveness to clients and local communities ■ Encourages ownership of reforms by agencies	■ Inertia due to lack of pressure to reform ■ Being more difficult and time consuming to implement ■ Lack of co-ordination of reforms ■ Lack of information at the centre to make decisions ■ Lack of consistency in reform efforts and presentation of data

Fig. 4.2 Potential benefits and risks of alternative implementation approaches (OECD, 2007, p. 34)

	Advantages	Disadvantages
'Big bang' approach	■ *Creates strong pressure and momentum for change* ■ *Offers an integrated package showing how reforms fit together* ■ *Communicates a consistent message and vision of desired end point* ■ *Takes less overall time to implement* ■ *Can provide uniform training and assistance to ministries* ■ *Allows for trade-offs among different interests*	■ *Potentially high-risk* ■ *Can result in costly mistakes* ■ *Needs significant resources* ■ *Runs the danger of overwhelming management and staff* ■ *Needs high-level political commitment* ■ *No time to give individual attention to ministries*
Incremental approach	■ *Opportunity to learn from experiences and to refine the system as it moves forward* ■ *Capacity to adjust the system for unintended effects* ■ *Spreads cost of reform over a longer period* ■ *More time to build support for reforms* ■ *More time to build management capacities* ■ *More time to give individual assistance and attention to agencies*	■ *Takes longer time to implement* ■ *Risks loss of momentum of reforms* ■ *Risks dissipating interests and energy* ■ *Can result in less coherent reforms* ■ *Can result in piecemeal reforms with limited or even conflicting impact* ■ *Can require running two budget systems simultaneously*

Fig. 4.3 Potential advantages and disadvantages of 'big bang' and incremental approaches (OECD, 2007, p. 36)

CASE STUDY 3: THE UK GOVERNMENT

In 1997, the election of a new government in the UK led to an overhaul of the public spending framework. This included the introduction of a medium-term expenditure framework as part of a Comprehensive Spending Review (CSR) in 1998. The CSR 'placed a high emphasis on performance through its public service agreements between ministries and the Treasury, which set measurable targets for public expenditure programmes' (OECD, 2007, p. 25).

The stated aims of the 1998 CSR were to reallocate money to key priorities, change policies so that money is well spent, ensure that departments work better together to improve services, and weed out unnecessary or wasteful spending.

The 2007 CSR (CSR07) introduced a new performance management framework aimed at supporting 'a sharper focus on key priorities, a more collaborative approach to achieving outcomes, and a reduction in burdens on front-line services' (HM Treasury, 2007a, p. 5). This new performance management framework included the following elements:

- *a streamlined set of 30 new Public Service Agreements (PSAs), which articulate the Government's highest priority outcomes for the CSR07 period and span departmental boundaries, setting out a shared vision and leading collaboration at all levels in the delivery system [The PSAs are thematic – grouped under four broad long-term goals (see box 4.5)];*
- *a single Delivery Agreement for each PSA, developed in consultation with frontline workers and the public, and published to strengthen accountability and ownership across organisational boundaries; ...*
- *a small basket of national, outcome-focused indicators to support each PSA ensuring robust and transparent performance measurement alongside genuine rationalisation, with a significant reduction in the overall number of priority indicators attached to PSAs;*
- *targets used where appropriate to deliver improved performance and accountability; with nationally set targets reserved for a small subset of PSA indicators that require firm central direction, and far greater space for increased local target setting;*
- *a more comprehensive approach to performance monitoring, with each department publishing a set of Departmental Strategic Objectives (DSOs) for the CSR07 period, alongside the smaller, prioritised set of PSAs.*

HM Treasury, 2007a, p. 36

The framework is admirably public and accessible to all, placing the government firmly on the hook for delivery. The PSAs in particular are worth studying. They are based on four principles of public service performance – principles that any service-providing organisation would do well to adopt:

- *clear, outcome-focused national goals, set by the government*
- *devolution of responsibility to public service providers themselves, with maximum local flexibility and discretion to innovate, and incentives to ensure that the needs of local communities are met*
- *independent and effective arrangements for audit and inspection to improve accountability*
- *transparency about what is being achieved, with better information about performance both locally and nationally.*

OECD, 2007, pp. 194–95

The format used for the PSAs – adopted for all 30 – offers one very good model of how to set out a performance contract despite the complexity of the subjects covered. Note from box 4.5 that each PSA is expressed as a desired public outcome. Its orientation is to the top of the results chain – to outcomes and impact. Each PSA is set out in three sections that enable the reader (including funders, beneficiaries and administrators) to answer the five fundamental questions that any strategy must address.

- What is the problem?
- What is the goal?
- How do you intend to reach the goal?
- How will you know what progress you are making?
- Who is accountable for performance?

Box 4.5   UK government goals and example public service agreements

- *Sustainable growth and prosperity*
  - *Raise the productivity of the UK economy*
  - *Promote world class science and innovation in the UK*
- *Fairness and opportunity for all*
  - *Halve the number of children in poverty by 2010–11 on the way to eradicating child poverty by 2020*
  - *Raise the educational achievement of all children and young people*
- *Stronger communities and a better quality of life*
  - *Increase long-term housing supply and affordability*
  - *Make communities safer*
- *A more secure, fair and environmentally sustainable world*
  - *Lead the global effort to avoid dangerous climate change*
  - *Reduce poverty in poorer countries through quicker progress towards the Millennium Development Goals.*

HM Treasury, 2007a, pp. 187–96

The three PSA sections are as follows.

- **Section 1: vision:** This one to two-page section sets out the context of the current reality, summarises progress made to date, and provides an overview of the intended future state towards which progress is intended in the three-year period covered by the CSR.

- **Section 2: measurement:** The second section lists those indicators that the government intends to use to measure progress. It includes between two and eight indicators and lists each one, together with a definitional paragraph to help manage expectations about how the measure is compiled and the rationale for its inclusion. Explicit, measurable targets are set for some, but not all, of the indicators. A measurement annex offers technical detail about data sources, frequency of reporting and baselines.
- **Section 3: delivery strategy:** The final section of the PSA lays out the key actions that the government intends to take in order to address the challenge identified in Section 1, and to reach the targets listed in Section 2. Again, the text sets the context before describing assertively, in short paragraphs, what the government will do. The document addresses accountability, with the lead minister for each PSA explicitly defined.

In 2007 (before the 2007 CSR, which introduced the 30 new PSAs) the OECD carried out a review of how the UK government has sought to develop and use a performance management framework. This review offers some valuable lessons to any organisation embarking on introducing a similar set of disciplines in order to oversee how it tackles its top priorities. Its reflections cover delivery, measurement, incentives and relevance. In particular, the OECD states that:

- *Understanding the delivery chain at the target-setting stage is important for ensuring that any targets that the government sets are achievable and realistic ... Delivering the irreversible step change in UK public services ... requires ambition, focus, urgency and clarity. As government strives to deliver increasingly complex outcomes that cut across organisational boundaries, understanding implementation and how a target will be operationalised becomes increasingly important.*
- *It is important to have timely, high-quality information about developments in the delivery chain to enable monitoring and challenge by senior management.*
- *Ensuring that departments have access to high-quality, robust and timely performance data that help the government relate resources to outcomes is crucial.*
- *Failure to gain the support of key agents can lead to problems with perverse incentives and gaming.*
- *It is important to ensure that national targets remain relevant at the local level if local partners and delivery agents are to continue to see national targets as a priority.*
- *Focusing on outcomes enables decentralised decision making by allowing other departments and agencies to decide what mix of outputs is best for achieving those outcomes.*

OECD, 2007, pp. 202–24

Key stewardship questions

1. What lessons can be learned for the organisation from the examples of Sightsavers International and OECD countries, including the UK Government?

2. What is the appropriate implementation strategy for the organisation – top-down or bottom-up, comprehensive or partial, incremental or 'big bang'?

3. What is an appropriate performance management framework for the organisation?

Part 2: Robust financial framework

5 The overall financial framework

Charged with the task of maximising the conversion of resources into impact, it is tempting for leaders to focus immediately and exclusively on expenditure when assessing the finances of the organisation. It is, after all, through expenditure that the organisation will finance the activities through which welfare impact will ultimately be generated. However, successful financial stewardship requires a more balanced, longer-term focus. To achieve impact over time, organisations are forced to worry not only about how effectively their current spending behaviour is contributing to achieving the desired welfare outcomes, but to focus on ensuring their future viability. Climbing the results chain requires organisations to align their ambitions with their current and future resources, to generate income cost-effectively, and to protect the precious income raised until it can be expended wisely.

The good news is that the well-defined sets of guidelines and statutory regulations that determine how organisations should report their financial position historically also provide a ready-made framework to define financial intentions. One example is the UK's *Accounting and Reporting by Charities: Statement of Recommended Practice (revised 2005)* known as SORP 2005 (Charity Commission, 2005). Financial stewards can effectively oversee the financial success of the organisation by maintaining four perspectives: income, funds, assets and expenditure. Through these four lenses it is possible both to assess actual financial performance and to set finance strategy.

DEFINING THE FINANCE STRATEGY

The purpose of a finance strategy must be to define how the organisation intends to reach its intended financial position if it is succeeding in meeting its mission. There are three prerequisites for the definition of a successful finance strategy.

1. The organisation must have a mission and a corporate strategy describing how it intends to deliver that mission.
2. There must be an understanding about what the financial picture – expressed in terms of what statements such as the income and expenditure statement, balance sheet and cash flow would look like if the organisation were delivering the mission optimally.
3. There must be an understanding of how the organisation intends to get from its current financial position to the ideal one.

The finance strategy should, therefore, describe how the organisation intends to move from its current financial performance and position to its intended performance and position (see fig. 5.1).

The balance sheet describes the financial position at a particular date – it is a snapshot in time. Performance, which is achieved over time, is reflected in the income and expenditure statement and the cash flow statement. These statements describe how the balance sheet position has been reached, and therefore are historical records, which can no longer be influenced. In contrast, the balance sheet is still 'live', defining the financial resources that still have to be stewarded as at the date at which the statement is prepared.

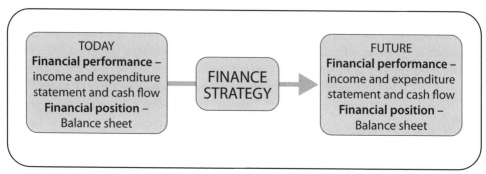

Fig. 5.1 Moving from the current to the intended financial performance and position

THE ROLE OF FINANCIAL STEWARDSHIP

Financial stewardship is about managing the financial resources at the disposal of the organisation. These are defined on the balance sheet. The distinction between financial performance and position highlights the constant need for the organisation to manage two principal, competing demands on its financial resources: spending them to meet the objectives of the organisation (its purpose) today, versus investing or retaining them in order to be able to meet its purpose in the future. The steward's finance strategy must explain how the organisation intends to manage its financial resources optimally, so that it maximises its impact today while maintaining the organisation as a going concern so that it can have impact tomorrow.

The aim is to maximise impact over time – not just today. Ultimately, this simplifies the key decision of the finance steward – what should be done with the financial resources at their disposal – down to one of four choices (see fig. 5.2).

1. Should they be spent on activities (including grant giving) in furtherance of the organisation's objectives?
2. Should they be spent on the management and administration of the organisation?

3. Should they be invested in activities to generate future income?
4. Or should they be retained for use at a later date, in order to maintain the organisation as a going concern?

These are the only four choices, other than giving the funds back to the donor – which, in certain circumstances, the organisation may be required to do.

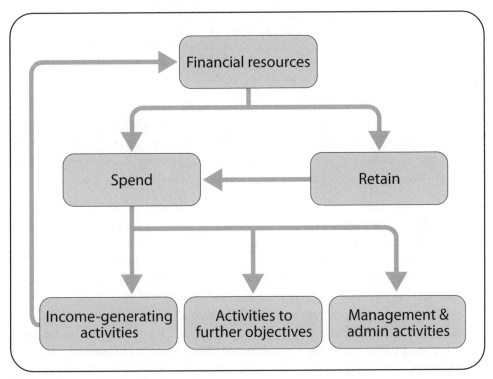

Fig. 5.2 Four choices for financial resources

FUND ACCOUNTING AND THE SOFA

There is a fundamental difference between the financial statements of private sector organisations and those of public sector or not-for-profit ones, reflecting the distinct purpose and orientation of the two types of organisation. Whereas private sector companies have a focus on net income (profit), the financial statements of public and not-for-profit sector organisations must focus on the receipt and application of income to achieve a non-financial objective (see box 5.1). They must demonstrate how well the organisation is able to generate income, protect the funds received until they can be used wisely, and then expend them as intended by the donor. In short, the statements must show how the organisation administers the funds that it receives.

> ### Box 5.1 Private sector versus public and not-for-profit sector financial statements
>
> *The difference between for-profit and nonprofit Operating Statement titles is more than symbolic. It reflects the nonprofit organizations' focus on the flows of financial resources, rather than on net income. The primary objective of nonprofit organizations is to provide services, not to earn a profit. Financial operations support and enhance their ability to provide services by balancing sources and uses of financial resources. Nonprofits must manage their financial operations prudently to ensure that they own financial resources adequate for continued service provision. For them, financial success should not be an end in itself.*
>
> *Herzlinger and Nitterhouse, 1994, pp. 96–97*

These statements highlight the most significant concept underpinning how public and not-for-profit organisations account – that of fund accounting, whereby each fund of resources held by the organisation must be accounted for separately. (For more information about management of funds, see chapter 7.)

There is a key implication of managing financial resources for an ultimate purpose that is not financial: a surplus of income over expenditure or a deficit in the operating statement (which shows income received and expenditure incurred during the year) is often not telling. A surplus or deficit in the year is not the critical measure. Much more important is the impact that this inflow or outflow of funds has on the level of fund balances held. For this reason, public and not-for-profit organisations augment the traditional income and expenditure statement with additional information that explains the effect of the resource flows on fund balances. In the United States, the statement is typically called the Statement of Revenues and Expenses and Changes in Fund Balances. In the UK charity sector, it is the Statement of Financial Activities (SOFA – see box 5.2).

> ### Box 5.2 The Statement of Financial Activities
>
> *The Statement of Financial Activities is a single accounting statement with the objective of showing all incoming resources and resources expended by the charity in the year on all its funds. It is designed to show how the charity has used its resources in furtherance of its objects for the provision of benefit to its beneficiaries. It shows whether there has been a net inflow or outflow of resources, including capital gains and losses on assets, and provides a reconciliation of all movements in the charity's funds.*
>
> *Charity Commission, 2005, p. 14*

Reading SOFAs and balance sheets

Good financial stewardship does not require advanced knowledge of accountancy. Nevertheless, it does demand a willingness and ability to understand and to work with financial concepts and key reports, such as the financial statements. Figure 5.3 and box 5.3 describe how to read the SOFA and balance sheet, and the relationship between them.

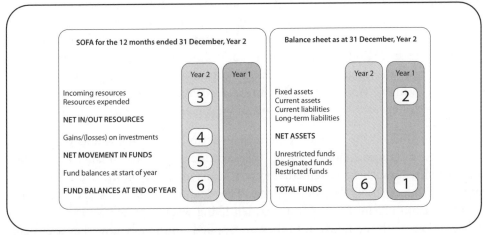

Fig. 5.3 The relationship between the SOFA and balance sheet

Box 5.3 Reading the SOFA and balance sheet

1. The current year starts with the balance sheet as at the end of Year 1. The total fund balances held by the trustees at the start of the year are shown in the bottom half of the Year 1 balance sheet column. In this example the balances are categorised into three types of fund, reflecting the nature of any restriction imposed on the fund by either the donor (restricted funds) or the trustees (designated funds).
2. The form in which those fund balances were held is shown in the top half of the balance sheet. Each fund balance must be in the form of fixed assets, current assets or long- or short-term liabilities.
3. Moving to the SOFA, the left-hand column shows the income received and expenditure incurred in the latest year (Year 2). Normally this column would be split into three, with unrestricted, designated and restricted funds shown separately. Income raised in the year adds to the fund balances, while expenditure incurred depletes them. Comparable figures for the preceding 12 months (Year 1) are shown in the right-hand column.
4. The fund balances are affected not only by income and expenditure, but also by changes in the value of any market investments held by the trustees. Gains in investments (whether realised or not) add to the fund balances, while losses in investments reduce them.
5. The combined impact of income raised, expenditure incurred and gains/losses on investment charged results in a net movement in fund balances in the year, showing by how much the opening fund balances have increased or fallen in the current year. These are the closing fund balances.
6. The same closing fund balances appear on the bottom half of the left-hand column of the balance sheet. Under the heading Year 2, the left-hand column shows the fund balance position as at the balance sheet date (31 December, Year 2). The bottom half of the balance sheet shows the fund balances by type of fund, and the top half the asset form in which the fund balances are held.

Using the financial statements

To define the objectives of a finance strategy, it is necessary to look at the financial statements included in the statutory annual accounts (the primary statements), acknowledging that these objectives only have relevance in relation to the organisation's purpose. It is not possible to write a finance strategy without reference to the corporate strategy – it is the continuum of the same, single, strategic planning process. Hind's diagram (see fig. 3.3) shows this clearly. So, determining a finance strategy is about deciding how the organisation plans to use the financial resources available now and in the future to deliver the intended results of the corporate strategy, and what that will mean the organisation looks like in the future.

These intended results should be defined in terms of the SOFA and the balance sheet. As discussed above, doing this assumes that the financial strategist understands how these statements are constructed, what information they give, and what information they do not give. The statements tell the story of the flow of funds from receipt to expenditure, identifying what income has been received, what is done with the funds until they are applied, and finally how they are spent.

However, financial information alone cannot tell the reader how effective the expenditure is or what impact it has. Measuring impact involves collecting and interpreting information about the organisation's services, and the effect of those services on addressing the organisation's mission. The financial statements only tell the reader what funds have been received, and how they have been applied. They do this from the perspective of income, funds, assets and expenditure. These are the key areas that any assessment of financial performance and any future finance strategy must address (see fig. 5.4).

SOFA	Balance sheet
Income The SOFA defines what income has been received during the period being accounted for, categorised into several groups that define the broad sources of receipt.	**Assets** The funds held at the balance sheet date are classified in terms of the form in which they are held.
Expenditure The SOFA shows what funds have been expended and in what broad directions, as a minimum split between welfare activity, including management and administration of the organisation, and reinvestment in further income-generating activities.	**Funds** The balance sheet confirms what income already received has not yet been spent, categorised in terms of the extent to which the donor has applied some restriction as to how the funds can be used by the organisation.

Fig. 5.4 The four perspectives of the primary statements

The following four chapters consider these four areas. The order reflects the flow of funds through the organisation, from the arrival as income, their management as fund balances and assets, through to their expenditure in furtherance of the organisation's purpose.

Key stewardship questions

1. What future financial position should the organisation reach?

2. How does it intend to get there?

3. How does the organisation intend to manage the competing demands of spend versus retain?

4. Do the organisation's stewards understand the primary statements?

6 The level, type and source of income

When assessing the adequacy of the income earned, the financial steward must first ask the following question: 'Is the organisation generating appropriate levels of income, of the right type, from sufficiently varied sources?'

There are three key characteristics of income to be sought.

1. **The level of income:** This must be sufficient to enable the organisation to meet its purpose. It must cover all the costs that are going to be incurred in undertaking the activities through which the organisation's impact is delivered.
2. **The type of income:** This, crucially, refers to the extent to which the donor imposes a restriction on how the organisation can apply the funds received.
3. **The source of the income:** Any organisation should aim to have a diversity of income sources in order to avoid the risks associated with putting all their eggs in one basket.

Any organisation's income strategy must reflect all three factors, and requires an understanding of the trade-offs between them. Arguably, there is an opportunity cost associated with any income-generating activity, since resources devoted to generating income from one source could otherwise be deployed to generate income from another. For example, the organisation must be sure that the benefits of restricted income exceed the opportunity cost of missing out on potential unrestricted income.

At times it may be a sensible strategy to trade off unrestricted income for restricted. However, once the true costs of servicing the requirements of the restricted funder are understood, the organisation may conclude that it would be better to raise, say, £1 million of unrestricted income than £1.5 million of income with restrictions attached that would be difficult to comply with.

LEVEL OF INCOME

Two issues in relation to the level of income raised deserve some discussion here: generating contribution, and cost recovery – particularly in relation to covering core costs.

Generating income contribution

As any experienced steward of a commercial organisation knows, 'gross margin not sales constitutes the real income of a business' (Warnes, 1984, p. 27). Similarly for a not-for-profit organisation, the resources needed to finance the welfare work by which its purpose is served are provided by the income contribution generated from the fundraising or other income-generating activities – not from the gross income.

Income contribution can be defined as the net income available for use once the costs of generating the income have been deducted. An organisation's income-generating aim must be to maximise the contribution made available for furthering the organisation's objectives over time. Remember that income-generating activities only break even once the contribution from them covers the management and administrative costs incurred by the organisation (such as audit fees), many of which will be fixed or may change in discrete steps, irrespective of the levels of operational activity. The real income of the organisation is the income that is available for activities that further the organisation's objectives (in other words, what remains after deducting income that is reinvested in further income-generating activities, or that pays for management and administration costs).

Box 6.1   Break-even point
Break-even point = management and administration costs ÷ gross margin percentage from income-generating activities

It is worth carrying out a periodic review of the organisation's break-even point – the level of income at which the contribution covers the fixed costs (see box 6.1). If it is rising over time, then either the profitability of income-generating activities is falling and/or the level of fixed costs is rising. Either scenario requires attention.

Crucially, the organisation needs to understand the solution to the problem of how to increase the contribution available to finance welfare activities. This does not necessarily mean increasing income, but reducing the break-even point. Conceptually, this is a fundamental point to understand. If the organisation wishes to increase the funds available for activities that further its objectives, then it must either make its income-generating activities more profitable or it must reduce its management and administration costs. It may make sense to reduce its gross income if that enables it to eliminate unprofitable income-generating activities and to scale down the related management and administrative effort.

It costs money to generate income – and the organisation needs to know how much. Sustaining or increasing the level of welfare activity requires available resources to increase over time, which in turn depends on continuous investment in income-generating activities. Some of the organisation's funds must be directed towards marketing and publicising the organisation to current and potential donors. However, different income-generating activities incur very different costs, and the organisation must reassure itself that the income contribution generated by each is adequate and improving. Any deterioration needs to be identified and understood carefully.

This assumes that the costs associated with generating income can be attributed accurately to each separate activity. That can be difficult – not least because of the time lag between income-generating activity and receipt of income. Assessing the return on legacy promotional activity is an extreme example of this, as the return on investment may not be realised for many years. The investment may not all be borne up front either, with administrative costs conceivably incurred throughout the life of the activity for which the funding was given – for example, in order to meet reporting requirements.

However, at a strategic level it should be possible for financial stewards to reassure themselves that, during any given period of time, the organisation is not investing too much or too little in income-generating and publicity activities. Monitoring the relationship between income generated in a period and the level of funds invested in income-generating activities during the same period (the cost–income ratio) can be a misleading metric, as this implies a direct relationship between the two. More sophisticated analyses now measure lifetime value. Nevertheless, tracking the trend of the cost–income ratio over time can be very valuable. If the investment was sound, then the return on investment will come through at some point, with a consequent improvement in the cost–income ratio. Prudent trustees and management would be wise not to accept too long a lag before expecting to see this occur. Relatively early paybacks on income-generating investments are appropriate, given the alternative, beneficiary-orientated uses to which the funds invested could have been used.

Cost recovery

There is now a generally accepted definition of core costs, based on a list of 22 types of cost. These include 'management, research and development, and support services such as premises, IT and finance as well as administrative, personnel and training charges' (Unwin, 2001, pp. 10–11). The challenge of covering these kinds of costs is a perennial one, and one that has dogged not-for-profit organisations in particular for many years. However, the difficulty of cost recovery is not unique to not-for-profit organisations by any means. Any organisation accepting restricted funds faces the challenge of negotiating to cover indirect costs that have to be incurred by the organisation, but that are difficult to attribute sufficiently directly to the programmes of interest to the funder.

Funding Our Future: Core Costs Revisited (Unwin, 2001) provides a comprehensive overview of the funding environment for not-for-profit organisations, offering a perceptive insight into the concerns that funders have about funding core costs.

While organisations can legitimately insist that the activities generating core costs are an essential component of their work, they also have an obligation to manage those costs tightly, in order to address the understandable funder concerns detailed in box 6.2.

Box 6.2   Why are many funders reluctant to provide funding for core costs?

1. Funders find it difficult to be satisfied that the grant is good value for money and achieving desired outcomes. There is anxiety about the ways in which 'backroom' costs can be justified.
2. Support for core costs has no easily understood justification for being time-limited. Funding programmes that have long-term or open-ended commitments restrict funders from being responsive to new and emerging needs.
3. Funders fear that they will be captured by the organisation to which they are making such a central contribution, from which it will be politically or emotionally difficult to disengage.
4. Funding core costs offers considerable scope for double or even triple funding of certain costs.
5. Offering support for core costs distorts the pricing structure of voluntary organisations offering services, which are purchased hiding the real costs of the services being bought.

Adapted from Unwin, 2001, pp. 23–24

While every organisation should apply whatever pressure and influence it can on the funder to include an element of the funding for core costs, ultimately it will face a 'take it or leave it' choice. If it takes it, it must do so with a clear understanding of how the core costs required to support the activity will be financed. There may be risks to take. The organisation may have sufficient unrestricted funding to be able to finance the core costs of an activity for a certain length of time but no longer, and perhaps less than the natural length of the activity. In this circumstance, should it even start the activity? This involves a judgement about how likely it is that it will be able to raise funds to finance the core costs of the remaining period of the activity, and on the implications of stopping the activity midstream.

Unwin's research identified four 'survival' strategies for financing core costs (Unwin, 2001, pp. 15–16, adapted).

Box 6.3   What is full cost recovery?

Full cost recovery means recovering or funding the full costs of a project or service. In addition to the costs directly associated with the project, such as staff and equipment, projects will also draw on the rest of the organisation. For example, adequate finance, human resources, management, and IT systems, are also integral components of any project or service.

The full cost of any project therefore includes an element of each type of overhead cost, which should be allocated on a comprehensive, robust, and defensible basis.

ACEVO, n.d., n.p.

---

1. **Cost recovery** – the price charged to the funder covers the full cost of activities, including an appropriate allocation of core costs [see box 6.3].
2. **Cost diversion** – activities incurring core costs are packaged to funders in the form of discrete projects (e.g. the reception desk activity is marketed as an information service; the policy department is broken down into a number of research projects).
3. **Cost donation** – voluntary, unrestricted income is raised which can be used for core costs financing.
4. **Cost reduction** – the level of core costs is driven down thereby reducing the funding requirement.

All these strategies assume that the core costs are known, and that there is a reasonable basis for apportioning them over the operational activities. The latter is not easy, and requires both a good understanding within the organisation of the techniques of activity-based costing and accounting, and a well-designed and maintained accounting system to capture the costs in the most appropriate way.

Since Unwin's publication, efforts to ensure that the price of contracts

> ### Box 6.4 UK government endorsement of full cost recovery
>
> *There is no reason why service procurers should disallow the inclusion of relevant overhead costs in bids. Furthermore, funders or purchasers should not flatly reject or refuse to fund fully costed bids. Funding bodies must recognise that it is legitimate for third sector organisations to recover the appropriate level of overhead costs associated with the provision of a particular service.*
>
> *HM Treasury, 2006, p. 6*

and grants reflects the full costs of delivery – full cost recovery – have increased apace. However, actual practice lags well behind intent. Nevertheless, the UK government's endorsement of full cost recovery is important (see box 6.4). Aware of funders' concerns with regard to core costs, the UK government now promotes the following three funding models proposed by Unwin (2001, p. 8), and strongly encourages funders to adopt one of them:

- *Full project funding, in which all reasonable associated costs are met as part of a funding package*
- *Development funding through which an organisation's infrastructure costs are met for a time in order to enable it to develop and grow*
- *Strategic funding through which the funder recognises the need for an organisation to exist – in order to meet its own objectives – and is prepared to contribute over an agreed period of time.*

In the UK, the overall funding relationship between the government and not-for-profit organisations is governed by the principles set out in the *Compact on Relations between Government and the Third Sector in England* (HM Treasury, 2009). The Compact is complemented by HM Treasury guidance in its publication *Improving Financial Relationships with the Third Sector: Guidance to Funders and Purchasers* (HM Treasury, 2006), which endorses the principle of full cost recovery. The government's review of the third sector in 2007 (HM Treasury, 2007b), carried out partly to inform the CSR, reinforces the commitment to full funding, but notes explicitly the perspective of the funder, echoing Unwin:

> *Government funding should allow an organisation to recover the full cost to it of providing a service, including an appropriate element of its organisational overheads. The Government remains committed to the principle of full cost recovery, however a further NAO review into full cost published in June 2007 [National Audit Office, 2007] acknowledged that Departmental practice towards cost recovery will vary with the purpose of the funding and the environment it takes place in. The Office of the Third Sector and HM Treasury accept the recommendation in the report to develop more sophisticated statements on full cost recovery that reflect funders' responsibilities for fair treatment and risk management.*
>
> HM Treasury, 2007b, pp. 90–91

The *Joint Compact Action Plan 2008–2009* (The Commission for the Compact *et al*, 2008) includes a proposal to 'produce more sophisticated guidance on implementing the Government's commitments to full cost recovery' (p. 10). Prudently, the Compact also counsels that 'it is important to plan ahead for the end of funding, in order to reduce its negative impact on the people involved, the stability of the third sector organisation and future partnerships' (HM Treasury, 2009, p. 24).

Ultimately, much energy has to be devoted to developing and maintaining relationships between the recipient of funding and the funder, and Unwin appeals for funders and funded to forge a 'win–win' partnership – a settlement (see box 6.5). This offers much food for thought, both to the funder and the funded.

Box 6.5   A new funder/funded settlement

It is in the interests of funders and operating voluntary organisations to reach a new settlement. This will have implications for both funders and funded organisations. It will require voluntary organisations to:

1. *Improve internal accounting, financial management and business planning*
2. *Develop benchmarking on overhead costs*
3. *Demonstrate effectiveness and capacity*
4. *Develop their own ways of measuring effectiveness and organisational change*

It will require funders to:

1. *Meet the overhead costs associated with managing a piece of work*
2. *See their funding as part of a programme of long-term investment*
3. *Manage change within their portfolio of grants*
4. *Develop new ways of evaluating effectiveness*

Unwin, 2001, p. 6

TYPE OF INCOME
Unrestricted income

What should be an organisation's strategy with regard to generating unrestricted income? Clearly, the more discretion the board has over the funds placed in its trust, the greater the extent to which it can expend those funds as it sees fit, in furtherance of the organisation's objectives. The ideal income is unrestricted, where the funder places no restrictions (within the objectives of the organisation) on how those funds are applied. Unrestricted income is the most precious income of all, and organisations should adopt a 'first in, last out' principle with respect to this type of income. This means that generating unrestricted income is treated as a first priority, and spending it a last resort. The latter should occur only once the organisation has exhausted any of the restricted funds that could be spent financing the same activity.

Restricted income

While no one would doubt the value, from the organisation's point of view, of having the discretion that unrestricted income provides, the donor perspective will be different. One of the core aims of any proposition to funders will be to reassure them that their financial contribution will have impact – in other words, that it will make a difference. It is understandably attractive for funders to be able to trace their particular contribution through to the final impact, and there lies the tension: the organisation wants unrestricted income in order to maximise its flexibility, while the funder wants to see as precisely as possible what their funds will be used for, and may be comforted by placing a restriction on their use to ensure that they are used as intended.

The reality for most organisations is that they cannot rely solely on unrestricted income to finance their activities, but neither should they. Arguably, every organisation has an obligation to generate whatever funds it can in order to further alleviate the need for which it was established in the first place, as long as it can do so cost-effectively. This means that it must endeavour to source income from statutory funders such as government departments and multilateral institutions, which will be subject to restrictions, as well as from non-statutory sources, such as the private sector, trusts and foundations.

Many organisations' restricted fund portfolios have changed significantly in recent years, becoming increasingly diverse as the needs of donors and recipient organisations alike have grown. New types of funding instrument have increased the complexity of managing these types of income. The World Bank is no exception, and as restricted funds have grown as a percentage of the total resources available to the institution it has become ever more important 'to introduce a more orderly and explicit approach to the rewards and risks associated with partnerships with money' (World Bank, 2008, pp. 5–6). Noting that some funding instruments are 'often uniquely complex inventions', the World Bank identifies four areas that need explicit consideration (see box 6.6).

Box 6.6   Handling trust fund complexities: four considerations

- ▪ ***Results*** – *what does the Bank want to accomplish in accepting to administer these resources, including having to ensure that such activities align with the Bank's mandate and strategic priorities, and what is the value added to the Bank?*
- ▪ *Are the **resources** on offer, and their allocation, adequate for the job to be done, including a sufficient funding envelope for the Bank to play its assigned role well?*
- ▪ *What are the **risks** to the Bank from accepting to be involved with these activities, and how will they be managed?*
- ▪ *What is the Bank's **accountability** associated with ensuring the highest and best use of these resources, including fiduciary standards, and who in the Bank specifically is accountable for the Bank's role(s)?*

World Bank, 2008, n.p.

The issues to be considered include the following:

- ● **Results:** New funds can be so complex and customised that they require the organisation to develop new skills and procedures, making them difficult to integrate with other activities undertaken. This can dilute the degree of alignment of income with strategy. Such funds also can make it difficult to promote cooperation with other donors. The governance arrangements can also inhibit the ability to deliver results.
- ● **Resources:** The resources needed to accomplish the stated objectives of the trust fund may be dictated by what funds are available, rather than what is known to be necessary. What is more, the cost of developing, and subsequently managing, innovative financing initiatives is high.
- ● **Risks:** Potential risks include financial costs, conflict of interest and reputational risks. Financial risks include the risk that programme or cost commitments will continue after the financial resources from the trust fund have been exhausted. Conflicts of interest can arise if the recipient of the fund acts as both trustee and implementer. Reputational risks can arise if the intended objectives of the fund do not materialise. Some of the initiatives financed by trust funds can be highly political or visible.
- ● **Accountability:** Accountability issues can be complicated in certain situations – for example, where more than one organisation acts in partnership in establishing the fund, where the organisation as trustee is responsible for the resources mobilised through the fund (including allocations to recipients), and where the organisation is the recipient of the funds.

The implications of sourcing restricted income need to be clearly understood. Any restricted income raised should be in addition to unrestricted income – not instead of it. The greater the restriction, the less discretion an organisation has over how the funds are used, so the organisation needs to be sure that sourcing restricted income does not detract from the organisation's ability to attract unrestricted income, and does not displace existing work programmes or priorities.

If the funder does require restrictions, the recipient organisation should seek to make these as broad as possible, to give it maximum discretion over the use of the funds. Whatever happens, the organisation must be sure that it is willing and able to comply with the terms of the restriction. There may be onerous reporting requirements, and the right decision may be to decline the funds being offered in these circumstances. Such a decision could be difficult for those individuals with stiff income targets to meet. It may well be worth reviewing the decision-making process by which funds on offer are accepted or refused, to ensure that the recipient organisation does not feel undue pressure to accept income proposals whatever the cost. It is also worth assessing whether there is an incentive for any staff member to turn down restricted income. There will also be accounting requirements associated with tracking restricted funds – for example, discrete coding – which equally need to be understood.

Endowment funds can be particularly burdensome in terms of administration. They may need to be held in separate bank accounts, and require separate disclosure and explanation in published accounts, irrespective of their size. They may last in perpetuity, creating problems years down the line, even where the original trustees of the fund and the relevant paperwork are no longer accessible. They may also may set awkward conditions: for example, requiring an organisation to accumulate the interest earned on the capital sum for the first five years, expend the interest earned on the capital in years 6 to 10, accumulate interest in years 11 to 15, and so on.

It is important to remain aware of the accounting implications of accepting restricted funds. Yet the challenge of complying with the demands of statute or recommended and best practice on fund accounting relates less to questions about how to account for and manage the fund income than to how it is expended. There may be questions about which fund to charge income to if the nature of the restriction overlaps with existing funds, but it should be possible to ensure that the details of income received are entered into the accounting system under the fund to which that income relates. When the organisation receives the funds, it must be able to determine whether these have a restriction placed on them or whether they are unrestricted. Some of these may need to be designated in accordance with trustee instructions.

Of course, every organisation would much prefer to raise unrestricted funds, as these offer the organisation maximum freedom to make choices within its mandate about resource allocation, but that seems to be increasingly difficult. Take statutory funding, for example. Reliable grants with undemanding conditions from statutory funders have been replaced with increasingly stringent funding contracts. Organisations now have to prepare increasingly detailed applications, giving considerable detail about the proposed activity, and must endure lengthy process times before decisions are made.

It may be necessary, in effect, to underwrite projects that need to begin before the organisation has received a funding decision. Of course, that can only be done if the organisation has funds available to use at its discretion if the application is denied, and the organisation must consider carefully the risks of beginning activities without funding secured.

In such circumstances, the importance of unrestricted reserves as a strategic financial tool cannot be overstated. Funds may be received well after the expenditure to which they relate is incurred, and this can cause some serious cash flow and accounting headaches. How should the organisation account for restricted income received retrospective to the expenditure that it has been granted to cover (expenditure which, precisely because of the delay in confirmation of funding, has had to be treated as unrestricted in an earlier accounting period)? The answer may be a transfer between restricted and unrestricted funds that is rather difficult to explain, in order to show the income and expenditure against the same fund. Box 6.7 describes the sequence of events under one scenario and the accounting challenges that are posed.

Box 6.7   Accounting for retrospective income

1. Expenditure is incurred in year 1, and has to be shown against unrestricted funds because the decision on the funding application (which if successful would be classified as restricted income against which the expenditure would be matched) is outstanding.
2. In year 2, the funding application is approved by the statutory funder (subject to stringent conditions). Income is either received or accrued – in either case, as restricted income, as the grant is only eligible to finance the activities of the organisation detailed in the application.
3. No expenditure is incurred in year 2 (having been completed in year 1). The restricted income recognised in the year is unspent, and is included in restricted fund balances. However, there is no future expenditure to finance that meets the terms of the restriction. The income sits in one fund while unrestricted funds remain depleted by the expenditure incurred in year 1. Hence the transfer. The restricted fund balance is transferred to the general fund, replenishing it to its previous level. The more attentive reader of the accounts might question what the trustees are doing by moving funds that the donors have given with restrictions attached into the unrestricted funds where no such constraints exist.
4. From a fund balance point of view, all is well. General funds are at the right level and the restricted fund is empty. Note, however, that at the end of year 2 both income and its matching expenditure ended up being treated as unrestricted. This is not ideal by any means.

The fundraising appeal determination process

Within the major fundraising charities, the process of managing the tension between the organisation's desire for unrestricted income and the donor's interest in attributing their funds to specific activities has become highly professionalised, with advanced marketing techniques used to appeal to the donor.

Appeals are designed around a particular theme – for example, using case studies showing how the charity has improved people's lives, in order to focus the donor's attention on how their contribution will help. However, they are in fact carefully worded to ensure that, in practice, the organisation can treat the income generated from the appeal as unrestricted and use it as they see fit – quite possibly on an activity that is not explicitly referred to at all in the appeal. In such cases, strict attention needs to be paid to the wording of the appeal to make sure that its income can be treated as unrestricted funds, both legally and morally, without diminishing the impact of the message. It may be, of course, that an appeal's image does encourage some donors to respond with a request that their funds are restricted to use only for the nature of the work highlighted in the appeal. So, an unrestricted appeal may generate restricted income.

The process by which appeals material is determined internally – whether printed literature for mailshots or billboards, or television advertising – needs to be defined and supported by all the relevant individuals. In most organisations, there will be some tensions to manage between the perspectives offered by those staff charged with generating income and those responsible for delivering services. The images and messages of the appeals have to promote the organisation's beneficiaries in a dignified, unpatronising way that is in keeping with the organisation's values, without unduly compromising the power of the image. By way of illustration, box 6.8 quotes from a statement of principles signed by members of Bond – a network of more than 350 UK-based NGOs working in international development.

Box 6.8   Using responsible fundraising methods

In their fundraising activities, Bond members aim to portray the realities and complexities of the situations with which they are involved, as inappropriate methods, simplistic images and messages can undo the positive impact of their work. Bond members recognise that the stereotypical image of southern people and countries held by many in the UK is often simplistic and potentially damaging; Bond members' fundraising publicity aims to avoid exploiting and reinforcing these stereotypes, and aims where possible to challenge them. Bond members aim to control all fundraising activities carried out on their behalf.

Bond, 2004, p. 3

The role of auditors

Add to this mix the question of determining the degree of restriction on the funding, and it is easy to see how important the appeal design sign-off process is. There is a great deal of sense in including the organisation's auditors in this decision-making process before finalising the design. At the time of the statutory audit the auditors will make their own judgement on the nature of any income raised, and on the degree to which that income should be restricted in use. So, it would be better to receive that judgement before plans are finalised, rather than after the income is raised or – worst of all – spent. However, this rarely seems to happen.

The most appropriate split of responsibilities would be for auditors to determine the nature of any restriction, and for the charity to determine the distribution of income within the boundaries of the restriction. In extreme cases the auditors may not feel qualified to judge, and may wish to refer to a legal opinion. Invariably, creating new fundraising appeal designs is a process that seems to operate to tight deadlines. Nevertheless, time must be given to enable auditors to comment on how any income raised from the appeal would need to be classified. If the relationship with the auditors is a good one, this needn't take long – a 48-hour turnaround time for an opinion is realistic.

SOURCE OF INCOME

Diversifying sources of income is common sense, simply to avoid over-dependence on any one source. That is a well-established strategy of managing risk. It reflects the fact that no income source is 100 per cent secure indefinitely; the four 'survival' strategies for financing core costs promoted by Unwin (see p. 86) are all time limited: government funding can change with the political climate, and so on. However, since diversification has its own costs (for example, increased management effort), the organisation must understand at what point the benefits of additional diversification are outweighed by the drawbacks. Each source imposes its own particular management demands, and income sources that are inappropriately costly or restrictive can easily be chosen in order to reduce risk through diversification.

Certainly, the more diverse the income sources, the more likely that one of those sources will be a cause for concern at any given time. The organisation may wish to impose some parameters that place an indicative ceiling on the proportion of total income that should come from any one source. As income from one source grows, there certainly needs to be a watchful eye to ensure that that the leverage of such income does not turn inadvertently to over-dependence.

This chapter has already encouraged income-seeking organisations to think from the perspective of the funder, both when attempting to increase the level of income (to cover core costs) and when trying to attract different types of income. However, the funder perspective can also be instructive when considering the source of income, as illustrated by the following two examples relating to government and to the private sector.

Sourcing from government

Outcome Funding (Williams *et al*, 1996), which critiques the public sector funding process, promotes the concept of 'government as investor', encouraging statutory funders to assess potential funding applications using private sector investment disciplines. The advice offered is pertinent to all funders, whether statutory or not, and funding applicants would be wise to understand how the investor, rather than the funder, views applications. Just as this book advises organisations to think from the top of the results chain, so *Outcome Funding* promotes a focus on impact not input:

> *When government views itself as a funder, it is primarily concerned with distributing money. When it sees itself as an investor, it becomes more focused on what happens after the grant.*
>
> Williams *et al*, 1996, p. 45

Thinking of funders as investors does have some intuitive attraction. It introduces the concept of return on investment, and helps applicants understand the value to the funder of diversification. Applying the concept of financial return on investment – the relationship between the money that goes into an organisation and the revenues that come out – has some obvious challenges for the public and not-for-profit sectors. However, it is appealing to invite organisations to reflect rigorously on whether the investment made by funders is preserved in order to keep producing beneficial impact rather than expended and lost (Williams *et al*, 1996, p. 46).

The investor notion also introduces the concept of portfolio, and with it the need for balance. This can be considered from several perspectives:

- programme intensity
- investing in proven methods versus new approaches and divergent thinking
- big programmes or small programmes
- established or new providers
- ameliorating symptoms versus attacking causes
- funding study or action
- risk versus predictability.

Note the assertion in *Outcome Funding* that 'government can handle low or even no gain from a project much more readily than it can handle the unexpected outcome that draws taxpayer ire' (Williams *et al*, 1996, p. 49).

95

Perhaps most helpful of all, *Outcome Funding* presents an alternative to the ubiquitous funding proposal – the target plan (see box 6.9). This is of value both to the investor, in judging where to make funds available, and to the recipient, in managing the project to deliver the desired outcomes successfully. The focus of the contents, and the language used, have an outcome and client orientation and emphasise delivery.

Box 6.9   The target plan

- **The market and your customers.** *Define the number and characteristics of the customers your program will serve. Indicate how they are different from the broader population of those with the need you address.*
- **Performance targets.** *Specify the performance targets you are committed to achieving, and indicate the reasons for not setting lower or higher levels.*
- **The product.** *Specify your product, its key features and its comparative advantages over other products offered to achieve the same performance targets and outcomes.*
- **Milestones.** *What are the critical milestones which you must achieve if you are to reach results?*
- **Key individuals.** *Profile those individuals who will have the most responsibility for shaping your product, connecting it to customers, and achieving performance targets. Focus on energy, capacity, and commitment.*
- **Organisation support.** *Note the two most similar projects undertaken by the agency and the extent to which they stated and achieved performance targets.*
- **Verifications.** *How will you verify the extent to which your performance targets are achieved?*
- **Financial projections**. *Specify project costs on the basis of milestones and performance targets.*
- **Plan for self reliance**. *Show how your program will continue without investment from this source.*
- **Customer evidence**. *Provide names of individuals who have expressed a strong interest in being a customer for your program.*

Williams et al, 1996, extracts from chapter 7 pp. 53 to 69

Making markets work

Crutchfield and McLeod Grant's excellent study of 12 highly successful US not-for-profits, *Forces for Good* (2008), led them to articulate six practices which have enabled these organisations to have unusually high levels of impact (see box 6.10). The practices include 'harness[ing] market forces' and seeing 'business as a powerful partner, not as an enemy to be disdained or ignored' (p. 6). The authors advise that 'tapping into the power of self-interest and the laws of economics is far more effective than appealing to pure altruism' (p. 21).

Working with business is clearly about much more than simply about generating income. Nevertheless, in the most successful corporate not-for-profit alliances the monies generated can be huge.

The 12 organisations studied in *Forces for Good* have worked with the private sector to achieve social impact by influencing and changing business practices on the back of clear business rationale. They have also built corporate partnerships. These often start with a donation of money, volunteer time or other contributions in kind before becoming more strategic alliances,

> **Box 6.10   The six practices of high impact nonprofits**
>
> - *Advocate **and** serve*
> - *Make markets work*
> - *Inspire evangelists*
> - *Nurture nonprofit networks*
> - *Master the art of adaptation*
> - *Share leadership*
>
> *Crutchfield and McLeod Grant, 2008, p. 21–22*

through social cause marketing or sponsorship agreements, in which both players can benefit from increased visibility. This in turn prompts increased resources in support of both organisations. The key insight would seem to be for not-for-profits to 'move away from seeking charitable contributions and towards building *strategic partnerships* with companies' (Crutchfield and McLeod Grant, 2008, p. 72).

Trading (where not-for-profit organisations run commercial enterprises that undertake trading activity in order to generate profits which can be donated as unrestricted income to the charitable entity) is also featured, though helpfully with a warning of the potential difficulties of running businesses successfully. Crutchfield & McLeod Grant's general assessment of the inherent risks associated with building corporate relationships include distraction from the mission of the organisation, reputational damage (a risk that the authors suspect will diminish as the social and private sectors become more comfortable in their relationships), and tensions with the organisation's other activities (such as advocacy).

Key stewardship questions

1. Is the organisation generating sufficient income to cover all the costs facing it, including core costs?

2. Are the income-generating activities profitable enough? Are they making a sufficient contribution?

3. Is the break-even level of income low enough?

4. Are funders giving the organisation sufficient discretion over how the income is applied?

5. Does the organisation have an adequate number of income sources? Does it have too many?

6. What should be the trade-off points be between the levels, types and sources of income?

7. How does the organisation intend to achieve these aims?

7 The level, form and matching of funds

Funds are nothing more than income already raised that has not yet been spent – what the UK Charity Commission defines as 'a pool of resources' (see box 7.1). These unexpended resources are the capital of the organisation: the injections of funds that will finance its future activities and assets. The only way that funds can be created is by generating income that is not (yet) spent.

It is often assumed that public sector and not-for-profit organisations aim to deliver a balanced bottom line each year, with income and expenditure offsetting each other. However, in reality, what inflow or outflow of resources is desirable on the SOFA depends on the existing funds position, and on the cash situation. It may be appropriate instead to either add to or deplete the existing funds or cash balances. The issue of cash is considered in the following chapter.

Once income has been raised, thereby becoming part of the fund balances, the organisation should turn its attention to the issue of how to manage those fund balances. What level of balances is it appropriate to hold, in what form, and how should the balances best be spent in line with the wishes of the donor (if defined)? These are the questions the finance strategy has to answer.

THE LEVEL OF FUND BALANCES

Fund balances should be kept, rather than spent, until it is appropriate to spend the funds in accordance with the wishes of the donor. In the unusual circumstance that it is not possible to comply with a donor's wishes, the organisation should return their funds to them. An exception to this is permanent endowment funds, where the trustees are not permitted to spend the fund but instead must maintain the whole of the fund permanently – normally the income derived from such a fund *is* expendable.

Restricted funds

In the case of restricted funds, the challenge is how best to match income with expenditure given the likely circumstance that more than one restricted fund will be eligible to finance a particular activity (see Matching funds and activities on p. 110). Once it is clear which activity a fund will be used to finance, the question of when to spend that fund is a relatively straightforward one, determined by terms of the funding agreement and/or the needs of the activity. So, the appropriate level of restricted fund balances to hold is entirely related to expenditure on the activity to which they are restricted.

Unrestricted funds

Unrestricted fund balances pose bigger questions than restricted funds. The organisation has to maintain itself as a going concern in order to have impact over time as well as in the present, and achieving this will require it to build and maintain a financial reserve. Unless the terms of the restriction dictate otherwise, it is not appropriate to use restricted fund balances as such reserves, so unrestricted fund balances have to be used instead. As a result, their level will be determined not only by the expenditure demands of the organisation but also its need to continue as a going concern.

Why hold reserves?

Increasingly, trustees are being encouraged or required to explain their reserves policy and to justify the level of reserves held by the organisation. The UK Charity Commission, in its publication on charity reserves (Charity Commission, 2010), emphasises that responsibility for establishing a reserves policy rests with the trustees, and that an organisation should be judged on whether its level of reserves (whatever that is) is justified and clearly explained. SORP 2005 recommends that the trustees' report should include a description of 'the charity's policy on reserves stating the level of reserves held and why they are held' (Charity Commission, 2005, p. 9).

There are four main reasons to hold reserves (see box 7.2). For most organisations, the first of these objectives – protect the continuity of the organisation's work – will be the most significant in monetary terms. A strategy of building unrestricted funds is a crucial way of guaranteeing continuity so that even in the event of disappointing income, expenditure can be financed from reserves. Not that this is a long-term option – reserves can only be spent once. Eventually, the funds will be exhausted unless they are replenished.

Box 7.2   Why hold reserves?

Organisations need to hold reserves in order to do the following:

- **Protect the continuity of the organisation's work, in spite of uncertain future income streams** – in other words, to provide a source of funding in the event of unexpected funding shortfalls.
- **Protect the organisation's funds from loss in value of the asset form in which they are held** – so, if the organisation's trustees choose to hold the funds placed in their trust in a form that can lose value as well as gain it, such as market investments, then they must have contingency funding available so that in the event of the former happening, the fund value can be restored. This is particularly true of endowment and restricted funds which, by definition, have been donated for a specific purpose.
- **Provide the capital needed to finance expansion of the organisation** – if the organisation is to grow it needs injections of money to finance investment in income generation for example. It can either borrow this money or use its own funds.
- **Provide the funds needed to replace assets** – where the historic cost of the asset understates its replacement cost. In order to purchase new computers, vehicles and other fixed assets the organisation needs funds. Unless the purchase of the assets is itself to further the objectives of the organisation, it is unlikely that the organisation will find specific (restricted) funding for such investments. The organisation must therefore generate unrestricted income that is not spent on operational activities – in other words, unrestricted fund balances, or reserves.

So, reserves management demands also that the decision makers have a sufficiently clear understanding of future income flows to anticipate when reserves are likely to be needed to honour expenditure commitments. In a period where committed expenditure is running higher than income (and therefore reserves are falling), the organisation must be sure that any further expenditure commitments can be financed without reserves being excessively depleted or, worst still, exhausted. Unless the organisation wants to reduce the level of its reserves, it has to know when to stop spending.

The public attention paid to the issue of reserves is entirely appropriate in the context of public accountability for funds placed in the trust of the trustees (hence the term 'trustee'), from the point of view of both donors and beneficiaries (see box 7.3). In prior guidance, the Charity Commission has specifically flagged up that some charities' sizeable reserves are likely to attract attention (Charity Commission, 2008b). As a result of this highlighting, such organisations risk being accused of being self-indulgent: of hoarding rather than spending. Organisations which are vulnerable to this exposure (if they have high levels of reserves) include those operating in areas where there is clear evidence of immediate human need, those which rely on a strong emotive appeal and those which claim an urgent need for new funds. Some high-profile charities that are often quoted in this respect (whether justified or not) fuel this public perception for the sector as a whole. However, for the majority of charities the problem is quite the reverse. For them, the priority is to find a way to generate unrestricted income that would give the trustees discretion not to spend the income, but to build an appropriate level of reserves.

Box 7.3   Designated funds
Where unrestricted funds are earmarked or designated for essential future spending, for example, to fund a project that could not be met from future income alone they can be excluded from reserves. In such cases the reserves policy should explain the nature and amount of the designation and when the funds set aside are likely to be spent. It is never acceptable to set up designations simply to reduce the stated level of reserves.
Charity Commission, 2010a, p. 7

The level of reserves must be necessary, as the Charity Commission rightly stresses, but equally they must be sufficient. There must be enough reserves to meet the objectives stated in box 7.2. For charities with insufficient reserves, discussions about what to do with unrestricted funds must recognise the legitimacy and importance of building those reserves alongside the more exciting expenditure options. Again, this highlights the importance of maximising impact over time. Regrettably, most charities do have to consider how they will have impact tomorrow as well as today: the cause will not have disappeared. So, there is much education needed in the public domain to legitimise the building of reserves.

How are reserves defined?

The Charity Commission uses the term 'reserves' to describe those financial resources over which the trustees have full discretion and which are not yet spent, committed or designated and 'that part of a charity's unrestricted funds that is freely available to spend on any of the charity's purposes' (Charity Commission, 2010a, p. 7).

The Charity Commission explains that this definition therefore normally excludes permanent endowment, expendable endowment, restricted funds, any part of unrestricted funds not readily available for spending (specifically income funds that could only be realised by disposing of fixed assets held for charity use) and programme-related investments. This is understandably so, since such funds clearly are not available to be spent at the trustees' discretion. For example, funds that have been designated to protect those assets held in a form that could only be realised if disposed are clearly not available for general use by the trustees.

Helpfully, the Charity Commission also notes that while both expendable endowment and restricted funds are excluded from the definition of reserves, 'holding such funds may influence a charity's reserves policy' (Charity Commission, 2010a, p. 7). As it rightly counsels, many charities with expendable endowments rely on the income generated from investment of the endowment –

a dependence that prevents the endowment as being regarded as 'free' for expenditure.

The case for excluding designated funds from a definition of reserves is less clear cut, as the Charity Commission recognises (see box 7.3). For example, trustees can designate funds into a continuity reserve in order to provide a bank of resources to draw on in the event of unforeseen difficulties or opportunities arising. The purpose of the designation is to ensure that the organisation keeps in mind the need to maintain such a reserve, and that such funds are spent not inadvertently, but only after conscious trustee consideration. Such funds, by intent, are 'free' for expenditure. So, the organisation needs to consider why the designation has been made, and in what form these funds are held. Ignoring designated funds that could be used by the trustees in extreme circumstances would encourage the trustees to build higher reserves than are necessary.

Determining what reserves to hold

Determining the appropriate size of reserves (so that they are both sufficient and necessary) must be related to the four objectives listed in box 7.2. The first two of these relate to the management of two risks. First, there is the risk that the continuity of activities cannot be sustained because of unexpected shortfalls in income. Second, there is the risk that funds are held in assets forms that might lose market value.

The exposure to market value losses (objective 2) can be easily assessed. What would be the monetary value of a loss of, say, 20 per cent in market prices of investments? The need for judgement comes in when assessing how big a possible market drop to protect against. The financial crisis that erupted in 2008 will have made trustees much more aware of the potential volatility of the markets. Similarly, calculating how much funding will be needed to finance expansion (objective 3) or pay for the replacement of fixed assets (objective 4) ought to be uncomplicated, based on a rudimentary business plan outlining what will need to be purchased and the anticipated costs of doing so.

However, determining the exposure to unexpected falls in income (objective 1) is more difficult. Gillingham and Tame (1997) propose a number of ways to consider this, including actuarial forecasting, risk assessment and scenario planning. Each has its merits, although most organisations would find the risk-assessment or scenario-planning approaches most logical and practical to undertake, and suitable to quote when explaining the level of reserves held or targeted. It is possible to make relatively crude judgements – this does not have to be a complicated, scientific exercise. After all, the aim is only to give the organisation an indicative feel for the size of funds that it should put to one side in case an uncertain event happens in the future.

The risk-assessment approach assesses how much the organisation can rely on having available funding to cover the costs of its planned activities, and therefore how much it faces a risk from funding that it cannot yet rely on. It is possible to determine the appropriate level of reserves to hold through a three-stage process. In simple terms, the organisation:

1. assesses what funds it needs
2. compares this to how much it can already rely on
3. makes a judgement about the risk attached to the remainder.

These three stages are described below.

Such an assessment could change frequently as new expenditure commitments are made or funding agreements signed, and the organisation must adopt the discipline of reviewing its funding exposure regularly (at least once a year). The annual discipline of writing the trustees' report should encourage this.

Stage 1: identifying funding requirement

This is a question of identifying the organisation's expenditure commitments. These can be assessed from three levels, each one subsuming the previous one.

1. The first level of commitment relates to the costs that the organisation will have to incur in the future, in order to honour its legal commitments. For example, they would include the costs that would have to be incurred if the organisation closed down, such as meeting staff statutory and contractual terms of employment.
2. The second level of commitment relates to those costs to which the organisation is morally committed, even if there is no legal obligation. This often includes project or grant agreements, where the organisation is contracted to provide defined services or funding over a stipulated period of time, but is subject to clauses that enable the contract to be terminated in the event of particular unforeseen circumstances arising. These *force majeure* clauses can include funding shortfalls as grounds to end a contract. The organisation may conclude that it is morally obliged to complete all the activities currently being undertaken. This may be a mixture of those activities with a finite life and any general activity that is ongoing.
3. The third level assumes the most liberal definition of funding need, including not only legal and current commitments but future commitments too. This refers to costs that the organisation intends to incur but to which it is not yet committed. So, this level assumes that organisation wishes to continue as planned, completing current activities and starting new ones as well. It therefore reflects the organisation's overall expenditure plans.

Both levels 2 and 3 require the organisation to make some judgement about the timeframe for the funding of running costs, such as payroll for permanent staff, which continue indefinitely. Since the general activity is undertaken in support of the specific project-based activities, the length of the project sets the timeframe for the organisation's funding requirement. This, in turn, requires the organisation's management information systems to be set up to provide costed data over activity-based timeframes. However, they may well not be set up like this. An alternative might be to exclude from consideration those activities that will only be undertaken if specific (and therefore, by definition, restricted) funding is received. With such activities, reserves are not needed. The contingency plan is that without funding, the activity does not happen.

While acknowledging the relevance of considering activity-based timeframes and ignoring activities that are dependent on restricted funding, many organisations will find it adequate to determine their funding requirement by simply using the forecasted total costs of the organisation over, say, the next 12 months. They can be confident that one year's cover will provide ample lead time to reduce commitments in the event of a funding downturn – even if that means terminating some existing commitments before their completion.

Stage 2: identifying funding secured

Identifying funding that is already secure should be straightforward. By definition, there should be some form of written agreement that confirms the commitment of the donor to make an income payment to the organisation. The exercise can be completed by considering what funding agreements are in place, either by donor or by activity. This stage should also identify any endowment, restricted and possibly designated fund balances that are available to fund the proposed activities.

Stage 3: identifying funding risk

The final stage in the reserves determination process is to consider the risk of failing to generate the balance of funding required.

The organisation must complete two tasks. First, it must identify the funding sources from which it anticipates generating the income. Again, this may be best done by activity – particularly for those organisations reliant on restricted funding. Then, it must make a judgement against each possible funding source on the degree of risk associated with the funding. This is expressed as a percentage of the total funding required from the source. It may be very low. For example, the income from individual donors whose donation is made in a committed, indefinite form such as direct debit might be considered to be a very low risk, given the low rates at which such donors typically withdraw their support.

Other funding sources, such as legacy income, should be regarded as a much higher risk, given the uncertainty associated with them. Once the degree of risk has been judged, the value of funding at risk by source can be calculated.

For ease of presentation and discussion, it is worth setting out the three stages at a summary level in a simple matrix (see fig. 7.1). This could be annotated to explain to the reader, for example, what rationale was used to identify a particular degree of risk.

	A		B	C = A − B	D	E = C x D
Activity	Total funding required	Income source	Secure funding	Total at risk	Degree of risk	Risk
	£'000		£'000	£'000	%	£'000
Specific activity 1	200	Funder X	120	80	30%	24
Specific activity 2	100	Restricted fund Y	100	0	0%	0
General activity 3	300	Funder Z	200	100	50%	50
	——		——	——		——
TOTAL	600		420	180		74

Activity	Identification of the activities on which the organisation incurs cost. This will be a mixture of specific activities and general activity, such as departmental running costs
Total funding required	The total cost of the activity over the defined time period
Income source	Identification of the funder or existing fund balance from which the funds will be sourced to cover the cost
Secure funding	The income from the source that is already secure and can be relied on because it has already been received, or for which the funder has a contractual commitment
Total at risk	The balance of the total funding that is therefore not secure
Degree of risk	The percentage of the insecure funding that is at risk
Risk	The exposed insecure funding expressed in monetary terms

Fig. 7.1 Estimating income risk

Writing a reserves policy

Under the SORP 2005, trustees need to explain their thinking on reserves and to justify the levels held (see box 7.4). The policy should show clearly how the ideal level of reserves compares with the current reserves position. It should also outline what action is proposed if the current position is not as intended and the arrangement for monitoring and reviewing the policy.

Box 7.4   What a reserves policy should explain

A good reserves policy will explain how reserves are used to manage uncertainty and, if reserves are held to fund future purchases or activities, it will explain how and when the reserves will be spent. A reserves policy provides assurance that the finances of the charity are actively managed and its activities are sustainable. In particular, a reserves policy can help to:

- *give confidence to funders by demonstrating good stewardship and financial management;*
- *demonstrate the charity's sustainability and capacity to manage unforeseen financial difficulties;*
- *give voluntary funders, such as grantmakers, an understanding of why funding is needed to undertake a particular project or activity*
- *give assurance to lenders or creditors that the charity can meet its financial commitments; and*
- *manage the risks to a charity's reputation from holding substantial unspent funds at the year-end without explanation.*

Charity Commission, 2010a, pp. 9–10

Expressing reserves in relation to expenditure

Typically, reserves are expressed in relation to expenditure, given that the main rationale for holding reserves is to counter the risk to expenditure from uncertain funding. Often, the expression is in terms of the length of time that the reserves would cover the expenditure (weeks, months or, in extreme cases, years). Less often, the calculation is rightly expressed in relation to expected future expenditure, rather than actual historic expenditure. It needs to be the former. In the example in figure 7.1, the level of free reserves required (to cover the funding risk of £74,000) would be expressed in relation to the funding requirement (£600,000) – in other words, 12.3 per cent. If the funding requirement referred to, say, a 12-month period, then the percentage could then be expressed as 45 days' cover.

The reserves are the 'piggy bank' available for the future. In a period of rapid change in expenditure levels (either up or down), expressing reserves in relation to historic expenditure may be misleading. Trustee bodies should express reserves in relation to expenditure in a way that gives a clear guide to their intentions without inhibiting their ability to make judgements in light of the particular circumstances that they might find themselves in. This means avoiding setting rigid, absolute maximum or minimum reserves levels (for example, stating that 'reserves should be no more than/no less than three months of future expenditure').

As the purpose of holding reserves in the first place is to substitute for income that has not been generated, there may be an occasion in which the reserves are actually used, resulting in low reserves. Equally, the reserves policy should not inhibit trustees from allowing reserves to increase to a high level at a particular time as a result of the sudden and unexpected receipt, say, of a sizeable legacy. If the reserves are viewed just after the receipt of such a donation, they might justifiably look high.

So, the reserves policy should indicate what level of reserves is expected and desired, while acknowledging that actual circumstances may leave the reserves higher or lower than this. The trustees' report should explain this circumstance and what action is proposed to get the reserves to the desired level.

The statement presented in box 7.5 shows that the trustees have assessed what approximate level of reserves they want to see held at any particular point in time. It is not a precise number – it is expressed as a range, with short-term circumstances determining what level, in practice, is held. Note also from the statement that the policy seeks to cover only a percentage of the future expenditure that is likely to be spent from unrestricted funds, rather than all of it.

Box 7.5   Extract from a reserves policy

The trustees are of the opinion that to safeguard the continuing work and commitments of Sightsavers, the level of unrestricted reserves (excluding pension deficit) at the balance sheet date should normally equate to 25% ± 5% of the projected total resources due to be expended from unrestricted funds in the following 12 months ... The trustees recognise that it may be appropriate to allow the level of reserves to rise above or drop below this benchmark at times as a result of short-term cash inflows or in order to ensure continuity of programmes.

Sightsavers International, 2008, pp. 26–27

THE FORM OF FUND BALANCES

The greater the degree of restriction, the greater the importance of ensuring that the fund is held in the right form. The acceptance of income with restrictions imposes obligations on the organisation – certainly in terms of how the funds are spent, but quite possibly also in terms of how they are protected until they are spent. The organisation will have an obligation to return the funds to their donor if they cannot be used in accordance with the terms of any restriction imposed by the latter. This means that it has to ensure that the funds do not end up in a form that makes them difficult to realise – or, worse still, spent on activity that falls outside the restrictions.

For this reason, it may be necessary to hold the funds in a discrete asset form, such as a separate bank account, to guarantee their protection. The organisation must be looking to keep these fund balances in as liquid and realisable a form as possible, so it cannot hold them in the form of, say, tangible fixed assets that could only be realised if sold, as this would prevent the organisation from functioning effectively.

The classification of fund balances by asset form can be very helpful (see fig. 7.2). Ask yourself the question: 'How easily could the fund balance be converted from its present asset form into cash?'

	General	Designated	Restricted
Fixed assets			
Current net assets			
TOTAL NET ASSETS			

Fig. 7.2 The classification of fund balances

In the above table, only the shaded box (representing general unrestricted funds held in an asset form other than fixed assets) can genuinely be defined as 'free' – in other words, truly at the discretion of the trustees. The assessment of the health of a balance sheet can change markedly if funds prove to be in a form that is either unrealisable, or if the timing of the realisation of the fund is not solely at the discretion of the trustees. For example, consider what would happen if the trustees were holding the funds either in a market-based form that had lost value at the time that the funds were needed, or in a fixed asset that could not be sold without affecting the operating capacity of the organisation.

Dealing with movements in market values

What if the organisation holds funds in an asset form that is shown on the balance sheet at market value rather than historic cost? What should it do if the market value drops? Potentially, it will have to replenish the fund balances to the previous value. Will it be able to say to the donor that the fund balance has reduced, not because of expenditure, but because of lost market value? This will depend on the terms under which the funds were given.

Unless the donor has explicitly agreed that its funds can be invested in assets that may fall in value, the organisation may believe that there is a moral obligation at least to replenish the fund for any market value losses attributable to it. Unless explicitly agreed to the contrary, the organisation might assume that the donor does not want its funds to be 'spent' on, say, investment losses. On the other hand, it may make its judgement in the light of movements in the market value of the funds' assets in previous years. If a year of losses follows several years of gains that were attributed to the restricted fund, a legitimate stance may be to charge the loss to the fund in the exceptional year in which it occurs. However, this is much less credible if several years of losses occur consecutively.

Protecting fixed assets

Having protected the organisation's restricted and endowment funds, what is the nature of the assets that are left (which, by definition, will represent the designated and unrestricted funds)? Very sensibly, some trustee bodies choose to designate funds that are equal in value to those assets that cannot be realised without jeopardising the organisation's ability to continue to function. This minimises the risk that general funds are depleted, whether intentionally or not, to such an extent that restricted and/or endowment fund balances end up being held in the form of fixed assets that cannot be easily realised. Consequently, it is much easier for everyone – trustees, management and actual and potential supporters – to see what unrestricted funds are genuinely at the trustees' disposal.

MATCHING FUNDS AND ACTIVITIES

If all the organisation's funds are unrestricted, the issue of which funds to use for which activity does not arise. Similarly, where the organisation has funds with tight restrictions that have been given specifically for one precise purpose, there is no decision to make about how those funds are spent once the funds have been accepted. Managed prior to use, yes, but expended, no.

How should an organisation best decide how to use all the funds that fall somewhere between these two extremes? It needs a process by which it can make decisions about which funds are used to finance which activities. It must be clear about what is paying for what. If not, there is considerable risk that particular activities will be either be double funded, or even treble funded, or not funded at all. As Unwin (2001) indicated, this risk was one of the reasons that funders gave for their reluctance to finance core costs (see box 6.2, p. 86).

Ideally, the attribution of expenditure to fund would take place at the time that the expenditure is incurred. This would ensure that at any time it was clear what balance was held in each fund. However, in practice it is rarely that straightforward. For example, how should the organisation account for an activity that costs more than any restricted funding received for that purpose? At least some of these costs will have to be met from another fund – perhaps from the unrestricted fund. This raises the following question, when any particular expenditure is incurred: which of the funds is being depleted?

Often, the terms of the restriction do leave room for choices about which project to finance. For example, a donor may simply impose a geographic restriction that requires the funds to be spent only in, say, Africa. Then, any of the organisation's activities that are undertaken in Africa would be eligible to be funded from the fund. The organisation may well not want to decide which fund to use at the time that the expenditure is incurred – for example, it may prefer to wait until the end of the financial year (when it will have to make a choice), when the complete funding and expenditure picture is clear.

This decision is not simply a political issue, but a financial stewardship one too. Guided by the principle that the unrestricted funds should be spent last, the organisation should assign the expenditure to the fund with the tightest restriction whose criteria it matches. However, it may wish to assign it to a highly restricted fund that it has not yet received – hence the preference to avoid matching cost to fund until the latest possible moment.

It is essential to have some central coordination of the matching process, to include the perspectives of service providers, fundraisers and finance. This coordination will help to manage the jostling between fundraisers within the organisation, who compete to get first call on the more marketable projects. Such a coordinating body serves as a forum at which the fundraisers and service deliverers meet to coordinate the matching of income and expenditure and match costed activities to funds.

To an observer, this sort of forum might resemble a market square, where stallholders (the service deliverers) endeavour to sell their wares (the charitable activities) to the customers (the fundraisers). A brokering process is conducted. Participants inform themselves as to which activities currently being undertaken or planned do not have secured funding attached to them, and fundraisers – aware of the expectations, wishes and interests of their donors – bid to secure or reserve these available activities. At any time the following information must be clear.

● **The cost of the activities (actual or proposed) to be covered:** This reiterates the importance of understanding the true cost of each activity. The structure of most accounting systems makes it easy to slip into believing that the direct costs of undertaking an activity (those directly attributable to the activity) are the only ones that need to be covered, leaving all the indirect costs unfunded. Activity-based costing is needed.

- **The timeframe over which the funding is needed:** It is helpful to know how much expenditure requires finance – from the start of the activity to its finish, however long that is – and whether it fits neatly in one financial year or straddles several. The organisation should be appealing to donors to finance the costs of the complete activity. It may be helpful to think in terms of the donor timeframes. Funders such as the institutional funders will think in financial years – their financial year, not that of the organisation – and the organisation will unquestionably have to appeal for funds and report on actual expenditure in financial years. Unless the organisation is lucky, those periods will not coincide with its financial year, and as a result it makes sense to think in terms of periods that are divisible in any financial year, such as quarters.
- **Which donors and funds are expecting to finance an activity:** It is often the case that more than one donor is interested in funding an activity, and more than one fund is suitable. In such cases the organisation has choices to make, with consequences.
- **How much funding is predicted from that donor:** And therefore what balance, if any, is still likely to be unfunded.
- **The status of the financing:** For example, each activity might have one of four descriptors against it, indicating the proximity of secure funding being received:
  - Available: no specific funding even in the pipeline yet
  - On offer: in discussion with one or more specific donors to provide funding for that activity, but nothing yet guaranteed
  - Committed: commitment obtained from donor to provide funding, but not yet received.
  - Received: income received and therefore available for expenditure as and when activity that meets the terms of any restriction can take place.

Managing the matching process

To be effective, such a process has to be carefully managed. It is not a free-for-all. Maintaining accurate, up-to-date information on each activity is critical if the organisation is not to risk inappropriate approaches to funders to finance activities that already have other funding or are inaccurately costed. Given that the future is uncertain, the anticipated cost and timing of activities will change over time.

So, the organisation must establish how to handle the funding implications of these changes – both in terms of internal fund management decisions, and in terms of the funder. It is important to have in place high-quality information systems, with responsibility clearly assigned for their maintenance. However, this does not necessarily have to be technologically sophisticated: a well-designed spreadsheet may be adequate.

Most critical of all is the decision-making process through which funds and activities are matched. At times there will inevitably be competing funding demands on the same activities. In this case there needs to be a clear internal process to determine which funding source is matched with the activity. The organisation must be clear whether a particular activity is to be matched with funder A or funder B – especially if the funding is not yet secure. For example, it must understand the consequences of reserving the activity for submission to funder A and subsequently being unsuccessful in that bid, by which stage income from funder B may no longer be available.

It also needs to consider the nature of funds that have already been received and are available before determining what future income is sought, since there would be no value in seeking funding that would be restricted to activities for which adequate funding is already available.

A final issue is the need to recognise the benefit of matching long-term, ongoing expenditure with funding sources that are also long term and stable. The alternative is to risk facing a funding shortfall for long-term expenditure that was matched with short-term funding source that is no longer active.

These issues can cause difficulties for those responsible for generating income. The same activities often appeal to a range of funders who (for all sorts of reasons) are reluctant to switch their interest to other, equally important, activities performed by the organisation. There may be considerably less room for negotiation with such funders than at first appears to be the case – particularly if they are unwilling to finance core costs.

Key stewardship questions

1. Are the reserves at an appropriate level, given the future intentions of the organisation?

2. Are the fund balances (restricted and unrestricted) in an appropriate form?

3. Are restricted fund balances being appropriately matched to expenditure?

4. How does the organisation intend to achieve these aims?

8 Managing assets for financial health

An organisation's assets describe the form in which the fund balances are held. Many assets will not be in the form of cash. They will have been converted into other forms such as computers or buildings (tangible fixed assets), or invested in products such as equities or bonds (investments). The fund balance may not have even been received yet, and may still be owed to the organisation (debtors). Similarly, the organisation may have incurred costs that commit it to paying the funds to another party but may not yet have done so (creditors). However, it is unlikely that many fund balances will have been converted into stock, unless the purpose of the organisation is met through the supply of goods. (Trading subsidiaries might also hold sizeable stock values.)

Irrespective of the form in which the fund balances are held, the finance steward must be confident that such a form is appropriate. The key to successful asset management revolves around understanding cash and how it moves. The organisation has to assure itself that sufficient cash is being generated, and that the assets of the organisation – its resources – are being appropriately used in pursuit of its purpose.

The finance strategy of a not-for-profit organisation will have many features that distinguish it from its commercial counterparts, but when it comes to cash the two should be very similar. The importance of cash is common to all businesses from every sector:

> Cash is to a business what blood is to a living body. Allow it to drain away and the body becomes weak and sickly and eventually dies. The more cash that can be generated ... the more healthy the company becomes. Rapid generation, conversion and effective utilisation of cash is the whole foundation on which a business rests.
>
> Warnes, 1984, p. 39

So it is with not-for-profit organisations.

ASSESSING FINANCIAL HEALTH

There are two key factors to consider when assessing financial health: liquidity and solvency.

Liquidity

The quickest way to understand the immediate financial health of an organisation is to determine how easily it could meet its short-term liabilities.

This is done by assessing the liquidity of its assets, reflecting the ease with which assets in a non-cash form could be converted into cash. The current ratio – the ratio of current assets to current liabilities – should, as a rule of thumb, exceed one. (In other words, there should be more current assets than liabilities.) A very high ratio might imply that the organisation has excessive liquidity – that is, that assets are being retained in an easily realisable form rather than being spent in furthering the welfare purpose.

Box 8.1   How cash flows in not-for-profit organisations

The start of the process is the arrival of cash from donors, the shareholders of the organisation investing their funds in order to generate a welfare impact. Those funds may arrive immediately in the form of cash (1) or, if committed earlier than paid, may be in the form of debtors (2) until cash is received (3).

If the funds are not immediately needed, the cash can be converted into investments (4) in order to generate investment income (5). At a later date the investments can be sold, thereby generating cash (6). Any realised gains or losses on the sale would be reflected on the SOFA.

Some cash will have to be used to purchase fixed assets (7) in order to provide the infrastructure to run the organisation. Only the cash generated from any sale of these fixed assets will re-enter the cash flow (8). In the case of most assets the resale proceeds will be less than the original purchase price. Cash spent on fixed assets is unlikely to be recovered and will eventually be recognised as expenditure by being charged as depreciation. As well as fixed assets being bought with cash, credit can be used (9), the value of creditors representing the value of cash to be paid out at some time in the future to repay the debt (10).

With fixed assets in place, and funds not yet needed suitably invested, the remaining cash sums are spent in one of three directions running the organisation. Some payments of cash will be invested in further income generation activities (11), such fundraising investment thereby feeding back into donor funds (12). At least some cash will have to be used to pay for essential management and administration costs (13), such as fees associated with regulating the organisation as a legal entity (e.g. audit fees). As much cash as possible, however, should be devoted to financing the welfare services that the organisation exists to provide (14). As with fixed assets, in all of these cases, the payment of cash out of the business can be delayed by financing the transactions through creditors (15).

At its simplest, there are only four options for deciding what to do with cash received from donors. It can be: kept in the form of cash; converted into another asset form in order to protect it to provide future value to the organisation; used to settle debts held with creditors; or spent on income generation, management and administration or on delivering welfare services. There are no other choices.

Solvency

Assessing the longer-term financial health of the organisation requires a somewhat more sophisticated understanding of the structure of its financing. Essentially, the total assets of the organisation – its total capital – must be financed from just three sources: fund balances, creditors and borrowings. The more the financial structure of the organisation is dependent on creditors and borrowings, the less secure its solvency. Borrowings can be arranged either formally, using financing facilities such as overdrafts and mortgages, or informally – for example, by using monies owed to creditors. If there is a net outflow of cash, this has to be financed either by allowing borrowings or creditors to increase, or by allowing fund balances to reduce.

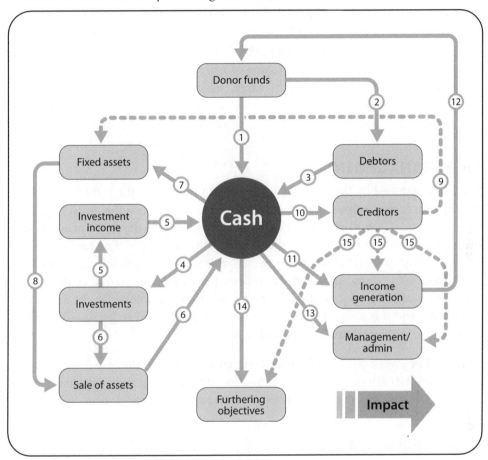

Fig. 8.1 Cash flow in a not-for-profit organisation

Long-term solvency demands that the organisation can generate positive operational cash flows. This means that it generates at least as much cash from its daily operational business as it spends, without the need to rely on cash generated from the sale of assets on the balance sheet. However, liquidity ratios will not necessarily highlight this. The short-term liquidity position can be quickly improved – for example, by the sale of fixed assets, such as computers or vehicles. Nonetheless, on the assumption that these assets are required for operational purposes, such action would quickly render the organisation ineffective.

To understand how much of its assets are being financed from borrowings rather than from its own fund balances, the organisation needs to compare the level of borrowings and creditors (total liabilities on the balance sheet) with the size of the fund balances. This is the debt to equity ratio – in other words, the total liabilities to fund balances. The larger the borrowings, the greater the financial strain on the organisation to generate cash to meet the principal and interest repayments due. A very low ratio (where fund balances are high compared to levels of debt) could lead the financial strategist to conclude that the organisation was in a position to expand its level of activity by taking on more debt or by reducing the fund balances.

However, if an organisation takes on debt that has consequent interest obligations when it has healthy fund balances (some of which may be invested – for example, in equities), it exposes itself to the charge that it is borrowing money to invest. So, it must be ready to defend its policy of accepting debt, as this is likely to command higher interest charges than it can earn by investing fund balances.

CASH MANAGEMENT

The funds handled by the organisation must not only be of the right type, held in the right form, and subsequently used in the right way, but all this must happen at the right time. Cash management is about understanding the flows of funds into the organisation, onto the balance sheet and out through the SOFA (see box 8.1 and fig. 8.1). Why? Because although the SOFA will state how much income has been raised, and may show that there have been net inflows of resources during the accounting period, it does not tell its reader whether the income has been received in cash yet; and it is cash, of course – not surpluses – that is needed to pay staff and suppliers, to make grant payments, and so on.

There can be a very critical difference between surpluses on the SOFA and cash. To understand the cash position, the organisation steward must go to the balance sheet and the cash flow statement. This is worth spending some time understanding.

Cash requirement

Most organisations require cash to cover two types of cost:

- **Operational expenses:** such as grants, salaries, rent, supplies, printed materials and fees. These items appear as expenditure on the SOFA.
- **Capital expenses:** such as property, computer equipment, fixtures and fittings and vehicles. These costs appear as fixed assets on the balance sheet.

The operational and capital expenses are the items for which cash will flow out of the organisation. Cash will flow into the organisation as a result of generating income, which is also shown on the SOFA. However, referring only to the SOFA will disguise the cash position of the organisation, potentially leading to a false sense of security. The following section (based on material presented by Warnes, 1984) illustrates the key principles.

Illustration of the key principles of cash flow

An organisation's primary statements show that during the period it raised £1 million in income, incurred £950,000 on operating expenditure, and spent £200,000 on capital items. All would appear to be well. The SOFA shows a surplus, and the organisation has £200,000 of new capital assets (see fig. 8.2).

The real picture is less positive. Even on the assumption that all the figures above were represented by cash, the organisation would be showing a cash outflow of £150,000. However, not all the income will have been received in the form of cash. Some funders will not have met their liability yet and, as a result, the organisation will have some debtors. Similarly, the organisation will not have met all its liabilities to suppliers yet for items that appear as either expenditure or capital.

Although the circumstances will differ from one organisation to the next, it is likely that many will have larger debtors than creditors. This is simply as a result of the fact that the funders will be relatively powerful compared to many not-for-profit organisations, and will have greater control over the timing of their payments to the organisation than the organisation does over the

SOFA	£'000
Income	1,000
Operating expenditure	950
	–––––
Net incoming resources	50
Balance sheet	**£'000**
Fixed assets	200

Fig. 8.2 Primary statements sample 1

SOFA	£'000
Income	1,000
Operating expenditure	950
	–––––
Net incoming resources	**50**
Balance sheet	**£'000**
Fixed assets	200
Debtors (20% x income)	200
Creditors (10% x operating expenditure and capital)	(115)
	–––––
Total net assets	285

Fig. 8.3 Primary statements sample 2

timing of its payments to creditors. Assume in the above example that 20 per cent of income is in the form of a debtor rather than cash, and that 10 per cent of payments are still showing as creditors. The primary statements would now look like figure 8.3.

SOFA	£'000
Income received in cash (80% x £1,000,000)	800
	———
Cash inflow	**800**
Operating expenditure incurred in cash (90% x £950,000)	(855)
Fixed assets bought with cash (90% x £200,000)	(180)
	———
Cash outflow	**(1,035)**
	———
Net cash outflow	**(235)**
	———

Fig. 8.4 Primary statements sample 3

The total net assets of £285,000 have to be financed with money from somewhere, with only £50,000 generated from the surplus of income over expenditure, leaving a £235,000 shortfall. That is perhaps more obvious if these results are reflected in terms of what has happened to cash (see fig. 8.4).

The performance has, in fact, resulted in a cash outflow of £235,000, which has to be found from somewhere. Study of the figures in the primary statement format will show that this has been caused by the increases in capital (£200,000) and net current assets (debtors – creditors = £85,000) exceeding the surplus generated on the SOFA (£50,000). The total cash paid out (£855,000 + £180,000) is £235,000 greater than the cash received in (£800,000).

Where can the organisation find the £235,000 that it needs to close this funding gap? The answer is from one of three sources. It could pay fewer of its creditors, it could borrow funds from a third party (such as a bank overdraft), or it could reduce its own fund balances. All three options have obvious dangers. The greater the creditors, the greater the strain on the organisation's resources, since they will use increasingly punitive measures to recover their debt. Borrowing money incurs costs such as interest payments, which further increase the expenditure payments needed, as well as accumulating potentially major cash flow problems when the principal sum has to be repaid. Meanwhile, as we have seen, reducing fund balances results in a permanent depletion of the organisation's capital base – which is fine if fund balances are healthy, but a problem if they are not.

It is important to note from the above illustration that the effect of the organisation's business over the period on cash is much greater than the SOFA surplus, hence the need to track cash movements so carefully. Note, too, that trying to resolve the cash problem by expanding the operations to generate more income is likely to have precisely the opposite effect. Gearing the organisation up

→ Calculate Cashflow - After Depreciation removed).

to raise twice the income would leave the primary statements showing a funding gap of £470,000 (see fig. 8.5).

What emerges from the above illustration is that cash flow (the change in cash during a period) is influenced by just three factors.

- **The surplus or deficit incurred on the SOFA:** which should be calculated after removing non-cash items such as depreciation charges.
- **The change in an organisation's net current asset requirement:** where this is measured by debtors less creditors (and if the organisation has stock, this should be added to debtors to calculate the net current asset requirement).
- **The level of capital expenditure on fixed assets:** such as computer equipment, fixtures and fittings and vehicles.

SOFA	£'000
Income	2,000
Operating expenditure	1,900
	———
Net incoming resources	**100**
Balance sheet	**£'000**
Fixed assets	400
Debtors (20% x income)	400
Creditors (10% x operating expenditure and capital)	(230)
	———
Total net assets	**570**
Cash flow statement	**£'000**
Net cash outflow	**(470)**

Fig. 8.5 Primary statements sample 4

All three have to be monitored assiduously. Before the organisation takes any action that will have cash implications, it has to understand and cover those implications. For example, if the organisation wishes to expand, that will place cash demands on it (at least temporarily, in terms of net current assets and capital), so it must be clear where it will find the cash to finance those demands. What is crucial is that action is taken continuously, to prevent the cash requirement stimulated by the above three factors from spiralling out of control.

The cash flow statement (the third primary statement, which is so rarely used or understood) can play a key role here. It is structured precisely to show what has happened to cash with respect to the three factors, and helpfully shows the reader how the cash movements are derived from the SOFA and balance sheet. For cash-starved organisations, it deserves far more attention than it gets.

Cash flow monitoring and forecasting

The tighter the cash situation, the more important the need to monitor closely historic cash movements and forecast anticipated ones. Tracking historic cash movements should not be difficult – particularly with the help of computerised bank facilities that monitor daily the movements of automated and cleared items in and out of the account. This can also greatly help with very short-term cash flow forecasting. The bank should be able to identify what transactions are already in the system and due to be charged or credited to the account over the following working days.

To the extent that the organisation's business in the future will be similar to its recent past, tracking cash history should help it to build up a good picture of the nature of its transactions, and the cash demands that are likely to be imposed. For example, within any month there are likely to be cash outflow peaks that coincide with the timing of the cheque runs, the payroll or grant payments. Comparing the historic cash flow with the expenditure pattern could also prove informative.

It is important to take great care to ensure that cash is not confused with income or expenditure. An organisation's income and expenditure plan/budget is not the same as its cash flow forecast, and if decisions are made in, for example, the mistaken belief that the phasing of anticipated income on the SOFA identifies when cash will be available, this could have disastrous consequences. For accuracy, a cash flow forecast has to be derived from the income and expenditure forecasts, with assumptions built in about when cash will be received in or be paid out.

ASSET MANAGEMENT

Identifying what drives an organisation's cash requirements has highlighted the importance of tight management of all the assets and liabilities on the balance sheet. Some key trends have to be tracked. What is important is that the steward of the organisation understands why each asset and liability exists, and what is an appropriate size of each, in relation to the financial position and performance of the organisation. This can be done through monitoring a set of key ratios that define the relationships between certain assets, liabilities, income and expenditure.

There is no ratio that, by definition, represents an absolute measure of success. The organisation must make its own judgements about, for example, how much it should be investing in fixed assets taking into account its level of activity, past record, financial position and industry benchmarks (if these are available). However, analysis of ratio trends over time will give a clear indication as to whether asset management is improving or deteriorating.

Asset turnover

Are the assets of the organisation working hard enough? If they are not, then funds invested in the assets could otherwise be released for expenditure to support beneficiaries, or the productivity of the assets should be increased. Asset productivity, or turnover, is measured by the ratio of total expenditure in the period to average total assets in the period. The appropriateness of the level of investment in capital – in other words, fixed assets, which has been identified as one of the three determinants of cash requirement – can be assessed using average total fixed assets in place of average total assets.

The usual aim is to see a high measure of output (income or expenditure) in relation to assets held. This would suggest that the assets are being productive. However, too high a ratio could be a sign of old assets with low balance sheet values, and may flag the imminence of significant asset replacement costs. Meanwhile, a very low ratio would suggest that the assets are insufficiently productive, and might be better converted into another form, such as cash, to be used on welfare expenditure. What is an appropriate asset turnover ratio will be very dependent on the business of the organisation: some will require significant investment in assets in order to function effectively, others much less so.

Debtor control

Is the organisation collecting funds owed to it at an appropriate speed? This is measured by tracking over time the relationship between income and debtors – the aim being to reduce the proportion of income that is in the form of debtors. At its simplest, debtor control is measured by total debtors to total income, although sometimes the relationship between the two is expressed in terms of the number of days' income that the debtors represent. Good debtor management will see the organisation chasing the funder to meet the terms of the funding contract or, at the very least, being aware of how outstanding the debt is.

As income grows, while the absolute value of debtors will also grow, it is essential for cash flow purposes that the level of debtors in relation to income remains at least constant. That is equally true of creditors so that, whatever the level of income, the ratio of net current assets to income should remain constant. A deteriorating debtor control ratio will indicate that the organisation is taking longer to collect funds owed to it than previously, and this should be investigated.

Creditor control

Is the organisation settling its liabilities with third parties at an appropriate speed? Good creditor control means ensuring that the organisation takes advantage of any payment terms that are offered by suppliers, and negotiates favourable terms where there is scope to do so. However, this should not extend as far as unreasonably withholding legitimate payments – even if many not-for-profit organisations lack the muscle to prevent some funders (especially statutory ones) from behaving similarly.

Nevertheless, at times when cash is very tight, delaying making payments to creditors is an obvious tactic – albeit a potentially dangerous one. Focusing on net current assets, where creditors are deducted from debtors, can deflect attention away from a worrying level of creditors, since the higher the creditors, the lower the level of net current assets. As Warnes (1984) advises, a very good indicator of the cash flow strain in the organisation is to measure the 'creditor strain' – the value of creditor payments that are overdue. It is important to track creditors (and debtors), aged by month, according to when the liability was incurred.

INVESTMENT MANAGEMENT

This book is not the place to detail how to manage investments. Nevertheless, there are a number of key issues that the financial strategist needs to consider carefully before investing any of the organisation's funds.

The first of these is to determine whether the organisation has any fund balances that are appropriate for investment. Although investments such as equities and fixed interest securities can be realised into cash very quickly (making them a relatively liquid asset), they are only an appropriate location for fund balances if certain conditions prevail. The funds must not be required by the organisation for other purposes in the short term – that is, for at least six to 12 months, and it has to be possible to anticipate the need for them to be realised with a reasonable lead time.

The overriding aim of investing funds must be one of protecting the real value of the asset. If either of the two conditions above exist, then the organisation exposes the investments to the risk that they will have to be realised suddenly, and at a point when the investment markets are depressed. In such circumstances the fund balances may have lost value.

The ideal scenario would see investments being realised in a managed way, for use in financing welfare expenditure after they have exhibited real growth in value. As this suggests, it is crucial that the objectives of investing fund balances are determined and documented before the investments are made. For example, do the investments need to generate short-term income that will be used to finance operating activity?

The organisation also needs to reassure itself that it is within the terms of any restriction imposed by donors for their funds to be invested, and to be clear what investment powers it has as an organisation. It is important to take professional advice in order to ensure that any decisions about investments are appropriate. This will centre on understanding and managing the tensions between risk and return. For example, the trustees of charities will have an obligation both to protect funds placed in their trust, and to generate an adequate return on balances not required for operational purposes.

It is also important to consider how the investments will be managed, and to articulate clear ways of measuring performance. The performance of professional investment managers should be compared to one of several published industry benchmarks, and for them to be set objectives in relation to those benchmarks. The most useful objectives are expressed in relative terms (for example, the performance should be in the top quartile of organisation portfolios) rather than absolute ones (for example, the portfolio should deliver total growth of at least 10 per cent per annum). These objectives must be set in recognition of the long-term nature of such investments, as short-term investment performance can be very volatile.

Key stewardship questions

1. Are the assets of the organisation sufficiently liquid?

2. Is the debt/fund balances funding structure of the organisation appropriate?

3. Is the organisation's cash flow being well managed?

4. Are the assets sufficiently productive?

5. Is debtor and creditor control adequate?

6. Is the organisation managing its investments properly?

7. How does the organisation intend to achieve these aims?

9 The level, distribution and effectiveness of expenditure

Expenditure refers to the costs incurred by the organisation that are recognised on the SOFA as 'resources expended'. It is discussed here as the last of the four elements of finance strategy (income, funds, assets and expenditure) – but it is just as important as the other three. The organisation must attend to all four perspectives of finance strategy if it is to demonstrate good stewardship of its financial resources.

In fact, expenditure is discussed last because it is the ultimate destination of the flow of funds through the organisation – and the start of the conversion process up the results chain. Funders donate income to the organisation in order to see their financial contribution have beneficial welfare impact on those that the organisation was established to serve. The organisation delivers this impact by climbing the results chain, starting with the generation and receipt of funds, and ending with impact on beneficiaries.

Chapter 2 established the overall performance contract that is needed in organisations – that of maximising beneficial impact, expressed in terms of the rate of conversion of income into impact:

$$\frac{\text{Impact}}{\text{Income}} = \text{Return}$$

This overall return, otherwise known as 'value for money', can usefully be broken down into the component elements of the results chain, in order to help define and assess performance in terms of economy, efficiency and effectiveness (see fig 9.1). Expenditure can be assessed in terms of all three. For the purposes of determining the finance strategy, the organisation's financial stewards must address three issues relating to expenditure:

- its size or level
- its direction
- its effectiveness.

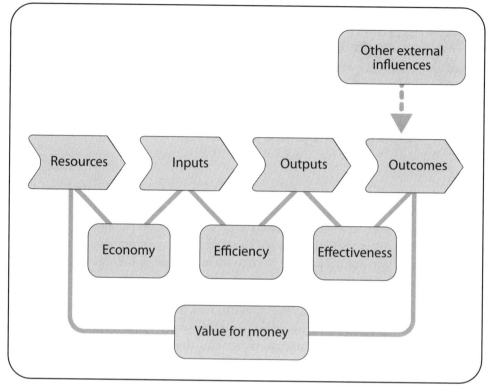

Fig. 9.1 Value for money (OECD, 2007, p. 194)

Control of expenditure is dependent on managing all three of these issues. This is not an easy task – especially in a public or not-for-profit environment, with the associated accountability challenges. As we shall see in chapter 11, the level of spending often attracts much more attention than either the direction or the effectiveness with which it is spent. Financial stewards have a critical role to play in ensuring that success is not measured simply by how much has been spent (as important as that is), but also by whether it has been spent on the right work programme and has been spent effectively on the elements of that programme.

THE LEVEL OF EXPENDITURE

The first strategic question to ask about expenditure relates to its total. Is the level of expenditure appropriate given the resources available to it? There are potentially three sources of funds to finance expenditure:

- income
- fund balances
- creditors (including borrowings).

The structure of the a typical SOFA, which places expenditure underneath income generated over the same period, can mislead its reader into believing that the expenditure has been financed solely from that income. That would be rare, and opening fund balances in particular provide a valuable supplement to new income.

Determining what resources are available to spend must be made in the context of the dual responsibility facing organisational leaders: maximising impact today, while maintaining the organisation as a going concern. Unless the purpose of the organisation has been met (in which case, the fund balances should be returned to the funder) it is the second of these responsibilities that must be addressed first. Maintaining the organisation as a going concern must have first call on the resources.

In practice, this means addressing the balance sheet issues discussed in the previous two chapters, principally ensuring that the level of reserves is sufficient, that the fund balances are in an appropriately liquid form, and that borrowings and creditors are not excessive. Income generated may be needed to increase reserves.

Alternatively, the level of fund balances may be greater than is needed, thereby enabling them to be depleted and made available for expenditure in addition to the income generated. Arguably, some of the wealthier organisations are far more prudent in terms of the funds that are made available for expenditure than is appropriate. Whatever, it is only once these issues have been addressed, and the balance sheet is appropriately healthy, that it is possible to identify the level of resources that are really available for expenditure purposes.

Once this is clear, a second question arises. Are those financial resources adequate to fulfil the operational plans of the organisation – or indeed are they more than adequate? This is a question of the closeness of the match between the available resources and the activities that would be funded by those resources. A judgement needs to be made as to whether the ambitions of the organisation seem reasonable in terms of what impact the expenditure could have (Herzlinger and Nitterhouse, 1994, pp. 133–34).

THE DIRECTION OF EXPENDITURE

In introducing the results chain, chapter 1 proposed that strategy and work programme should be designed from outcomes backwards. Implementation, it suggested, should take place from inputs forwards. This approach argues that determining which financial resources will be used to finance expenditure follows the determination of what activities the organisation will undertake, and which ones therefore need funding. The chronology of matching funding and activity is activity-led – activity (the cause, the output) defining the funding requirement (the effect, in this case the input).

Ideally, of course, leaders would wish to be needs-driven. However, in reality many organisations have found themselves having to question whether they should alter their proposed activities in order to make them more palatable to potential funders. In these cases, the cause and effect is reversed: activities follow funding.

The dangers of being funding-led are obvious, and yet it is easy to be seduced into spending resources on activities that do not best fulfil the organisation's mission as a result of the charms or demands of funders. Once more, this highlights the value of generating unrestricted funds that enable the organisation's decision makers to spend resources as they see fit, so that they can be truly needs-driven.

Whether needs-driven or funding-led, the finance strategist must picture what expenditure profile the organisation should have. This presupposes that the organisation knows how it wishes to categorise the areas of expenditure (activity) – both for presentational and management purposes.

> **Box 9.1 Activity classification of costs**
>
> An 'activity classification of costs' is the aggregation of costs incurred in pursuit of defined activity (e.g. provision of services to elderly people or counselling), and is achieved by adding together all the costs (salaries, rents, depreciation etc) relating to that specific activity.
>
> The three main 'high level' activities that charities preparing accruals accounts will report on are generating funds, charitable activity and governance costs of the charity.
>
> Charity Commission, 2005, p. 65

Usually, the expenditure classification reflects the structure of the organisation, which in turn reflects the distribution of work internally. It needs to identify the main ways in which the organisation meets its purpose. UK charities, for example, use an activity classification of costs defined in the SORP 2005 (see box 9.1). Most organisations will pursue a whole host of activities in furtherance of one or more purposes. For example, many medical charities established to support those living with a particular medical condition will offer services to individuals needing support today, while funding research towards finding a cure for tomorrow. The alternative expenditure classifications are discussed further in chapter 14.

Expenditure distribution

Supporting multiple purposes or services is not unusual, as can be seen from the Sightsavers International strategic framework (see p. 58). The charity highlights distinct strategies for delivering against four change themes (health; education; social inclusion; and community participation and development), and challenges itself to excel at developing effective partnerships, ensuring high-quality programme delivery, developing effective and joined-up advocacy, and establishing strong strategic networks and alliances.

It is worth noting that the relative importance of activities within the organisation in terms of meeting purpose and having impact may not be well reflected in terms of expenditure. Crucial activities may be inexpensive, and vice versa, and expenditure may not be the most appropriate way to measure the degree to which the organisation's resources are invested in them. For example, international charities can find that comparable activities in different parts of the world incur very different costs. One programme could have much lower expenditure than the other, although both have similar impact.

So, expenditure does not measure impact. For true comparability, non-financial measures need to be used and possibly more sophisticated financial techniques applied, such as adjusting to reflect purchasing power parity. Accepting that point, the financial steward must determine what relative proportions of the financial 'pie' different activities of the organisation should consume, and must seek assurance that there is a strategy in place to enable the pie to be cut in this manner.

It may be useful to consider what profile would be desirable on the SOFA in terms of the three high-level activities defined in box 9.1. For example, how much of the organisation's expenditure should not be on furthering the objectives of the organisation? Once the organisation has determined this top-level profile between the three main categories of expenditure, it can begin to discuss the extent to which it should support activities within each category – for example, how much should be allocated to direct services, advocacy and research. (We will talk more about allocating funds for expenditure in chapter 17.)

Comparisons with other organisations may offer some guidance as to what expenditure distribution to aim for, but it is important to use these comparisons with care, even using statutory information. For example, although the SORP 2005 has brought consistency to the format of UK charity accounting, there is still considerable discretion available to charities as to how costs are charged between the various expenditure headings. What one charity recognises as governance costs, another might treat as expenditure in furthering the charity's objectives. There is a danger of comparing apples with oranges.

Apart from differing operating efficiencies, even if identical accounting policies are used there are good reasons why different organisations' ratios may differ. For example, the costs of generating income will be heavily determined by the nature of the fundraising being undertaken, and the degree to which the organisation is investing in growing its support base. Organisations that receive a large proportion of their income as investment income, grants or legacies are likely to have a lower cost–income ratio than those that rely on direct marketing. Similarly, organisations that are in a phase of investing for income growth, rather than simply investing to maintain current levels of support, will incur relatively heavy costs and have a correspondingly high cost–income ratio in the short term.

Achieving the desired expenditure profile

Where the desired profile of expenditure differs significantly from the current profile, this raises some key strategic questions.

- Are the funds equally available for the desired profile as for the current one – in other words, do the terms of any restriction prevent the funds being applied in the way that the organisation now wishes?
- Is the organisation going to reduce actual expenditure in some areas, or is its strategy to hold expenditure constant (or at least restrict the level of increase) in order to divert more funds elsewhere?
- What is the lead time needed, operationally, to change the expenditure profile of the organisation?
- How long will it take to set up new projects or services, or to conclude existing commitments? How far into the future is it sensible to commit funds now?

The issue of dispersal of funds becomes particularly pertinent when resources are tight, when the funds available from income and from fund balances are stretched and it is difficult to cover the expenditure. In these circumstances, stewards of the organisation must guard against making expenditure decisions that solve a short-term problem (a funding gap) at the cost of long-term damage to the organisation's capacity to continue to have impact. This can be characterised as the expenditure strategy of the 'have-not' organisations (see box 9.2).

Box 9.2 Characteristics of the 'have-not' organisation	
Perspective	Short-term rather than long-term
Language	'Cuts' rather than 'growth', 'change' or 'investment'
Priority	Urgent rather than important
Sacrifices	Newest rather than lowest priority
	Investment rather than short-term impact

A preoccupation with reducing expenditure – or at least, avoiding new commitments – means that the 'have-not' organisations focus on the urgent costs rather than the important ones. They tend to sacrifice activities that lack quick impact, even though in the long term they are crucial. These are typically the investment activities of staff training, fundraising development and building membership and so on.

The 'have-not' organisation shies away from shutting down current activities that are of declining priority, to the detriment of new, higher-priority activities. The vocabulary internally (and possibly externally) is of 'cuts', rather than 'growth', 'investment' or 'change'. The organisation might have to judge between stopping one activity to release funds for another, or to continue both by drawing down on fund balances or increasing borrowings. It has to understand the implications of each option, the possible risks, and the consequences if those risks materialise.

THE EFFECTIVENESS OF EXPENDITURE

Measuring the level and destination of expenditure does not measure its effectiveness. It is the assessment of expenditure effectiveness that takes the reader up the results chain towards 'impact', addressing the question posed right at the start of this book: 'What beneficial impact has the organisation had given the resources available to it?' In answering this question, it is useful to distinguish between the efficiency, effectiveness, consistency and impact of an intervention.

> *The first of these analyses the relationship between the resources put into a given project or programme and the outputs and outcomes achieved. Thus, an efficiency assessment helps to decide whether the same results could have been achieved at less cost, or whether significantly better results could have been achieved with only a small amount of additional resources. An effectiveness assessment looks at the degree to which a project has achieved what it set out to do. Third, one can evaluate the degree to which the process or methods adopted were consistent or in harmony with the outcomes achieved: for example, a non-participatory project design and implementation would not be consistent with intended outcomes that sought to strengthen people's capacities to solve their own problems. Impact is then assessed by analysing the degree to which an intervention's outcomes led to change in the lives of those who it is intended to benefit.*
>
> Roche, 1999, p. 22

Chapter 2 has already exposed the challenge of measurement and attribution, as leaders seek to understand the extent to which their organisation is contributing positively to its intended beneficiaries. The importance of gaining this understanding is a must (see box 9.3), and the difficulty of adequately measuring impact simply adds to the pertinence of the need to try. Indeed, organisations are trying: investing considerable funds, time and political capital in developing better ways to assess the effectiveness of their contribution.

Box 9.3   Measuring impact

*If you are proposing a project, or founding an organization, you **must** say what effect you expect it to have on your individual intended beneficiaries, people with names and faces. You **must** say it with figures. You **must** then check up to see if it had that effect. You **must** calculate the return to the beneficiaries. Otherwise all your efforts are just vanity.*

Argenti, 1993, pp. 131–32

The international development sector is an excellent case in point. Three broad themes are emerging from the sector's considerable work on improving aid effectiveness through results – themes that are relevant to all organisations in the public and not-for-profit sectors.

Box 9.4   IDA results measurement system

■ *Tier 1 country outcomes* – Are IDA-eligible countries making progress on core development indicators?
■ *Tier 2 IDA contribution to country outcomes* – Does IDA programming support countries in making progress?

World Bank, 2007b, p. 2

- **Increasing focus on outcomes and impact that extends much further up the results chain than the traditional emphasis on inputs, activities and outputs:** To this end, organisations are developing new techniques, processes and systems – such as logical frameworks, results chains and impact evaluation – that enable them to assess their ultimate contribution to beneficiaries. The International Development Association (IDA) – part of the World Bank Group – is one example of an organisation that has introduced a results measurement system that measures results at two levels, explicitly acknowledging the need to track both beneficiary outcomes and, further down the results chain, organisational contribution (see box 9.4). Both are necessary. The former provides the essential context and driving force for organisations, while the latter offers scope for learning and performance evaluation.

- **Recognising the need to strengthen the capacity of developing countries to self-manage programmes to achieve the desired outcomes:** Much work is being undertaken to better enable developing countries to define their own desired outcomes, design and implement the programmes by which such outcomes can be achieved, and to develop the monitoring capacity to measure and assess progress. There is also wide appreciation of the importance of 'stronger capacity for strategic planning, accountable management, statistics, monitoring, and evaluation' (Managing for Development Results, 2006, p. 7).

- **Fostering partnership:** Wisely, if somewhat belatedly, organisations are recognising the value of collaboration: of building strategic alliances to solve problems that are well beyond the scope of influence of any single organisation, however large. For example, in the international development sector there is increasing recognition of the need for agencies to harmonise their operational procedures and align their support with the priorities and strategies of their in-country partners.

Impact evaluation

As both Roche and Argenti indicate, impact is about change. Impact is commonly defined in terms of the effects – whether positive or negative, intended or not – on people, institutions and the environment brought about by a given action, activity (such as a project) or series of actions (Roche, 1999, p. 21). So, impact evaluation is concerned with systematically identifying and analysing these effects. The World Bank describes impact evaluation in terms of 'the difference between what happened with the project or program and the situation if the intervention had not been made, i.e., the counterfactual situation' (World Bank, 2010, n.p.).

There are a wide range of evaluation tools available to organisations that wish to measure their effectiveness at different stages of the results chain. Impact evaluation is the ultimate activity, focusing right at the end of the chain on final impact. The World Bank's Independent Evaluation Group (IEG) provides a list of evaluation tools, which includes the following elements:

- **Project reviews:** that assess the effectiveness of individual projects or programmes
- **Country evaluations:** that examine the performance of the organisation in a particular partner country, usually over a multi-year timeframe (usually four to five years), in relation to the country's strategies and priorities
- **Sector and thematic reviews:** that focus on performance and experience in particular sectors, such as agriculture or transport, or thematic areas such as poverty or gender. The reviews cover five to ten years
- **Process reviews:** that examine ongoing activities, such as aid coordination or development grant-making
- **Impact evaluation:** comprising several methods or models:
  - **Rapid assessment or review:** conducted ex-post. This method includes participatory methods, interviews, focus groups, case studies, analysis of beneficiaries affected by the project and available secondary data
  - **Ex-post comparison:** of project beneficiaries with a control group
  - **Quasi-experimental design:** involving the use of matched control and project (beneficiary) groups. For example, the International Finance Corporation reports that a quasi-experimental evaluation of an alternative dispute resolution programme in Serbia showed that the use of mediation led to significant time and cost savings for firms, compared with the regular court system (International Finance Corporation, 2008, p.3).

135

- **Randomised design:** randomly assigning individuals or households either as project beneficiaries, or as a control group that does not receive the service or good being provided by the project (see box 9.5). This is also known as the experimental method.

Box 9.5   Randomised trial of training of dairy farmers in Ukraine

The International Finance Corporation is running a randomized trial of a dairy project in Vinnyitsya, Ukraine, to evaluate the impact of a three-part training regime to help farmers improve milking practices, boost yields, and improve milk quality. A random sample of 14 farmers received advisory services at the beginning of the program and another 14 randomly selected farmers began participating six months later. A comparison of treatment and control groups found the treatment group had almost 20 percent more total output and 15 percent greater output per cow.

International Finance Corporation, 2008, p. 9

Principles to improve effectiveness

Managing for Development Results (MfDR) and the International Aid Transparency Initiative (IATI) are two examples of the huge degree of collaboration now being demonstrated by the international development community. Launched in 2008, IATI:

Box 9.6   Why is transparency of aid important?

When donors provide aid, they should tell the public about it in a way that people can easily understand.

Aid transparency means that everyone can see how much aid is being provided, what it is being spent on, and what it aims to achieve. Making aid open to public scrutiny helps to ensure it is used in the most effective ways. It also helps citizens in both donor countries and developing countries hold their governments to account for using aid money wisely.

Department for International Development, n.d., n.p.

---

aims to make public information on aid spending and activities more available and more accessible, worldwide. The initiative brings together donors, partner countries, civil society organisations and other users of aid information to agree common transparency standards for aid flows

Department for International Development, n.d., n.p.

The principle behind IATI is a simple one: 'we know that transparency helps to improve aid effectiveness' (Department for International Development, n.d., n.p.).

The MfDR joint venture emerged from a series of 'Roundtables on Results', which had been held since 2002 by representatives of aid recipient countries, together with multilateral and bilateral development agencies, all aware of the need:

> to harmonize development approaches among donors, reduce transaction costs for recipient countries by aligning donor resources, increase country-level absorptive capacity and improve financial management systems through capacity building, and increase local ownership in the design and implementation of poverty frameworks at the country level.
>
> Managing for Development Results, 2008, p. 98

Note the philosophy expounded by the initiative – a need to climb the results chain:

> MfDR centres on gearing all human, financial, technological and natural resources – domestic and external – to achieve desired development results. It shifts the focus from inputs ('How much money will I get, how much money can I spend?') to measurable results ('What can I achieve with the money?') at all phases of the development process. At the same time, MfDR focuses on providing sound information to improve decision making. This entails tracking progress and managing business based on solid evidence and in a way that will maximise the achievement of results.
>
> Managing for Development Results, 2008, p. 6

MfDR articulates five principles, agreed in 2004, for sound performance management. They are directly relevant to the task of assessing expenditure effectiveness facing any financial steward.

1. At all phases – from strategic planning through implementation to completion and beyond – focus the dialogue on results for … stakeholders.
2. Align actual programming, monitoring and evaluation activities with the agreed expected results.
3. Keep the results reporting system as simple, cost-effective and user-friendly as possible.
4. Manage for – not by – results, by arranging resources to achieve outcomes. This encourages all interventions to be planned from outcomes backwards, not inputs forwards, and from the top of the results chain, not the bottom.
5. Use results information for management learning and decision making, as well as for reporting and accountability. This fifth principle takes the reader back to an earlier theme explored in chapter 2 – that of using measurement as much, if not more, for the purpose of learning as for accountability. Used exclusively for measuring performance, results information can quickly discourage innovative behaviour.

IMPLICATIONS FOR FINANCIAL STEWARDSHIP

The content of the previous section, on the effectiveness of expenditure, illustrates the new realm within which financial stewards must operate. They cannot stay comfortably at the bottom of the results chain, monitoring inputs, divorced from an understanding of and an involvement in determining how the organisation is supporting the achievement of sustainable, intended outcomes. Further, individual organisations' agendas are increasingly being determined in partnership with other donors and aid recipients. Narrow, internally orientated goals, strategies and processes that may be at odds with the priorities and management systems of the beneficiary population are being superseded. Harmonising operational procedures and aligning support with others is now required. Definitions of success for individual organisations – of what effectiveness looks like in practice – may need to change accordingly.

Key stewardship questions

1. Is the level of expenditure appropriate given the resources available to the organisation?

2. What is the optimal distribution of expenditure between income generation, governance of the organisation and beneficiary-orientated welfare?

3. Are funds being spent on the right activities in each of these areas?

4. Is the expenditure cost-effective? How do you know?

5. How does the organisation intend to achieve these aims?

10 Establishing effective risk-control practices

How can financial stewards reassure themselves that the organisation is operating in a controlled way – in other words, that the decisions being made by individuals as they carry out the organisation's work are appropriate, given the circumstances in which they are being made? How can an organisation achieve its dual goals of maximising impact and maintaining itself as a going concern in a manner that is compliant, and that manages risk appropriately? It does so by maintaining effective internal controls and adopting effective risk management practices. These practices are particularly pertinent to public and not-for-profit organisations, which have responsibility for the stewardship of funds placed in their trust by donors in order to provide benefit to others.

THE REGULATORY DRIVE FOR INTERNAL CONTROLS AND RISK MANAGEMENT

There is a bewildering array of advice to follow. Corporate governance, internal controls and risk management have all become red hot topics in recent years, preoccupying the leaders of organisations in all sectors across the globe, fuelled in part by the high-profile, dramatic business scandals and failures of companies such as Enron and WorldCom. A whole welter of new legislation and 'best practice' codes have resulted, aiming to guide and, if necessary, force boards to address issues related to governance, control and risk.

In the UK, section C2 of the *Combined Code of the Committee on Corporate Governance* (Financial Reporting Council, 2008) requires publicly listed companies to maintain sound systems of internal control and report annually on the effectiveness of those controls. Specific guidance on complying with section C2, known as the 'Turnbull Guidance' (or more formally as *Internal Control: Revised Guidance for Directors on the Combined Code*, Financial Reporting Council), was most recently revised in 2005. In the United States, section 404 of the Sarbanes-Oxley Act of 2002, entitled 'Management assessment of internal controls', imposes similar obligations on listed companies there, as does Principle 7 on recognising and managing risk within the second edition of *Corporate Governance Principles and Recommendations* (Australian Securities Exchange, 2007).

Similar guidelines have been published for the public and not-for-profit sectors, as evidenced by *Standards for Internal Control in the Federal Government* (United States General Accounting Office, 1999), the code of good practice *Corporate Governance in Central Government Departments* (HM Treasury, 2005), and *Good Governance: A Code for the Voluntary and Community Sector* (National Hub of Expertise in Governance, 2005), both published in the UK.

> **Box 10.1   Statement on risk in the trustees' annual report**
>
> *A statement should be provided confirming that the major risks to which the charity is exposed, as identified by the trustees, have been reviewed and systems or procedures have been established to manage those risks.*
>
> *Charity Commission, 2005, p. 8*

Statements that obligate leaders to acknowledge their responsibility for maintaining effective internal controls, and to confirm that appropriate systems are in place to manage the risks facing the organisation, are now a standard feature of the public accountability exercised by boards in published annual reports. The UK charity sector is just one example (see box 10.1).

This legislative push has spawned a plethora of 'how-to-do-it' frameworks, cycles, models and scorecards – the best known of which, perhaps, are the US *Integrated Frameworks on Internal Control* and *Enterprise Risk Management* (Committee of Sponsoring Organizations of the Treadway Commissions (COSO), 1994, 2004). Meanwhile the UK Treasury's set of principles and concepts on risk management, drawn up in 2001, have become sufficiently implanted in central government practice to be referred to as simply *The Orange Book* (HM Treasury, 2004).

Limitations of the internal controls and risk management agenda

Despite the growing availability of guidance, there is increasing evidence that the added burdens of compliance with corporate or regulatory standards on internal control and risk management have not resulted in the intended added value. Control disciplines that, when first introduced, stimulated heightened awareness of the risks facing an organisation or the fragility of internal control processes, have lost that critical edge over time. Signs that they are not really working are not too difficult to identify in most organisations.

Typical symptoms include:

- Internal controls and risk management are regarded as distinct activities undertaken by a compliance-orientated unit within the organisation rather than by, say, operations teams.
- Overloaded senior executives, required to self-certify that 'all is well' within their span of control, find themselves signing statements of assurance with minimal review, as they juggle to prioritise 101 competing demands on their

attention. Leitch (2008, p. 110) identifies the following three problems with such statements: first, it's a loaded question (there is pressure to give the expected answer); second, the certification offers little learning; and finally, the experience can generate resentment, as the process looks like a 'systematic exercise in delegating blame in advance'.

- Stretched internal audit teams, driven by volume-based targets (such as the number of audits completed and tight completion dates) drive through predetermined audit programmes, reluctant to accommodate learning generated during the process.
- The trustee body's annual review of the risks facing the organisation, using a traditional risk register, becomes a stale, judgemental compliance activity that fails to influence the strategic thinking of the organisation.

THE AIM OF RISK-CONTROL DISCIPLINES

A brief review of the definitions of internal control and risk management provided by regulators and the consulting firms will confirm the difficulty of distinguishing between the two topics. The definitions illustrate the challenge (see box 10.2). Leitch (2008) suggests that there is no need to try to understand the difference – better, instead, to think in terms of 'risk control'.

Box 10.2   The challenge of distinguishing internal control and risk management

- **Internal control** – *designed to provide reasonable assurance regarding the achievement of objectives in the following categories: effectiveness and efficiency of operations; reliability of financial reporting; and compliance with applicable laws and regulations.*

COSO 1994, p. 3

- **Risk management** – *designed to identify potential events that may affect the entity, and manage risk to be within its risk appetite, to provide reasonable assurance regarding the achievement of entity objectives.*

COSO, 2004, p. 2

It is significant that both COSO definitions frame internal control and risk management processes in terms of assuring the achievement of objectives. While the importance of reliable financial reporting and compliance with regulations are unquestionable, the biggest added value of risk-control disciplines arguably comes from gaining assurance that the organisation has climbed the results chain from income to impact as efficiently and effectively as possible, and has maintained itself as a viable entity while doing so.

To that end, risk control refers to processes designed to assure that people and systems in an organisation act as intended, that they do the 'right thing' in the circumstances, and that the information is correct. These disciplines range from routine daily checks on data and business processes to strategic risk assessments that help the organisation's leaders determine corporate direction. Sayer Vincent (2006) refers to 'a portfolio' of controls (see fig. 10.1). It is immediately apparent that the types of processes that support effective risk control extend well beyond the traditional financially orientated controls such as reconciliations, authorisation procedures and segregation of duties.

Control type	Objective
Aims and objectives	Clear understanding of the intended strategic direction
Planning	Alignment of work planning with strategy, maintenance of 'ready to go' contingency plans
Accountability	Unambiguous decision-making authorities
Competencies	'Fit for purpose' skills and capabilities in the right place at the right time
Monitoring	Continuous reviews to inform learning
Employee welfare	Highly motivated people
Independent review	Objective verification of performance over time

Fig 10.1 Illustrative portfolio of risk controls (adapted from Sayer Vincent, 2006)

Since performance can only be assessed with hindsight, the litmus test of any system of internal control, or approach to risk management, is how people and systems handled the actual circumstances they faced and whether, in those circumstances, their achievements were maximised. However, organisations have to look ahead and plan how to move forward, despite uncertainty. Therefore, an organisation's risk-control processes can only be said to be fully effective if the following questions can be answered affirmatively at any time.

● **Historic:** Has the organisation maximised its impact over time given the circumstances it has faced, and has it remained viable? In other words – with hindsight, how good was the actual performance of the organisation in the circumstances that prevailed?

● **Counterfactual:** How well would the organisation have performed had the circumstances differed from those that actually occurred? Did it strike lucky, or was it ready to manage uncertainty, able to adapt to the circumstances?

● **Prospective:** How capable is the organisation of maximising future impact and sustaining itself, whatever future circumstances might prevail?

So, successful risk-control disciplines seek to assure that an organisation is geared up for success, whatever the circumstances. This assurance does not come principally from seeing that a single predetermined plan is implemented, come what may, but rather from establishing that the organisation is capable of making best use of the resources available to it given the circumstances in which it has to operate – whether anticipated or not. Organisations are far less in control of their circumstances than their planning typically suggests or anticipates. Leitch calls it 'uncertainty suppression' (2008, p. 36), while Taleb is less complimentary (see box 10.3). They are much less able to forecast ahead with accuracy than their systems recognise.

Box 10.3   Fooled by randomness

We underestimate the share of randomness in about everything ... probability theory is a young arrival in mathematics; probability applied to practice is almost non existent as a discipline. In addition we seem to have evidence that what is called 'courage' comes from an underestimation of the share of randomness in things rather than the more noble ability to stick one's neck out for a given belief ... Economic 'risk-takers' are rather the victims of delusions (leading to overoptimism and overconfidence with their underestimation of possible adverse outcomes) than the opposite. Their 'risk-taking' is frequently randomness [or] foolishness.

Taleb, 2004, p. xli

Insightfully, Leitch (2008) identifies a common factor in all risk-control work – that of uncertainty – for example, uncertainty about the possibility of human error, uncertainty that data might be wrong or incomplete, and uncertainty about the impact, both positive and negative, of technological or political changes on the organisation. In a certain, reliable world, risk control would be unnecessary. People and systems would perform consistently, and as intended. The future would be certain. Effective risk-control disciplines assure an organisation that it is managing uncertainty as best as it can.

In the wake of the global credit crisis, there is renewed recognition of the volatility of operating environments, and interest has soared in the phenomena demonstrated by the shape of a power curve (see fig. 10.2). Historically, economic events (such as banking crises) and natural events (such as earthquakes) have followed a similar pattern, characterised by a combination of small, frequent outcomes and rare, hard-to-predict, extreme outcomes that have huge impact. Belatedly, organisations are recognising that the range of possible outcomes that can occur at some future point is much broader than previously thought. Zanini (2009, n.p.) draws several generic conclusions:

- *Make the system the unit of analysis. You can't assess the behavior and performance of a specific agent ... without gauging the behavior and performance of the system in which it is embedded ...*
- *Don't assume stability and do take a long look back ...*
- *Focus on early warning ...*
- *Build flexible business models.*

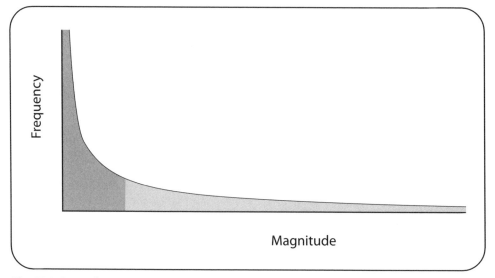

Fig. 10.2 Power law patterns (picture by Hay Kranen, public domain, n.d., n.p.)

FINANCIAL STEWARDSHIP RISKS

Asking the question 'What does effective risk control look like?' brings the reader to the five organisational principles to which this book is devoted. These are the five principles that are necessary to manage the organisation effectively, to handle the risks its faces and, ultimately, to maximise impact over time. They provide a ready-made classification of risk that any organisation must manage.

Using the financial stewardship map presented in chapter 1 (see fig. 1.2, p. 8) it is easy to illustrate the events that could derail the organisation's ability to climb the results chain effectively (see fig. 10.3). If the organisation does not have a clear strategic direction, if its financial framework is weak, if its resources are not aligned with its priorities, if its ability to deliver results through day-to-day financial management is poor, or if the internal environment inhibits or disables people or systems from acting appropriately, then poor financial stewardship will result – that is, the resources available to the organisation will be used sub optimally. The risk controls that the organisation must have in place need to assure the stewards that all five principles are firmly rooted in the way that the organisation operates.

Risk	Characteristics
Unclear strategic direction	■ Inappropriate targets ■ Insufficient prioritisation or sequencing
Weak financial framework	■ Insufficient income generated to cover costs ■ Inappropriate levels of reserves ■ Assets insufficiently productive ■ No evidence of expenditure effectiveness
Misaligned resources	■ Spending target trap ■ Diminishing horizon trap
Poor day-to-day financial management	■ Poor knowledge of the current state of play ■ Out-of-date or no forecasts ■ Inappropriate financial targets and/or parameters ■ Poor allocation decisions ■ Lack of dialogue on performance and action planning
Disabling environment	■ Ambiguous stewardship responsibilities ■ Insufficient in-house stewardship expertise ■ Inadequate communication and learning

Fig. 10.3 Example financial stewardship risks

THE TYPICAL RISK MANAGEMENT PROCESS

The traditional process for managing risks follows a simple, logical cycle, which begins with identifying the risk facing the organisation (see fig. 10.4). The task is to identify where there are control gaps (in other words, where the level of risk remains higher than is regarded as acceptable), and to take action to close them.

This cycle looks similar in most organisations. There are a variety of methods of identifying the risks facing the organisation, including workshops, consultations, benchmarking, scenario or 'what if' analyses, audits and inspections, research methods, and cause-and-effect diagrams (Chartered Institute of Management Accountants, 2007, p. 6). Risks are classified into major groupings, such as strategic risks, operational risks, reporting risks and compliance risks (Epstein and Rejc, 2005). The risks are assessed in terms of impact on the organisation and likelihood of occurrence, using a simple high–medium–low or traffic light scoring approach, and presented graphically in two-by-two diagrams. Those high risks, which are judged as likely to occur, and to have a significant impact if they did, appear in red and are shown in the top right quadrant of the diagram. They become the priority risks to be addressed.

Risk strategies are discussed and agreed to reflect the response of the organisation to the assessed risk. Risk responses include the following (Chartered Institute of Management Accountants, 2007, pp. 7–8):

- **Avoidance:** *action is taken to halt the activities giving rise to risk*
- **Reduction:** *action is taken to mitigate the risk of likelihood or impact or both, generally via internal controls*
- **Sharing or transfer:** *action is taken to transfer a portion of the risk through insurance, outsourcing or hedging; and*
- **Acceptance:** *no action is taken to affect likelihood or impact.*

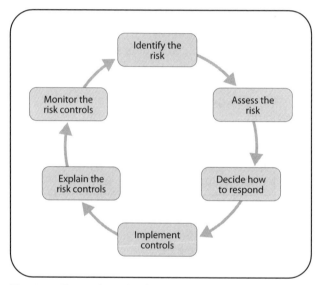

Fig. 10.4 The traditional risk management cycle

An organisation will typically maintain a register that lists the risks, the likelihood or impact assessment of each risk, and the strategies being implemented in response. This register is used periodically by boards and senior management teams to monitor the adequacy with which risk is being managed. The organisation then judges the residual risk – the level of risk that remains, taking into account any controls or risk responses applied – and uses it to help identify what action needs to be taken.

How useful is such a process? It can be hugely beneficial when there is a genuine effort within the organisation to grapple with the challenges facing it, and when there is a need to clarify what action to take and why, in a structured way. At its best, a process of this kind can determine the focus of strategy and work programmes and provide a mechanism for monitoring progress, while also maintaining active antennae to stimulate reaction to what is happening in and around the organisation.

Figure 10.5 illustrates the application of the risk management cycle to one key element of the financial framework – holding appropriate levels of reserves – and to step 1 of the day-to-day financial management that is needed: understanding the current position. What is the risk associated with these two issues? In both cases, the control risk is identified. The reviewer can confirm the controls that have been designed and implemented to manage the risk, and assess whether the design would be effective if complied with. The reviewer can test for compliance and reach a conclusion as to whether the risk has been successfully managed. If the conclusion is negative, this implies a weakness either in design or compliance, or both. Solutions can then be determined. A similar process for review could be undertaken for each of the five components of the stewardship model.

Identification	Response	Implementation	Monitoring
What's the uncertainty?	What response will give adequate control?	Are the controls in place?	Are the controls effective?
Inappropriate level of reserves	A reserves policy in place setting appropriate level of reserves (chapter 7)	Is there a reserves policy in place setting an appropriate level of reserves? Are financial decisions made that are consistent with the policy?	Are the reserves that are held appropriate in size, given the exposure of the organisation to uncertain future income and market losses and/or its need to finance expansion or replace existing assets?
Poor knowledge of current financial state of play, resulting in poor allocation decisions	Financial information that meets the eight characteristics of successful management accounting (chapter 14)	Is financial information generated that meets the eight characteristics of successful management accounting?	Are allocation decisions appropriate, given the financial state of play at the time the decision was made?

Fig. 10.5 Risk management by stewardship component

However, following the traditional risk management cycle does have potential limitations and flaws, and its use is no guarantee that uncertainty is being well managed by the organisation, for the following reasons (influenced by Leitch, 2008).

- The listing and classification of risks creates a false sense that each risk is distinct, can be rated individually, and can be managed independently from the other risks, often with just one defined solution.
- The approach is typically very unscientific. Participants often have a poor understanding of the real risks facing the organisation. They reach compromise agreements on risk assessments (such as high, medium or low) without evidence, with different attitudes to risk and with differing interpretations of what the various labels mean. If highly judgemental and potentially biased assessments divert attention away from major opportunities or threats, then the consequences can be significant. The reverse is also possible, with attention inappropriately directed towards inconsequential uncertainties.
- As with any framework, the design and execution of such a risk management process can inhibit fresh and innovative thinking about how the organisation should be run, what uncertainties it faces, and what action it should take. Not all risks may have been considered and in practice, the risk management strategies agreed for those that have been considered may not be the best ones. Things may have moved on since the process was last run.
- The process is often detached from the running of the organisation. It may be carried out by a few senior individuals relatively infrequently, and be at least partly driven by reporting obligations. In the worst cases the cycle is never completed. The risk assessment and identification of responses is registered, a statement on risk is included in the annual report, but the exercise has no meaningful influence on the strategies and work programmes executed day-to-day. No action plan arises from the assessment. The agreed risk responses never happen in practice.

ENABLING EFFECTIVE RISK CONTROL

To improve the effectiveness of the risk-control disciplines used in organisations, four qualities must flourish. They are linked. The organisation must cultivate:

- a finely tuned capacity to adapt
- risk-control practices that are embedded in daily operations
- an increasing willingness and capability to quantify uncertainty
- a culture that encourages people in the organisation to think openly and outside the box about how to manage uncertainty.

Capacity to adapt

Given uncertainty, the most important control that must be entrenched in any organisation is the capacity to adapt: to be able to react appropriately whatever the circumstances. This requires 'sense and respond' agility (Haeckel, 1999) both in its people and its systems. It requires what Leitch calls 'intelligent' controls (see fig. 10.6). Haeckel uses a helpful metaphor to illustrate the sense and respond capability that is needed to manage uncertainty, comparing a 'make and sell' bus company to a 'sense and

> **Box 10.4   Buses versus taxis**
>
> *Bus companies function as* **mechanisms** *for efficiently generating unchanging (or gradually changing) products and service. Taxi companies function as* **adaptive systems** *for responding to unanticipated requests.*
>
> *Haeckel, 1999, p. 62*

respond' taxi fleet (see box 10.4). The task for leaders of sense and respond organisations, says Haeckel, is to hone two skills. The first is to 'modularize their business *functions* to create capabilities that, in combination, can respond to a much broader (exponentially greater) spectrum of possible customer requests' (Haeckel, 1999, p. 67). This challenges leaders to reflect on their organisational design. The second is to enhance 'how people accountable for those capabilities process information' (p. 75). Effective risk control includes being able to collect and process data about what is going on both internally and externally and to convert that into information and knowledge that supports good decision making.

	Other controls	*Intelligent controls*
View of outcomes	■ *Things are either right (what we wanted/ planned) or wrong* ■ *Our objectives are fixed*	■ *There may be different levels of performance and outcomes may be evaluated in more ways than just right versus wrong* ■ *Our objectives may change*
Main mechanisms	■ *Preventing things from happening at all* ■ *Checking before something is done and giving a go-ahead if appropriate* ■ *Checking something after it is done and correcting if it is wrong*	■ *Cause–effect interventions* ■ *Doing things to learn, learning, and adapting in future actions* ■ *Assessing uncertainty* ■ *Exploiting statistical laws* ■ *Adapting internal control plans dynamically (especially in projects)*

Fig. 10.6 The characteristics of intelligent controls (Leitch, 2008, p. 25)

Embedding risk control

Embedding risk-control thinking and disciplines in daily work practices means that everyone in the organisation actively and consciously thinks about and addresses uncertainty as they carry out their work. It becomes an essential component of the job itself. So, risk control and managing uncertainty is tackled in two distinct ways. One is through an explicit programme of work, with clear terms of reference (including deliverables such as reports) undertaken by a designated person or team who manages the work programme like a project. Internal audit is an example of this approach; so is the formal risk management process described above. The other way is less obvious but potentially more effective: by tackling it as part of the daily activities undertaken by people throughout the organisation.

The famed Toyota Production System (TPS) is essentially a case study in this practice. Consider the following example, described by Johnson and Bröms (2000), which compares the concept of standardised work used in the TPS with the embedded controls exhibited by living systems:

> An immune system constantly detects and transforms or rejects abnormalities that enter the organism's continuously flowing metabolic system. The organism does not have to wait for a delayed 'report' from an 'information system' to learn about and act upon such abnormalities.
>
> Johnson and Bröms, 2000, p. 97

> By imposing agreed-on work patterns, standards ensure that a team member can see quickly and easily when something abnormal occurs. Abnormalities encompass not just product quality defects, but also deficient tooling, unsafe practices, and departure from productivity norms. Standardization provides benchmarks for 'normal' that enable one to see whether or not the same work is done differently each time it occurs. Because benchmarks make abnormal outcomes visible the moment they occur, team members are able to stop work and correct errors on the spot. Errors do not go undetected; they are not left to be remedied later by 'trouble-shooters' or, worst of all, identified by customers. Standardization creates a discipline that improves quality and holds costs in check not because work is done repetitively, but because work passes from hand to hand free of errors.
>
> Johnson and Bröms, 2000, pp. 89–90

There are countless ways to achieve this integration and these can be introduced in each process, function or activity that the organisation undertakes, whether as a part of a strategic planning exercise undertaken infrequently or daily operations. Some examples are given later in this chapter. As Leitch summarises: 'Controls occur everywhere. They are at every level of every organization, in some form. Sometimes they look the same in different places but usually they do not' (2008, p. 25).

Quantifying uncertainty

Leitch (2008, p. 244) argues that better quantification of uncertainty is a necessary evolution. It is an acknowledgement of the power of evidence-based management:

> *Internal controls thinking ... has paid almost no attention to quantifying risks or the benefits of controls in a credible, mathematically competent, and data-supported way. Most assessments don't get past high–medium–low. This is in huge contrast to the quality movement, with its vast array of statistical process control techniques and its emphasis on measurement and on results. However, as organizations spend more and more on internal controls they reach a point where intuition is not enough and reassurances that the work is worthwhile need to be backed up with facts.*

Encouraging thinking outside the box

Rather than encouraging open questioning of what is the right thing to do in light of the prevailing circumstances, many organisational practices are actually debilitating. Certainty is highly valued, and uncertainty discounted. Chapter 2 discussed the challenge of establishing appropriate performance contracts that give people incentives to 'do the right thing'. In that vein, the organisation's leaders and stewards have to encourage honesty so that risks, uncertainties and control deficiencies are highlighted and can be discussed and tackled openly, without fear of repercussion.

Similarly, undue pressure to hit targets and execute the plan can effectively blinker the organisation to what is actually going on and what is ahead (whether planned or not, and anticipated or not). The organisation's board and senior executives have a vital role to play in articulating their beliefs about uncertainty and their expectations about how it should be managed internally. Communications and training are essential. Leitch (2008, p. 22) goes as far as to define the objectives of risk control as being simply the following:

1. *To help people take off their mental blinkers and see the true range of possibilities they face.*
2. *To help people behave competently in a way that is consistent with that wider view.*

EXAMPLES OF EFFECTIVE RISK CONTROLS IN PRACTICE

Below are samples of six risk controls that can be easily implemented within any organisation keen to improve its management of uncertainty. They are taken and adapted from Leitch's collection of 60 ideas for cost-effective controls (Leitch, 2008), and are illustrative of the type of easy-to-implement, innovative risk controls that can add significantly to the organisation's understanding of how able it is to climb the results chain.

- **Evolving uncertainty lists:** List 'areas of uncertainty', consider their significance and decide what to do about them. Do this frequently, implementing controls as you go. This has two advantages: it keeps uncertainty in the forefront of action planning, and gets people testing controls early – in other words, learning by doing.
- **Matrix mapping:** Map controls and risks in a matrix rather than in a conventional risk register listing, so that you can see which controls are addressing which areas of uncertainty. This will clarify what controls are in place, and why.
- **Storytelling about the future:** Imagine a future situation after an event – either positive or negative – has occurred, however unlikely. Discuss how that event might have come about. This will help to identify the possibilities of what might be ahead, and will provoke thinking about what the organisation might do about it. Scenario planning is one form of this approach.
- **Healthy conversations about control performance:** Encouraging openness about uncertainty and thinking outside the box about how to handle it is best done through regular conversations about the controls which are actually being used in daily processes. These can be thought of as informal discussions about how things work, whether or not they work, and why. Establishing patterns of questioning helps to ensure that the conversations are focused and informative.
- **Agile documentation reviews:** Undertake early and rigorous reviews of sample controls documentation in order to improve documentation quality and promote learning. Leitch argues that reducing the review speed significantly increases the identification of defects which, with timely coaching, can be eliminated in the future.
- **Reporting with uncertainty:** Most reports used for decision-making purposes imply greater accuracy and certainty in the arguments, evidence and numbers presented than is actually the case. This diminishes the learning that is possible. Disclosing the extent of uncertainty by, for example, stating the information sources, survey sizes and confidence limits can help trigger a much better understanding of what is being presented, and how it should be used.

It is probably now apparent that the five principles detailed in this book, by definition, provide an encyclopaedia of controls and risk management techniques to enable organisations to manage uncertainty effectively. Dip into any chapter and you will find risk controls being expounded: establishing appropriate performance contracts or reserves policies, diversifying income sources, describing results in terms of trends and ranges, maintaining up-to-date forecasting techniques, cultivating dialogue, aligning resources to priorities, defining unambiguous responsibilities, building expertise in-house, and harnessing technology to spread knowledge.

Any activity that an organisation undertakes will benefit from a review of the risk controls that are in place, and an assessment of how they can be improved. Take just one example – that of procurement. Sayer Vincent (2009) provokes some important questions about how procurement controls may need to vary, depending on the degree of uncertainty present at the time that the procurement process is embarked on, if the intended outcome is to be achieved.

The conventional approach to procurement adopts a logical chronology, which starts with the development of a business case. This is used to define functional and technical requirements (a requirements definition) with which an invitation to tender process is carried out, to select a suitable supplier of goods and services. A contract is signed, committing both the customer and the supplier, and then detailed planning takes place to identify the changes to business processes and the configuration of new systems that are to be made. Finally, the plan is implemented.

What seems on the face of it to be a sensible process to follow in order to achieve intended benefits, through the provision of goods and services by an external supplier, is in fact laced with weaknesses from start to finish – largely resulting from a failure to adequately cater for uncertainty.

- The process assumes that the customer organisation and the potential suppliers all understand the process in the same way, and are ready to commit the resources necessary to complete it.
- It assumes that the customer organisation knows what it wants at the start of the process.
- It places huge pressure on the supplier selection process, during which prospective suppliers have strong incentives to over-promise, and comparative assessments of alternative bids can be difficult to make.
- It distances the successful supplier from the customer until a relatively late stage in the process.
- It crystallises the customer's requirements in a contract before implementation starts, thereby limiting the opportunities for change in the light of experience.
- It encourages both customer and supplier to focus on delivering the contractually agreed goods and/or services, rather than on the potential benefits to the organisation.

The comfort and apparent control of the conventional procurement model, where everything is neatly predetermined, does not reflect the reality of many procurement processes, which are full of risks and uncertainty. In many situations, advocates Sayer Vincent, a more adaptive procurement process would be beneficial – one that focuses on benefits, embeds learning in the process, and enables the customer and supplier to work collaboratively from an early stage so that both parties contribute to defining the business case, the technical requirements and the solutions as they go.

Trust (between customer and supplier) becomes an essential ingredient, but one that, if present, enables a clear understanding and agreement to be established between the parties early on, and permits the contract to be determined later in the process.

This example demonstrates again how effective risk control very often comes from adopting day-to-day practices that explicitly address uncertainty within them. Organisations have to have the willingness and capability to digest what is happening as a result both of their past actions and those of others, and to adjust future actions accordingly. That is what effective control in times of uncertainty means – not the rigid adherence to an unalterable plan.

INTERNAL AUDIT AND OTHER FORMAL ASSURANCE TECHNIQUES

The promotion of, and enthusiasm for, embedding risk control in organisations' day-to-day practices, as seen in this chapter, does not invalidate the important role to be played by more formal processes. The two complement each other, and independent assurance of the adequacy of risk controls within the organisation can be given only from outside the management structure. Most typically, this perspective is provided by the internal audit function.

Determining when it is appropriate to introduce an internal audit function is a decision governed largely by the question of the organisation's complexity. This could be a function of size or of some other operational complexity, such as geographic spread or funding diversity. However, in smaller organisations it is not the easiest function to resource, requiring specialist skills but perhaps only justifying part-time capacity. It may be worth considering contracting out internal audit – which may sound odd, but is possible and a pragmatic solution – or even sharing with one or more organisations.

The respective roles of internal audit and management

The apparently simple dichotomy between the roles of internal audit and management (see box 10.5) can mask how imprecise in practice the distinction can be at the point of interface between the two functions. Internal audit is not an easy role to play. The internal auditor is part of the organisation, and yet has to remain one step removed to be able to look at the organisation with an objective eye and to influence change without formal authority over colleagues whose systems have been reviewed. It is difficult to feel welcomed, as the role may generate anxiety, scepticism and even hostility. The internal auditor requires a good understanding of the organisation, must be empathetic to its aims and to how it functions, and should understand its politics and culture if it is to be able truly to assess the adequacy of the controls that are in place.

> ### Box 10.5 The respective roles of internal audit and management
>
> - It is the responsibility of management to establish and maintain the systems of internal control used in the organisation.
> - It is the role of internal audit to assess whether the controls and systems designed by management are adequate, being complied with as intended, and operating effectively, and to advise management to those ends.

Ultimately it is for the organisation's management to determine which areas of activity are covered by the internal audit function. Internal audit is a tool that managers can use to reassure themselves that the risk controls are effective; but who is 'management' in this context – the executive, or the board and trustees? Internal audit instils discipline into the evaluation element of any performance management system, but it definitely ups the stakes, given that internal audit reports are likely to end up being read by the organisation's leadership. No manager wants to find themselves defending a critical internal audit report in front of the chief executive or board.

This highlights the crucial difference between management review and internal audit: independence. An internal auditor is independent of those responsible for establishing and maintaining the systems, and has scope to review systems irrespective of the wishes of managers – but often that is the only difference. There are no reviews within the remit of the internal auditor that management would not want to be doing for itself. It is simply engaging a specialist to play this role.

Tension can arise if the internal audit programme feels imposed on management as a policing function, designed to highlight internal inadequacies rather than as a resource for them to steward. In such a circumstance, it is very easy for management to get into the habit of running ahead of internal audit, to ensure that risk-control weaknesses are closed or unnoticed. Yet if it is working well, there will be genuine collaboration between management and internal audit, with the shared goal of designing and maintaining a cost-effective risk-control system.

To this end, there is no substitute for frequent dialogue between the two. There will be a high degree of trust evident without compromising the objectivity of the internal audit function. In organisations that handle risk control well, managers welcome the internal audit function. They commission reviews without waiting to be told that their function is on the audit rota, and they engage fully in helping to focus the reviews on those areas of the organisation where the risk-control need is greatest.

In order to be effective, any internal review (whether labelled 'internal audit' or not) must meet the following criteria.

- It must be undertaken properly – formally, with terms of reference, a written report and a follow-up plan that both ensures that action is taken on the control issues raised and that subsequently advises that the issue is now closed. It needs the time that management, with their executive responsibilities for the organisation day-to-day, can rarely give.
- It must have the authority to effect change.
- It must be undertaken with sufficient objectivity to enable the systems' design and maintenance to be seriously reviewed afresh. It can be difficult for managers to stand sufficiently far back from their own systems to do this – but if they can, all well and good.

There is a danger of being over-anxious about separating the function of internal audit from day-to-day management, and it is worth being pragmatic. If management can meet the above criteria when completing a review, then it should be of little concern that it has not been carried out by an internal auditor. It is the quality of the review that is paramount.

It is also important to remember that the objective of internal audit is assurance of effective risk control within the organisation. The success of the internal audit function should not be measured in terms of the size of the control gaps identified. Bigger gaps do not mean better audit. Arguably, a 'clean' audit, giving management complete assurance of the effectiveness of risk control, should be the shared ambition both of management and of the internal auditor.

Internal audit etiquette

For any internal audit programme to be successful, expectations need to be managed. It must be clear who is responsible for doing what, and what the internal audit process is. Defining the etiquette that is expected may be helpful, outlining the key steps that should be taken at each stage of the internal audit process (pre-, during and post-audit), defining the authority of the internal auditor, and the format and timetable of audit reports (see box 10.6 for one example).

Box 10.6   Internal audit etiquette

Preparation pre-audit must include:

- consultative determination of the scope and timetable of the proposed audit within an overall audit plan
- written terms of reference, published at least x days before the commencement of the audit work on site.

Conducting the audit must include:

- face-to-face discussions at the start and end of the audit, with relevant management outlining the process and findings respectively
- unrestricted access throughout the audit to whatever systems, procedures and information are requested.

The audit report must:

- be written fairly, identifying where controls are effective in managing risk and uncertainty, or where action has already been taken or planned to address the risks identified, as well as highlighting control gaps
- be evidence-based
- distinguish between control issues that can be addressed locally, and those that relate to corporate policy or procedures
- include timetabled action agreed with management in response to the issues raised
- be written and signed off within x working days of the audit's completion.

Audit follow-up must:

- be timetabled and conducted within a timeframe consistent with the timetabling of action agreed in the audit report
- include a first draft progress report written by the management responsible for the risk controls that were audited, and a final report jointly signed by the auditor and management within an agreed timeframe
- articulate how to handle audit issues that are not closed. Audit follow-up cannot continue indefinitely.

Adapted from Sightsavers International, 2005

This etiquette should highlight the critical factors that must be approached effectively if internal audit is really to add value.

- **Expectations:** Individuals need to appreciate what process is to be followed, what scope the audit has, what their responsibilities are, and what authority the auditor has.
- **Ownership:** Management must feel and take ownership for getting effective risk controls in place by, for example, being responsible for closing control gaps identified.
- **Communication:** Control issues must be identified with evidence, set in an appropriate context, communicated fairly and, where possible, face-to-face.

Key stewardship questions

1. What does, or would, effective risk control in the organisation look like?

2. Is the organisation geared up for success, whatever the circumstances?

3. How well does the organisation understand, track and manage uncertainty?

4. What processes is the organisation using to assure itself that its risk control is cost-effective?

5. Does the organisation cultivate the qualities needed to enable effective risk control?

6. How embedded are the risk controls?

7. How intelligent are they?

8. How effective is the organisation's internal audit function?

Part 3:
Aligned resources

11 The allocation traps

ALIGNING RESOURCES

Having set a clear strategic direction with an agreed work programme and built a robust financial framework, funds must be made available to enable the work programme to be implemented. How should the organisation decide how much to make available? How are the funds 'handed out'? The objective of any resource allocation methodology is to enable units to plan, and then implement, the multi-year strategies and work programmes by which they will have their intended impact – and to be able to do with confidence that funds will be available. This introduces the topic of resource allocation (box 11.1). As will become evident, the choice of methodology by which spending units are given access to resources significantly affects how they behave.

Box 11.1 Resource allocation
The methodology and process by which money is made available to deliver organisational impact.

The task of the financial steward is to align the financial resources with the agreed work programme. It is through the work programme that strategic priorities are implemented, thereby enabling the organisation to achieve its impact goals. Alignment of resources occurs when there is consistency between how the resources available to the organisation are managed and its desired outputs and outcomes. It is a crucial component of strategic alignment (see box 11.2).

Box 11.2 Strategic alignment
Strategic alignment within an organisation is evident when its capabilities, decision making, configuration of resources, management information, incentives, behaviours of staff, organisational values and culture are all compatible and supportive of the achievement of the organisation's strategic objectives and its mission. Achieving strategic alignment requires units within the organisation to plan and manage within the envelope of strategic thinking and of decisions already being developed for the organisation as a whole by higher levels of management. Operational priorities, the allocation of resources, and investments in capacity development should all reflect and support the overall strategic direction. *Scott, 2001, p. 323*

THE ANNUAL BUDGET

Traditionally, the annual budget has played the major role in trying to align the organisation's resources with its work programme, strategy and objectives. The one-year allocated envelope reflects the traditional budget model where each year budgets are distributed up front, before the start of the financial year, by a central treasury department or budget unit (the budget distributor) to units (the budget recipients) in the form of 'envelopes' of money from which the units finance activity during the year. At the start of the following year, each unit receives a new envelope.

It is easy to see why the one-year budget has acquired such wide acceptance:

- In its consolidated form, it provides an overall financial picture of future expected results, as at the point in time at which it is prepared. To that extent it provides a forecast.
- It can be used as a target of, for example, income to be raised – and thereby becomes a measure of performance. It defines what would represent a satisfactory outcome at the time the budget was prepared, and based on the assumptions used. It becomes the benchmark against which actual results are compared. Typically, if the budget is achieved then this would be regarded as a good performance, while if it were exceeded (expenditure) or not reached (income), this is regarded as requiring explanation – the implication being poor performance.
- It can be used to guide resource allocation by outlining how the resources are to be allocated between the operating units and activities.
- It imposes a constraint on expenditure, so it acts as a ceiling on spending.
- It can also provide a marketing tool with which to appeal to donors – especially statutory, corporate and institutional donors – to provide funding to support particular activities. It says to them, 'This is what your funds would be used for.' It then becomes the key comparator, or control, against which actual results are reported.

The budget can therefore meet a number of the crucial demands of financial stewardship. Nevertheless, the experience of most organisations using annual budgets as an integral part of the way that finances are stewarded is dissatisfying. Consider the following observations:

- **Unpredictable factors:** Most organisations engage in very detailed financial planning, even though a wide range of factors that will be critical in influencing their future are entirely unpredictable. Whether planned or not, the organisation has to react to the circumstances in which it finds itself operating. Most find themselves needing to respond quickly to unforeseen circumstances: income streams are uncertain; unplanned opportunities arise; social, political or economic situations change unexpectedly; stock markets move unpredictably; and key suppliers' viability disappears – you name it. To the point where it is safe to say that the organisation at any time in the year is not where it expected to be, or if it is, it is the result of luck *and* judgement. As Bryson (2004, p. 16) states, 'Strategic planning is likely to result in a statement of organizational *intentions*, but what is *realized* will be some combination of what is *intended* and what *emerges* along the way.'

- **Out-of-date plans:** Most performance management systems continue to compare performance to a fixed plan, even though the plan is acknowledged to be out of date and no longer defines the best way forward. Then, success and failure are defined in terms of the plan rather than in relation to the actual circumstances in which the performance was achieved. A budget can be out of date before the year to which it relates even starts. How often do managers find themselves explaining large variances in the very first month of the year? It is not surprising. Much time has usually elapsed since the budget was prepared, and its construction will have been reliant on a variety of assumptions, any one of which may prove to be fallacious.

- **Spending surges:** Many organisations experience a surge in expenditure in the first couple of months, or the last few weeks, of the financial year. More often than not, this profile has nothing to do with the demands of the organisation's beneficiaries for the services provided. The reason: annual budgets based on negotiated targets and resources, which encourage a 'spend it or lose it' mentality in their holders. Cost centre managers find something to spend any spare budget on rather than lose it. The expenditure profile reflects the timing of the distribution of new allocations of money (budgets) at the start of the financial year, or their imminent withdrawal at the end. The result is sub-optimal cash management and resource allocation decisions.

- **The exclusive focus on the year end:** Most management teams rely on financial information that does not extend beyond the end of the current financial year, even if that year ends in a matter of weeks. There is a brick wall built at the end of the final accounting period of the year, over which the manager or trustee cannot see. For example, management accounts for period 10 of the year will typically not tell the reader anything beyond period 12, even though by the time the information is available period 12 probably ends in six or seven weeks' time. Why, as an organisation progresses through a financial year, does it make sense to shorten the forward perspective of management accounts until, by the final quarter, it extends no further than several weeks ahead? Predictably, obstacles and/or opportunities are, as a result, seen later than they could be and potentially too late.

- **The 12-month timeframe:** Most management information is presented in relation to 12-month periods of time, irrespective of the duration of the discrete activities by which the organisation delivers its mission. Service provision may need to be planned, and commitments made, over a significantly longer timeframe; fundraisers may legitimately argue that they cannot forecast with any degree of accuracy beyond the next six months. There may be no element of the organisation's work that fits a 12-month timeframe.

- **The budget bureaucracy:** The traditional budgeting process is typically drawn out and detailed over several months, involving literally thousands of numbers. Many a finance team finds itself moving straight from the year-end audit work relating to the previous year to the budget preparation work relating to the following year. What gets squeezed is any attention to what is happening now. The budget preparation process is a major distraction from running the business.

The frustrations of working with traditional budgets are deeply felt by managers in organisations in every sector. However sophisticated the budget preparation, it cannot predict the future with 100 per cent accuracy – and the greater the uncertainty about the future, the greater the possibility that what subsequently happens will not have been anticipated by, or caused by, implementation of the plan. As Haeckel (1999, pp. 2–3) says, 'traditional planning is useless in the face of great uncertainty'.

Hope and Fraser have led efforts to expose the deficiencies of the annual budget:

> *In its simplest form, budgets are no more than estimates or forecasts of income and expenditure and as such have few behavioural implications. Indeed they are essential for managing cash flows in every business. This is neither our meaning nor our problem. When we use the term budgeting, we mean an annual process that takes place inside most medium- to large-sized organisations that sets the performance agenda for the year ahead. This has much wider behavioural implications. In this form the budget is, in effect, a performance contract (either explicit or implicit) between two managerial levels. The purpose is to commit the subordinate or team to achieving a certain result and control the outcome. The terms of such a contract are likely to include a fixed target, a time period within which it must be achieved, the resources provided, the limits of authority, the reporting intervals, and any specified financial rewards that apply if the agreement is met. The problems caused by the budget-based performance contract are evident in most large organisations. Budgets lead to undesirable results, provide the illusion of control, and reduce responsiveness.*
>
> Hope and Fraser, 2001b, n.p.

ALLOCATING FUNDS: THE TRAPS

In making funds available to spending units, organisations typically fall into one or more of five traps. The one-year allocated envelope falls into all five.

1. **The spending target trap:** Budget recipients are given the incentive, implicitly or explicitly, to do whatever it takes to 'hit the budget'.

2. **The entitlement trap:** This creates a culture where budget recipients believe that the budget is to be protected for their exclusive use, or spent rather than lost, whatever the demands of the rest of the organisation.
3. **The accountability trap:** The organisation takes its eye off the ball by demanding accountability for performance only at infrequent points in time, such as financial year ends.
4. **The brick wall trap:** The organisation restricts its outlook to a relatively short time horizon, beyond which it chooses to be blind.
5. **The diminishing horizon trap:** The organisation allows its outlook to shorten over time by fixing the brick wall in time.

Each of these traps is now described in turn.

The spending target trap

The typical definition of a budget, explored further in chapter 12, barely hints at the agreement that the budget distributor and the budget recipient typically form in practice. On the face of it, the deal is simple: achieve certain objectives in return for funding. However, one question quickly dispels that belief: 'Under the terms of the deal, how much should the budget recipient have spent by the end of the year?'

The answer, of course, is: 'It depends.' It depends on whether the funds were in practice made available to the budget recipient (unanticipated circumstances, such as financial difficulties, may have prevented this), whether the actual work programme was as intended (many factors may result in the work programme being changed), and whether the funds were used wisely (flagrant misuse of budget should result in spending being stopped, for example). The best answer that can be given is typically: 'No more than the budget.'

Here lies the problem. When the deal is constructed, the intention of the distributor is that the budget is a means (financing a programme) to an end (achievement of objectives). However, in practice, it quickly becomes a definition of an end in its own right. The budget becomes a performance target to be hit – most typically, a one-year target. The budget recipient becomes principally accountable not for achieving the agreed objectives within the financial constraints imposed by the budget, but for spending the budget – and in many cases, for spending precisely the budget: no more, and no less.

The behaviour of the distributor tells all. If the distributor signals through their behaviour, whether overt or surreptitious, that the recipient is expected to 'hit' the budget, then the recipient will respond accordingly. How does this happen? The answer lies in the thorny issue of incentives.

Spending incentives

Consider the spending incentives associated with the one-year allocated envelope. What obligations do the budget recipients have, and how should they behave? The budget allocated is finite, and therefore defines a constraint on spending. The budget recipient does not have spending authority above this amount. This is shown by the line B in figure 11.1. To the extent that the spender acts within this authority, the budget (level B) defines a spending ceiling. There is downward pressure on spending from this hard ceiling, which results from the consequences of spending higher than this level – often labelled an 'overrun'.

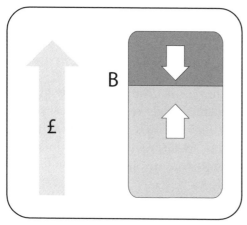

Fig. 11.1 The budget recipient's spending authority

The consequences may be self-imposed – for example, there may be sanctions applied by the budget distributor or senior management if spending exceeds the budget, or at least the requirement to justify the apparent profligacy. Consequences may also be externally imposed by the donor. In addition, funding constraints may mean that exceeding the ceiling would place the organisation in financial difficulties. So, the downward pressures are likely to be real and considerable.

Only a moment's thought is needed to realise that the allocated envelope defines not only a ceiling, but also a floor. There is considerable upward, as well as downward, pressure on a budget recipient. First, there is the very genuine pressure to undertake as large a work programme as possible, in order to have maximum beneficial impact on those that the programme seeks to support. Budget recipients always need more money – there is inevitably more to be done than is possible given the funding constraints.

Given this, not spending the budget received might be regarded at best as naïve, and at worst immoral, if the needs of the beneficiaries that the budget was intended to meet went unmet. 'The funds were allocated to achieve certain objectives through a defined work programme, not to be stockpiled' will be the accusation. 'If we had known that you were not going to spend the funds, we could have allocated them to other priorities.'

There is also pressure to protect future years' budget allocations, which are likely to be at least partly determined by the level of prior years' spending. The lower the level of spending actually incurred this year, the more difficult it is to justify a higher level next year, against the accusation: 'You clearly don't need the money.' Better, instead, to push this year's spending upwards – it will help the case to justify next year's bid. This often meets a political goal too – the size of budget is often synonymous with importance: the bigger the budget, the more important the budget recipient.

This upward pressure on spending is typically formalised by internal budget rules that prevent units from retaining allocated funds that remain unspent at the end of the budget year. A 'spend it or lose it' budget contract is in force.

The dual pressure on spending, up and down, drives actual expenditure levels inextricably towards the budgeted figure. Rational budget recipients will spend as much as they can get away with, constrained only by the effectiveness of the downward pressure applied by those to whom they account. If both forces are in place, then an implicit performance contract is struck – 'Hit the budget!' Behaviour that reflects such a 'hit the budget' culture will become increasingly overt as the close of the financial year beckons. Those whose anticipated full-year level of spending is currently lower than budget will do all that they can to increase spending before the year end.

This is likely to result in a marked spending acceleration, stimulated by one or more of several habits. The rigour with which spending proposals are assessed may fall, with less stringent criteria applied – deliberately. Spending that earlier in the year was deemed extravagant is now embraced as worthy. Spending that was planned for next year is brought forward (thereby exacerbating the rollercoaster trend of spending). In the internal market, the 'underspending' unit actively encourages last-minute charges from other units: anything to get the level of spending up!

In systems that permit transfers of budget, the underspender will also seek to offload spare budget, thereby reducing the under-run by reducing the size of the budget allocated, rather than by increasing spending. The organisation may witness the unseemly spectacle of unneeded budgets being shovelled from one underspending unit to another, each equally desperate to avoid being landed with funds that will simply worsen their under-run position.

This means that the value of the budget has fallen sharply. What was an extremely valuable asset earlier in the year (as witnessed by the intensity of the budget negotiation) has become a liability: unspent budget has negative value. In the run-up to the year end, the motivation to manage the numbers in order to 'hit the budget' almost completely obliterates the drive to meet the objectives of the programmes that the budget was distributed to finance (see box 11.3).

For the 'overspending' budget recipient, the incentives and consequent behaviours are inverted. The spender will seek to constrain or reduce spending. Proposed spending will be more rigorously assessed than earlier in the year.

Box 11.3 Balanced versus effective budget

More attention is placed on the balanced budget than on the effective budget. This may be the supreme (and certainly the most legitimized) form of procedural ends outwitting outcomes.

Williams et al, 1996, p. 33

Legitimate spending will be delayed until next year. Other budget recipients will be approached and encouraged to reduce earlier charges.

Arguably, the responsibility for this behaviour does not lie with the budget recipient – at least not primarily. They are acting perfectly rationally, given that their principal spending accountability is expressed in terms of the level of spending rather than in relation to the efficacy or effectiveness of it. They are judged in relation to the easy-to-measure *level* of spend versus the budget – not the very difficult-to-measure spending *effectiveness* (see box 11.4).

Box 11.4 The typical focus of accountability

The focus of spending accountability is typically on the relationship between the level of spending and the size of the budget (i.e. the size of the under- or over-run) rather than on the efficacy or effectiveness of spending. There is considerably more pressure to achieve a desired *level* of spending than to ensure that the spending has a satisfactory impact.

A typical set of management accounting reports used by management will be full of actual versus budget analysis, inviting the reader to assess the likelihood of actual spending matching the available budget at the end of the financial year. The report may be divorced from assessments of work programmes. In extreme cases, even the level of actual spending may be less important than the size of the gap between that level and the budget. If it results in a large underspend in terms of the budget, then successfully constraining spending may generate more questions than if expenditure had been higher – irrespective of the value of the additional spending.

However, many organisations exhibit an inherent bias towards underspending – in other words, spending less than the budget. Some risk-averse spenders may have a deep-rooted aversion to spending more than they have, and if this tendency is sufficiently widespread then it may become the dominant culture of the organisation, even if that is not intended corporately. Another example would be organisations that are strapped for cash, which will have to hold reserves as low as possible, and which may implicitly or explicitly promote spending conservatism, conscious that overspending the budget distributed could be fatal.

What explains the almost systemic underspending in organisations that have a healthy balance sheet and that could therefore afford (financially, at least) to overspend the budget? Why is the underspending bias prevalent here? The very question tells you something. If the level of spending is judged in relation to a predetermined number, then several incentives are invoked.

- **The incentive to negotiate as large a budget as possible:** Why wouldn't a rational budget recipient do that? The larger the budget, the greater the financial room to manoeuvre and, often, the greater the kudos of the budget recipient in the organisation. The budget recipient may succeed in their negotiations and receive a larger budget than they need or can sensibly spend. Underspending versus the budget will result.
- **The disincentive to spend more than the budget:** This is typically greater than the disincentive to spend less, whether this is perception or the reality. If sanctions are applied in the event of spending more than the budget, the signal will be a powerful one. Extreme sanctions, such as staff redundancies, will not be forgotten for a long time. Many years may have to pass before the fear of overspending dissipates. It is doubtful whether underspending has such consequences.
- **The tendency to try to minimise an under-run:** This merely increases the likelihood of an under-run occurring in the following year. It is a vicious cycle: a higher than needed budget is negotiated, actual spending is consequently low relative to the budget, there is a mad scramble to increase spending – if necessary by bringing forward activity from the following year – and the artificially boosted spending persuades the budget distributor to agree to a higher than needed budget for the following year. There is also the tendency for over-compensation, with a variance on one side being followed by an overreaction towards the other.
- **The incentive to be over-prudent in forecasting future spend:** It is commonly thought better to over-forecast spending than to under-forecast – testimony to the presumption that the consequences of underspending (both personal and organisational) are less significant than those of overspending. By the way, asking for forecast spending levels from budget recipients where a 'hit the budget' model is in place is likely to be worthless. Why would budget recipients indicate that they anticipate the level of spending to be anything other than the budgeted one? What would be their incentive to suggest that spending will be higher or lower than budget? Either indication could lead to sanctions of some kind.

Whether the budget is an allocation, a prediction or a target, the message for the recipient is the same: to spend as much as they can get away with – that is, until the disincentives to spend more equal or outweigh the incentives.

Meanwhile, the incentives for the budget distributor are not straightforward either. While you might think that their aim is to apply downward pressure on spending in order to drive down costs, they too may have an incentive to keep spending up. The downward pressure is triggered by a desire to eliminate cost inefficiencies, while the upward pressure stems from a desire to maximise impact. The distributor is usually an intermediary between the donor and the recipient and, just as the distributor demands explanations from the recipient if budget remains unspent, so they risk similar obligations in front of the donor.

The entitlement trap

The more the budget is distributed as an upfront allocation to the spending unit, the clearer the spending authority of the budget recipient. With an upfront allocation the budget recipient is offered funding certainty and is likely to feel a strong sense of ownership of the funds. A good thing, you may think. However, the more the funds are allocated up front, the less flexibility the distributor has to react to unexpected circumstances that were not anticipated at the time of the distribution.

In this event, access to the funds is complicated. Budget ownership on the part of the budget recipient turns quickly to budget entitlement. The proprietary instincts of the budget recipient, following the receipt of the allocation, are likely to be exhibited by a strong reluctance to 'release' the funds in the event either that they are no longer needed, or that higher organisational priorities emerge. There is a clear trade-off, in that providing funding certainty to the budget recipient comes at the price of inflexibility. Entitlements promote either spending profligacy or budget stockpiling. The impediment to flexibility raises serious questions about the sense of using upfront budget allocations as a means of making financial resources available to spending units, irrespective of the benefits of funding certainty.

The accountability trap

A further feature of the one-year allocated envelope budget is the almost-exclusive focus of accountability on one point of the year: its end. The logic of this is not difficult to understand. The budget is distributed to cover a pre-defined period, a single financial year, and at the end of the period it makes good sense to take stock, to review whether the budget has been well managed.

Management information guides the reader's attention towards this one point in time. Reports show the 'burn rate' – the proportion of the budget that has been spent to date – inviting the reader to judge whether the rate of spending is appropriate, given the elapse of time. Half-year reporting of low burn rates encourage the spender to 'hurry up', prompting the end-of-year spending acceleration that has already been described. The report is often accompanied by a narrative reassuring the reader that although the spending in the first two quarters has been low, it will pick up in the second half of the year. If there is any event at which accountability is sought mid-year, the budget distributor is easily placated with this assessment. The degree of real learning or accountability that has taken place is minimal. The spender knows all too well that they are able to 'spin a yarn' based on future promises.

Much of this can be attributed to the use of the budget figure as a year-end target against which the budget recipient is accountable. There is a once-a-year definition of success, and few organisations have found effective ways of making a meaningful assessment of performance at the six-month point. Part of the secret of overcoming this is not to regard it as the six-month point. Treat it instead as the just the latest month on a long-term journey.

The brick wall trap

The one-year allocated envelope model encourages the organisation to focus no further than one year on. This has two problems – both significant ones. The first is that, by definition, no funds are made available beyond one year: there is no 'envelope' of funds beyond the year, even though much of the work programme that will be financed from the envelope is part of a multi-year strategy that only makes sense if implemented in its entirety. In this case, medium- and long-term strategies and work programmes are being underwritten with one-year funding arrangements.

The second problem with this model, as we have seen, is that all the focus of attention will be on the year end. As the organisation moves forward, it will inevitably want to inform its ongoing decisions with as good a sense of what is ahead as possible. So, during the year, monitoring of actual spending is likely to be accompanied by regular forecasts that are designed both to project future results and to highlight forthcoming events to which the organisation must react. Almost certainly in this model the forecast will extend to the end of the year – but no further. It is as if the organisation has constructed a brick wall that artificially limits the horizon to one year. No one internally is looking beyond the wall. That seems odd, if you think about it. Why would an organisation voluntarily choose to blind itself?

The diminishing horizon trap

The brick wall trap is exacerbated if the wall is fixed in time. If all the focus of attention is on the end of the year, and this continues as the year progresses, then the organisation gets closer and closer to the wall. Towards the end of the year, the horizon is very short: one of weeks only. Action planning and decision making are likely to be undertaken ignorant of likely opportunities or difficulties that could reasonably be anticipated ... if only the organisation was looking.

THE CONSEQUENCE OF THE TRAPS

It is easy to see the consequence of the budget traps in the actual behaviour of organisations. This is particularly evident through the following tendencies as the organisation approaches the end of the financial year.

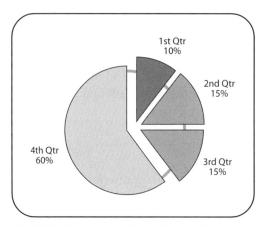

Fig. 11.2 Distribution of spending within a year

- **Bunching:** The profile of spending or output delivery may show the distribution within the year, as illustrated by figure 11.2. A slow start to the year ultimately ends in a gallop to the line in the final quarter, prompting a huge organisational sigh of relief and inevitable relaxation. This contributes to a light first quarter in the following year, thereby setting off the same tendency to try to catch up in the remainder of the year. The extent of the year-end bunching will depend on the force of the incentives in place – whether real or perceived – to those responsible for spending or delivery.

- **Short-termism:** Attention focuses predominantly on the short term, with strong incentives to concentrate on hitting the targets that will lead to favourable performance assessments.

- **Focusing on the bottom of the results chain, rather than the top:** Many managers describe the pressure to hit the number, and quarter 4 becomes a numbers management game, with considerable effort expended in order to try to finish the year with expenditure reaching a predetermined target. The principle of 'doing the right thing' is sacrificed as decisions are made with a focus on the year-end number rather than the long-term outcome.

The bottom line is that in any of these scenarios the organisation's use of its resources is sub-optimal. The conversion of resources into impact is less than it could be – and the real consequence is suffered by the organisation's intended beneficiaries.

Key stewardship questions

1. How well aligned are the resources of the organisation to its work programme, strategy and objectives?

2. Which allocation traps are prevalent in the organisation?

3. What incentives do spending units have?

4. What consequences are evident?

12 Allocation aids

The five allocation traps described in chapter 11 deeply impede the efficiency and effectiveness of organisations. All the individuals associated with an organisation have an obligation to its donors and beneficiaries to avoid the traps as best they can. This is particularly true of its leaders – including its financial stewards – who are responsible for the design of its governance and performance management frameworks and culture. That is easier said than done. Nevertheless, there are solutions that, as a minimum, dilute the consequences incurred from the traps. This chapter is devoted to identifying some of those, conceptualising some methods of resource allocation that encourage and enable those charged with delivering the organisation's impact to make efficient and effective decisions about how resources are used.

First, however, it is important to provide a definition of a budget that recognises the true enabling role of resources in the results chain, and that acknowledges the allocation traps identified.

WHAT IS A BUDGET, REALLY?

It may seem unnecessary to define a 'budget' but, as chapter 11 has exposed, it is crucially important to do so. There are several interpretations, and both the budget distributor and the budget recipient need to have a shared understanding. Is it an actual allocation of funds at the start of the year? Or is it an intended allocation of funds, which will be made if certain conditions prevail – a sort of commitment or plan, if you like? Or may be it is neither. Perhaps it is not an allocation at all, but rather a forecast or target of some sort.

The distinction is not just an academic one. It does matter, and both parties had better be clear which definition applies. The consequences of misunderstanding the intended meaning could be serious. If the distributor believes that the budget is a forecast of what level of spending will occur if certain conditions prevail (and that it will change if actual conditions differ from those assumed), while the recipient assumes that the budget is an allocation of funds made up front for their exclusive use, over which they have full authority, then trouble lies ahead. The spending authority of the budget recipient must be clear.

Whether the budget is an actual allocation, an anticipated allocation, a plan, a forecast or a target, what can be said is that the budget figure defines the level of spending which the budget recipient is expected to incur by the end of the financial year, given certain assumptions (see box 12.1). The rationale of the distributor is that the budget is needed in order to enable the recipient to undertake certain activities or programmes through which the objectives of the organisation can be achieved. For the distributor, the budget is a means to an end: the achievement of objectives. Think of it as an actual or intended allocation of funds, the expenditure of which is designed to finance the recipient's work programme by which the achievement of certain objectives is sought.

> **Box 12.1 What is a spending budget?**
>
> A spending budget is an actual or intended allocation of funds, the expenditure of which is designed to finance the recipient's work programme by which strategy is implemented and the achievement of certain objectives is sought. The budget defines the level of spending that is anticipated in a defined period, given certain assumptions.

AVOIDING THE TRAPS

What can be done to avoid the five traps? Various techniques can be used that weaken the traps, including those set out here. None of them offers a magic solution, but when used by attentive management as part of an appropriate accountability framework, the worst consequences of the traps can be significantly alleviated:

- **carry-over facilities** that enable budget holders to judge between spending and saving
- **contingency funds** that offer scope to replenish budget envelopes as needed
- **spending ranges** to define spending authority rather than precise budget numbers
- **rolling the envelopes:** rolling timeframes rather than static ones
- **multi-year** timeframes rather than single financial year ones
- **expenditure directions** rather than budget allocations.

Each of these is considered in turn.

Carry-over facilities

What happens if a budget recipient does not fully spend the budget allocated to them? Crucially, can they keep the unspent funds or not? If they cannot, the signal they are given is clear – 'spend or lose' – and in this circumstance, budget recipients will typically spend. For all the reasons previously discussed, they would rather spend the budget than lose it – even if the spending has questionable efficacy or effectiveness. The incentive not to spend in this circumstance is very weak.

In essence, the very distribution of a budget forces the distributor to decide whether unused funds can be carried over the brick wall into a new budget period, or not. Many organisations seek to overcome the 'spend or lose' behavioural problem by providing a carry-over facility that enables the budget recipient to retain budget that is unspent at the end of the year, and to be able to carry it over the year-end brick wall into the new year. The UK government is one example (see box 12.2). A variation on this is to limit the size of the potential carry-over – for example, by restricting it to 3 per cent of the budget distributed. Each of these two carry-over policies creates distinct incentives.

> **Box 12.2   Carry-over i
> the UK**
>
> *To encourage departments to plan over the medium term departments may carry forward unspent DEL [Departmental Expenditure Limits] provision from one year into the next and, subject to the normal tests for tautness and realism of plans, may be drawn down in future years. This end-year flexibility also removes any incentive for departments to use up their provision as the year end approaches with less regard to value for money.*
>
> HM Treasury, 2010, n.p.

Limited carry-over

Imagine that the budget recipient has been allocated a budget depicted by the 'B' line in figure 12.1. Level B is thus the intended spending ceiling. The budget distributor provides a carry-over facility that is effective once spending reaches level A. The maximum amount of budget that can be carried over is therefore shown by the white area between lines A and B.

As has been previously discussed, above level B there is downward pressure on spending, generated by sanctions that are imposed if the budget recipient over-spends. Until spending reaches level A, there is upward pressure. Level A becomes the new floor in the eyes of the budget recipient. Be in no doubt that a floor remains in this model; it has merely been reset at a lower level than was the case before a carry-over facility was provided. Until spending reaches level A, the 'spend or lose' incentive will continue to drive spending behaviour.

Once the level of spending is within the white area, the spending incentive changes to what can be labelled as 'spend or save'. The

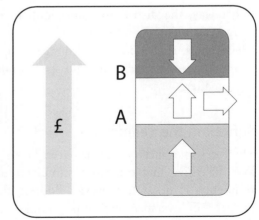

Fig. 12.1 Limited carry-over facility

budget recipient genuinely has the incentive to make a reasoned choice between spending and saving. They can choose, and are not penalised by their choice.

Unlimited carry-over

If we acknowledge that a carry-over facility creates helpful 'spend or save' incentives once a minimum level of spending has been reached, this invites the question as to how to maximise this incentive. 'Why not make the entire budget allocation eligible for carry-over if unspent?', you may be thinking. The effect of this would be to eliminate the spending floor, which in effect becomes set at a spending level of zero (see fig. 12.2). This is clearly attractive to the budget recipient. They can't lose! They keep whatever funds they do not spend.

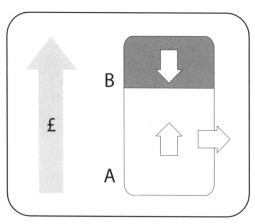

Fig. 12.2 Unlimited carry-over facility

However, the distributor may fear that the incentive to save will outweigh the incentive to spend. If the budget allocation is over-generous, then the budget recipient indeed has scope to stockpile unspent funds. The budget recipient has a strong incentive here to negotiate as large a budget as possible, irrespective of their real need. Adjusting future years' budget allocation in light of the carry-over of funds is a possible solution, but it risks imposing the very penalty that the carry-over policy sought to avoid. As long as the adjustment is sufficiently far into the future to avoid unreasonably interfering with plans already established, there should be no problem.

Either way, the distributor must look to ensure that the accountability of the budget recipient includes not only the level of spending but also efficacy and effectiveness. How well has the budget recipient used the funds made available to them? The budget recipient who spends nothing will achieve nothing – and that must matter.

Softening the ceiling

The carry-over facility that has been described attempts to address the 'spend or lose' incentive that otherwise stimulates upward spending pressure on budget recipients. It doesn't, however, address the issue of spending more than the budget – of 'overspending'. What should happen if spending exceeds level B? The argument to date has assumed that the budget is a 'hard' ceiling – that is, that spending cannot exceed the budget level without the spending unit incurring sanctions of some kind. The more severe the sanctions (in other words, the greater the downward pressure on spending), the more likely it is that actual spending will fall short of the budgeted sum.

If the aim is to see spending reach the budgeted figure by the end of the year, then the upward and downward pressures facing the budget recipient must offset each other, otherwise there will be a bias towards either under- or overspending the budget. The issue of how to soften the downward pressure on spending has to be addressed, or there will be an inherent bias in incentives – which is likely to lead to the units spending less than is made available to them. There is a natural tendency to negotiate a larger budget than is needed, 'just to be on the safe side'. Provision of a carry-over facility will merely accentuate

> The only way to avoid developing a chronic habit of spending less than intended is to accept the risk of spending slightly more than intended.

this bias. An unbiased budget would mean that the budget distributor is indifferent between the spending exceeding the budget and falling short of it. In the event of the former, the reaction of the distributor becomes critical.

Contingency funds

We have established that the budget recipient benefits from funding certainty ('I know where I stand and can make decisions accordingly'), while the budget distributor is likely to favour funding flexibility, particularly during times of uncertainty or ambiguity ('The more I hand out now, the less I have to use for future priorities that I don't yet know about'). One approach that endeavours to allow both to be achieved is to maintain and use contingency funds. These are funds that are held centrally, and distributed to budget recipients as needed in response to emerging priorities that were not anticipated at the time of the initial budget distribution. They are the reserves of the organisation, and act as the buffer, the bank or the rainy day fund.

It is important to remember four points in relation to contingency funds.

1. **Policy:** If they are going to be used, the organisation needs to have a contingency fund (or reserves) policy that articulates why these funds are held, what size they should be, under what circumstances they can be used, and how they will be replenished.
2. **Process:** There needs to be a well-defined and administered process to enable spending units to access these funds if the circumstances warrant it.
3. **Accessibility:** The funds need to be available as needed, to be distributed in a timely fashion to enable them to be used without unnecessary delay to address the issue that led to their demand. Often, contingency funds are managed

within the constraints of the single financial year deal, and they are distributed too late within the year to be spent wisely. The result is simply a transfer of unused funds from the centre to the units.

In a 'hit the budget' culture, the budget recipient would rather not receive contingency funds than receive them too late to be spent. There is little point handing out budget in the last days of a one-year model that does not permit carry-over. Be clear that the use of contingency funds does not change the incentives previously described in a budget allocation model – they simply allow the size of the budget (line B in the diagrams) to be increased.

4. **Management:** The management of contingency funds will differ greatly, depending on whether these funds are subject to the same spending rules as the budget. Contingency funds that are essentially reserves of the organisation held on the balance sheet until used can genuinely be used as and when needed, without the pressures imposed by the budget cycle. On the other hand, contingency funds that are merely a portion of the year's expenditure budget held back by the distributor, rather than being released to the spending units, will be subject to the same 'spend or lose' pressures as the distributed portion. The distributor will not want to hold a significant portion of the budget back if they are going to be penalised for not spending the budget, come the end of the year.

Spending ranges

A spending range defines the budget authority in terms of two parameters rather than as a precise number. In figure 12.3, the spender is given a budget of B but is advised that spending is intended to fall within the range defined by levels A and C. The introduction of ranges around the envelope influences the spending target and brick wall traps. By expressing the desired level of expenditure or available level of resources in terms of a range rather than a point, the precision of the target is helpfully reduced. Within the budget period, the budget recipient now has some discretion about the level and timing of expenditure. The need to hit the precise budget – to land actual expenditure 'on a dime' at the end of the period – has gone. The World Bank is one organisation that has adopted this facility in managing its administrative expenditure in recent years, albeit using a narrow band (see box 12.3).

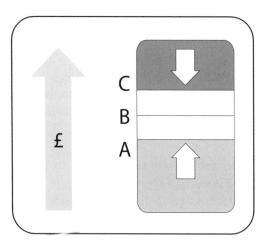

Fig. 12.3 Spending range

> ## Box 12.3   The World Bank's 2 per cent flexibility band
>
> The World Bank's senior management agrees a resource framework with the board that is valid for three years. The framework indicates the direction in which the Bank's administrative expenditure should move over the three-year period. Management is expected to ensure that the trajectory of spending follows the intended direction, while allowing short-term fluctuations within single financial years. Fluctuations permitted are defined by an expenditure range around the intended direction (for example, plus or minus 2 per cent around a target of 0 per cent change over three years). While expenditure stays within the range, management can proceed. Reaching the parameters triggers discussion and agreement with the board about management's intended response.

Rolling the envelopes

'Going rolling' means maintaining a consistent timeframe to review performance and to look ahead. The concept of rolling is therefore relevant both when looking backwards, in order to assess actual performance, and looking forward, to provide a planning horizon. In terms of looking forward, the aim is to make the horizon consistent in length, in order to give spending

> 'Rolling' means maintaining a consistent timeframe in which to look backwards to review performance and to look forward to plan ahead.

units the confidence to plan strategically over the medium term. The horizon is maintained consistently at, say, 12 or 36 months as time passes.

To this end, 'going rolling' weakens the brick wall and diminishing horizon traps. This is done by extending the horizon periodically as it diminishes, by adding extra planning periods to the end of the existing horizon. Most typically, the extensions are added quarterly or annually. In the former, months 13 to 15 are added at the completion of month 3, while in the latter, year 4 is added at the completion of year 1.

In terms of budget envelopes, 'rolling' means adding additional resources to the envelope in order to cover a period (quarter or year) equivalent in length to the period that has passed since the envelope was last replenished. In this way, the envelope always covers the same future horizon. This eliminates the diminishing horizon trap and also reduces the brick wall trap, in the sense that the wall keeps moving forward. To some extent, the budget recipient never arrives at the wall to face the carry-over decision. However, the decision becomes part of the consideration of how much resource to add to the envelope for the new extension. Rather than disappearing completely, the problem changes form.

How far forward should an organisation look? Looking forward, we have two objectives: short-term control and medium- to long-term planning. Each requires a different horizon. Short-term control is best served by quarterly or monthly rolling forecasts, with a 12 to 18-month forward-looking focus. Medium- to long-term planning is best served by rolling multi-year horizons. The precision of rolling a three-year planning horizon quarterly is probably worthless. Chapter 15 looks at forecasting in detail.

Going multi-year

Operating within a multi-year framework means that managers have access to funding over several years, to enable them to implement agreed strategies. Multi-year funding helps organisational performance in two ways:

1. it supports strategic planning by offering sufficient medium-term funding security to enable operational decisions that have multi-year implications to be made with confidence. In this way, funding decisions are made in relation to the period of the strategy – resources are made available in line with the needs of the business, rather than with the accounting calendar; and
2. crucially, it enables the budget distributor to signal the direction in which expenditure should move over time.

Moving multi-year can significantly reduce the risk of at least some of the allocation traps described. The diminishing horizon problem is certainly helped. As the months go by, the horizon does diminish but, for example, seven months into year 1 of a three-year framework, the visible horizon is still 29 months ahead rather than just five. The budget recipient now has clarity about future funding over a much more sensible period than just one year. There is much more consistency between the timeframe used to define strategy and the resources made available to finance its implementation. Arguably, the brick wall is now sufficiently far away not to be an impediment, although this depends on the consequences of under- or overspending the first year's budget.

Most typically, going multi-year means using a three-year timeframe, and the intended spending direction is expressed in terms of three annual budget envelopes. For example, the UK government sets three annual departmental expenditure limits (DELs) (see box 12.4).

> ### Box 12.4   Three-year budgets in the UK
>
> *Spending Reviews set firm and fixed three-year Departmental Expenditure Limits (DELs) and, through Public Service Agreements (PSA), define the key improvements that the public can expect from these resources.*
>
> *HM Treasury, 2008, n.p.*
>
> *Three-year budgets and end-year flexibility give those managing public services the stability to plan their operations on a sensible time scale. Further, the system means that departments cannot seek to bid up funds each year … So the credibility of medium-term plans has been enhanced at both central and departmental level.*
>
> *Departments have certainty over the budgetary allocation over the medium term and these multi-year DEL plans are strictly enforced. Departments are expected to prioritise competing pressures and fund these within their overall annual limits, as set in Spending Reviews. So the DEL system provides a strong incentive to control costs and maximise value for money.*
>
> *HM Treasury, 2010, n.p.*

Expenditure directions

More powerful yet is to combine going multi-year with some of the resource allocation techniques that eliminate the one-year budget envelope traps. The most potent approach is to replace budget envelopes completely, with spending direction signals. Adopting this resource allocation methodology is not straightforward by any means. A number of critical factors have to be in place for the methodology to be successful (see box 12.5), but it potentially offers the most effective control of expenditure of all – one that truly enables the level, direction and effectiveness of expenditure to be maximised over time.

Using expenditure directions, resources are not allocated up front to units. The direction is a signal – an indication of the level and direction that expenditure is expected to take over a multi-year timeframe, given the agreed strategy to be implemented. Units do not

> ### Box 12.5   Expenditure directions: critical success factors
>
> - Clear signals of spending expectations as part of overall performance contract
> - Excellent tracking
> - High level of accountability of spenders

'keep' resources that they do not spend, neither do they carry them over the financial year-end 'brick wall'. They draw down funds in line with an indicative expenditure direction, and are accountable for doing so as effectively and efficiently as possible over time. It is a 'spend as you need' approach. The accounting system coding enables accurate recording of who has spent what.

The implication of not pre-allocating budgets to units in envelopes is hugely significant. Units do not have an account of funds to exhaust or protect. In effect, all units have to draw from the same pool. The concept of fiscal year-denominated envelopes containing budgets that holders try to spend within the year (or to carry over the artificial timelines dividing years) disappears. Units spend as they need from a central source, in line with the indicative directions. They are judged on their performance in climbing the results chain, and on whether expenditure moves in the intended direction over time.

Imagine setting an expenditure direction expressed as a percentage change target to be met each year over a three-year period, such as a 2 per cent reduction per annum (aimed at stimulating productivity improvements). This target would be relevant over any 12-month period – not just at the end of the financial year – thereby avoiding the accountability trap. Accountability focuses on whether the direction of actual spending is following the intended trajectory over time rather than on the precise level of spending incurred in a particular financial year. Interest centres on what has been achieved with the resources spent, and what action is appropriate to take, rather than solely on the level of spending.

In practice, if the principal determinant of spending was operational business, and managers were not preoccupied with 'managing the budget', the spending pattern of most organisations would fluctuate over time. A fluctuating path would be normal (see fig. 12.4). The factors causing the actual path of spending to oscillate around the intended trajectory include both timing and price: if the actual timing of activities differs from those anticipated, or if actual costs differ, then an intended level of spending may not be met.

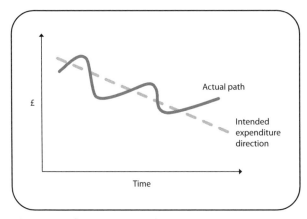

Fig. 12.4 A fluctuating spending pattern

Given these uncertainties, and the desire to see spending follow an indicative direction, managers need some licence to be either side of the intended spending path. This can be done only if managers are willing and able to run the risk of spending marginally more than intended. It is the role of senior management to ensure that, in aggregate, indicative spending levels remain within parameters. The preoccupation should be about whether the trend over time follows the intended path, rather than whether actual spending is at a precise level at a precise point in time.

The aim is not to give management an incentive to make knee-jerk reactions to short-term, minor fluctuations in order to hit precise, arbitrary financial year-end targets. Instead, it is to give managers authority to spend resources as they see fit day-to-day, in the best interest of the organisation's clients. Clearly, this must not be interpreted as a signal to spend however much they like whenever they choose. They must be accountable for moving costs in line with an agreed direction over time.

In recognising that actual expenditure is likely to follow an uneven path rather than a straight line, judgements have to be made about the degree of deviation from the intended direction that is permissible. For example, what should be the reaction in figure 12.4 to the actual path of expenditure at the end of the time period shown, when actual expenditure is both higher than intended and moving in the opposite direction?

One solution is to flank the intended direction with parameters, or bands, either side, creating an expenditure range within which the level of expenditure is expected to remain (see fig. 12.5). The upper band creates a spending ceiling: a level of spending above which expenditure is not intended to reach, even allowing for operational or pricing uncertainties. The bands – both upper and lower – signal a level of spending at which enquiry is triggered.

Maintaining a level of spending outside the bands should be the subject of explicit discussion and understanding. It should not be permissible for expenditure to stay adjacent to the upper band indefinitely. There should be explicit dialogue, supported by good analytics, to provide reassurance

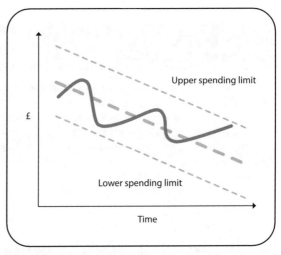

Fig. 12.5 An expenditure range

that expenditure will return in line with the intended trajectory and level within a reasonable time period. Note that from the point of view of implementing strategy, where each financial year begins and where it ends is irrelevant.

ACCOUNTABILITY WITHOUT BUDGET ENVELOPES

How is it possible to give clear expenditure directions without these being interpreted as budget envelopes, with all the consequent issues raised in the previous chapter? The positioning of the directional signal becomes all-important, for the following reasons.

- The direction – even if expressed in terms of annual amounts, much as a budget envelope – must be defined as the estimated amount needed by the unit in order to deliver the agreed strategy. There must be this explicit link between money and delivery (as provided in the definition of a budget given in box 12.1).
- Receiving units must be advised unambiguously that the sum is an indicative expenditure amount – not an allocation. They have no entitlement rights on it.
- Units must be required to track actual and intended use of resources quickly and accurately, in order to be able to assure themselves that the spending level and trajectory honours the intention of the spending direction.
- Accountability must be institutionalised through dialogue at all levels. It must be evident, through the focus of the dialogue, what units are being held accountable for.
- People in the organisation must be guided as to what is expected. Leaders and managers must engage with staff and volunteers to create a clear picture of how resources are expected to be managed. One approach is to articulate answers to frequently asked questions (see box 12.6).

Box 12.6   Accountability without envelopes: sample questions and answers

What happens if a unit spends more or less than the indicative amount?
It depends. Units are accountable for 'doing the right thing' for the client, using resources effectively and efficiently as possible, subject to the constraints of implementing within the agreed strategy and in line with the intended expenditure direction. They are not accountable for spending a particular sum within a particular time period. However, they are accountable for continually tracking actual and expected spending, and for alerting senior management to key trends. Whatever the level of expenditure, the organisation has to assure itself that the money has been spent wisely.

Can a unit keep what it doesn't spend?
No. They are not 'given' any funds to keep.

Is a unit punished if it spends more than the indicative amount?
There needs to be a rigorous dialogue about what is going on, but there needs to be this same dialogue at any level of spending. The ongoing dialogue and analysis needs to help management conclude whether the higher than anticipated level of spending is simply part of normal fluctuations in spending over time, or whether there is a performance issue that needs to be addressed.

What is the incentive for a unit to keep spending down?
The incentive is to know that management is holding the unit accountable for the decisions that they make with the funds used. They do this through dialogue with the units, challenging their results, plans and assumptions, and pushing them to demonstrate continual improvement. They support this dialogue with high-quality analytics, including trends and benchmark data. Units that have a well-thought-through strategy, that implement skilfully given the prevailing circumstances, and that demonstrate tight expenditure discipline, are rewarded over time through recognition, new business and new opportunities.

ENSURING COHERENCE

Whatever methodology is adopted, it is essential that the component parts are coherent. It is easy to get it wrong. If resources are allocated using budget envelopes, for example – whether distributed for one year or more – these must be accompanied by some form of carry-over if the 'spend it or lose it' behaviour is to be countered. Carry-over is incompatible, however, with a draw-down approach to funding, such as the one using medium-term expenditure directions.

Key stewardship questions

1. What does the term 'budget' mean in the organisation?

2. How can the organisation avoid the allocation traps described in chapter 11?

3. Is the organisation's chosen resource allocation methodology coherent?

4. How does the organisation intend to solve these issues?

Part 4:
Dynamic financial management

13 A new financial stewardship

GOOD FINANCIAL STEWARDSHIP

If good financial stewardship demands that organisations make crucial decisions about how the financial resources at their disposal are used, then the organisation must accept three prerequisites:

1. It should be able to identify: (a) where it is trying to get to; and (b) where it is now.
2. It must have as good a sense as possible about: (c) what is ahead of it.
3. It needs to accept that where it is now, and what is ahead of it, is continually changing – even if where it is trying to get to is not. So, it must be prepared to reconsider what resource allocation decisions it should make as it goes. That necessarily means that its notion of 'satisfactory performance' might also change as it progresses.

Good financial stewardship should be based on the use of up-to-date information about the current financial position, and latest thinking about the future, in the context of defined targets or goals. This information will be constantly changing. So, the crucial task is not to predict where the organisation will be at some point in the future: that is a near impossibility, and financial stewards have to accept that fact. Instead, the task becomes one of understanding the range of possible future circumstances in which the organisation may find itself and of developing a capacity to manage, come what may.

That last sentence is worth digesting carefully. The task is to develop an ability to react to the actual circumstances the organisation finds itself facing, rather than trying to predict accurately where that will be. It is about developing an 'ability to rapidly implement whatever strategy [is] necessary, rather than determin[ing] *the* strategy in advance' (Haeckel, 1999, p. 11).

If Haeckel's observation is accepted, then the whole basis of financial (and operational) planning changes and the methodology of financial management based on a detailed, fixed budget are likely to be too cumbersome, unwieldy and inflexible an approach at best. At worst, it will be a dangerous one, sending decision makers inappropriate signals about how resources should best be allocated.

> ## Box 13.1   The principles of planning
>
> 1. Planning and forecasting must be a continuous, participatory activity, not an annual event. The possible impact of opportunities and problems must be assessed when they arise.
> 2. The perspective and timeframe looking forward should reflect the nature of what the organisation does, not the requirements of accounting statute.
> 3. The organisation must have evidence-based metrics that between them are sufficient and necessary to show whether the financial performance and financial state of the organisation is satisfactory or not. The organisation should be stewarded using these critical measures of performance (i.e. on what it is really important to get right), not a mass of detail.
> 4. Information about the organisation's current financial performance and state of play that is accurate, appropriate and right up to date must be available at all times.

Financial stewardship methodology

To provide the flexibility and adaptability needed, the design of the methodology by which an organisation stewards its finances must be underpinned by four principles (see box 13.1). These principles translate into a cyclical five-step financial stewardship methodology that is logical and built on common sense. This is a straightforward approach that enables the organisation's decision makers to manage its finances as they go, taking on board circumstances and issues that present themselves on the way. At its simplest, it is no more than an adaptation of how a human brain behaves as an individual moves from A to B. The five steps are as follows.

1. **Monitor:** Understand where the organisation is now. Decide how and where to move forward in the context of where the organisation is now, and the adequacy of the performance that it has achieved to date.
2. **Forecast:** Look forward to see what is ahead. Before starting to move forward, the organisation has to check whether there is an obstacle in its path that is going to impede its progress, or an opportunity that would be advantageous to accept.
3. **Aim:** Decide where to go. Armed with the intelligence collected in steps 1 and 2, the organisation is now able to make a sensible decision about its intentions, such as where it wants to get to, and by when.
4. **Plan:** Decide how to get there. The decision makers must identify the alternative ways of reaching their destination, and choose between them, using criteria such as weighing up the relative importance of speed and cost.
5. **Act:** Set off towards the intended destination. The organisation implements the decisions made in step 4.

The steps are sequential, each step building on the previous one, and together creating a continuous performance management model. In practice, it is a continuous cycle of information gathering and decision making in reaction to that information (see fig. 13.1).

Following the cycle, each step requires the organisation to collect information that informs it about how to proceed to the next step. In order to provide this information, it needs to answer a number of key questions. In terms of financial stewardship, these are the kinds of questions shown in figure 13.2.

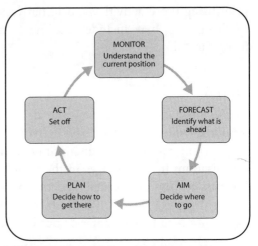

Fig. 13.1 The continuous performance management model

Step 1

First, the organisation needs to understand its current financial position: critically important is to assess the resources that it has available now and its recent financial performance.

Step 2

As part of the information gathering, before it moves forward, the organisation also needs to assess what is in front of it financially in terms of the commitments already made – especially in terms of future income generation and likely ongoing costs. This will enable it to assess the financial room it has to manoeuvre, by identifying those resources it anticipates having available over which there is still some discretion (in terms of how they are applied). Then, its financial stewards can set a sensible, realistic aim.

Step 3

Step 3 is where the organisation defines what success looks like in financial terms. Then it can worry about how it is going to get there (step 4). The risk of carrying out step 3 before the monitoring stage (steps 1 and 2) is that the aim may be unrealistic given the resources available to the organisation (see the first of the four fundamental questions on p. 246). Monitoring before aiming helps the organisation to ensure that its ambitions are realistic, given its starting point, and what it sees ahead.

Step 4

In particular, step 4 must enable the financial stewards to understand what resources they are able to commit now, and to what. A process for deciding where to allocate these resources has to be in place, including a way of prioritising those activities and initiatives that do not yet have funds committed to them. This may include deciding to stop some activities that are currently being funded.

Step 5

In the final step – step 5 – the decisions made in step 4 are implemented. Resources are committed, new activities and initiatives are brought on-stream, and current activities are discontinued, immediately shifting the position of the organisation. It is no longer in the same position as it was before it took step 5. Business reviews are needed, and this means that the monitoring and forecasting steps – steps 1 and 2 (understanding the current financial position of the organisation and what is ahead) need to be repeated. And the cycle continues.

Step	Questions/actions
1. Understand where you are now	What is my current financial position? What resources do I have? What is my recent financial performance?
2. Look ahead to see what's in front of you	What additional resources do I anticipate generating, and when? What commitments have I already made to new initiatives? What will they cost, and when will the cost be incurred? What ongoing costs will I have to incur? What spare resources will I therefore have available?
3. Decide where you want to go	What financial outcomes am I looking to achieve? What would success look like in financial terms?
4. Decide how you intend to get there	What 'available' resources can I commit now, either from reserves or from future income? What else would I like to do? What's the priority? What additional commitments is it appropriate to make now? What existing commitments is it appropriate to stop making now?
5. Set off	Make or stop commitments such as incurring expenditure or liabilities.

Fig. 13.2 Key questions

Attributes of the methodology

This approach has key attributes that differentiate it from traditional financial management methodologies using budgets.

- The five-step process is a continuous cycle, rather than a single event undertaken once a year. In particular, the planning stage – step 4, when resource allocation decisions are made – takes place when it is needed, whenever that is in the year, not when a budget timetable predetermines that it should happen. The annual event called 'the budget' disappears.
- The methodology does not assume that the appropriate timeframe over which to plan and look ahead is a 12-month one. It may be – but equally it may not be. Instead, the forward perspective is determined by the nature of the activities that the organisation carries out, and the timeframe over which funds have to be committed. Again, that may or may not be 12 months. It is essential that the organisation maintains a permanent monitoring capacity, both to be able to assess current performance and position, and to see what is coming ahead.
- The key controls in the methodology (the checks and balances that prevent expenditure, in particular, from spiralling out of control) are candid dialogue about performance and the outlook, supported by a few key indicators defined in step 3 – not by detailed budgets and variance analyses prepared line-by-line, period-by-period.

THE TWO TIMEFRAMES

In practice, organisations will need to undertake the five-step cycle over two timeframes: a strategic, multi-year one, and a shorter operational one. Just as organisations set an overall multi-year direction through strategy, and manage day-to-day performance using shorter-term operational planning and control processes, the task of aligning resources relies on the same two frames of reference. Figure 13.3 illustrates the concept.

In the medium term, the organisation needs to align resources with strategy. This means defining the financial boundaries within which the organisation will have to operate over the medium term. Think of this as defining the edges of the shaded arrows in figure 13.3. It also means defining the direction. In particular, this means defining the level and direction in which expenditure is expected to go over time. This is depicted by the trajectory of the arrow. Completing these two tasks requires the financial steward to undertake the five steps. This is likely to occur regularly but at infrequent intervals, as identified by the points A and B in the figure.

Meanwhile, in the short term, decision makers will complete the five-step cycle more frequently (this frequency is depicted by the dotted lines) – monthly, quarterly or perhaps annually – in order to maintain continual supervision of performance and of the short-term outlook.

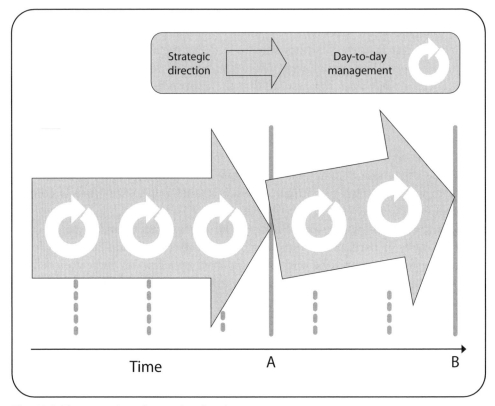

Fig. 13.3 The strategic and operational cycles

The short and medium term are described in more detail below.

The medium term

There is no hard-and-fast definition of what 'the medium term' constitutes. Its vital characteristic is that it is multi-year. The ultimate objectives of most welfare-focused organisations require a long-term perspective, reflecting the scale of beneficiary need and the magnitude of developing and successfully implementing solutions. For example, the Millennium Development Goals were established in 2000, setting targets 15 years ahead (see box 13.2).

> ## Box 13.2   The long term: the Millennium Development Goals
>
> *In September 2000, building upon a decade of major United Nations conferences and summits, world leaders came together at United Nations Headquarters in New York to adopt the United Nations Millennium Declaration, committing their nations to a new global partnership to reduce extreme poverty and setting out a series of time-bound targets – with a deadline of 2015 – that have become known as the Millennium Development Goals.*
>
> *The eight MDGs – which range from halving extreme poverty to halting the spread of HIV/AIDS and providing universal primary education, all by the target date of 2015 – form a blueprint agreed to by all the world's countries and all the world's leading development institutions.*
>
> *United Nations, n.d., n.p.*

In contrast, the medium term defines a timeframe over which multi-year strategies can be planned and implemented in pursuit of the long-term objectives. As a minimum, this is likely to mean maintaining an 18-month horizon. Most typically, a three to five-year timeframe is used. The case studies described in chapter 4 included Sightsavers International's five-year strategic framework and the UK government's three-year Comprehensive Spending Review, to give just two examples.

Adopting a medium-term perspective, the financial steward has two tasks:

1. To establish a set of financial parameters within which the organisation must operate over the medium term. These are the financial boundaries and targets that define financial performance for the organisation. The financial framework outlined in part 2 provides a ready-made structure to do this (suitable parameters are defined in chapter 16).
2. To define a resource allocation methodology by which funds are made available to finance the implementation of strategy. Spending units need clear multi-year signals about funding if they are to plan and then implement multi-year strategies and work programmes in order to have the intended impact. They must be confident of the level and type of funds that will be available. Otherwise, their planning and programme management will inevitably adopt a short-term orientation.

The short term

The short term defines a period within which strategies are translated into, and implemented through, operating plans. Business units agree work programmes with leaders and organise resources of all types, including human and financial resources. Plans are executed, day-to-day services delivered and change initiatives implemented. It is in the short term that the organisation moves forward step by step, continually reacting to new information about performance and outlook, within the defined medium-term parameters and in line with the medium-term direction.

Most typically, organisations use a static 12-month timeframe to define the short term – almost invariably based on the financial year. Unlike the medium term, where using financial years makes eminent sense, in the short term there is much more to be gained from using a rolling perspective that straddles financial years, in order to maintain a consistent horizon over the short-term outlook. (This is discussed more in chapter 15 on forecasting.)

Developing medium-term expenditure frameworks

A good example of how financial stewards in the public sector are endeavouring to fulfil the two tasks required of them in the medium term – setting financial parameters/direction, and providing an efficient/effective resource allocation methodology – is provided by recent efforts to reform public expenditure management. Governments around the world are increasingly developing medium-term expenditure frameworks (MTEF) to steward public finances, and their construction provides good evidence of the five-step methodology in action (see box 13.3).

Box 13.3   Medium-term expenditure framework

A MTEF tries to integrate policy with resource allocation decisions in a multi-year context to better reflect the effects of decisions on public finances, and generally lead to improved policy decisions. It also involves structuring the decision-making process to encourage economy and efficiency, and focus spending and policy on attaining the government's objectives. So a MTEF could be said to be about strategic allocation of resources in line with government priorities and the opportunity costs of decisions.

Dorotinsky, 2004, p. 1

Dorotinsky summarises a MTEF process in three stages:

1. *Estimating total available resources for the public sector over a multi-year period – usually within a multi-year macroeconomic and fiscal policy framework.*
2. *Estimating the actual cost of current government policy and programs by sector, again in a multi-year context.*
3. *Reconciling the information in steps 1 and 2 to align policies with available resources, and using this information as a basis for improved policy and funding choices and, ultimately, improved outcomes.*

Dorotinsky, 2004, p. 1

These three stages demonstrate the complete 'Monitor, Forecast, Aim, Plan, Act' cycle, as follows.

- **Monitor:** Governments are encouraged to understand the current state of play. This is in terms of understanding current economic conditions, and current revenue collection and expenditure performance.
- **Forecast:** Based on macro-economic forecasts, multi-year revenue estimates enable ministers to establish a revenue envelope. The government tests the sensitivity of broad expenditure estimates to changes in various assumptions, including the continuation of current policies. This helps create an overall picture of expenditure trends and enables affordability to be gauged.
- **Aim:** Decisions are made about the general policy directions of the government, and the specification or modification of government objectives for each sector.
- **Plan:** These directions are translated into multi-year allocations across sectors (such as health or education), followed by allocations of spending by each ministry among its activities and programmes to attain its objectives.
- **Act:** Ministries implement agreed policies, immediately prompting the need for business review and updated tracking of latest results and trends.

Integrating the two timeframes in one continuous process

The World Bank provides one example of an organisation attempting to integrate the two timeframes in one continuous planning and performance management process. The annual calendar identifies a series of engagement points between the Bank's board, including its committees, and senior management. These points include an annual assessment of the Bank's three-year outlook – labelled internally as the Medium-Term Strategy and Finance (MTSF) discussion – and an ongoing quarterly business review process. Through these two events, the Bank leadership undertakes the five steps required of good financial stewardship:

1. reviewing regularly actual performance, including financial performance
2. presenting short-term forecasts and medium-term financial outlooks
3. reaching agreement on financial parameters within which the Bank is expected to operate
4. making allocation decisions
5. using those allocation decisions to prompt implementation of the agreed work programme, in line with overall strategic priorities.

The MTSF discussion

The MTSF discussion uses a forward-looking three-year horizon to present the strategic context facing the Bank and, in that context, to define the intended strategic and financial direction of the institution. A paper, tabled to inform discussions among the board and senior management, offers three medium-term perspectives.

1. It articulates the strategic priorities of the Bank in light of the external environment and its mandate from shareholders.
2. It discusses the three-year financial outlook for the Bank in terms of its income and capital adequacy position. It examines the sensitivity of the financial prospects to key assumptions and scenarios.
3. Based on this analysis, the MTSF discussion recommends how much funding is available, both for lending and for administrative expenditure. This recommendation underpins the third component of the discussion on the Bank's multi-year resource framework – a framework that provides a summary of the proposed level and trajectory of the key elements of administrative expenditure over the forthcoming three years. The discussion is used to reach consensus about the overall level of resources to be available, and the degree of budget flexibility around that indicative level that will be permitted. This is defined in terms of a percentage range around the target trajectory.

The quarterly business review

The quarterly business review follows the completion of each quarter. This process brings members of the board and senior management together to review latest performance and to assess the short-term outlook. The discussion, and the report tabled to inform that discussion, adopt a results chain logic, examining progress in implementing selected Bank strategic priorities, historic trends in the delivery of lending and knowledge-based products, staffing and administrative and capital expenditure. An issues note, prepared in consultation with the chair of the review meeting, focuses the agenda.

Key indicators are provided for each of these topics, together with illustrative examples to emphasise particular messages concerning performance. Trend data is presented showing both latest quarter and moving four-quarter historic totals, enabling readers to understand the medium-term trends as well as short-term oscillations. However, the short-term outlook is financial year-based, reflecting the institution's continued focus on end-of-year results and the continued presence of several of the resource allocation traps described in chapter 11.

Applying the five steps in the short and medium term

The following chapters explain the essence of each step – where necessary, distinguishing between the short- and medium-term perspectives. The methodology makes no presumption about issues such as the characteristics of the organisation, the nature of its work or the state of its finances. What all organisations have in common is the need to steward themselves through an uncertain future so that they maximise impact over time with the finite resources available to them.

Key stewardship questions

1. How able is the organisation to react appropriately to circumstance?

2. What principles underpin the organisation's planning?

3. Is the organisation's financial stewardship methodology effective?

4. When and how does the organisation undertake the 'Review, Forecast, Aim, Plan, Act' cycle?

14 Step 1: monitor

UNDERSTANDING THE CURRENT POSITION

At this stage, what is relevant is history – and the obvious place to start is the statutory accounts. These offer income and expenditure history over a 24-month period (the last financial year and its prior year comparative), the balance sheet as at the end of the last two financial years, and a cash flow summary over the same period.

To understand the financial state of play of any organisation, start with the balance sheet, not the SOFA. It is the balance sheet that will show, crucially, what assets and liabilities the organisation has as it moves into the future from the balance sheet date. However, not many lay readers of statutory accounts find them easy to read, so a key role of the senior finance professionals involved in the organisation is to help users of the published accounts to understand what they say.

As time progresses, the statutory accounts at the end of the previous financial year end will be increasingly uninformative to the reader searching for an understanding of where the organisation is now. Other information is required, which is normally produced under the label of 'management accounts'. As its name implies, such information is prepared solely for the benefit of internal management and trustees: it is not required statutorily, neither is it accessible outside the organisation. Nevertheless, the information held in the primary financial statements of the statutory accounts must be kept in mind throughout the year – if only to be aware of how the public would interpret the organisation's performance and state of play.

THE ROLE AND CHARACTERISTICS OF MANAGEMENT ACCOUNTING

Management accounting refers to any information about the financial performance and state of play of the organisation that is prepared for its decision makers (see box 14.1). Such information, and those who provide it, have a particular role to play in contributing to the financial stewardship of any organisation. The role of management accounting extends far beyond simply generating numbers. It is about supporting good financial stewardship – one of the key tools needed to maximise impact.

Box 14.1   Definition of management accounting

The application of the principles of accounting and financial management to create, protect, preserve and increase value so as to deliver that value to stakeholders of profit and not-for-profit enterprises, both public and private. Management accounting is an integral part of management requiring the identification, generation, presentation, interpretation and use of information relevant to:

- *Formulating business strategy*
- *Planning and controlling activities*
- *Decision-making*
- *Efficient resource usage*
- *Performance improvement and value enhancement*
- *Safeguarding tangible and intangible assets*
- *Corporate governance and internal control.*

Chartered Institute of Management Accountants, 2000, pp. 15–16

So, what should a financial steward be looking for to make the management accounts successful? The information contained in the management accounts, and the advisory service that should accompany that information, must demonstrate eight characteristics (see box 14.2). We now consider each of these in turn.

Relevant

Management accounts must refer to whatever financial information the reader needs to plan and control the financial resources for which they are accountable. That may mean a cost centre report – but if the management accounting team members interpret it as such, then they had better make sure that they are correct in doing so. They need to ask, 'Who am I doing this for, and what information can I provide that will make a crucial difference to the quality of the decisions they have to make?'

Box 14.2   The eight characteristics of successful management accounts

1. Relevant
2. Up to date
3. Accurate
4. Intelligible
5. Accessible
6. Informative
7. In context
8. Dynamic

The issues that may require most attention are those raised in part 2 on funds and assets. Understanding and managing cash flow may be a much more serious issue for the organisation than income and expenditure. Is the balance sheet position satisfactory? Is there adequate debtor or creditor control? What impact have changes in the market value of the investment portfolio had on the reserves position? Has each restricted fund been used in accordance with the wishes of the donor? If these are the critical questions, the key financial information tool – the management accounts – must provide the answers.

Up to date

How quickly can the decision makers in the organisation see the management accounts? Typically this will take place 10 to 20 days after the end of the month. Many organisations accept management accounting deadlines that result in their making decisions using information that is six weeks out of date. If it is the middle of the month, and the management accounts are published monthly but have not yet been published for the previous month in your organisation, then yours is one of them.

How many well-run organisations rely on six-week-old information in order to make decisions? It is not necessary. Any well-organised competent finance team should be able to produce information within three to five working days, and their readers must be dissuaded from believing that somehow the circumstances of their particular organisation make this standard impossible. The production of fast actuals is a crucial component of the methodology: they provide the best indicator of where the organisation is now. Tight reporting deadlines can be achieved, even for international organisations. Worldwide multi-currency organisations should be aiming for management accounts deadlines of five working days at most, national and single-site operations less. Technology should enable this to be reduced further, to the point where management accounts are available online in real time.

Achieving deadlines

Achieving such tight deadlines requires discipline and a clear sense of what information is important, and what information isn't. This requires excellent information systems, both to generate and communicate information. There are a number of critical success factors.

- Get the culture of the organisation right. This is the most important factor. Buy-in is needed from the top on the importance of ensuring fast, accurate publishing of management accounting information. The more valuable the management accounts prove to be, the more the operational management will demand the information they provide.
- Restrict the management accounts to key data only. Operating sites should get the key information to the location of consolidation quickly – detail and hardcopy can follow later.
- Reconcile the balance sheet after the income and expenditure information is published, if it cannot be done before. There is a risk that the key summary

data published is inaccurate – errors that would be picked up when the detailed reconciliation work is done. However, the relevant question is whether the error is likely to be of a magnitude that would change the decisions made in its ignorance. Trade 100 per cent accuracy for speed.

- Keep on top of the trial balance by dealing with queries and reconciliations as quickly as possible – and certainly before a further month's data obscures it.
- Ensure commitment to getting the accounts information processed on time throughout the organisation.
- Get the finance team committed to delivering a high-quality service to the organisation, and recognise their achievement when they do it.

Do not underestimate the importance that should be attached to understanding quickly where the organisation is now. It is difficult to steward the organisation forward in the appropriate direction if information is not available to identify where it is currently. There is definitely a trade-off between accuracy and timeliness. The more accurate the recipient wants the information to be, the longer they are going to have to wait to get it. Delaying the publication of management accounts in order to ensure greater accuracy can be justified only if that greater accuracy would affect the decisions that will be made using those accounts. That trade-off needs to be understood well enough to determine at what point further accuracy will no longer affect the decision to be made.

Accurate

Arguably, to produce inaccurate information is worse than not producing any information at all. Accuracy in this context means not only minimising the data-handling errors – miscoding, data entry errors, incorrect totalling or transfer of figures – but also eliminating errors of omission.

Intelligible

Irrespective of how timely and accurate the accounts are, if they don't inform the reader then they are not useful. Many management accounts contain too many numbers, presented in a layout that discourages the reader. It must be clear who the audience is, and what information they need to make the decisions expected of them. Trustees need different information to that which is needed by a manager, and it is usually appropriate to present financial information (whether actual results, or future plans or forecasts) to trustees on only one or two pages: like the format of a SOFA and a balance sheet, for example. If nothing else, that absence of detail forces the trustees to focus on the big picture.

It is worth considering why many recipients of management accounts struggle to use them effectively. Often, it is because the accounts obscure the key messages in unintelligible language or presentation. Do not accept the word of the accountant who tells you that the finances are complicated to understand. Demand simplicity.

Accessible

The user of the accounts should be able to access this management tool at the time they need the information – not when the system is designed to prepare it. That is unlikely to coincide with the pre-set monthly management accounting reporting deadlines. At the very least, 'on tap' must mean being able to request a standard report when it is needed, but it should mean much more than that. Staff should be able to have appropriate access to relevant parts of the accounting system from their screens, enabling them to make ledger enquiries or request standard reports. There is no reason why this self-service approach should not extend into data entry or report design, provided that appropriate controls are in place.

Informative

The accounts must tell the reader what is actually going on. For example, what do the users of the information understand 'actual' to mean? Expenditure and payments are not the same thing – but do readers realise that?

In context

Management accounts that report that '£x has been spent on legal costs' explain very little. The information begins to be interesting, and useful, once the reader compares that figure to a benchmark. It is not possible to reach a judgement about whether expenditure of £x on legal costs was satisfactory without a context. However, even with a good financial context, it is not possible to have a thorough understanding of the financial performance of the organisation without understanding the operational performance as well. Not only is it inadequate to know only that £x has been spent on legal costs, it is also inadequate to know that expenditure of £y on legal costs was planned. We need an explanation as to why £x has been spent on legal costs. What impact has this expenditure had?

We have already explored some of the challenge this creates at a strategic level, as organisations seek to climb the results chain and understand their influence on beneficiaries. Equally, at a more operational level it may be very difficult to identify what impact a particular activity has had on the organisation's intended beneficiaries – but at the very least there should be a clear sense of the outputs from the activity. That might mean knowing how many delegates attended a conference, how many people are subscribing to a publication, how many calls have been taken by the helpline, how many blind children have received mobility training and so on. In each case, these measures of output should be accompanied by context. How many were expected? How many were achieved in the last year or month? How many do the best in the business have? Why not compare the income-generating performance against the best in the business?

It may not be possible to match that performance, but it is an informative exercise to ask why another organisation can achieve a higher level of excellence, in order to understand the answer and to see what can be done to close the gap. The performance of athletes is always compared to their personal best, or to the relevant record performance for the event. Why not management accounts?

One answer may be paucity of benchmark data, as we shall see.

Using benchmarks

The use of benchmarks to aid performance assessment has been growing steadily in recent years, promoted vigorously by, among others, the Beyond Budgeting Round Table, the Hackett Group and the American Productivity and Quality Center (APQC). Benchmarking refers to 'the process of continuously comparing and measuring against other organisations anywhere in the world to gain information on philosophies, policies, practices, and measures which will help an organisation take action to improve its performance' (APQC, n.d., n.p.). Benchmarks provide points of reference; standards against which to compare results. There are three comparators.

1. **Self over time:** The yardstick in comparing the unit or organisation against itself is to look for improvement over time.
2. **Internal comparisons:** These go beyond measures of self-improvement or deterioration over time, by comparing against internal peers. Unit-to-unit comparisons provide powerful incentives for performance improvement. (This is explored further in chapter 16.)
3. **External comparisons:** Looking outside the organisation offers the potential of being the most valuable comparator, enabling the organisation to assess its performance against other organisations that are regarded as 'the best', the highest performers in either overall results or in particular operations/processes (see box 14.3).

Box 14.3   External benchmarking

Most leading organizations use some form of external benchmarking, whether it be high-level metrics based on best-in-class industry standards or more specific KPIs based on operational measures. Benchmarking at the operational level entails analyzing in detail the performance of companies deemed to be best-in-class in performing certain processes and activities.

Hope, 2006, p. 170

Benchmarking to expose internal deficiencies or highlight high-quality practices in-house can be highly appealing – almost seductive. It has obvious merit – and in the right circumstances, its results can be an extremely powerful stimulus to performance improvement. In the political arena, in which public sector and not-for-profit organisations have to operate, the results of benchmarking can also provide the crucial legitimacy for action.

The secret to using benchmarks successfully – as with all measurement aids – is to appreciate both their purpose and their limitations. The difficulty of ensuring that inter-organisational comparisons are fair (organisations often claim to be unique, making benchmarking difficult or unhelpful) emphasises the key role of benchmarks – to provoke assessment of the adequacy of relative performance:

> *The objectives of the benchmark are to establish relative performance, not develop an absolutely precise measure. By setting appropriate expectations up front, it is possible to agree that a reasonable degree of accuracy but not absolute precision is all that is needed. Establishing the benchmark as 'directionally correct' is quite sufficient to allow an organization to identify and prioritize the opportunities for improvement.*
>
> Axson, 2003, p. 229

Nevertheless, benchmarking can be an expensive, time-consuming distraction from the often already-known need to improve performance in-house. Participating in benchmarking exercises must not be at the expense of taking prompt action to address obvious performance deficiencies. Rather, the two can be tackled simultaneously. Formal benchmarking may not be necessary: informal exchanges may suffice, and the public and not-for-profit sectors offer considerable scope for collaboration between organisations by sharing data, practices and experiences.

Dynamic

The accounts and the advice must be alive and forward-looking, and must take into account the inevitability that unexpected events will affect performance.

THE FORMAT AND STRUCTURE OF MANAGEMENT ACCOUNTS

Fundamental to the success in generating useful management accounts for the reader is being clear about what information they want. The data must then be put into the accounting system in a way that enables it to be extracted in the format they want. As already acknowledged, trustees require different management accounts from managers. Each requires a different level of detail. It may be helpful to think of a hierarchy of detail, with the accounts becoming more summarised at each level until, ultimately, expenditure can be quoted as a single figure for the whole organisation or group (see fig. 14.1).

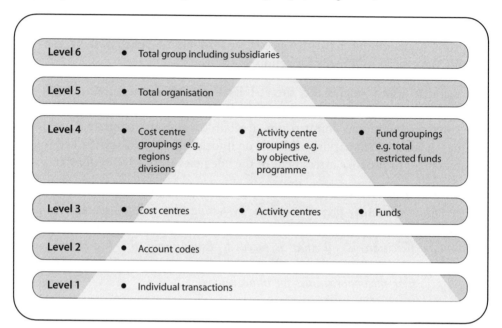

Fig. 14.1 A hierarchy of detail

- **Level 1:** The base level is that of the individual transaction. All the accounts rely on the base level of data entry: from it, all the summary information must be generated. At its simplest, the accounts could be a list of the individual transactions entered.
- **Level 2:** The first level of summary is to group transactions by account code. This is the conventional nominal account code, giving a traditional classification of expenditure. It explains what the money has been spent on (for example, salaries or rent).
- **Level 3:** The third level is to group account codes into some form of classification which reflects units that can be managed discretely. There are usually three types of classification needed at this level. Most typically, this means categorising expenditure into cost centres that reflect the operational structure of the organisation. However, it can also mean activity centre. This classification groups costs into the activities by which the organisation meets its objectives to beneficiaries (see box 14.4). It tells the reader what money has been spent *for*, rather than *on*. The third classification of costs at this level could be by fund. In complying with the requirements of fund accounting, this classification groups costs (and income) into the funds by which the organisation must account to donors.
- **Level 4:** This level groups cost-centre or activity-centre totals into broader categories, such as regions or divisions (in the case of cost centres), or perhaps

into the objectives (in the case of activity centres – for example, education and support for beneficiaries).

- **Level 5:** This level combines these category totals into a single organisation figure.
- **Level 6:** This level adds in any subsidiary figures, to give a group total.

Creating the right coding structure is absolutely critical to the success of producing such a hierarchy of management accounts. If a changed coding structure is needed, it is much easier to do the hard thinking up front before going live than to do it piecemeal later. Nevertheless, it is inevitable that users of the system and codes learn as they go. For example, adopting an activity-based costing system, with each transaction coded to one of a number of predetermined activities, may not be easy. It may be difficult to reach a sensible classification of activities. Some activities are easy to define (such as one-off income-generating events) but others are not (such as general parliamentary activity undertaken to influence and inform policy-makers).

Ideally, each level 4 activity would have a unique link to one objective – but how should the organisation account for activities that straddle more than one objective? It will need some sensible bases for allocating costs by activity.

> **Box 14.4 Activity classification of costs**
>
> An 'activity classification of costs' is the aggregation of costs incurred in pursuit of a defined activity (e.g. provision of services to elderly people or counselling), and is achieved by adding together all the costs (salaries, rents, depreciation, etc) relating to that specific activity.
>
> The three main 'high level' activities that charities preparing accruals accounts will report on are generating funds, charitable activity and governance costs of the charity.
>
> *Charity Commission, 2005, p. 65*

Management and statutory accounts

Recognising that readers of management accounts and readers of statutory accounts may well be two different audiences, many organisations produce the two types of information in significantly different formats. This makes sense if the statutory accounts do not categorise income or expenditure in the most useful way for management use. However, it would be worth checking that this is true before devoting time and energy to generating management accounts formats that differ from the statutory ones, and then being obliged to reconcile the two. The format of Sightsavers International's top-level management accounts is almost identical to that of its statutory accounts (see box 14.5).

> **Box 14.5   Sightsavers International's internal and external SOFA**
>
> Sightsavers International publishes two versions of the SOFA as part of its management accounts: an internal version, reflecting the organisational division of accountability for income and expenditure (with expenditure classified by cost centre), and an external version (which presents the same data classified by activity in accordance with statutory requirements). The internal SOFA report forms the apex of the management accounts reporting pyramid on expenditure within the charity. On a single page, it provides information at levels 4, 5 and 6 of the hierarchy described in figure 14.1.

Managers and trustees must have a continuous understanding of what impact the resource allocation decisions that they take would have on the statutory accounts. It is highly desirable that the top-level management accounts are presented in a similar format to those of the statutory accounts, for two reasons.

- It minimises the risk of misunderstanding, which can occur when the statutory and management accounts look very different. Much time can be taken up trying to reconcile management accounts and statutory accounts.
- It forces the readers to focus on few numbers – the numbers that will make the crucial difference.

Accounting by fund and activity

We have already seen the importance of understanding how the various activities in the organisation are being funded (see chapter 7 on funds). The organisation must understand 'what is paying for what' – as demonstrated by the format of the SOFA prepared by UK charities, which requires columnar analysis by type of fund.

In a similar way, one way of ensuring that the question of 'what is paying for what' is understood is to present the income and expenditure results in the form of a two-dimensional matrix: funds appear on one axis, and either cost type (for example, salaries) or activity on the other (see fig. 14.2). This approach enables the reader to see whether restricted funds are fully covering the costs of the activities for which they are earmarked, and how those precious unrestricted funds are being used. However, it may not be possible or appropriate to identify which funds are being used at the time that expenditure is incurred (see matching funds and activities, p. 110).

	Fund 1	Fund 2	Fund 3	Fund 4	Total funds
Activity 1					
Activity 2					
Activity 3					
Activity 4					
Total activities					

Fig. 14.2 Expenditure by fund matrix

COMMUNICATING MANAGEMENT ACCOUNTS

Presentation of the management accounts is critical if the reader is to feel enthusiastic about the information they receive. A typical set of management accounts is communicated in a written report format that shows actual results versus budget both for the latest month and cumulatively, the annual budget and, perhaps, the projected full year actual. However, the philosophy of dynamic adaptation required by the methodology requires rather more imaginative thinking about how best to communicate the key financial information with which decisions will be made. Alternative ways of presenting the results, using trends, graphs and face-to-face presentations, must be experimented with.

Consider the simple table shown below (fig. 14.3). It could be an extract from most organisations' management accounts reports, generated each month. This example, which reports actual expenditure results as at the end of the third quarter of the financial year, Year 4, shows two pieces of data: expenditure in Q3 and the cumulative expenditure year to date (YTD).

The actual levels of expenditure might be compared to a budget – for the quarter and, more often, for the full financial year. YTD expenditure will often be expressed in terms of a 'burn rate', showing the

£m	Year 4 Q3	
	Last Q	YTD
	————	————
Expenditure	19.8	58.2

Fig. 14.3 Expenditure example 1

percentage of budget, or of the fund balance, spent so far in the year. By implication, any YTD information orientates the reader towards the financial year end. That can be important, as expenditure must not exceed fund balances – but in truth, with such limited information, very little understanding of what is really going on is possible. Only rudimentary analysis and interpretation can be achieved.

By adding more reference points, the organisation can provide a better context for learning how well the spending unit or organisation is performing. Consider figure 14.4. Figure 14.3 has now been augmented with two additional data references: the cumulative total of expenditure incurred in the last four quarters, and the expenditure charged in the financial year Year 3. Expenditure of £81.0 million straddles two financial years, being the sum of the final quarter of Year 3 and the first three quarters of Year 4.

£m	Year 4 Q3			Year 3
	Last Q	YTD	Last 4Q	4Q
Expenditure	19.8	58.2	81.0	75.7

Fig. 14.4 Expenditure example 2

By framing actual expenditure in four-quarter totals, the reader is able to assess performance in relation to other figures that are typically presented in annual totals. These include prospective totals (such as financial year targets or estimates) as well as historic totals (such as the level of expenditure in the last full financial year, Year 3, as shown in the table). The four-quarter total provides a clear picture of financial changes since the last statutory year end. In this example, the growth in expenditure during Year 4 becomes apparent. The consistent use of a four-quarter total helps to steward spending along a desired trajectory. For example, it is very obvious what direction spending must take if the aim is to avoid a year-on-year increase in expenditure.

Trend analyses

While two data points enable comparisons to be made, they are insufficient to enable conclusions about trends to be drawn. It is trends that provide the crucial insights into performance over time. Organisations need to be looking to achieve continuous improvement over time. 'Is performance improving?' is one of the critical questions that they must be asking continually.

Trends are important for a number of reasons (see box 14.6). First, at their most basic level, they enable the reader to see whether the factor being tracked (in this example, expenditure) is increasing or decreasing over time and, if so, how quickly or slowly this has occurred. By assessing the indicator's movement over time, it is possible to

> **Box 14.6   The value of trend data**
>
> *Trends in observed rates provide invaluable information for needs assessment, program planning, program evaluation, and policy development activities. Examining data over time also permits making predictions about future frequencies and rates of occurrence.*
>
> *Rosenberg, 1998, p. 191*

make judgements about the possible impact of a particular event, such as a change in policy or the launch of a new programme. It is only by following the trend in data over time that the organisation can assess whether the action being taken is having the desired impact.

In addition, when comparing data of one factor against other benchmarks, assessing a trend over time rather than making the comparison solely at one point in time reduces the risk of making a misleading assessment. One data point is insufficient for meaningful performance assessment.

Finally, trends enable changes in both absolute and relative results to be reviewed. Two data sets may both show declining trends, but there may be a reduction in the discrepancy between the two.

Once the data shown in figures 14.3 and 14.4 is presented as part of a longer trend, it becomes a potent management tool. In figure 14.5 the previous data at the end of Year 4 Q3 is incorporated into a series of trends extending back seven quarters, to the start of Year 3. The scope to prepare meaningful analytics has now increased significantly. This has the following impact.

- Patterns emerge. Note, for example, the quarter-on-quarter growth in expenditure during each financial year. Both years show relatively low expenditure in Q1.
- Specific comparisons are possible. For example, a comparison of Q1, Q2 and Q3 in Year 4 with the equivalent quarters in Year 3 reveals expenditure increasing.
- Showing data in short time periods (in this case, in quarters) as well as annual aggregates provides two perspectives. The quarter-by-quarter trend will highlight quickly the impact of decisions about expenditure. Shifts in expenditure will, by definition, appear more marked in the first column of data than in the rolling four-quarter total column. However, the latter offers a better sense of the trend over the medium term.

£m	Expenditure		
	Last Q	YTD	Last 4Q
	————	————	————
Year 3 Q1	16.3	16.3	77.9
Year 3 Q2	18.0	34.3	77.1
Year 3 Q3	18.6	52.9	76.1
Year 3 Q4	22.8	75.7	75.7
Year 4 Q1	17.4	17.4	76.8
Year 4 Q2	20.9	38.3	79.7
Year 4 Q3	19.8	58.2	81.0
......			
Year 6 Q4			90.0

Fig. 14.5 Expenditure example 3

- By presenting data over more than one financial year, the focus on the financial year end (Year 3 Q4 in the shaded row in figure 14.5) reduces. Q4 becomes just another data point. Instead, attention can focus on the medium-term trend. If the organisation wants to place particular emphasis on the end-of-year position, it can highlight the relevant data, as shown in the table.
- The trend data can be presented alongside a target or planned result. This can be powerful, illustrating starkly what has to be accomplished to reach that figure. Imagine, for example, that policy-makers have decided to invest additional funds into the particular sector or programme represented by figure 14.5. The inclusion of an annual expenditure target of £90 million by the end of, say, Year 6 signals that a significant growth in expenditure above current levels is required. Sightsavers International uses this approach in reporting progress in relation to financial performance indicators. The eye can follow the recent history of performance in relation to the selected financial indicators and consider the adequacy of the performance in the context of a pre-defined future target.

A variation on the above is to present both historic and prospective perspectives in the same table. This can be done by showing actual results for completed periods and forecasts in future periods. As each quarter is completed, actual results replace forecast ones. Both could be shown next to each other in relation to the latest quarter, as indicated by the two highlighted rows in figure 14.6. In this example, actual expenditure in Q3 (£19.8 million) was less than the forecast of £20.1 million.

Using graphics

Pictures often give a clearer message than numbers or words. If used selectively for the critical information only, graphic representation of financial information can be a very useful addition to the management accounts portfolio. Consider figure 14.7, which reproduces the quarterly data shown in figure 14.5 for Year 3 and Year 4. In addition, it includes two earlier years of data by quarter, thereby giving a continuous quarter-by-quarter trend since the beginning of Year 1: a total of 15 quarters.

£m	Expenditure	
	Last Q	Last 4Q
	▬	▬
Year 3 Q4 Actual	22.8	75.7
Year 4 Q1 Actual	17.4	76.8
Year 4 Q2 Actual	20.9	79.7
Year 4 Q3 Actual	19.8	81.0
Year 4 Q3 F/cast	20.1	81.2
Year 4 Q4 F/cast	23.1	81.3
Year 5 Q1 F/cast	17.7	81.6
Year 5 Q2 F/cast	21.5	82.2

Fig. 14.6 Expenditure example 4

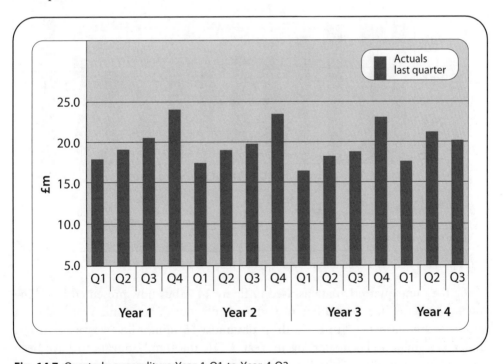

Fig. 14.7 Quarterly expenditure Year 1 Q1 to Year 4 Q3

The expenditure pattern within each financial year that was referred to earlier is now very stark. Within each year, during the Year 1 to Year 3 period, expenditure shows a quarter-on-quarter growth, culminating in a surge in the final quarter. The trend is a typical one in organisations that are focused on the financial year end, and that trigger 'spend it or lose it' behaviour on the part of spenders. However, expenditure in Year 4 Q3 (the final quarter shown) breaks the pattern, falling short of the Q2 total. Is this a blip, or the emergence of a new trend? The answer is not yet apparent – but the question warrants discussion.

However, the most important trend may not even be visible yet in either the data table or graphic format. This trend is not represented by the pattern of expenditure quarter by quarter – it is the medium-term trend that results from those quarterly results. In this example, this trend is pronounced, as can be seen in figure 14.8. The figure captures a rolling picture of four-quarter totals, as in the right-hand column of figure 14.5.

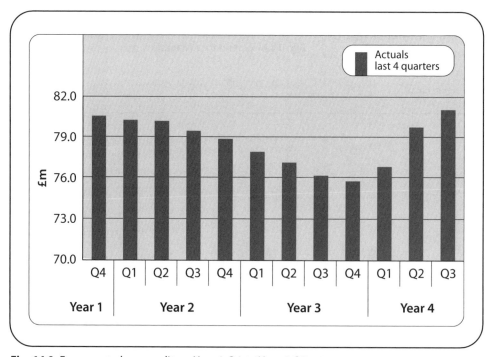

Fig. 14.8 Four-quarterly expenditure Year 1 Q4 to Year 4 Q3

Using the same quarterly data as used in figure 14.7, but now presented in rolling four-quarter totals, a very different pattern is obvious. Year 2 and Year 3 show a steady decline in expenditure – a drop of almost £5 million in two years, to just under £76 million. Then, starting in Year 4 Q1, the trend appears to have been reversed dramatically. With three successive quarters of annual growth, a new trend has started. Some event or events have triggered a change in expenditure direction – whether intended or not.

Note the effect of the choice of scale on the value axis (Y axis). Scaling the axis from £70 million rather than £0 exaggerates the relative change in the bars. Expenditure in the four quarters to Year 3 Q4 appears to be about half the level of the four quarters to Year 4 Q3, although the actual difference is less than 7 per cent. The scale can help focus attention on the key issues, but it does risk misleading the reader.

Many management accounts reports focus on explaining why the expenditure incurred in one particular quarter or year differs from that in the previous period or the equivalent period one year earlier. Such preoccupation may impede a clear understanding of the real trend.

Face-to-face presentations

One of the key messages of this book is the importance and power of dialogue in managing performance. As far as possible, information should be seen as a resource for all that is made openly accessible without compromising individual privacy. That extends to provision of news. The methodology requires an organisation's staff, management and trustees to have a good understanding of its financial position. If there is bad news, they need to hear it.

One option is to communicate orally – in the form, say, of a monthly 20-minute management accounts surgery to which staff are invited. At the surgery, the relevant management can provide a headline-only overview of the income and expenditure results, and can talk through the balance sheet slowly and simply. They can outline any key financial decisions taken by the trustees, and their impact on the overall financial position of the organisation, such as reserves levels. It is also an opportunity for staff to quiz management on issues affecting the financial performance and state of play of the organisation, or to obtain clarification on how to use the management accounts reports that they receive as a manager. Sophisticated presentation tools are not necessary for such an approach – a flipchart will do.

Access to management accounts

The more the user of the management accounts owns the accounts, the more they will value the information they provide as a decision-making aid. Increasingly, the supplier–customer relationship between the finance team and the decision maker can be modified, in an effort to make the user as self-sufficient as possible. Self-sufficiency might be demonstrated by expecting the user to be involved in, or even lead, the following sorts of tasks:

- designing reports or coding structures
- inputting data
- generating reports
- accessing the accounting system to make enquiries.

There is no reason not to give the users appropriate access to the accounting system so that they can access information whenever they wish to, rather than according to a predetermined management accounts publication timetable.

UNDERSTANDING THE PRESENTATION OF INFORMATION AS ACTUALS

It is worth stressing the importance of being clear about what information is presented as actual results. Are the readers of the organisation's financial information clear what is meant when they see a column headed 'actual'? In part 2, we saw the distinction that must be made between income and expenditure that appear on the SOFA and cash transactions. Under an accrual accounting policy (see below), expenditure will include non-cash transactions, such as depreciation and accruals, but will not include cash transactions such as purchasing property and equipment and other fixed assets.

Accounting for transactions

Good financial control means knowing what funds have been received, and what has happened to them. The earlier it is known that some of those funds received have been spent (or at least earmarked), the less likely it is that the organisation's decision makers will believe that those funds are still available at their discretion. Throughout the period between making the commitment and meeting the liability, there is a risk of overestimating the size of the funds available. The longer the gap, the greater the risk. What the reader of the management accounts sees in the 'actual' column will depend on the method of accounting for transactions that is adopted (see fig. 14.9). If the reader does not clearly understand what transactions are included, there could be a serious misinterpretation of the true financial position.

Cash accounting

Using a cash accounting policy, an amount will appear in the actuals column as expenditure only once a payment has been made – for example, once a cheque has been written. This may be some time after the legal liability has been incurred, and well after a commitment has been made to spend the funds. If management accounts only reflect the commitment once the liability has been met, then the risk of overstating the 'free' funds is considerable.

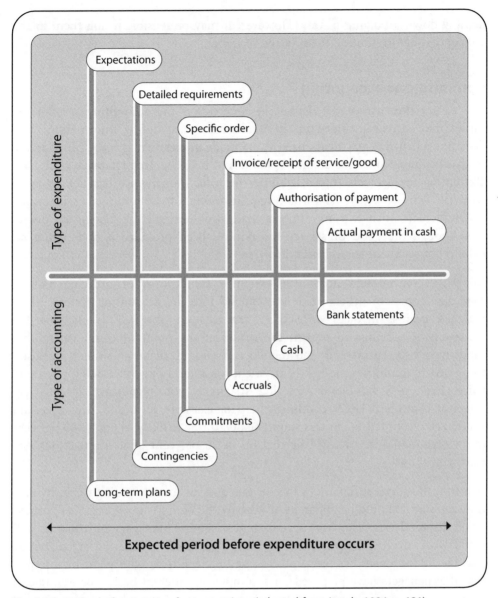

Fig. 14.9 Method of accounting for transactions (adapted from Lynch, 1994, p. 131)

Accruals accounting

The first step in rectifying the risk of overstating 'free' funds is to move to accruals accounting – by accruing liabilities when they are incurred, rather than recognising them only when they are met. This means, for example, charging invoice values as expenditure, and coding payments to creditor balances. It is worth looking at the flow of documentation through the organisation. Often, invoices are routed first to the recipient of the good and service, and may sit halfway down a bulging in-tray. However, it may be sensible to log them in the system first before routing them to the recipient.

Commitment accounting

The earlier the invoice details can be entered on the accounting system, the earlier they can be included in the management accounting information. This does not mean that payments need to be made any earlier. Invoices provide the ready document to enable creditor liabilities to be recognised relatively easily, but accounting for accruals (those liabilities for which an invoice has not yet been received) is more tricky. This would require a switch to commitment accounting, where 'actuals' include commitments made (for example, by placing an order) even though the good or service has not yet been provided and therefore no liability for payment has yet been incurred.

Adopting commitment accounting requires some form of ordering system. Typically, copies of orders made are entered into the accounting system, to be matched against invoices once these are received. As well as enabling the management accounts to inform the reader at the point of commitment that funds have been earmarked, and therefore are not 'available' for other purposes, using orders minimises the risk of payment for a good or service being processed twice. Even if a full-blown ordering system is not introduced, it can help financial controls if larger commitments (for example, all orders over a certain value) are accounted for in this way. The 80/20 rule is likely to apply: 80 per cent of an organisation's costs will be tied up in 20 per cent of its transactions. So, start with those.

Just from this brief summary of the various options for accounting for individual transactions, it should be apparent how easily the figures shown as 'actual' can be misunderstood. This can have serious repercussions. Managers and finance staff could work at cross purposes for months, unwittingly comparing actual results that the finance team has prepared on one financial basis with plans or forecasts that the managers have prepared on a completely different basis. For example, if forecasts were prepared on an accruals basis and actuals on a cash basis, it would not be surprising if significant differences often arose between the two.

For this reason, an important rule of thumb is to make sure that actuals and forecasts or plans are prepared on the same accounting basis, if the latter are to be of any value in informing the decision maker. Many readers of financial information simply are not aware of the different methods of accounting that could be used, and have conceptual difficulty grasping how, for example, depreciation of assets is accounted for. So, it is crucial that the reader is guided and supported in interpreting the accounting information they receive, and yet most finance professionals allow themselves so little time to carry out this task.

What effect would it have on the quality of decision making if the time currently spent on generating information was instead devoted to interpreting it?

Key stewardship questions

1. Do the organisation's management accounts have the eight required characteristics?

2. Are both the format and structure of the management accounts the most appropriate for their audiences?

3. Is the internal communication of management accounting information as effective as it could be?

4. Are actual transactions recorded using an appropriate accounting policy that is understood by the organisation's decision makers?

5. How does the organisation intend to achieve these aims?

15 Step 2: forecast

SEEING WHAT'S AHEAD

Step 2 changes the perspective on financial management, and looks forward. Its purpose is to collect as much relevant information as possible about what is ahead. The organisation can then use this information alongside its understanding about where it has come from and where it is now (step 1), to decide on an appropriate way forward (steps 3 to 5). The first action within the step is to answer two questions.

1. What financial resources can the organisation reasonably anticipate having available in the future?
2. What expenditure commitments has the organisation already made that will use some of these resources?

This step is about forming a view about the future – an assessment that needs to be made continually. The ongoing reassessment of the future is incorporated into updated forecasts of the future income, expenditure and cash results (and any other important financial performance) that can be reasonably expected. These forecasts serve decision making.

> **Box 15.1   Definition of 'forecast'**
>
> *A financial view of the future derived from a manager's best opinion of the 'most likely outcome' given the known information at the time it is prepared. Thus it should be unbiased, reflect all known events (good and bad), and be realistic.*
>
> *Hope and Fraser, 1999, p. 7*

THE PURPOSE OF FORECASTING

The purpose of financial forecasting needs to be clear in all participants' minds. In this methodology, the forecast's only rationale is to help guide decision making about resource allocation. If forecasts are not influencing decisions, then they have no value. If this is the case, they can be abandoned. However, if you do use forecasts, make sure that they don't become negotiated targets against which management is accountable.

Forecasts help an organisation to understand what resources it can reasonably anticipate having available in the future. At any time, this sum will be a composite of fund balances that are available now and future income that it can reasonably anticipate generating. The organisation can use this information to inform decisions about how much of these resources it can responsibly afford to commit now.

Bearing in mind the continuous need for organisations to have a short-term operational focus and a medium-term strategic outlook (see fig. 13.3, p. 194), forecasts help decision makers to maintain short-term control and set medium-term strategic direction.

Although the only resources that can be spent now are the existing fund balances, the decisions about what future income to commit now will need to be informed by expectations about future resource availability. If the financial stewards know that the organisation has some sizeable financial liabilities to meet on the horizon, and that income streams will dry up, they will probably be far more cautious in their judgement about deploying resources for other high priorities than they would otherwise.

Box 15.2   The price of inaccurate forecasts

Large forecast errors can lead to significant budget management problems, such as expenditure arrears and a stop-and-go expenditure policy, and pose an important obstacle to the development of a meaningful medium-term budget plan. Moreover, unrealistic budget plans are inconsistent with basic principles of transparency and diminish public accountability of fiscal operations.

Danninger, 2005, p. 3

Armed with good forecasting information, decision makers can take action that is appropriate to the current and anticipated circumstances. The lack of such a radar screen – or an inaccurate one – can be costly both to operations and to the organisation's reputation (see box 15.2).

This means that the methodology requires judgements to be made about future income streams, along with establishing a clear understanding of the commitments already made. With these pieces of information in hand, it is possible to determine the level of resources that the organisation is likely to have to spend in the future, and therefore how much of those resources it is appropriate to commit now.

However, forecasting is not about crystal ball-gazing. There are too many variables influencing the future to be able to anticipate precisely what will happen. The forecaster can only take account of known events and accept that there will be some unknown circumstances that will affect the results. The greater the uncertainty, the greater the need for organisations to develop the following capabilities.

- **Absorptive capacity:** the capacity to assimilate new information quickly. Perfectly efficient forecasting incorporates new information instantly. In the real world, information gathering takes time, and it is worth assessing how actively the organisation is on the lookout for fresh signals, and how capable it is of digesting and translating that data into useful information for management. The faster an organisation's ability to react to new information, the less important is the need to forecast ahead. So, the first question to ask is 'Is the radar screen turned on?'

- **Management capacity:** the capacity to react appropriately, however unexpected the circumstance. How ready is the organisation to cope with the unexpected? Several factors contribute to establishing a dynamic, highly responsive state of readiness. These include the clarity of organisational purpose, values and strategic priorities; the degree of decentralisation of decision making; and the efficiency of business processes. This capacity is also cultural (see box 15.3).

- **Financial capacity:** the capacity to handle a variety of financial outcomes. Recall from chapter 13 the advice that organisations need to be able to cope with arriving at any of a variety of financial destinations that may result from taking certain action. It cannot be sensible practice to assume that action taken can only result in one outcome. For example, it is better to build in prudence to estimates

> **Box 15.3   Slow assimilation**
>
> *'We tend to break the good or bad news to ourselves slowly, taking too long to allow surprises to be incorporated into our forecasts' [Nordhaus, 1987, p. 673] … The evidence shows that forecasters are unwilling or unable to signal that the economy is heading down the wrong track until a crash is imminent; and even then they initially underestimate the extent of the damage.*
>
> Loungani and Rodriguez, 2008, n.p.

of future resource availability, and to face the possible prospect of greater than expected fund balances, than to base spending plans on highly ambitious, best-case income forecasts. The reserves policy adopted and executed is a critical component of establishing and maintaining this capability.

ELIMINATING FORECASTING BIAS

A good forecast describes what a forecaster expects to happen – not what they expect the recipient of the forecast to want to happen. It is an important difference. Honesty must replace the political gamesmanship that accompanies most budgeting and forecasting processes. This poses some tough challenges, as it is necessary to develop an internal culture that discourages playing such games. Hope and Fraser's definition of forecasting (see box 15.1) is a good one, highlighting the importance of basing the forecast on known information – however unpalatable that information might be.

Forecasts will be biased if there is an incentive for the forecaster to skew their best estimate in one direction or the other. Two causes illustrate this.

1. **The asymmetry of the cost of making forecasting errors:** The cost of actual results exceeding, or falling short of, the forecast may not be the same. As a result, managers may not have an incentive to provide unbiased forecasts; instead, the incentives may encourage them in either an optimistic or pessimistic direction. For example, if the cost of actual income falling short of forecast is greater than the cost of it exceeding the forecast, then the forecaster will have an incentive to reduce the risk of an income shortfall by offering a

prudent forecast. The higher the cost (whether political, economic or personal) of failing to deliver income forecasts, the greater the incentive to provide prudent forecasts in order to minimise the likelihood of a revenue shortfall. This explains Dorotinsky's counsel to beware of politicised forecasts (see box 15.4).

2. **The use of forecasts as targets:** Target-setters can overstate income forecasts or understate expenditure forecasts in order to create performance pressure. If they believe that the performance improvement from over- or under-forecasting outweighs the costs of reduced credibility (from an inaccurate forecast) – in other words, that the targets stimulate improved performance – then it becomes rational to bias forecasts intentionally. Two observations come from this point. First, the credibility of organisations is at least partly defined by the reliability of their plans: 'Have they done what they said they would do?' This is particularly true in the public sector, and does put pressure on organisations to hit the plan or forecast. Second, organisations do use targets as incentives in an effort to drive performance, however ambiguous the behaviour that such targets encourage in practice.

> **Box 15.4   Political estimates**
>
> *It is important to distinguish between political estimates – estimates of desired or hoped for growth – and sound estimates for budget development. The former are optimistic estimates prepared for public consumption ... to build optimism ... these are not good estimates to use in developing the budget.*
>
> Dorotinsky, 2004, p. 2

The challenge of cultivating and maintaining an environment that encourages and enables unbiased forecasting is a major one, intimately linked to the whole issue of the implicit or explicit performance contract that is in place. Those who request forecasts have to be clear why they are doing so. Any hint that the forecast will be used to measure the performance of the forecaster will create immediate incentives for bias.

Similarly, as discussed in chapter 11, demanding spending forecasts from units that have received single-year budget envelopes, with an implicit 'spend it or lose it' contract, provokes an obvious but important question: what is the incentive for the budget holder to forecast any level of spending other than the budgeted amount? If they forecast spending less than the budget, then they risk having their budget taken away or reduced in future years. On the other hand, if they forecast spending more than the budget, then they risk being criticised for exercising insufficient expenditure control.

FORECASTING CHARACTERISTICS

Before considering how to make judgements about future resources and current commitments, it is important to think about three characteristics of the forecasting process:

- how far forward to look (the forecasting timeframes)
- how often changes in the outlook should be reflected in judgements (updating forecasts)
- the level of detail required.

Each of these characteristics is explained below.

Forecasting timeframes

The question of how far forward to forecast must be determined by the following four factors.

1. How far into the future the organisation intends or needs to commit resources that are currently available now. To avoid the risk of giving stop–go messages to project managers mid-project, it is important to be clear about whether the organisation can underwrite the costs of the whole project before it starts – in other words, whether the costs could be financed from estimated future resources. If the organisation has to make three-year commitments, then that is the timeframe over which it must forecast resources before making those commitments.

2. The investment lead time that the organisation needs to establish new projects, activities and/or services. Resource availability guarantees need to be made to those within the organisation who are directly responsible for service provision, with sufficient lead time to enable new projects to be set up. The forecasts enable decision makers to give messages about the likely future resource availability so that the programme management can determine what level of activity to cultivate within their area. Without committing any funds, programme staff can be informed that overall programme growth of, say, 5 per cent per annum in expenditure terms would be realistic over the following three years. This enables the programme staff to be active in developing new partners and sowing the seeds of new projects that could be brought on-stream within two years.

3. The lead time that the organisation needs to make critical changes to the way it operates. Having, say, a three-year forecast of income enables the organisation's decision makers to ask a critical question. If that is the size (financially) that the organisation is likely to be in three years' time, what buttons need to be pressed now to enable it to manage that size most effectively? Research and development activities to grow a new income stream, create a new membership profile, or develop a new cadre of management (for example) will take several years to achieve.

4. How far forward the organisation's donors want to look, or want the organisation to look. If long-term funding agreements are being negotiated, the donor will want a long-term picture of how its funds will be used.

Within the overall forecasting timeframe of, say, three years, it is important to consider what time periods the forecasts should be broken into: should it be months, quarters, operating years? Reaching a conclusion will be helped by thinking about resource allocation decisions, public relations requirements and rolling forecasting.

Resource allocation decisions

Resource allocation decisions must be made with regard to not only how much resource there is to allocate, but also to when it is available to be allocated. The timing of cash flows is an important factor for all but the most cash-rich of organisations. The tighter the cash position, the more important the understanding of future cash movements. This means that, for treasury purposes, very short-term forecasts of receipts and payments (rather than income and expenditure) can be crucial if the organisation's financial stewards are to ensure that funds are in the right place at the right time. Tight treasury management will prevent cash from sitting idle, thus ensuring that it is working (in other words, generating interest) until it is needed. These forecasts could have a timeframe of just days or weeks, and will require updating daily.

In terms of the costs relating to individual projects, overall expenditure control may not require forecasts to be broken down into shorter timeframes than the total project life. As long as the overall estimated project cost is acceptable, there is no expenditure control issue. However, cash flow management will almost certainly demand some breakdown into shorter time periods. To the extent that the project is being financed from future income streams, it is critical that the timing of receipt of that income, and of its expenditure, is understood. The organisation cannot spend the income if it has not yet received it. So, the tighter the cash position, the shorter the forecasting timeframes will need to be.

Public relations requirements

While the activities of the organisation may not be run neatly in the timeframes of the organisation's statutory accounting year (resource management will need to reflect the nature of the organisation's activities, not the accounting calendar – see the specific projects on p. 236), the public relations aspect of the statutory accounts cannot be ignored. The results in this timeframe will be published in the public domain, and what those published accounts say does matter. To the extent that the financial stewards want or need to guide the organisation towards delivering a particular income and expenditure position, or balance sheet, in the statutory accounts, the decision makers will need to be conscious of what the forecast results in that timeframe would say.

Rolling forecasting

Chapter 11 identified the risks of focusing exclusively on the end of the financial year – a practice that falls into the 'brick wall' and 'diminishing horizon' traps. Using rolling forecasts enables leaders to overcome these two traps by maintaining a constant time horizon that straddles financial years (see fig. 15.1). Irrespective of when it is undertaken in the financial year, a rolling forecast offers the same perspective: one that is neither limited by the end-of-year brick wall, nor reduces over time. This maximises the near-term visibility of decision makers, offering the following important benefits.

- Rolling forecasts provide business intelligence beyond the financial year end, to support decision making. Decisions affecting this time period are informed ones.
- Rolling forecasts support an organisational culture that strives to maximise beneficiary impact, rather than one that focuses on hitting year-end input or output targets. For example, in choosing between spending in Q4 this year or Q1 next year, decision makers have the information that they need to decide when an action will best contribute to climbing the results chain. Without this outlook, any decision will be uninformed.

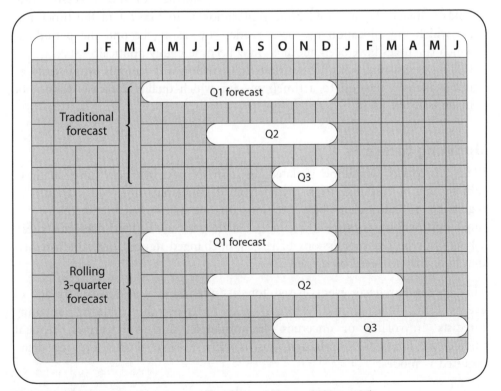

Fig. 15.1 Traditional forecast versus rolling forecast (Axson, 2003, p. 196)

However, introducing rolling forecasts is not easy, and not always sensible:

Box 15.5 Requirements for successful rolling forecasting

Rolling forecasts can have a place in the management process providing you heed certain design considerations:

- *Match your desire for detail with your predictive capability. Recognize that organization's ability to predict the future declines the further out you look; therefore demand less detail in the later periods of the forecast and add additional detail as your visibility improves*
- *Limit the time horizon of the rolling forecast to a period that is relevant for decision-making – for many companies this may only be one or two quarters.*

David Axson, n.d., n.p.

- While it makes sense to adopt rolling quarterly forecasts for short-term control, medium-term strategic direction-setting is best served by annual forecasts. The precision of adopting quarterly forecasting, say, three years ahead, is an illusion. It is neither feasible to forecast with such precision, nor useful to do so. Strategic direction-setting is not guided by quarter-to-quarter movements in forecasts.
- Rolling forecasting does not work well together with allocations denominated in relation to financial years. The natural tendency of the forecaster who holds a financial year-based budget allocation is to forecast in the timeframe for which the allocation has been made. Forecasting beyond the period for which resources have been allocated may become highly political.
- Rolling forecasting will offer spurious information if it requires estimates to be undertaken in relation to a timeframe for which quality forecasts cannot be made (see box 15.5).

Updating forecasts

Ideally, forecasts would be updated as soon as circumstances have changed, rather than in response to a predetermined timetable. It would certainly be regrettable to continue to base decisions on one assessment of the future if a more appropriate assessment could be made and used. This does not mean asking for repeated submissions of largely unchanged figures: only the forecasts that have changed need be revised.

This approach reflects events-based forecasting, where it is the occurrence of events (both internal and external) that provokes the value of updating forecasts. In volatile or uncertain circumstances, this may warrant frequent updates of forecasts – although this is only feasible if the level of detail required is modest.

Broad-brush forecasting: the level of detail required

A traditional budget would typically break down the total allocation of an operational unit (or cost centre) into detailed income or cost types, such as salaries or consumables. The real danger of adopting a rolling forecasting methodology is that the process, which used to be an annual exercise of planning in great detail what would happen, becomes instead a much more frequent exercise of similar effort. So, how does the organisation avoid producing four or more detailed budgets each year?

The key to success is to make forecasting broad brush and intuitive, rather than detailed and 'scientific'. Short-term forecasting for cash management purposes does require careful consideration (if cash is very tight, potentially thinking payment by payment). However, forecasting for any timeframe beyond that ought to be – and can be – a quick, top-level exercise completed by very few people.

The forecasting detail discussed at senior level may not need to extend beyond the detail included on summary financial information used by organisational leaders. A director should have a good intuitive feel as to how much is needed in their areas of accountability, given the current expectations of future activity.

When determining how to allocate resources, it is not necessary to produce a detailed forecast function-by-function, cost centre-by-cost centre and account code-by-account code. If there is any detailed forecasting being undertaken, it is in the area of income generation. What is needed is an assessment of future resource availability – not a forecast of how those available resources will be spent. Once a judgement about future resource availability is made, the expenditure 'forecast' is simply a top-level assessment of how those resources are likely to be distributed. It is about saying, for example, that the organisation expects to have £x million to spend, rather than forecasting how that allocation would be spent.

Encouraging managers to move from a tradition of preparing detailed, static budgets to one of submitting intuitive, broad-brush, rolling forecasts is not easy. Mindsets are deep-rooted, and managing the pace of change is important if staff members are to be engaged emotionally. Managers need to learn to trust their intuition. Many need the comfort of preparing the top number from detail – at least initially. Only the evidence of time, where it can clearly be demonstrated that intuitive feel is good enough, may give a manager the confidence to let go of the detail. They need to be sure that it is understood that they cannot forecast the future with 100 per cent accuracy, and that it does not matter if they do not. So, it is crucial to be able to dissociate accurate forecasting from performance measurement. Performance cannot be measured by the accuracy of a forecast, only in relation to the circumstances in which it was achieved.

FORECASTING FUTURE RESOURCE AVAILABILITY

The format of income and expenditure statements such as the SOFA risk misleading the reader, by implying that expenditure in the year is necessarily funded from the income received in the year. The requirement to show the balance of income less expenditure (operating inflow/outflow) encourages the reader to believe this.

As discussed in part 2, the reality, of course, is that there are also other crucial sources of funding: opening fund balances and, if necessary, borrowings. In assessing likely future resource availability, it is important to consider not only future income streams, but also how much – if any – of the fund balances held by the trustees could be expended.

Making reasonable assumptions

The aim is to identify how much resource the organisation is prepared to release for future expenditure now, recognising that some of those resources are secure (for example, some fund balances are already in the hand, while some future income may be contractually guaranteed), but that some – maybe the majority – is not.

This is about risk management. The organisation cannot commit more than it can guarantee to finance without the risk of having to renege on some of those commitments – not that minimising risk is appropriate in this case. If an organisation were to commit to spend only when income was safely in the bag, or was at least guaranteed to come (a risk-minimisation policy), it would be more likely to end up with unspent income than to have to exercise the opt-out clause on expenditure commitments previously made. Why? Because for most organisations, to assume no future income at all is unreasonably pessimistic.

The general advice to be given here must be to ensure that assumptions about future funding availability are reasonable rather than over-optimistic or pessimistic, and to understand the risk–return trade-off for the organisation (see box 15.6). At what point does the risk of over-committing funds that are not yet secure outweigh the returns (in the form of additional activity in

---

Box 15.6 The importance of realistic income forecasts

The estimates need to be the best, objective estimates possible by technical staff in order to form a sound basis for setting ... policy and for budget development.

Overly optimistic revenue estimates can lead to excessive spending.

By differentiating the different sources of revenue and their likelihood of materializing, better judgments can be used in setting fiscal policy as well as in ex post assessment of the quality of estimates used in budget formulation.

Dorotinsky, 2004, p. 4

furthering the objectives of the organisation) that could be offered if those funds were, in fact, to be generated?

Prudence will serve the financial steward well. It is much better for the organisation to find itself with more funds than expected than to deal with all the problems associated with being overstretched. Most organisations will find it relatively easy to increase the level of expenditure as a result of having cash in the bank (albeit perhaps over a long period of time, if they are to use it wisely) than to reduce raised expectations or possibly withdraw from existing commitments. It is possible to test the reasonableness of forecasts by placing them under the spotlight, exposing them to the scrutiny of others and the scope for benchmarking (see box 15.7).

Box 15.7   Contributors to assuring reasonableness of forecasts in the public sector

- *Comparison with private or other forecasts*
- *Vetting of forecasts through academic or non-government fora*
- *Early release of forecasts to Parliament and the public*
- *Using the median forecasts of several reputable non-government organizations as the government forecasts*
- *Technical rules for making the forecasts more conservative*
- *Economic updates prior to budget enactment that allow modifications to the budget proposals to fit emerging trends*

Dorotinsky, 2004, p. 3

The philosophy of the methodology is to allow future resources to be committed up to a level that could be underwritten in the event that the future income forecasts on which those commitments were predicated do not materialise. If insufficient income is generated, then the organisation's only sources of funding with which to underwrite expenditure commitments already made would be reserves and borrowings. The greater the organisation's ability to underwrite expenditure in the event of income not being generated, the more liberal it can be in determining the level of future resources that can be committed now.

The winning approach is undoubtedly to have unrestricted, general reserves to call on. With the confidence of those funds as contingency, the organisation can market itself vigorously to potential donors in an effort to secure the income that will render accessing the reserves unnecessary.

Forecasting income

The ability to forecast future income streams accurately is critically dependent on the degree of reliability inherent in the income stream. Some streams offer much greater certainty than others.

Reliable income streams

Ask a not-for-profit fundraiser how far into the future they can accurately estimate income streams and they will most likely say (and with some legitimacy) that the horizon quickly becomes hazy. Six months ahead may be as far as they can see. On the other hand, there may be particular income streams that are very reliable and predictable. Typically, the more committed the form of income, the greater the predictability.

Take direct marketing, for example. Organisations that are successful in fundraising through direct marketing are able to persuade an increasingly large proportion of their individual donors to support the organisation in a committed way by contributing a regular sum of money – for example, by direct debit. The payment continues indefinitely until the donor cancels the instruction. Very quickly, the organisation can build up a picture of the speed with which donors do cancel their payments, known as the attrition rate, and thereby make accurate forecasts forward of income from that source. Sensitivity testing of the key variables – the number of donors, the mean value of donation and the attrition rate – can be used to assess the volatility of the forecast to changed assumptions. Increasingly sophisticated techniques, such as lifetime value (see box 15.8), are being used in this field of fundraising to infer the future performance of donors.

> **Box 15.8   Lifetime value**
>
> *Lifetime value is the total net contribution that a donor generates during her/his lifetime on the donor list.*
>
> *Aldrich, 2007, p. 3*
>
> *LTV [Lifetime value] = The net contribution by each donor each year [×] the expected duration of the relationship in years [×] the discount rate*
>
> *Sargeant and Jay, 2004, p. 144*

Other sources of income

Forecasting of other sources of income may have to be less analytical. Restricted income – often agreed contractually, especially with the statutory funders – is predictable only until the end of an existing agreement. Beyond that the organisation may be required to tender competitively for future contracts and grants, a process that is by no means assured of success.

Legacy income is notoriously difficult to predict, and no wise organisation would base plans on the assumption that a sizeable legacy will appear in the future. Such an event would have to be treated as a bonus, and the sum handled in a manner that was appropriate at the time it happened.

Two sources of information can help forecasting legacy income. The first is past legacy income trends. Here, the question to ask is whether it is reasonable to expect the historic legacy income stream to continue into the future. Is there any reason why it would not? There may be. A large individual bequest may have distorted the overall picture, the size of the supporter base may have changed markedly, or the level of legacy promotion undertaken may have altered significantly. The second is the current notifications from solicitors of legacies that are yet to be received, although the size of the legacy (in the case of residual legacies) and the date at which it will be received can be very difficult to ascertain with any confidence.

Crucially, future investment income relies on the size of the capital sum to be invested and the future rates of return that the investments can attract.

Forecasting expendable reserves

If an organisation wants to estimate how much of its future reserves it can afford to expend, it must judge how large those reserves will be, and how large they should be, given the purpose for which they are held. This need not be complicated, and is only difficult if the current level of reserves is higher than the organisation would like. If it is not, there are no expendable reserves. Given that reserves policies are typically expressed in relation to percentage of expenditure, an organisation can make broad estimates of future expenditure levels simply from an understanding of likely future income streams and current reserves levels. A simple spreadsheet model would enable it to estimate how much of the reserves level is in excess of the stated policy at any point.

UNDERSTANDING EXPENDITURE COMMITMENTS

What is a 'commitment'? The methodology requires the financial steward to identify what costs the organisation is already obliged to incur at some point in the future. However, this is not a watertight definition: some judgement is required.

There may be some future costs towards which the organisation has a clear legal and/or moral obligation, and those commitments are relatively easy to identify. Less straightforward are all those costs for which there is no such obligation but that it would be reasonable to assume the organisation will have to bear: its intentions. What needs to be clear is what the organisation is already committed to spending – not what it anticipates that it will spend in a particular period.

Thinking in terms of commitments tends to lead, in turn, to an activity-based approach to costing. In practice, it is important to distinguish between individual initiatives or projects, with discrete costs that directly result from carrying out the project work; and general activity, which cannot be attributed neatly to any one project. Individual initiatives will typically have a finite life, with specific objectives and direct costs, while support activity tends to be ongoing.

Within individual cost centres, there is almost certainly a mix of the two types of activity, whether the cost centre's role is one of service delivery, income generation or administration and support. Identifying the costs to which the organisation is already committed is a task that needs to be addressed differently, depending on whether the reference is to specific projects or general activity.

Specific projects

The organisation should not have embarked on any initiative without some understanding (however broad) about its purpose, intended outcomes, expected length of life and cost implications. A project proposal should outline these areas. The perspective that needs to be adopted is the project life, not the accounting calendar – recognising that funding arrangements, or the project's activities, may require consideration over a period of time concurrent with the accounting calendar. In determining whether to begin a proposed project, the organisation needs to consider the implications through to the completion of the project, not just to the end of the next accounting period.

The work of many organisations is almost entirely project-based – with each project lasting, say, three to five years, with an agreement between the organisation and the local partner (through whom services will be provided) in place before it begins. This memorandum of understanding places moral commitments on both parties to deliver the objectives of the project over the project's lifetime. While there are get-out clauses relating to funding and *force majeure* circumstances that would enable the agreement to be terminated earlier than planned, this is very much seen as a last resort and is exercised infrequently. No project agreement is signed without a firm expectation that the project will be funded through to its completion, assuming satisfactory delivery of the project objectives.

The agreement does include indicative top-level costings, giving an overall project cost, and it is this project cost that is recognised as the organisation's financial commitment and the baseline against which any future changes in expected cost is assessed. These projects are not designed with the organisation's statutory accounting requirements in mind: the majority of the project agreements do not start in line with the start of the accounting year, and the project life never fits neatly within one statutory accounting year. The driving forces in project design and management are, rightly, the needs of the beneficiaries of the project, and the capacity of the partner organisation to meet those needs.

Specific projects, in areas such as income generation and general management functions, must be considered in a similar vein and should be managed in relation to the overall project life and its objectives. The organisation should consider the total costs of a particular fundraising appeal, event or major IT development against the proposed benefits of the initiative before pressing the button. There is no point thinking only as far as, say, the end of the current financial year. Once the initiative has the go-ahead, the methodology requires the organisation to recognise the full costs of the project right through to completion as already committed.

General activity and support service functions

Thinking about the situation today, what financial commitment has the organisation already made with regard to, say, running the chief executive's office or the HR department? There will be no one straightforward answer. Conceptually, it is far easier to identify commitments already made in relation to specific projects, with firm start and end dates, than it is for general activities that underpin such projects. Yet in all units of an organisation – and particularly the support or central service functions – much of the activity will be ongoing and general in nature.

So, identifying the current cost commitments of general activity cannot be done in the same way that it is done for specific projects. However, there are several different approaches that can be used instead.

- Estimate the level of general activity (running costs) needed to support the specific projects already committed to – in other words, showing the change in running costs in relation to the decrease in current commitments over time.
- Assume that the current absolute levels of running costs will continue over a defined future period.
- Impose a cost target that reflects the level of running costs that the organisation believes it will allow over a defined period. This target could be determined in absolute terms or relative to total expenditure, for example. In this case, the expenditure forecast for the total costs of the support service functions can be simply a derivative of the cost target imposed (in the form of a metric – see chapter 16), which places a percentage ceiling on these costs in relation to overall expenditure.

Determining which approach to adopt to value the current commitments of general activity has an important influence later in the methodology in step 4. Step 4 will assume that the costs identified in this step are committed, and are not subject to further negotiation. A useful rule of thumb when considering whether running costs are already committed is to question the extent to which they would be eligible for future negotiation. If they are, then it is more helpful to not regard them as among the current commitments.

MAPPING FUTURE AVAILABLE RESOURCES AND EXPENDITURE COMMITMENTS

Ideally, the level of future resources will increase, reflecting growing income streams. In addition, the further into the future the organisation looks, the further the level of existing commitments will usually fall – until, at some future date, there are no specific projects and therefore no general activity needed to support them. In these circumstances, there will be a growing gap between future resources and current commitments.

Consider figure 15.2. Line AB defines the indicative level of available resources anticipated in the future. Line AC defines the level of future spending already committed by the organisation with the funding made available (declining over time). The gap between the two, shown by the area ABC, represents the level of anticipated available funding not yet committed. The emergence of a new priority must be funded either from anticipated available resources (the ABC area), or by reducing existing commitments (lowering the AC line) or by increasing future resources (raising the AB line).

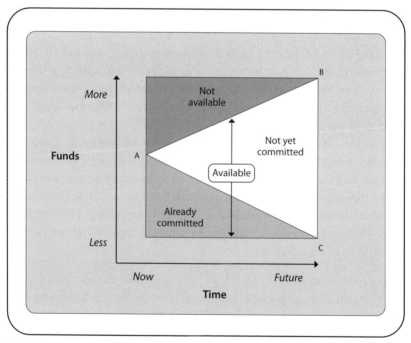

Fig. 15.2 Future available resources exceed committed resources

However, what if the future resource availability was very uncertain or insecure? In this instance, it is likely that the organisation would nevertheless have ongoing expenditure commitments, such as employee salary costs, rent and other general activity. Any activity currently undertaken has to be financed, and if current commitments exceed current resources then something has to give immediately.

That is a relatively straightforward, if uncomfortable, decision. More difficult is deciding how to move forward when the anticipated future resource availability raises questions about how the current future commitments are going to be financed.

The key question is whether to commence or continue with an activity already under way that can be financed today but that may not be affordable tomorrow. The financial stewards have a choice. They could continue with the activity, drawing on whatever funding they already have, in the hope that they are successful in raising further funds. This approach must make sense if the funding is heavily restricted so that it cannot be used for an alternative purpose. Alternatively, they could discontinue the activity as quickly as possible, in order to free up those resources that they were intending to spend on it. Such an option becomes particularly relevant where the funds being used are unrestricted and therefore, could be diverted to another purpose.

Figure 15.3 illustrates the point. Anticipated future resources are shown by the line AB, and current commitments by the line AC. So, the anticipated level of available resources is expected to fall faster than current commitments. Unless the level of available resources rises above the level of existing commitments, some activity or activities will have to be stopped. Commitments will have to be reduced.

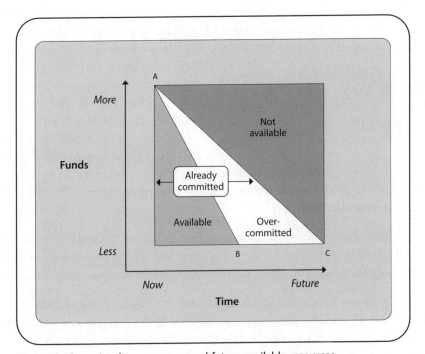

Fig. 15.3 Committed resources exceed future available resources

In such circumstances, should an organisation seek to reduce the commitments immediately to release the resources, or should it continue until it has to reduce the commitment? The more important the activity is to the organisation, the more likely it is to conclude that the activity should continue – the decision to stop being made only when it must. If a priority activity is stopped earlier than it has to be, there must be a clear understanding of the reason why. In determining a priority activity, do not make the mistake of assuming that the urgent activities are necessarily the priority ones. It rarely makes sense to turn the tap off for activities that are of an investment nature, such as investment in future income growth, membership growth or staff development – and yet where short-termism takes over, these are the easiest to chop.

ENSURING QUALITY FORECASTING

Forecasting what might happen in the future is a notoriously difficult exercise for organisations, and its inaccuracy is the source of much frustration. Much management practice seems to expect precise forecasts, and to rely on their submission – particularly in times of uncertainty. However, it is at such times, when trends, results and history change course, that accurate forecasting is most difficult to achieve. The global economic crisis that emerged in 2008 offers the most pertinent evidence possible of this (see box 15.3).

So, what can stewards of organisations do given this forecasting reality? The key is to strive for quality of process rather than precision in the forecasting outcome. The quality of forecasts reflects the reasonableness of the assumptions, the robustness of the forecasting process, the consistency with which that process is followed across the organisation, and the degree to which it fits within the whole approach adopted by the organisation to climb

> Forecasting is the perfect forum for testing alternative views of the future.
>
> *Axson, 2003, p. 200*

the results chain. A high-quality forecasting process requires management to consider its business drivers and operating environment, and to think about possible courses of action.

Crucially, high-quality forecasting approaches recognise the reality of forecasting error, acknowledging that the range of factors that influence financial results are such that any forecasting model – however sophisticated – over-simplifies reality.

Forecasting errors, where actual results deviate from those forecast, occur for two reasons: random variation and bias. Dougherty (n.d.) offers a two-step solution to forecasting error: attack the bias, then plan for variation. This chapter opened by recognising the importance of generating unbiased forecasts. This is a big challenge, intimately connected to the issue of the performance contract that is in place within the organisation. The incentives to provide honest forecasts have to be in place.

However, it is also essential to recognise and plan for normal variation in results. Requesting and using forecast ranges, rather than single-point forecasts, makes intuitive sense. Decision makers should expect results to vary within defined limits. The organisation has to be confident that it could handle being anywhere within these limits. To this end, forecasting is a risk management tool: the organisation can assess the impact of alternative assumptions on the decisions it intends to make and the results it can expect.

Planning for variation also means developing the capabilities mentioned earlier in the chapter. At some point, organisations are better served by investing in agility – in their reactive capacity – rather than their forecasting capability. The organisation must be ready to react to unexpected information. It must have the systems, culture and financial wherewithal to change course quickly. The more agile an organisation, the less dependent it is on forecasts.

Key stewardship questions

1. Why is the organisation forecasting? What decisions are the forecasts supporting?

2. How capable is the organisation of reacting to forecasting error?

3. What incentives are in place for those preparing forecasts?

4. Are the forecasts being prepared for the right timeframe and to the right level of detail?

5. What expenditure commitments has the organisation already made?

6. What is the relationship between the future available resources and expenditure commitments already made?

7. How high is the quality of the forecasting process?

16 Step 3: aim

DECIDING WHERE TO GO

Establishing financial boundaries and targets

Steps 1 and 2 of the methodology concerned themselves with monitoring the current financial state of play of the organisation – its current financial position, and what future financial commitments it has already made. Those steps are the crucial forerunners to the remaining three steps which, looking ahead, determine a destination, a plan of how to get there, and then set off in pursuit of that destination.

Step 2 ends with an understanding about which of the resources currently available the organisation can afford to commit, given the level of resources that it can reasonably anticipate having available in the future. This next step – step 3 – guides the decision maker in determining how best to commit these resources by establishing explicitly what financial performance and position is required. It does this by translating the organisation's finance strategy into KPIs.

As we saw in part 2, it is the role of finance strategy to define what intended financial performance and position is sought and how the organisation aims to achieve those aspirations. By writing a finance strategy, the organisation will have defined the areas of the its finances to which it must pay strategic attention. These are the areas for which metrics are now needed. In this way, the metrics provide a medium-term financial performance framework – a set of financial boundaries and targets within which shorter-term, and more operational decisions can be made.

Chapter 13, which introduced the five-step methodology, explained the need for both a short-term and medium-term perspective in managing organisational performance. In particular, it stressed the importance of establishing a financial set of parameters within which the organisation must operate over the medium term. These parameters guide decision making, ensuring day-to-day consistency with longer-term ambitions.

By the end of this third step, the decision maker should have all the information needed to determine the direction in which resources should be allocated. The following information should be clear:

- what funds are currently available
- what funds are expected to become available
- what financial parameters the organisation must operate within
- what financial targets the organisation aims to meet.

SETTING FINANCIAL KPIs

As we saw earlier, one of the principles by which an organisation should conduct its financial stewardship is to use critical measures of performance not a mass of detail (see box 13.1 on p. 190). These KPIs must, between them, be sufficient and necessary to inform the organisation's financial stewards about whether its financial performance and financial state is satisfactory. It is these KPIs that replace the target-setting and control roles of budgets. Actual performance is expressed in terms of the KPIs rather than in comparison to a budget, and the KPIs guide the reader's judgement about how satisfactory the results are.

It is worth recalling from chapter 2 that if the KPIs have been well defined, they will reassure when all is well and flag up when corrective action is needed. Used as targets, the KPIs reflect the financial aspirations of the organisation, while as parameters they identify the boundaries within which performance is expected.

In writing a finance strategy, the organisation's financial stewards will have identified what aspects of the organisation's financial performance are most important. They are, by definition, the key indicators of performance that must be tracked. This means that the indicators naturally fall out of the finance strategy. They are valid as long as the strategy is valid: it is not sensible to keep altering the financial boundaries or targets. Each selected indicator needs to have a boundary or target attributed to it.

For example, consider the key stewardship questions summarised at the end of each chapter in part 2. Each of these could be an area of the organisation's financial activity for which an indicator is established. For each indicator, the organisation could agree a target performance level or a parameter against which actual results would be tracked, as in figure 16.1. It would also establish deadlines for reaching each required standard, as measured by the target or parameter.

Perspective	Indicator	Target/parameter
Income	Sufficiency of costs covered	X% of funding agreements fund[ ] core costs
	Growth in fundraising contribution	X% of last 12 months, +/or in X percentile of comparable organisations
	Cost–income ratio	Between X% and Y%
	Break-even level of income	No greater than £x
	Degree of income restrictions	X% of income unrestricted
	Diversity of income sources	Income from any source at least X% and/or no more than Y% of total income
Funds	Reserves	± 3 months expected expenditure
	Form of funds	X% of funds realisable within Y weeks
	Fund/activities match	No greater than X% of activities subject to competing funding bids
Assets	Liquidity	Ratio of current assets to current liabilities at least X:1
	Funding structure	Ratio of debt to fund balances no greater than X:1
	Cash flow	£x cash inflow or outflow required
	Asset productivity	Ratio of total expenditure to average total assets no less than X:1
	Debtor control	Ratio of debtors to income no greater than X:1
	Creditor control	Ratio of overdue creditors to total creditors no greater than X:1
Expenditure	Level of expenditure	X% of available resources to be spent
	Distribution of expenditure	Costs of generating income as % of total expenditure to be at least X% and no greater than Y%
	Prioritisation of activities	At least X% of costs in furtherance of objectives spent on activity A
	Cost-effectiveness	Qualitative impact assessment indicator

Fig. 16.1 Indicators and target performance levels or parameters

Since the indicators will be used to guide future decision making, they must not only help inform the organisation retrospectively as to whether satisfactory performance has been achieved, but should also act as early-warning systems, to alert management if the organisation is going off course, in sufficient time to enable corrective action to be taken. So, effective financial stewardship requires two kinds of indicators: lag indicators, to record with hindsight what performance was like (in other words, to measure actual results); and lead indicators, to highlight what future performance can be expected in light of events occurring now that will influence those results (performance drivers).

To set appropriate lead indicators, the organisation must identify what information would provide reassurance that the future outcome, as defined by the lag indicators, was on course to be achieved. For example, it is essential that organisations that are heavily reliant on direct marketing income (a lag indicator) can anticipate whether income will be generated from this source. So, they need to track closely any activities that will contribute to determining whether the direct marketing income outcome sought will be achieved. These lead indicators include the number of individual donors recruited and the average donor yield. If these lead indicators give poor results, the organisation has early warning of disappointing income figures to come, and can act accordingly.

Arguably, each of the four perspectives of finance strategy could ultimately be measured by just one metric:

- **Income:** growth in contribution
- **Funds:** reserves levels
- **Assets:** liquidity of assets
- **Expenditure:** the percentage of total costs on activities in furthering the organisational objectives.

If all four of these metrics were moving in the desired direction, the organisation would be enjoying increasing expenditure on activities in furtherance of its objectives, financed by growing income and underpinned by an appropriate level of reserves held in a relatively liquid form. If the organisation achieves good performance against these four metrics, it will be demonstrating good financial stewardship. It is possible to set metrics not only at a corporate level by which to steward the organisation, but within particular operating units of the organisation, in order to steward performance more locally.

The four fundamental questions

Herzlinger and Nitterhouse (1994, pp. 133–35) believe that 'four fundamental questions' must be asked to assess an organisation's financial performance.

1. 'Are the organization's goals consistent with the financial resources it needs to finance them?' This question invites organisations to assess whether they can achieve their goals, given their financial position.
2. 'Is the organization maintaining inter-generational equity?' This is the 'spend or save' question. Expenditure today depletes resources available for the future.
3. 'Is there an appropriate match between the sources of resources and the uses to which they are put?' Organisations need to match sources and uses – for example, in order to avoid the exposure of having long-term capital commitments financed by short-term grants that may expire.
4. 'Are present resources sustainable?' As discussed in chapter 6, the more dispersed the sources, the better the organisation's ability to maintain them.

Rules of thumb

In setting financial targets or parameters for the metrics, the following guidelines may help.

1. Recall from chapter 2 the challenge of target setting. The way in which the KPIs are used needs to be carefully thought through, understood and communicated.
    a. They can be a predetermined measure of performance which, at the extreme, represents the absolute definition of the boundary between acceptable and unacceptable performance.
    b. They can be a target that defines an intended outcome to encourage certain behaviour, but which does not represent a (predetermined) measure of performance, which will be determined retrospectively.
2. It is much easier to establish KPIs as boundaries and aspirations, rather than as predetermined measures of performance. Imagine setting targets solely for the purpose of inspiring the staff to aim to achieve results that they had previously considered unachievable. That can only be possible if the targets are divorced from performance measurement – in other words, if the staff will not be held to account if they do not achieve the target. Instead, they will be held to account for the actual performance in light of the circumstances in which it was delivered, and in relation to comparatives such as the previous year, or competitor performance. The KPIs, set with the purpose of the organisation in mind, provide the targets, the goals and the aspirations.
3. It is important to have a good sense of what is out of bounds – in other words, what unacceptable performance looks like. Metrics can be set to define this boundary so that once it has been reached, steps can be taken to ensure it is not crossed. These boundaries could be regarded either as strictly out of bounds (that is, under no circumstances would it be acceptable to end up here) or as trigger points to stimulate enquiry into whether corrective action is needed. Example boundaries could be:

a. A cost–income ratio in any year of at least 1:3. The concern here would be to ensure that investment in further income-generating activities is not forgotten.

b. Expenditure on activities in furtherance of organisational objectives as a percentage of expenditure to be a minimum of, say, 60 per cent. This would, in effect, place a ceiling on the costs of other activities.

c. Free reserves not to exceed six months' worth of future expenditure plans.

Again, it is important to note the need for lead indicators to inform decision makers in advance that they are likely to move out of bounds in time for them to take some corrective action. It would not be satisfactory to rely on a lag indicator that would simply tell them that they had already gone out of bounds.

4. Within the extremities of the boundaries, in most cases it is not helpful to be overly prescriptive about the metric target. Many organisations now develop target ranges for their key indicators rather than precise outcomes in recognition of the impossibility of forecasting with 100 per cent accuracy. In effect this approach sets a minimum and maximum for each indicator. It is simply an extension of defining out of bounds, allowing the organisation to acknowledge the imprecision of the exercise by saying 'we want to see this indicator somewhere in this sort of range' without being overly prescriptive.

5. It might be necessary or desirable to change the metrics goal in light of actual circumstances. There is nothing sacrosanct about the metrics' target, although changing them must not become a means of 'shifting the goalposts' in order to dress up an unacceptable performance.

Targets, transparency and accountability

Chapter 2 highlighted the potential pitfalls of setting targets, in terms of the behaviours that they can stimulate in those being controlled or performance managed. Financial stewards are more likely than most to run the risk of setting inappropriate targets. There are three principal reasons for this.

1. **The fear of financial mismanagement:** Financial stewards face an awkward dilemma. Clearly, it is important that the organisation has sufficient financial controls in place to ensure its ongoing viability and reputation. Horror stories abound of organisations which have failed to establish or maintain sufficient oversight of financial management, resulting in financial failure or severely damaged reputations. The fear of such an event can lead financial stewards to overreact by imposing targets in an effort to control behaviour.

2. **Pressure to find efficiency improvements:** Stewards can find themselves under considerable pressure, both from within the organisation and externally, to demonstrate efficiency improvements. It is a common political mandate to

promise such improvements. Sceptical boards, or senior management, may not be content to see overall levels of expenditure moving in the intended direction. Their own impressions of the efficacy with which the organisation is run may provoke them to demand evidence of cost savings – for example, of changes in spending policy in traditional areas such as travel, consultants, space and IT.

3. **The inherent 'controller' tendency of the accountant:** The truth is that many leaders of organisations on the board and in senior management positions are more comfortable overseeing the performance of organisations by micro-managing operations and finances than by strategic leadership. Many financial stewards are willing and able to play a traditional financial controller role that promotes and sustains centralised decision making, a focus on the input end of the results chain, and the imposition of micro-controls.

The consequence of these pressures may be an appetite to impose micro-level spending targets. These targets are typically expressed as per capita spending targets, predetermining from the centre how much the organisation believes it is appropriate to expend on particular line items. Policy is defined through expenditure caps such as 'no more than £x per staff member on travel, training or computer equipment'.

These impositions may be helpful organisationally for two main reasons. First, they simplify the application of policy: those subject to the policy do not have to worry about making judgements or choices. Second, they can help reinforce organisational values and establish a desired internal culture. The policy says 'this is how we do things here', establishing important behavioural norms. This can be particularly helpful in times of dramatic change or crisis, when uncomfortable but decisive action needs to be taken.

However, micro-level spending targets will also have undesirable consequences. Since they are centrally imposed, by definition they fail to take account of local circumstances. All units are subject to the same policy. The policy may be more appropriate, and its application more successful, in some units than others. What is more, as chapter 2 showed, such targets will focus attention in their direction. Unit managers will do what is necessary to comply, including game playing. In addition, the centre will be preoccupied by the targets. Its focus of attention will be on policy compliance rather than on understanding the units' business and on assessing the extent to which they are maximising impact over time.

Given the legitimacy of the need to control spending, and to maintain some broad compliance with institutional policy and/or values, the solution lies in the power of transparency and accountability. Transparency is almost universally recognised to be a powerful means of highlighting behaviour and performance, and of providing the incentive for improvement. Rather than imposing targets and caps centrally, it may be more effective to give discretion to units to determine their own spending choices, and for the centre to focus on highlighting comparisons between units and on understanding the rationale and consequences of the choices made.

The approach is one of allowing units discretion within parameters, publishing the results of choices made, and holding units accountable for the consequences of those choices. The fact that a particular unit chooses to spend more per capita than its peers is transparently evident, and the unit has the expectation and obligation to explain its decisions in the context of a broader discussion about the use of resources and the results achieved.

In this way, peer comparison can be a crucial and effective driver of performance, as individual units and the organisation as a whole seek to do better than their peers. Transparent reporting of performance in terms of the selected indicators among a community of peers highlights relative performance, and acts as a spur to performance improvement.

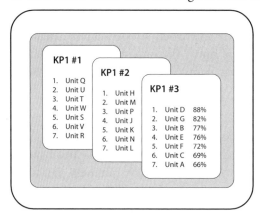

Fig. 16.2 Internal comparisons of financial indicators

Financial indicators are often common to units and so lend themselves to internal comparisons. Merely presenting the comparisons provokes discussion (see fig. 16.2). The KPI target becomes one of out-performing peers – at least relatively:

The objective is to create a performance league table at every level. It is the pressure that arises from a unit's position in the league table that drives performance improvement ... Finding that your business unit is lying in a lowly position in one or another performance league table should tell you where to look in terms of improvement.

Hope, 2006, pp. 170–71

KPI GOVERNANCE

KPI governance refers to the processes through which KPIs are developed, selected, defined, reported and monitored. The purpose of sound KPI governance is to ensure that the indicators are decision-relevant, valid, reliable and timely. In addition, it is highly desirable that indicators can be aggregated from unit level to institutional level, and can be benchmarked against suitable comparatives.

Without good governance, it is easy for KPIs to distract from good performance management rather than contributing to it.

There are several symptoms of poor KPI governance (see box 16.1) and, particularly in large organisations, there is a high risk of these symptoms being evident. Only then does it become apparent that a governance process is needed at all. The larger the organisation, the more likely it is that a formal process (with clear decision-making points) is necessary.

To maximise the value of the KPIs, the following issues have to be tackled. If they are not, the subject of reports and discussions that include KPIs will descend into dispute about the indicators themselves.

- **Selection:** Who is the decision maker? Who decides which KPIs are used, and which are added or dropped? How is that decision

> ### Box 16.1 Poor KPI governance: symptoms
>
> - Ambiguous or no indicator ownership
> - Too many indicators
> - Irrelevant indicators
> - Unused indicators
> - Disputes about definition
> - Disputes about data accuracy
> - Slow, labour-intensive production

made? It is not uncommon for business units and senior management to disagree as to which indicators best inform the topic being discussed – particularly if the topic in question is the performance of that unit. Senior management often want to use a common set of indicators across business units in order to be able to make internal performance comparisons, while units will explain why they are unique and should be assessed using tailored indicators.

The obvious compromise is a mix of common and unit-specific indicators. Determining who is the decision maker will have a profound impact on ownership. The more centralised the decision making, the more the business units will feel that the exercise of maintaining and reporting on KPIs is a corporate requirement rather than a genuinely valuable contribution towards performance management.

- **Timeframes:** Over what timeframes will the selected indicators be tracked and reported?
- **Definition:** What calculation methodology will be used for each indicator and, again, who will decide? Financial indicators are particularly vulnerable to internal debate over which numbers are included.
- **Measurement:** How will the data for the indicators be captured? Survey and data entry processes will be needed, and coding structures may have to be revised.
- **Production/storage:** How will the indicators be generated? Often the indicators require data to be sourced from different systems and housed in a depository

of some kind where ratios, formulas and trends can be calculated. This has to be managed. Who in the organisation is best placed to do that?

- **Quality control:** It is very easy for incorrect indicators to be published – errors that potentially misguide decision makers. It is important to have clear quality control protocols for ensuring the accuracy and integrity of data and calculation.
- **Reporting:** Version control is a related challenge, given that the data used in many indicators is changing on a daily basis. There must be unambiguous responsibility for ensuring that the correct version of KPI reports is available and used.
- **Communication and access:** Who in the organisation would benefit from seeing the KPI data and trends? How can they access them? It is worth thinking hard about how to make the information as transparent and accessible as possible, recognising always that the data needs to be interpreted.

KPI REPORTING

Using a few KPIs to inform assessments of progress towards future goals lends itself to tracking progress over time. Chapters 14 and 15, on monitoring actual results and forecasting, provide the relevant perspectives to report and interpret KPIs. Trends – historic and forecast – help organisational leaders and decision makers to make assessments about actual performance, and judgements about what future action to take. Reports need to show how these trends and forecasts are taking the organisation towards its stated goals. The trends invite management to ask whether appropriate progress is being made, whether the financial boundaries are being respected, and what further action is needed.

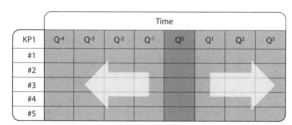

Fig. 16.3 Historic and prospective trends

The financial KPIs that are defined will largely be relevant over the medium term. Individual indicators may be added or dropped, targets and/ or boundaries defined may alter, and the five-step methodology expounded in this book encourages decisions to be made when they are needed – not necessarily when they are planned.

However, the fundamental finance strategy, on which the KPIs are based, is likely to remain valid for an extended period. So, the reporting timeframe used to track KPIs needs to mirror this. The sort of perspective offered by figure 16.3 is one possibility. In this format, a series of KPIs are shown together across an eight-quarter timeframe. The latest quarter (Q^0), which is highlighted, is flanked by actual data to the left and forecasts to the right, thereby providing a historic and prospective trend for each indicator.

Sightsavers International adopts a similar approach in tracking a small selection of financial KPIs each month. Most of the KPIs use a 12-month moving ratio, and all have a pre-defined target. The eye can follow the recent history of progress in relation to the selected indicators that are shown moving left to right towards the target (see fig. 16.4). In several cases the target is expressed as a range rather than a precise number.

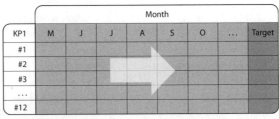

Fig. 16.4 Moving historic trend with target

Both extremities of the defined range set threshold points at which action is triggered. These include the following:

- **Free reserves as a percentage of direct charitable expenditure:** The use of a range recognises that, at any point in time, the actual level of reserves may vary from the precise level intended, and that there is a level above which and below which the organisation would not expect to go.
- **Fundraising cost–income ratio:** The organisation recognises that there is a minimum level of investment needed in order to generate future income, but also a minimum return necessary. The use of a range rather than a precise target recognises both.

Integrating financial KPIs

Acknowledging the fundamental message of this book – the primacy of maximising impact as the objective of any organisation, and the pivotal role that the financial steward has in achieving this objective – requires the steward to consider how to integrate financial planning and reporting with the other elements of the results chain. Finance is an integral component of the chain. It is meaningless, in the true sense of the word, to disconnect it. Organisations have to show how they align the financial resources to the work programmes and strategies by which they intend to have impact.

Efforts to integrate the measurement and reporting of the financial and non-financial components of organisational performance management advanced dramatically with the evolution of Kaplan and Norton's Balanced Scorecard (Kaplan and Norton, 1996) in the mid-1990s. While its name implies a focus on measurement and indicators – both financial and non-financial – the real benefit of applying the scorecard concept comes through understanding what the intended results chain of the organisation is, and how measures can help performance reviews and action planning.

The scorecard and strategy map force organisations to look at plans and performance from different perspectives. Finance is just one of them. The others are the internal business operations perspective, the customer perspective and the learning and growth perspective. Not-for-profit organisations have learned to adapt the scorecard – in particular, replacing the customer perspective with the dual perspectives of donors and beneficiaries.

	Short-term/operational context	Longer-term/strategic context
Activity/programme level — what we do (Is it working?)	1. Indicators of current goal achievement. Information to answer questions concerned with 'are we doing what we said we would do?'	2. Indicators of underlying performance. Information to help answer 'is it worth it, and what else should we be doing as well or instead?'
Organisational level — what we are (Is it well run?)	3. Indicators of financial and administrative soundness. Information concerning ways in which the organisation is or might be 'at risk'.	4. Indicators of renewal or decline. Information to help consider 'are we building up our capabilities or at least sustaining them — or are they wasting away?'

Fig. 16.5 Integrating financial indicators in a performance dashboard (Paton, 2003, p. 141)

Paton (2003) offers a variation on the scorecard: a 'dashboard for social enterprises' (p. 139) designed to answer two basic questions, acknowledging the need to nurture programmes and the organisations by which they are delivered, across both the short and medium terms (see fig. 16.5). The first question is 'Does it work?' – in other words, does the organisation achieve the intended results through its work programmes and strategies? The second is 'Is it well run?' – in other words, is the organisation administered efficiently?

To these four perspectives Paton adds a fifth: the need to plan and report on major change projects that affect the organisation itself, for which the organisation's leaders, trustees and senior managers may be directly responsible. The result is a general architecture for dashboards of 'social enterprises' that contains five areas (see fig. 16.6). Finance is inherent in all of them.

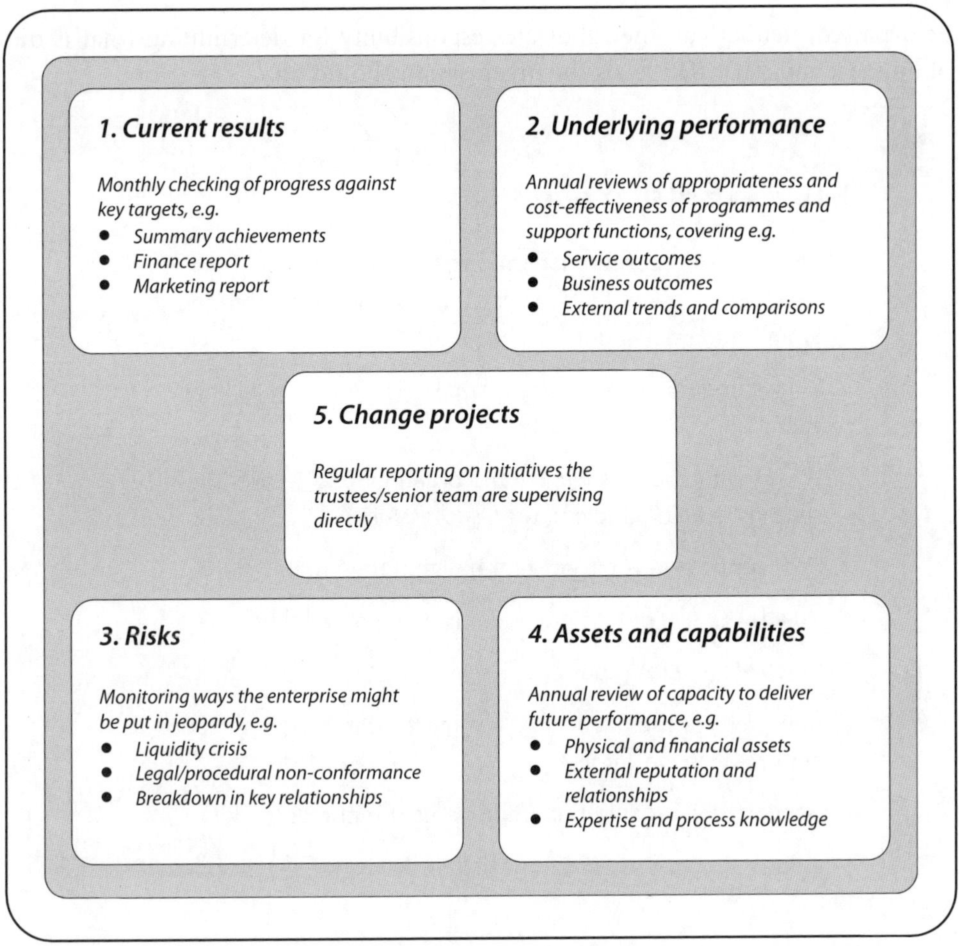

Fig. 16.6 A dashboard for social enterprises (Paton, 2003, p. 142)

The dashboard contains the following sections:

1. Current results

Monthly checking of progress against key targets, e.g.
- Summary achievements
- Finance report
- Marketing report

2. Underlying performance

Annual reviews of appropriateness and cost-effectiveness of programmes and support functions, covering e.g.
- Service outcomes
- Business outcomes
- External trends and comparisons

5. Change projects

Regular reporting on initiatives the trustees/senior team are supervising directly

3. Risks

Monitoring ways the enterprise might be put in jeopardy, e.g.
- Liquidity crisis
- Legal/procedural non-conformance
- Breakdown in key relationships

4. Assets and capabilities

Annual review of capacity to deliver future performance, e.g.
- Physical and financial assets
- External reputation and relationships
- Expertise and process knowledge

COMPLETING STEP 3

Hopefully this chapter has demonstrated the power of using financial KPIs as part of a wider suite of performance measures. KPIs will guide the financial steward in managing resources and, if properly defined, between them can indicate whether the organisation is being successful in financial terms. Financial performance can be seriously tracked in as few as half a dozen indicators. Equally crucially, all resource allocation decisions can be guided by the impact that those decisions would have on the KPIs.

Such is the influence that the KPIs have on the whole issue of resource allocation (and thereby performance of the organisation) that the most senior players in any organisation – trustees, board members and senior management – must be involved in establishing, setting and monitoring them. The governors cannot be bypassed, neither can they abdicate responsibility for determining what is out of bounds, and what KPI goals the organisation should set.

Key stewardship questions

1. What should be the organisation's financial KPIs? (In other words, which elements of the finance strategy is it critical that the organisation gets right?)

2. What target or parameter is it appropriate to set in relation to each KPI?

3. What lead indicators will tell the organisation whether the strategy is being implemented successfully?

4. How centralised is target-setting within the organisation?

5. How is the use of KPIs governed in the organisation?

6. How are the KPIs reported?

7. How well are the financial KPIs integrated in a broader set of performance indicators?

8. How can the organisation improve its use of KPIs?

17 Step 4: plan

DECIDING HOW TO GET THERE

Step 4 is the decision-making step of the methodology: the stage at which the organisation makes resource allocation decisions. Crucially, it assumes that in step 2 the organisation has determined how much resource it is willing and able to commit now for future expenditure, recognising that some of that resource will be future income that has not yet been generated (see box 17.1). The logic of the methodology is that before determining the available resources it is willing to commit now, the organisation must have addressed its need to maintain an appropriate level of reserves as contingency, in case future income does not materialise. So, by this stage, the organisation should be confident that it has access to contingency funds (reserves, or as a last resort, borrowings) in the event of anticipated income not materialising.

The aim of step 4 is to determine what commitments to make now with regard to fund balances and future expected income that are currently available. This involves making decisions about the gap between future resources and current commitments, as determined in step 2, and using the KPIs agreed in step 3 to guide those decisions. If current commitments exceed future resources, then the decisions relate to how to reduce the former and/or increase the latter. If future resources exceed current commitments, then the decisions must focus on determining what additional activities to take on. It is this latter scenario to which the remainder of the chapter is devoted.

Box 17.1   Calculating the resources available
Available resources = current spare fund balances + future income – existing commitments not yet met

There are three distinct stages to this step. Again, it is necessary to think in terms of two timeframes: a three to five-year, medium-term, strategic timeframe and a short-term, operational timeframe. The first stage is to determine the top-level allocations that are needed at a corporate level in order to achieve the financial profile described by the KPIs in step 3 – in other words, the SOFA and balance sheet profile. This stage addresses the medium-term need to define the level of expenditure and the direction in which it is expected to go over a multi-year timeframe.

Stage 2 – also relevant across financial years – ensures that the organisation gives clear signals about its sectoral or policy priorities in furthering its objectives. Finally, stage 3 determines how to use the resources within each of the main expenditure categories: a process that is dynamic and takes place as needed, as the organisation moves forward.

STAGE 1: TOP-LEVEL ALLOCATIONS FOR THE MEDIUM TERM

There are four ways in which the decision maker can use the resources available. They can be used to assess:

- how much of the organisation's available funds should be devoted to activities in furtherance of the organisation's objectives
- how much should be reinvested in income-generating activities
- how much should be spent on the management and administration of the organisation
- how much should be retained in reserves for future contingency purposes.

The question here is which option to adopt.

Such decisions are made on the basis of which allocation best serves the objectives of the organisation, as guided by its KPIs. The decision maker can make appropriate and quick decisions about top-level resource allocation decisions if they know:

- what the current financial position of the organisation is (step 1)
- what financial commitments it has already made that still have to be met (step 2)
- what resources the organisation is able to commit now (step 2)
- what KPI targets have been set (step 3).

These decisions about resource allocation can be made as and when the need to make them arises – whenever that is – rather than at a predetermined time when an event called 'writing the budget or the plan' occurs. Traditionally, resources would be allocated on the basis of a budget. Spending units would submit detailed financial plans that would be consolidated into a total budget. Once the overall budget was agreed, the components that made it up would become allocations. This approach, in contrast, enables and expects allocations to be made continuously in the light of the current situation and the latest expectations of the future.

At its simplest level, choosing how to allocate available resources between the four options can be determined by KPIs that set targets for the proportion of expenditure that should be committed to each. In other words, it becomes simply a matter of slicing the cake according to the KPIs. However, the KPIs – which reflect financial strategy – are likely to be long-term aspirations that will take time to achieve. So, decision making will need to be thought-through more carefully than simply allocating, say, 75 per cent of the funds in the direction of activities that further the organisation's objectives in line with a KPI target.

In the short term, there may be good reason why the organisation cannot sensibly spend funds in those proportions. For example, it may need to build the capacity of those staff who manage service delivery to handle growth before the KPI target can be achieved. Whatever allocations are determined, the decision makers must be confident that they move the organisation in a direction that is consistent with the intended KPIs at an appropriate pace, and stay at all times within the boundaries defined by those KPIs. The ultimate test is to be confident that the chosen allocations represent the optimal distribution of resources at the time that the decision is made. No alternative distribution should offer greater progress towards successful implementation of the finance strategy.

There is a natural order to determining the four-way split of allocating available funds, as follows. When the organisation has calculated the response to the first question, it should move on to the next to consider how to divide up the remainder of its funds, and so on.

1. How much does the organisation need to retain as reserves to maintain its financial stability?
2. If the organisation is to have the funds to enable it to have impact in the future, how much does it need to reinvest in income-generating activities?
3. How much does the organisation have to spend on managing and administering itself (like it or not)?
4. How much is left for activities that further the organisation's objectives?

Note the obligatory tone of these first three questions. If the organisation is to maintain itself as a going concern, there is no choice but to commit precious funds to these activities. The art is to maximise cost-effectiveness: keeping these allocations as low as possible, without sacrificing effectiveness.

As the questions above suggest, the allocation for activities that further the organisation's objectives becomes a balancing number. In practice, the process of allocation is likely to be reiterative. There will be negotiation at the margin – at least there should be. The managers responsible for service delivery should always be finding scope to press for additional funds, and endeavouring to persuade the fundraisers that they can improve their return on investment (in other words, generate the same or higher levels of income with fewer resources). Fundraisers and service deliverers alike are likely to be eagle-eyed over costs incurred on the organisation's management and administration.

Nevertheless, there are three essential ground rules to note.

1. At this stage the allocation of total resources available is simply into four: there is no detailed allocation whatsoever. To avoid the risk of stop–go management, the allocations have to be regarded as secure – as minimum funds available. Once the decision is made, it is not meant to be reversed. Once made, allocations should not be retracted.

2. The allocations must be reviewed frequently – at least quarterly – and may be increased in light of new information about current state of play or future outlook.

3. The allocations are indicative of the expenditure profile wanted, but not of spending contracts against which performance will be measured.

Allocations to reserves

The organisation cannot expect to have long-term impact unless it is run on a sound financial footing. So, of the competing demands for the organisation's available funds, the issue of reserves must come first. However, this does not mean prioritising reserves at the total expense of the other three competing demands. Diverting significant funds to reserves in order to reach a desired level of reserves quickly, rather than allowing the funds to be used for expenditure purposes, may not be practical without a serious detrimental impact on the continuity of activities. More realistically, if the current reserves are substantially less than the level required, as identified in the finance strategy, then the organisation's stewards will need to build the reserves up over time, making modest allocations to reserves year-by-year.

Allocations for income-generating activities

With regard to allocations for income-generation purposes, the key constraint should probably not be an absolute sum of money, but a relative one. Generating income must be judged on return on investment, long-term return, and – to a lesser extent – short-term return. So, allocations for these activities can be set with reference to the return on investment ratios. There will be a natural constraint on how much the organisation can raise in a defined period of time, be that an internal one (such as management capacity) or an external one (such as the fundraising environment). Cash flow will probably be relevant, given the time lag in the receipt of income following income-generating activity. Even if the long-term return on investment looks excellent, if the short-term cash resources would be excessively depleted, further investment in income generation would have to be delayed.

In the process of determining the level of investment to make in income-generating activities, it would be profitable to understand fully the sensitivity of income to alternative levels of investments. What would be the short and long-term impact of spending an additional £0.25m on income-generating activity in the next six months? It would be worth knowing and understanding the impact on the rest of the organisation's performance. What would happen to the percentage of expenditure devoted to welfare activity? Would that percentage still be defendable publically?

Each area of operation is so interdependent on the others that any one of these resource allocation questions requires an understanding of the whole. What is clear is that the concept of return on investment – however it is measured or interpreted – does provide an inherent self-regulating tool: how much is invested in income-generating activity is judged in relation to how much that activity raises to pay for itself, and more.

Allocations for management and administration

Apart from the fundraisers, none of the units within an organisation are directly responsible for generating income. They are genuinely cost centres, rather than profit centres relying on funding given to them from elsewhere to finance their activities. It is not possible to identify at the level of an individual budget line what expenditure will be required 12 months away – but doing this is not necessary in any case. What is necessary, however, is to give the managers of these units some parameters within which to work. They must know, without having to go continually cap in hand to a higher authority, what resources they can rely on. Determining the corporate allocation for management and administration activities can usefully be set at a strategic level in one of two ways.

1. **Set an absolute sum of money:** This is probably best done in relation to historic expenditure levels, and provides a means of setting tight expenditure targets – for example, a 2 per cent reduction on last year.
2. **Set a relative allocation in relation to overall expenditure:** An example would be to decide that a maximum of 7 per cent of the total organisation expenditure in a particular period should be spent on administration. This approach requires corporate cooperation, since all units in the organisation affect the achievement or otherwise of a relative target through their own expenditure behaviour – not just that part of the organisation responsible for management and administration.

This option is a zero-sum game. The higher the level of spend in one area, the lower the proportion of total spend represented by another area. In reality, the ability of the management and administration units to react to lower than anticipated expenditure elsewhere – with consequent upward pressure on the relative percentage spent – will be limited. Many of the management and administration costs are fixed in the short-term: the organisation is committed to incurring them, irrespective of whether the welfare or income-generating activities take place. Nevertheless, setting some constraint on funds spent on management and administration to be met over the long term, or over a rolling basis, is highly valuable.

Such a strategic level parameter can be quickly set, based on broad assessments of the likely level of activity given the operational plans of the organisation. No detailed numbers, consolidated bottom-up, are necessary. Once allocations are made, those responsible for managing the sums allocated must be allowed to get on with it, and their success in doing so will be evident from the actual results and the consequent impact on KPIs.

Allocations for activities in furthering the organisation's objectives

Once the financial stewards are clear about how much of the organisation's funds they wish to reinvest in generating income, devote to management and administration activities, or retain, establishing how much to commit to activities in furtherance of the organisation's objectives falls out automatically. It is the balancing figure: the funds that remain after the other demands have been met.

As described in step 2, determining how far ahead to commit funds for these activities is driven by the second principle of planning, outlined in chapter 13 (see box 13.1 on p. 190). The perspective and timeframe looking forward should reflect the nature of what the organisation does – not the requirements of accounting statute. In practice, this means making commitments that reflect the length of the activities that the organisation is undertaking or supporting, and the lead time involved in developing them.

Time-limited project-type activities have a timeframe by definition: for ongoing activities, a reasonable timeframe has to be assumed for the purpose of determining the future level of resource consumption. The timing of the allocation must be determined by the lead time needed to bring new activities to a point of ready to go. If it takes, say, two years to develop a new activity, then the organisation must give notice (confirming that funds will be available) of at least that length in order to ensure that the activities are ready when the funding is available. The tap cannot be turned on instantaneously.

The importance of the existence of free reserves, to act as contingency in the event of income not materialising to cover the costs of commitments made, cannot be over-stressed. An organisation can only commit resources to the spenders that it has not yet raised if it has spare funds available that it would be willing and able to use if it needed to underwrite the expenditure commitment. The only source of those funds (without establishing obligations to third parties through any form of borrowing) is the organisation's own reserves. At the risk of stating the obvious, it is not possible to underwrite expenditure without guaranteed funds to draw on if this became necessary.

Lead times for multi-year resource allocations

For most public or not-for-profit organisations working to tackle long-term social, medical and environmental issues, determining how far in advance to commit funds is a critical question. Programme staff tend to operate with lead times to set up new programmes that extend well beyond the 12-month planning and reporting cycles of organisations. This means that they need long notice about funding availability if they are to proceed with confidence. It is not sensible to operate programmes that are all about long-term sustainable impact on the basis of short-term stop–go decisions in light of income ebbs and flows.

So, the organisation needs to provide a context about resource availability that is sufficiently long term to enable the programme staff to plan programme development and growth in line with these lead times. In effect, this means being willing to underwrite the costs of any commitment signed by the organisation, even though future funding is not certain. In other words, the level of funding is guaranteed, so that the senior programme management can promote programme growth without the fear of funding shortfalls once the projects are ready to be implemented.

As was outlined in chapter 12, providing clarity about funding availability over a multi-year timeframe often means using a three-year timeframe over which recipients receive clear advance funding signals. This has two principal benefits: the distributor can align resources with intended priorities across several years, and the recipients can make strategic and operational plans with confidence of the funding that will be available.

STAGE 2: ALIGNING ALLOCATIONS WITH POLICY CHOICES

The high-level allocations described in stage 1 must align with the priorities of the organisation. In particular, funds made available to further the objectives of the organisation need to be allocated in directions that reflect the medium-term choices about how best to add value to beneficiaries. The financial steward should never underestimate the influence of the signal of intent provided by financial allocations (see box 17.2).

Box 17.2   Allocation signals
Budget allocations have crucial if not overriding significance for the implementation of strategies and plans. Budgets often represent the most important and consequential policy statements that governments and nonprofit organizations make. Not all strategies and plans have budgetary significance, but enough of them do that public and nonprofit leaders and managers should consider involving themselves deeply in the process of budget making. Doing so is likely to be a particularly effective way to affect the design, adoption and execution of strategies and plans. *Bryson, 2004, p. 244*

In this way, governments can reflect 'at least general policy directions of government (e.g. additional education spending) and specification or modification of government objectives, in broad terms, for each sector' (Dorotinsky, 2004, p. 7). Similarly, in not-for-profit organisations, governing boards and senior management can use medium-term expenditure allocations to signal clear prioritisation of organisational objectives. Once leadership signals its intent to direct its finite resources towards certain types of services or beneficiaries, the policy choices of the organisation become sharper and more real. As with stage 1, it is high-level, broad messaging that is needed here. Too much granularity and/or short-termism dilutes the policy signal, and interferes with the dynamic allocation of resources to activities that takes place as needed in stage 3.

In making allocation decisions based on strategic choices, it is worth addressing explicitly the question of the link between performance and resources. Does good performance mean more resources? Not necessarily. The financial steward would do well to remember the wide range of factors that influence such choices. Performance is certainly important, and it is reasonable to assume that there should be a positive correlation between performance and resources over a certain time period, while the programme is supported.

However, performance is by no means the exclusive determinant of what gets funded: figure 3.5 on p. 51 listed 13 factors, one of which is 'track record'. Disappointing programme results may lead decision makers to conclude that *additional* resources should be invested in order to achieve the desired impact. On the other hand, if it is judged that in the circumstances, the return on investment has been unsatisfactory and there is no plausible outlook of improvement, then the organisation might decide to *reduce* the level of resources invested. Excellent results will be similarly inconclusive in determining the future level of resources. Those results do not necessarily ensure that the programme remains a priority in the future.

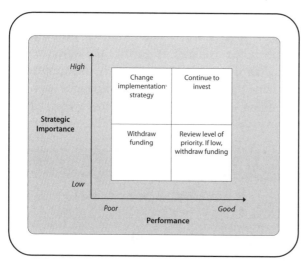

Fig. 17.1 The influence of strategy and performance on funding

The likely funding allocation choices influenced by strategic importance and performance are shown in figure 17.1. Converting income to impact optimally means investing in high-performing activities that address strategic priorities. Continuing to finance any other activity – whether high-performing or not – should be questioned.

STAGE 3: COMMITTING THE ALLOCATED RESOURCES AS NEEDED

Once such decisions have been made about how much of the available funds to retain, and how much to allocate for income generation, management and administration, and furthering the organisation's objectives, the management responsible for each area of the organisation needs a decision-making process by which to determine how the resources at its disposal are used. So, the next allocation decision to be made – the third stage of the allocation process – is how to use the funds allocated to furthering the organisation's objectives, to income generation, or to the management and administration of the organisation.

Ideally, this should maximise the discretion with which management can make its decisions, subject to any constraints imposed by the KPIs. These decisions are not made at a corporate level: the centre concerns itself only with the overall finance strategy and the results chain of the organisation.

Other than at the very top level, resources are committed as the need to spend arises. The methodology allows the decision to be made at the latest possible moment, when the current situation and knowledge about the future is as up to date as it can be, and is reflected in the latest information available. There is no value in making the decision earlier. This means that decisions are not made at the time of a pre-defined event called 'the budget approval', as this can result in two risks emerging. The first is that the decide-as-you-go approach paralyses the spenders, who end up coming 'cap-in-hand' for every expenditure decision. The second is that the approach leads to '*first* come, first served' rather than '*best* come, first served' allocation decisions. Each risk can be managed.

The 'cap-in-hand' risk

The 'cap-in-hand' risk is overcome by recognising that a certain amount of funds need to be spent on general day-to-day activity, and by classifying these costs as committed. Responsibility for managing these costs can then be delegated to the spenders, who would then need funding approval only for new specific projects (see box 17.3). This would mean that each operating unit would have access to guaranteed funds to enable them to deal with the routine expenditure incurred in running the unit. In an effort to drive down costs, this sum could be set at a lower level than in a previous equivalent period.

Box 17.3   Example: committing funds at an operating unit level

How does the chief information officer (CIO) know whether £x million can be spent on IT?

■ A guaranteed allocation of funds for general activity within the IT department over a defined time period (such as the next 36 months, as in the case of three-year expenditure frameworks described in chapter 13) is agreed. This could be higher, lower or unchanged from the immediate history of expenditure on such costs. The sort of items to be included in such departmental running costs is agreed in advance. The CIO can approve such costs without reference elsewhere, subject to a threshold above which higher approval is required.

■ Projects or activities that are not part of the defined running costs of the department have to be presented to the relevant senior manager with a funding proposal outlining the objectives, components and costs. Such projects are discrete, specific, time-limited, and comprise major activities. If more than one project is proposed, the projects are prioritised by the CIO.

■ The relevant senior manager determines which project submissions to approve, from within their top-level allocation.

■ Total funding of approved IT projects is guaranteed to the CIO, who manages the implementation of the projects. Costs of the projects as incurred are approved within normal authority limits.

The 'first come, first served' risk

The 'first come, first served' risk has to be managed by those responsible for applying the funds in the area for which the top-level allocations have been made. They must decide whether to approve options on the table now, or to postpone a decision in the expectation or hope of finding more attractive options in the future. In effect, the question being asked is: 'Would you prefer what might be round the corner to what is on offer now?' There is a trade-off between, on the one hand, not being able to finance an activity that is added to the shopping list late in the day because all the available funds have already been committed and, on the other, delaying financing projects that are currently on the list in the hope or expectation that something better may be added to it.

It is for the relevant management to determine whether all the available funds are distributed in one go, quickly, or are released more slowly, drip-fed over the course of a period of time. Either course of action is necessarily subject to any constraints imposed by cash requirements, which may dictate the timing of expenditure. It would be useful for decision makers to be able to see what is on the horizon if they are to help management in making such determinations (see box 17.4). The decision will be also heavily influenced if a 'spend it or lose it' budget contract is in force (see chapter 11 on allocation traps): the shorter the time available to spend the funds before they are lost, the greater the pressure to approve options already on the table, rather than wait.

> **Box 17.4   How to get expenditure early warnings**
>
> Expenditure early warnings can be generated by asking operational managers not only to compile a prioritised list of activities that are ready to go, but also to identify activities that are in the pipeline. Early warning of activities that are under development and likely to appear on a future shopping list helps inform decisions about whether to commit resources now to activities already on the shopping list, or to hold them back to finance activities still to come. It also provides an effective early means of reviewing whether the strategic direction of the organisation is being translated into the right activities at the operational level – in time to influence what gets done.

ENSURING OPTIMAL USE OF RESOURCES

So, how does the organisation ensure that all the resources within each high-level category are used optimally? It needs to follow a decision-making process designed to enable competing demands on those resources to be assessed, compared and conclusions reached. With the three main expenditure categories – income generation, management and administration, and activities in furtherance of the organisation's objectives – the methodology requires the management responsible for distribution of the allocated sums to determine which activities are funded and which are not, by answering the following questions.

1. What resources have we been allocated?
2. What financial commitments have we already made that will use up some of those resources?
3. Therefore how much resource do we anticipate having left?
4. What else would we like to do in addition to those commitments already made – in other words, new activities?
5. What are the highest priorities for our resources?
6. So, what activities should we start or stop?

In effect, each area of the organisation maps available resources and expenditure commitments to identify the gaps between the two, over which they have discretion. The process is essentially an activity-based one, in which costs are considered in relation to discrete activities, rather than in terms of the cost classification of a typical general ledger. As in step 2, the process of understanding the existing expenditure commitments of each area lends itself to an activity-based approach to costing.

Determining priorities: specific projects

Identifying the highest priorities for the organisation's resources is best done by comparing activities, so question 5 in the list above requires the decision makers to compile a prioritised 'shopping list' of activities that can be continuously updated as new ideas and/or requirements come to light. For example, a priority

267

list for the income-generation allocation could be built from prioritised lists submitted by managers of the operating units within the relevant directorate (see fig. 17.2).

However, the implication of question 5 is that all activities – including current commitments and proposed new activities – need to be prioritised. Only in this way can the organisation identify whether some of the activities currently commanding precious resources should, in fact, be stopped because they are no longer a priority. Remember Porter's observation that 'strategy renders choices about what not to do as important as choices about what to do' (see box 3.1 on p. 39). Stopping current activities does not represent failure, and yet that can be a common interpretation of a decision to discontinue existing commitments – especially if they are long-established ones, and if the decision has implications for the future employment of staff.

Nevertheless, it would be a mistake to assume that current activities necessarily represent a higher priority than others. Activities that were appropriate and high priority when they were started may not be so any longer, and must not be assumed to be if the resources are to be applied optimally in furthering the organisation's mission. This must, of course, be considered in relation to the extent to which the board of trustees has discretion over the application of funds.

Determining priorities: general activities

As we have seen, determining priorities by activity is comprehensible for specific projects with particular objectives to be delivered within finite timeframes – but what about those general activities that were referred to in step 2 (see p. 237), such as the 'back office' functions of finance, IT, HR and facilities management? How can the organisation determine within this approach what resource to commit to activities that are undertaking all sorts of daily activities?

Such functions exist in all parts of an organisation: in the directorates heading up income generation and the operational programmes arms of the organisation, the management functions within each operating unit, and so on. On the assumption that the functions already exist, there will be current commitments, which can be separately identified in step 2. Recognising this, any additional resource that is requested for these areas might be required on the 'shopping list' for consideration against specific projects. This is certainly an obvious way of assessing the proposed start up of such a function where it does not already exist.

Alternatively, the organisation could make decisions on general activity within any unit before considering specific projects. This may be the more realistic approach – recognising, as it does, that the business of coordinating and prioritising projects requires some support and general management. In theory, the level of general activity should depend on the number and complexity of projects that need to be supported. However, in practice, once there is a broad understanding of the level of activity that the function has to support, then approximating the size of resource that must be committed to its support is relatively straightforward.

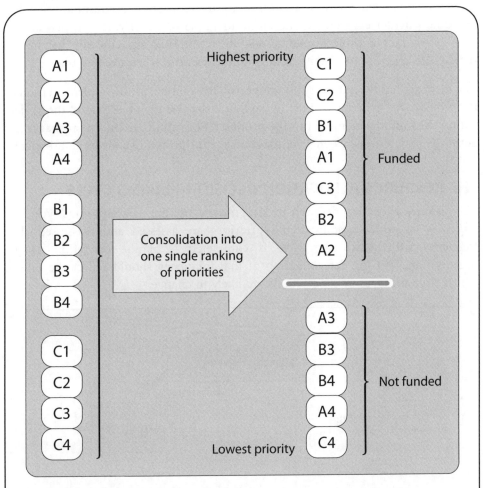

Operating units A, B and C are within the span of control of one senior manager. Each unit ranks its activities by importance, top-down, into one list according to its priorities. The senior manager consolidates the three priority lists into one single listing maintaining the *unit* ranking of activities (for example, A1 remains a higher priority than A2, B2 higher than B3, and so on) but now determining the ranking of activities between the three units' projects. Activities C1 and C2 are ranked as the highest of the 12 activities. A funding 'guillotine', defined by the level of available funds, determines which activities are funded (C1 to A2).

Fig. 17.2 Prioritising activities

Approving activities

Assuming that the project is delivering what was intended, the funding for prioritised activities that are approved is guaranteed for the duration of the activity at the time of approval. This funding security enables the activity's manager to manage the pace of implementation of projects according to the project's circumstances, not according to the corporate accounting calendar. Deciding whether expenditure should occur in period 12 of year 1 or period 1 of year 2 becomes a project matter, not an accounting one, thereby helping to replace the 'spend it or lose it' culture with a 'spend it when needed' one.

The manager has the authority and responsibility to manage the implementation of the project over the course of its life, so that it delivers the objectives of the project within the funding submitted in the proposal. So, within reason, the manager has authority to determine when, over the course of the project life, the funds are spent.

THE RESOURCE ALLOCATION DECISION-MAKING CYCLE

The resource allocation decision-making process becomes a continuous cycle (see fig. 17.3) in which resources and priorities are assessed and reassessed. The frequency with which the cycle is completed is at the discretion of the organisation, and the determination of that frequency should reflect the rate at which circumstances or expectations are likely to change.

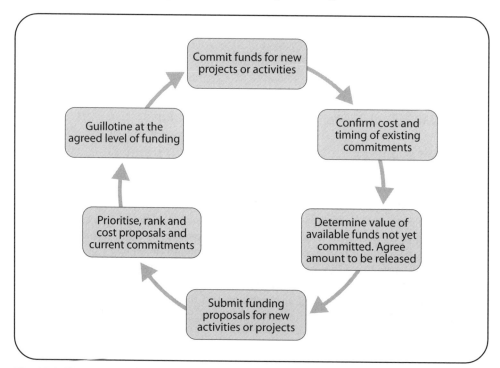

Fig. 17.3 The resource allocation decision-making cycle

One option is a quarterly cycle. Here, all stages of the cycle can be completed each quarter, meaning that operating unit managers can propose new activities and/or projects four times a year as and when it is appropriate from a programme point of view, rather than when it fits into the accounting/planning timetable. However, it may not be straightforward to move an organisation towards such a process. It is asking for a number of sacred cows to be sacrificed. The pace of change needs to be thought through, balancing the competing merits of the sharp shock associated with rapid change against those that would accompany a slower, more evolutionary development of new principles. It may be beneficial to develop a troubleshooting guide to answer the obvious questions that spenders might have.

As with any planning process (including traditional budgeting), the system requires proposed activities to have been properly thought through prior to submission for funding. One risk of being able to propose new ideas frequently is that the discipline of good activity planning can loosen. This will happen if the culture becomes one in which it is acceptable for submissions to be incomplete, and where omitted components can simply be added to the shopping list next time round.

The resource allocation decision-making process in practice

The process progresses as follows.

1. Within each of the three top-level expenditure areas (income generation, management and administration, and activities to further the organisation's objectives) the relevant managers determine how much of the guaranteed resources to use on general activity in the operating units within their span of control, and thereby how much to make available for specific activities.
2. Operating unit managers within each area submit a prioritised list of activities that they wish to be funded, plus lists of activities that are in the pipeline, to give early notice of what is on the horizon.
3. Decision makers within the three expenditure areas decide how much of the allocated funds at their disposal to release. This funding 'guillotine' determines the level to which funding approval will be given, within the ranked projects listing.
4. Approved projects' funding is guaranteed for the duration of each project, thereby reducing the size of the available funds that are not yet committed.

SEQUENCING THE DECISION MAKING

Which should be fixed first: the work programme or the resource plans? The downward design logic of the results chain, from impact to resources, would suggest that it should be the work programme. The work programme, planned to deliver outputs and outcomes that generate the organisation's intended impact, should determine the application of resources. However, in practice, the scale of the work programme that is implemented will be heavily influenced by the level, type and sources of resources available.

So, it becomes crucial to establish financial parameters up front, within which operational planning can be undertaken sensibly. This avoids the inevitable frustrations that otherwise result from allowing spenders to plan beyond their means, their initial excitement about possible future programme expansion then punctured by the subsequent financial reality. Box 17.5 illustrates the point.

Box 17.5   Aligning policy to known resources: an example

Assume a health ministry wants to develop a health policy for the country, and it convenes expert groups as well as various groups involved in the sector, such as the Chamber of Doctors, hospital administrators, nurses organizations, etc. Collectively these groups will use their best professional judgment in devising an optimal health policy. This policy may include specific targets of number of beds per capita, physicians per hospital, etc. It may also specify vehicles for advancing the policy, such as the nature and type of health benefits included in the national health insurance plan, or assume certain modes of service delivery (e.g. expansion in government-owned clinics).

Now, when it comes to financing the policy, it is commonly the case that the entire package is unaffordable. If the policy is retained as formulated, the best that can be hoped for is, for argument's sake, 60 percent of the total cost of the policy. The result is that the policy cannot be implemented, objectives cannot be achieved, and even the reduced funding level may be too low for individual elements of the policy to be effective (e.g. funding for vaccines may be too low to assure adequate coverage of the population).

In contrast, if the overall funding level were known in advance, framing the policy discussion, entirely different objectives, programs, or means of production may be explored. Instead of government-owned clinics, perhaps the government would contract with private clinics to provide services at lower cost. Or, vaccination programs would be considered essential and fully funded. The package of health benefits covered under the health insurance plan might be adjusted. The point is that both objectives and means of achieving the objectives will be different under different resource constraints.

Dorotinsky, 2004, pp. 10–11

CREATING FISCAL SPACE

One of the challenges facing any budget distributor is that of creating fiscal space. Emerging priorities and new mandates need funding. That is easy to provide if funds available for expenditure are growing. However, if they are not, then the organisation needs a clear approach to creating financial room to manoeuvre. This requires funding to be redistributed away from current destinations. Recipients have to make trade-offs – that is, choices. If the exercise is not well managed and based on an intelligible, reasonable and transparent rationale, then this exercise quickly becomes highly political and fractious.

There are a number of ways in which funding space can be created:

Uniform spending reductions across all units

This approach can be dressed up in different ways often to avoid using the term 'cut', which is easily pejorative. 'Productivity tax' is one label, the intention being to indicate that reduced spending is expected to result from improved productivity rather than reduced work programme. It reflects a belief that efficiency improvements are possible in any unit.

Whatever the approach is called, the message is clear: reduce spending! Obviously this is a blunt instrument, and the charge is always that it fails to discriminate. All units face equal reductions, irrespective of the relative importance of the work programme or of the efficacy with which funds are currently being used. However, the decision to apply uniform spending reductions is quick and easy to make and administer. It can also be surprisingly effective. Such reductions do force every part of the organisation to look at how it can increase its return. Requiring spending reductions of, say, between 1 and 3 per cent for as few as two or three successive years can quickly generate sizeable funds for emerging priorities without having a noticeably deleterious effect on the impact made by units.

It is a practical, effective way – for a limited time – to start 'tightening the belt' in any organisation that is generally inefficient, bureaucratic or lacks agility. Simultaneously, more precise instruments and approaches can be developed to enable decision makers in the future to better target spending reductions.

Expenditure policy changes

Otherwise known as 'line item controls', this approach focuses on making changes to specific organisational policies that define the spending parameters within which units and individuals are expected to operate. Any policy relating to one or more expenditure or budget lines may warrant review and possible revision. These include policies determining compensation and benefits, facilities, IT, travel, consultants, representation and hospitality.

In all of these cases, organisations have to make judgements about what level of cost to allow – recognising that, at its simplest, expenditure is influenced by both price and volume. For example, expenditure on salaries is determined by the number of employees and the salary levels awarded to those employees. Policies might be written to guide the determination of either factor. Units can be constrained both in terms of the number of employees that can be engaged and the salaries that can be awarded.

The potential for cost savings can be high. However, exercising central control over spending behaviour in units comes with risks, as we saw in chapter 16 (see pp. 248–50). It is critical that the organisation determines the extent to which it wishes to decentralise decision making. The potential benefits of imposing policy from the centre – uniform policy, hard constraints on behaviour and cultural norms – can be easily offset by the dissatisfaction of the units having controls imposed on them. The outcome may not be the desired one, even if the policy change is sensible – which, in any case, it might not be.

Pricing policy

In larger organisations, it is likely that the centre will use a form of internal pricing to charge units for goods and services that are managed centrally. Facilities are a good example, with units charged an internal rate for use of space. A central facilities unit manages the overall relationship and contract – for example, negotiating rental agreements with landlords. The internal price may be varied, dependent on whether the organisation wishes to subsidise the utilisation space by units, fully cover costs, or generate a 'surplus'. Just as prices in the marketplace create consumer incentives and disincentives to purchase products, so internal pricing can be used within organisations to stimulate desired behaviours. The higher the internal rate for space, the lower the appetite of expenditure-constrained units to demand it.

Business process reviews

This approach focuses on improving the efficiency with which business processes (which are major drivers of operating cost) are completed end-to-end. Such processes tend to run across organisational structures, and this crossing of functional boundaries can generate errors and create inefficiencies in the completion of work.

The goal of process reviews is to design and operate systems and procedures to ensure that activities are performed efficiently, avoiding unnecessary steps, and avoiding errors first time. Efficient processes also need to embed the ability of the organisation to adapt to abnormal conditions, correcting problems when they occur. Many organisations' business processes are over-complex and inefficient. They need to be simplified.

Programme reviews

All of the above approaches focus on improving the efficiency of business through productivity improvements or pricing changes. Significant cost savings are possible – at least initially – but the returns will diminish as efficiency improves. Of course, inefficiencies can return, and there is an ongoing need to remain vigilant. However, usually, to achieve more dramatic and larger cost savings, major changes in the organisation's strategy and/or work programme are required.

Eventually, attention on efficiency improvement must be replaced by strategic assessments of the content of work selected by the organisation. These reviews must ask fundamental questions about the added value of particular activities, work programmes or strategies. Cost–benefit analyses must inform decision makers' judgements about whether programmes should or should not continue and, if the former, whether or not they should continue to be run in the same way.

What information is required to inform such reviews? It is information about how successfully organisations climb the results chain for particular programmes, coupled with assessments about the external environment. Paton (2003) offers one example, used by US-based Pioneer Human Services, a not-for-profit organisation supporting a range of people, including those with substance misuse problems, people with housing needs and ex-offenders (see fig. 17.4).

	Social performance	*Business performance*
Internal information	• Activity and output levels; completion rates / client feedback / complaints data / trends in client profiles ...	• Trends in key indicators of financial and operational performance (e.g. cost-activity and cost-output trends, margins)
External information	• Outcome studies • Benchmarking data (e.g. reoffending rates, or data from comparable projects/organisations) • Innovations developed by others • New patterns of social need	• Market share, and competitor analysis (e.g. how much 'people recovery work' is being funded, by whom? Who else is getting and doing this work and why?) • Market trends (e.g. regarding public policy)

Fig. 17.4 Programme review information matrix (Paton, 2003, p. 144)

In 2002 the US government's Office of Management and Budget introduced the Program Assessment Rating Tool (PART) in an effort to establish a consistent approach to assessing federal programmes. It is perhaps the most extensive use of programme review in the public and not-for-profit sectors, intended to enable all US government programmes to be assessed every five years. The PART is a structured questionnaire, which is designed to evaluate the effectiveness of programmes, and results in an overall effectiveness rating, which is published:

> The Program Assessment Rating Tool (PART) was developed to assess and improve program performance so that the Federal government can achieve better results. A PART review helps identify a program's strengths and weaknesses to inform funding and management decisions aimed at making the program more effective. The PART therefore looks at all factors that affect and reflect program performance including program purpose and design; performance measurement, evaluations, and strategic planning; program management; and program results. Because the PART includes a consistent series of analytical questions, it allows programs to show improvements over time, and allows comparisons between similar programs.
>
> Office of Management and Budget, n.d., n.p.

TRADE-OFFS

Predictably, the focus of attention when determining resource allocation decisions is often the margin – the delta – rather than the whole. There is often far greater interest and debate about the last 2 per cent of intended spending than there is in relation to the first 98 per cent. Assessing future resource allocation starts from a baseline of current allocations or spending levels. The principal interest is on what redistribution should occur in order to finance new priorities. This is particularly true in flat or declining funding environments, when there are no extra funds on the table to distribute.

The decision makers focus on change. They rightly want to understand what efficiency improvements are being made in the units – evidenced by maintaining or improving service delivery while spending less. They also need to understand intended work programme changes, to demonstrate shifts in spending as evidence that they are making hard choices about how the funds available to them are used. It is all part of the due diligence required of the financial steward, in the ever-present task of ensuring that resources are used optimally, maximising the conversion into impact.

Key stewardship questions

1. How much funding is it appropriate for the organisation to commit to expenditure now?

2. How is the allocation between the main expenditure categories determined?

3. How is the organisation signalling its policy choices?

4. Is there a cost-effective process for committing funds within each expenditure category?

5. Do the resource allocation decisions reflect relative organisational priorities?

6. How satisfactory is the alignment of resources with the organisation's objectives and mission?

7. How does the organisation create fiscal space?

8. How is the organisation making trade-offs?

18 Step 5: act

SETTING OFF AND REVIEWING PROGRESS

The organisation's stewards have now decided where they are trying to get to, and have expressed the financial goals in terms of medium-term expenditure directions and financial metrics. They have a good understanding of where the organisation is now (with reference to actual income and expenditure results, balance sheet, cash flow reports, and so on) and have compiled their best collective sense of what is ahead of them from top-level income forecasts and expenditure commitments. Using all three sets of information, they have now decided on the allocation of those resources over which they have discretion. They have made decisions about what levels of general activity and which specific projects to finance.

The organisation can now act on these decisions and press the buttons that actually commit funds as agreed, so that activities are undertaken that contribute to the delivery of the mission.

THE BUSINESS REVIEW PROCESS

The spenders are now getting on with the spending. Time to sit back and relax? Far from it! The answers to the questions 'Where is the organisation?' and 'What is ahead of it?' will be always changing. Every day, the income and expenditure position, the balance sheet, the cash flow and the judgements about the future will be changing. Just as the traveller reacts to what is happening around them as they move forward, the organisation must react to continually updated operational and financial information about results and expectations. The steps become inextricably linked and completed, almost simultaneously. As soon as action is taken, the position of the organisation will have changed.

Meanwhile, the environment in which the organisation is operating will have altered as a result of internal and/or external factors. What is ahead will be constantly evolving and changing, and may persuade the financial stewards to adjust their sights, thereby influencing their resource allocation decisions. The speed with which the cycle is completed will depend on the degree of uncertainty and change that is present in the operating environment of the organisation, but it is unlikely to be evenly paced.

> The business review process must be a performance review and action-planning forum: the primary management forum driving performance improvement. The key to success is accountability and dialogue – not forms and templates.

So, the organisation needs to design and run a business review process, in order to enable periodic performance review and action planning. Monthly or quarterly is the norm, timetabled to coincide with end-of-period milestones. The business review provides an opportunity for decision makers to meet, supported by high-quality, focused and timely information. Its design and execution should enable it to become the primary management forum driving continuous performance improvement within the organisation. It should be designed in a way to facilitate learning, by stimulating thinking and sharing information, but its focus must be on problem-solving and improvement. Information must be shared before the forum to enable participants to arrive ready to tackle issues.

The review process needs shepherding – particularly in organisations that struggle to maintain a high-accountability culture, and in those where the key participants are handling multiple priorities with heavily time-constrained diaries. The process will not run itself.

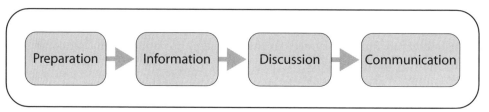

Fig. 18.1 The four business review phases

Each review process has four distinct phases (see fig. 18.1). Each of the stages shown in figure 18.1 is described below.

Preparation

The process must be designed, and warrants being run as a project. There are a surprising number of tasks that will have to be completed. As well as being the phase when all participants can be made aware of elements such as schedules and reporting requirements, at this stage it is valuable to determine the focus of the documents that will be tabled and discussions that will be held. Meeting early with the overall owner or sponsor of the process is important – as is maintaining dialogue with all the contributors, to ensure that they are familiar with what is required of them. The logistics of preparing documents and meetings can be complicated, and there may be a challenging coordination role for a secretariat.

Information

Certain information needs to be prepared and distributed as part of the process. This information can take several forms.

- **Analytics:** We have already looked in some detail at the issue of data, metrics and trends. It is sufficient to say here that data that informs discussions needs to be tabled. This is particularly true of trends in relation to key metrics that help participants answer the question of whether desired outcomes are being achieved, outputs delivered, and inputs deployed wisely. These metrics can be effectively presented in graphical forms. More detailed analytics can be provided in data tables. Up-to-date data needs to be collected so that a contemporaneous picture of performance and issues is available. It is important to pay attention to ensuring that the data is accepted as accurate and appropriate by the participants. Debates about the validity of the data, and the appropriateness of the calculation methodologies, need to take place beforehand.

- **Project plan summaries:** The project summary should portray what has been achieved to date, whether the project is on schedule to deliver the intended benefits, and the forthcoming milestones. The state of performance can be flagged in a way that is easy to interpret, using simple colour coding.

Box 18.1   Examples of World Bank Quarterly Business Review report formats

- **President's Briefing.** This is a two-page performance summary prepared each quarter end. The report focuses on providing headlines on results, trends and latest forecasts in relation to key outputs (the Bank's lending and knowledge products) and inputs (staffing, income and expenditure). Simple graphics illustrate results trends and coloured arrows provide an instant signal of the trajectory of performance.
- **Quarterly Business Review – Report to the Board**. Organised in terms of a results chain, this report to the Bank's board members provides a detailed account of the institution's performance in terms of strategic priorities, outputs, activities and inputs. The report is narrative-based, offering a detailed picture of key developments in the areas of strategic focus; the volume, trend and quality of the Bank's products; and on staffing, income and expenditure trends. Extensive use of examples is made.

- **Reports:** Narrative-based reports, such as those described in box 18.1, enable recipients to gain an up-to-date understanding of performance and future action in relation to any part of the results chain. Examples, illustrations and anecdotes can play a valuable role alongside more analytics-based assessment, as Denning (2005, p. 5) argues:

  Analysis is what drives business thinking. It seemingly cuts through the fog of myth, gossip and speculation to get to the hard facts. It purports to go wherever the observations and premises and conclusions take it, undistorted by the hopes or fears of the analyst. Its strength lies in its objectivity, its impersonality, its heartlessness.

Yet this strength is also a weakness. Analysis might excite the mind, but it hardly offers a route to the heart. And that's where you must go if you are to motivate people not only to take action but to do so with energy and enthusiasm. At a time when corporate survival often requires transformational change, leadership involves inspiring people to act in unfamiliar and often unwelcome ways. Mind-numbing cascades of numbers or daze-inducing PowerPoint slides won't achieve this goal. Even logical arguments for making the needed changes usually won't do the trick.

But effective storytelling often does.

- **Issues notes:** A perceptive, well-written issues note prepared ahead of the discussions can significantly contribute to the success or otherwise of the business reviews. The note should advise on any contextual matters that are relevant, highlight particular issues that need to be tackled, emphasise specific data that should be referenced, and provide an outline of the meeting objectives, agenda and participants. Ideally, a pre-meeting briefing with the chair of the discussions should be held to prepare them for the meeting and guide them on where to focus the discussions, and what outcomes to aim for.

Discussion

Phase 3 comprises the discussions: the heart of the process. This is where decision makers meet and candid conversations must take place with honest, outcome-orientated assessment of current performance and intended action (see box 18.2). It is powerful to frame business reviews from the top of the chain downwards by assessing organisational performance in terms of the welfare outcomes that are sought.

> **Box 18.2   UK government stocktakes**
>
> *Central to any process for managing performance is a meeting in which those responsible for delivery are held to account.*
>
> Barber 2007, p. 91

For example, the UK government focused its 'stocktake' meetings around 14 public service priorities under the responsibility of four government departments: health, education, transport and the Home Office. Framing the discussions in terms of whether the organisation is achieving its intended outcomes will stimulate the right discussion. Positioning the meeting as an opportunity to assess whether achievement of outcomes is happening – or at least improving – forces the participants to be clear about design of work programme down the chain, and the adequacy of progress up it.

The discussions should focus on one or more of the questions listed in box 18.3. Every one of the 10 questions listed warrants the time of the organisation, with the focus shifting depending on the stage of the business cycle reached. The questions move down the results chain, driven from desired impact. Initially, time must be spent on the first three questions to establish the purpose, the focus of the efforts that will follow. However, over time attention must move down to the latter questions, eventually specifying exactly who has to do what.

> **Box 18.3 The key business review questions**
>
> 1. What outcome are we seeking to influence?
> 2. What will success look like?
> 3. What is our strategy to get there?
> 4. What are the priorities, and what trade-offs must we make?
> 5. What is our plan, and what are the key milestones?
> 6. What progress have we made so far?
> 7. How satisfactory is current performance:
>   a. over time, and is it getting better?
>   b. given the circumstances?
>   c. compared to others?
> 8. What's the evidence?
> 9. What's on the radar screen?
> 10. Who needs to do what, and when?

Note the focus on trade-offs, the use of a project plan approach to assessing performance (through milestones and interim assessments of progress), and the retrospective perspective taken to assess performance. Performance is assessed in relation to comparable organisations, and over time to determine whether improvement is evident. In both cases, the assessment must be made in the context of the circumstances in which it was delivered.

The discussions must spend time analysing specific results that have been achieved, the root causes of actual performance, the latest outlook of what is ahead, and consequent action that is planned. The agenda should enable participants to understand how well they and their peers are doing, and to agree on what further action to take.

The people who need to be round the table are those who are accountable for successful delivery of the intended outcome. It is an opportunity to bring together colleagues across functions, and they must collaborate to ensure end-to-end delivery. Possible action includes agreeing changes to goals (unlikely), strategy (possible), the implementation of strategy (likely), or the resourcing of it (likely).

One of the many challenges of these discussions is to get to action planning. It is easy and intellectually satisfying (to some, at least) for the conversation to remain conceptual – to have extensive debates about the logic of the chain, the strategy of the organisation, or the most appropriate metrics to use. However, for the discussion to reach the practical question of who needs to do what, there must be a direct connection between the organisational outcomes and the work programmes of units and individuals within the organisation.

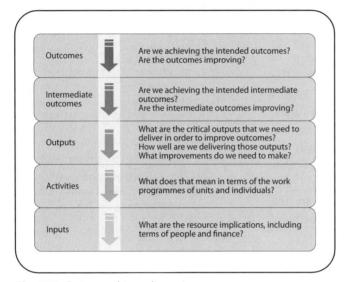

Figure 18.2 illustrates how the discussion can be driven from a performance assessment of outcomes to the implications for the activities undertaken by units and individuals in the organisation. The consequence of the discussions, and the action agreed, must be reflected in the work plans of those who deliver the outputs by which the outcomes are achieved.

Fig. 18.2 Outcome-driven discussion

The key to success is accountability and dialogue – not forms and templates. Getting colleagues together to look at evidence of current performance and discuss how things are going, and what needs to be done next, can be extremely powerful if, as a result, clear action plans emerge accompanied by an unambiguous definition of who is accountable for what. Investment in the phases of the process should be distributed accordingly. If necessary, time allocated to gathering information must be sacrificed in order to make time for interpretation and discussion.

Communication

Following the discussions, there is a communications task: to make sure that salient points are captured and disseminated. This can include publishing the information and summaries of the discussion to a wider audience. The agreements made in the meeting must be channelled into the day-to-day work programmes of the organisation. There is an opportunity for leaders to use the content of the business review to account transparently to the organisation, to develop a shared understanding of how well the organisation is performing, and to ensure that everyone is fully aligned with future action plans. Everyone needs to be clear about what action needs to be taken in relation to identified issues, and to understand the priorities and trade-offs in light of the resource implications of agreed action.

ENSURING CANDOUR

If the business review process is going to be successful in focusing on holding individuals accountable for actual performance and action planning, it has to be driven with a tight hand. The more bureaucratic the organisation and the weaker the culture of accountability, the more the process requires stewardship. It also requires as much objectivity and candour as possible. There is a role for independent assessment of performance in order to achieve this.

One of the key tasks played by the UK government's Delivery Unit, headed by Michael Barber, was to provide the chief executive – in this case, the prime minister – with an objective, evidence-based evaluation of whether performance was improving, and to highlight the critical issues that needed to be tackled with those accountable for performance (see box 18.4). A key decision of the chief executive is to determine who should report on progress and issues. The likely trade-off is between gaining ownership (by requiring those accountable for performance to report on it) versus gaining candour and objectivity (by asking an independent party to provide the report).

Box 18.4   UK government stocktakes: the key ingredients

To succeed, the Delivery Unit-organised stocktakes had to have certain key ingredients. The first was [a] focus on performance; the second was regularly focusing on the same handful of priorities; the third was the regular attendance of the Prime Minister himself and the relevant secretary of state; and the fourth was ensuring that the data presented to the meeting was shared and accepted by everyone present. Each of these characteristics seems relatively straightforward, but the combination was revolutionary.

Barber, 2007, p. 92

Such evaluations can advise on strategy and policy, and can be a crucial interpreter of the data. They can also be simply a presentation of the facts. Doing no more than presenting a quantitative review of the number of deliverables achieved is helpful. For example, highlighting simply that in a given quarter 35 deliverables were planned and 20 were delivered successfully, raises some important questions. Is 35 deliverables a sensible number? Are they the right deliverables? How satisfactory is the delivery of 20 of those deliverables? What happened to the remainder? What should happen now?

BUSINESS REVIEW IN PRACTICE: WORLD BANK HR VICE-PRESIDENCY

In 2008, the World Bank's HR vice-presidency developed its own strategic framework (see fig. 18.3). The framework has three aims:

- to enable the unit to define how it contributes to the Bank's delivery of its mission as an institution
- to ensure that its strategy, ongoing work programme, staffing model and use of resources aligns with Bank priorities
- to provide a structure for assessing and reporting on its performance.

The framework defines the *raison d'être* of HR as enabling the Bank to establish and maintain the staffing and organisational capabilities required in order to provide flexible, rapid and effective responses to its changing business environment. These capabilities (which themselves must change over time) help enable the institution to deliver appropriate lending and knowledge products by which it has impact.

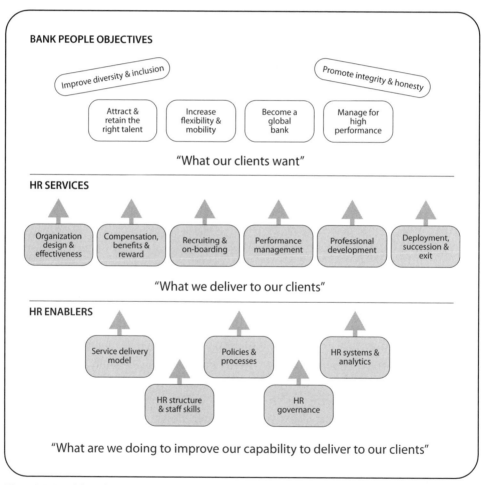

Fig. 18.3 World Bank HR vice-presidency strategic framework (World Bank, 2009, n.p.)

The Bank has defined four principal people objectives:

- attracting and retaining the right talent
- increasing flexibility and mobility
- becoming a global bank
- managing for high performance.

These are supported by two underpinning values: improving diversity and inclusion, and promoting integrity and honesty.

These objectives – strategic imperatives for the Bank – define the intended outcomes of its HR strategy and work programme. An overall HR strategy is developed for each objective. The work programme is then defined in terms of six business lines, used to classify the many different services provided by the vice-presidency. The key areas of focus internally to the unit are shown on the strategic framework as five enablers.

At the completion of each quarter, business review meetings are held, chaired by the vice-president of HR. Each quarter, the subject of the meetings is the same. The meetings focus on the bank's people objectives. These meetings ask one overriding question: 'Is the Bank moving in the right direction in terms of the objective?'

The first part of the discussion focuses on performance. Trend data of relevant metrics is presented as an easy-to-read set of 'dashboard' graphics, to inform the discussion. Using the metrics and qualitative feedback, participants debate the adequacy of performance in terms of the objective, asking questions such as: 'Are we becoming more flexible and mobile as an institution?', 'How do we know?', 'What has been the evidence?', 'Is the rate of progress satisfactory?', and 'Is there any reason why it will, or will not continue?'

The second half of each meeting focuses on action. This places pressure on the participants to be clear about the HR strategy by which the objective, such as increased flexibility and mobility, will be supported. Participants offer diagnoses and share lessons of recent experience implementing the agreed strategy. The key HR services and initiatives by which the strategy is being implemented are reviewed. 'How well are we providing these services, and implementing these initiatives?' asks the vice-president. Gaps in critical services are identified, together with possible efficiency improvements. Action is agreed, and responsibilities assigned.

The meetings also focus internally on HR's enablers, asking whether HR's capability to deliver to clients is increasing. Again supported by metrics, attention focuses on the efficiency of service provision and on the implementation of key cross-functional initiatives by which the vice-presidency is aiming to improve services.

Within 48 hours of each meeting, the vice-president distributes a note to the participants confirming what has been agreed and next steps. Directors and managers work with their teams to revise work programmes and initiate project plans in light of the action agreed. At the completion of the series of meetings, the metrics dashboard is published to all HR staff. Town hall-style forums allow all HR staff to hear first-hand from the vice-president and directors on the state of play and the intended short-term action plan, and to engage in question-and-answer sessions on HR performance, strategy and plans.

The value of review

The description above of the HR quarterly business review process suggests that these processes are typically well honed, running seamlessly from start to finish. In fact, they often are not – but that is acceptable as long as the process increases in efficiency and value in each quarter. In practice, the business reviews can feel untidy, laborious, confusing and distracting. Unclear definitions of success can impede good understanding about the state of the bank's HR objective. The strategy's limitations can be exposed. Precious time can be used in debating the ideal set of metrics, ignoring the reality of what is available. Responsibilities can be ambiguous and agreed action imprecise. Progress can feel slow and detached from the day-to-day need to provide unglamorous but essential services.

The process of business review is not an easy one to establish or maintain. However, above all, the process brings key players together, forces the right conversations and, by assessing performance and planning action through a client-focused lens, enables units and organisations to channel their efforts optimally in support of the mission they serve.

INCORPORATING THE FINANCIAL IMPLICATIONS

Of course, any organisational business review must involve consideration of the financial results and position, and it is a key role of the financial steward to translate the business decisions into financial implications. It is also essential to translate all the decisions that have been made into an overall financial forecast. Leaders must continually appreciate the likely financial consequence of the choices made, and it should be possible for the relevant management to prepare a financial outlook based on broad indicators of future activity level and cost trends without having to build it bottom-up from detail.

It is well worth organisations developing the skill and capacity to prepare and maintain high-level, broad-brush, indicative financial forecasts (which can be done quickly by just a few individuals) that are accurate enough to support decision making while not requiring an onerous micro-orientated process that distracts everyone from getting on with the task of delivering impact to beneficiaries.

Particularly helpful to management is financial information that presents a moving picture over time of the actual results achieved, together with the latest financial outlook as prepared in the forecasts. As we saw in the discussion on trends in chapter 14, presenting both a historic and prospective picture in the same report offers the organisation's financial stewards all the critical information regarding income and expenditure on one sheet. It creates a powerful information tool which, together with the balance sheet, becomes the single most important financial planning and control tool of senior management and the governance body (neither of which should be considering detail as a matter of course).

The process of re-forecasting

How should the organisation react if the financial forecasts differ from prior expectations? What if the financial projections of a particular project climb above the estimates included in the funding submission completed under step 4 of the methodology? The first relevant point is to acknowledge that decision makers will need to know that the forecast has changed, if they are to react. The process and culture of the organisation must be such as to enable operating managers to advise when their expectations about future financial performance change.

The process of re-forecasting at operating-unit level is built into the resource allocation decision-making cycle (fig. 17.3 on p. 270) described in step 4. Periodically, unit managers are required to reconfirm the cost and timing of existing commitments. Within the five-step methodology, this is replicated at a corporate level in step 2, when the financial stewards of the organisation look forward and, among other things, identify the expected cost of commitments already made but not yet met.

The culture of re-forecasting

The culture of re-forecasting is determined by how the organisation chooses to react to information from the line that previous estimates (about, for example, income or expenditure or cash) have changed. That reaction will depend on the extent to which the forecasts are regarded as predetermined performance contracts. The more they are so regarded, the greater the likelihood that the reaction to news that costs are likely to be higher than previously expected or income lower will be one of criticism.

The organisation has to understand that a certain culture is required to promote best-estimate forecasting rather than desired-outcome forecasting. Such a culture is almost certainly going to require forecasting to be divorced from performance measurement, with an acceptance that in some circumstances costs may exceed expectations. That is not to imply that managers should not be expected to exhibit high-quality forecasting skills: a culture in which the accuracy of the forecast does not matter cannot be allowed to develop. It does matter, because decisions will be made on the back of those forecasts.

Systems must be in place to require managers to demonstrate that their funding submissions, and subsequent income and expenditure forecasts, are reasonable and complete. Simultaneously, the organisation must be in a position to handle the unexpected financially. Managers should be expected to explain any major changes to forecasts, and distinctions must be drawn between factors that are within the control of the manager and those that are not.

However, it is best to avoid the attempt to predetermine an acceptable level of variation against the last forecast. Such a level simply ends up being interpreted as an acceptable margin of error that is added onto the approved sum. This breeds complacency. At all costs, the temptation to override a manager's best-estimate forecast, and impose instead the desired outcome, must be resisted. The organisation needs to listen to and understand what its managers really think is going to happen, however undesirable. There needs to be a continuous incentive to maintain tight costs in the pursuit of maximum cost-effectiveness.

Good reporting systems that inform the organisation's management and leadership of actual and forecast financial results alike should prevent a cost-complacent manager from causing undue financial difficulties. If anticipated costs exceed the agreed funding level without good reason, the operating manager could be asked to resubmit a funding proposal so that a new understanding of the activity's cost–benefit can be agreed. However, a manager needs to have discretion, within reason, to allow the costs of an activity to vary from the level of funding approved at the time of the project funding submission (see box 18.5). Managers need incentives to keep costs tightly under control while having discretion to allow costs to be managed (both up and down) in line with the demands and impact of the activity or project.

Box 18.5   Understanding changes to activity costs

- Understand the reasons for the new level of anticipated costs.
- Understand what impact the activity has had to date, and what impact it is expected to have if all the anticipated costs are incurred.
- Understand what scope there is to reduce the costs and the implications on impact of doing so.

Such discretion must be offered in the light of the individual manager's competence to handle the responsibility of devolved project financial management. They need to understand the financial context within which they are managing activities, understand the implications to the organisation of poor cost control, and appreciate that, ultimately, they are being judged on impact at the top of the results chain.

Accountability is the single most critical component of any performance management framework. There must be consequences of the business review – at unit and individual levels alike. Spending units must be rewarded for using resources effectively and efficiently, as evidenced by demonstrable added value to their clients. The more effective and efficient they become over time, the more recognition they receive. Ineffective and inefficient use of resources becomes an accountability issue. Managers that consistently deliver high-quality activities that further the organisation's objectives cost-effectively should be rewarded – not necessarily financially, but with further opportunities within the organisation. Future funding submissions made by these managers can be assessed with confidence, professional development opportunities can be extended and, of course, they should be well placed to assume other roles internally.

THE FIVE-STEP PROCESS IN ACTION

The acid test of the methodology is whether the steps, between them, provide an effective management tool. For example, a key question would be 'What would happen if the forecasts of the future are wrong?' – as they may well be. Imagine that a major investment in income generation fails to deliver and that income is significantly lower than anticipated. The chronology of the steps that would be taken is shown in box 18.6.

Box 18.6 Testing the methodology: a scenario

1. A decision to invest in fundraising activity is made (step 4) following consideration of a funding proposal from the fundraising department in terms of its impact on KPIs already set (step 3).
2. The fundraisers implement the investment decision, which becomes a current commitment (step 5).
3. Fundraising expenditure increases, and cash levels fall (step 1).
4. Ongoing reports indicate that donors are not being recruited in response to the fundraising initiative as expected (step 1).
5. The future costs of current commitments increase and the size of 'still-available' funds drops correspondingly (step 2).
6. The future income implications of low recruitment are assessed and forecasts of income are reduced (step 2).
7. Forecasts of resources that are likely to be available are reduced (step 2).
8. Metrics are reviewed in light of this new information but are reconfirmed (step 3).
9. The future allocation for service delivery 24 months ahead is reduced (step 4), with consequent implications for the level of general activity and/or the number of specific projects that are implemented (step 5).

In this way, the approach enables decision makers to react in good time to the information collected and, as a result, to steward the organisation forward appropriately. The key to its success is to act judiciously in the management of the financial risks associated with future resourcing uncertainty. Committing the organisation to future expenditure of funds (at least some of which will not yet have been generated) must be done with the assurance that the financial consequences of those commitments can be managed. Preventing the organisation from either over- or under-committing itself financially requires careful judgement.

Key stewardship questions

1. How does the organisation review business performance?

2. What is the focus of the review?

3. How much importance is attached to dialogue?

4. How well are the financial implications of business decisions understood?

5. How does the organisation react to changes in its outlook?

6. What are the consequences of accountability – for units, and for individuals?

Part 5: Enabling environment

19 Roles: determining the spread of responsibility

The preceding chapters have sought to define how organisations must steward the precious financial resources available to them, if they are to have the impact required by their beneficiaries and intended by their donors. But who within the organisation should carry out the tasks of financial stewardship? To some extent, the answer will depend on the size of the organisation. For example, small organisations without paid employees will rely heavily on volunteers, including trustees, to undertake the financial stewardship tasks that are, in larger organisations, vested in management. The larger the organisation, the more scope there is to distinguish between the roles that different positions within the organisation should play. Good financial stewardship assigns discrete responsibilities to a board of trustees, senior executives and managers. Finance specialists have yet a further role.

THE ROLE OF THE GOVERNING BODY

There are many sources to guide the reader on the legal role of an organisation's governing body in relation to financial stewardship. Try, for example, the UK Charity Commission's website (see box 19.1) or *The Good Trustee Guide* (Dyer, 2008). Note that despite the different names given to this body, the principles of good governance are common to all.

The Charity Commission's definition of responsibilities affirms the central role that trustees must play in financial stewardship. This is true for the governors of any not-for-profit organisation. Two aspects of the Charity Commission's definition are worth highlighting. The first is recognition of the need to ensure solvency. This takes the discussion back to one of the themes of this book: how the organisation manages the tension between having impact today and maintaining itself as a going concern so that it can have impact in the future. The second is its focus on outcomes: this is what financial stewardship is actually for.

The duty of prudence further emphasises the need to maintain a robust financial framework. Receiving assets, safeguarding them and applying them are exactly what implementing a finance strategy and climbing the results chain are all about: to have impact, the organisation must successfully implement a finance strategy that establishes performance criteria in relation to the flow of funds through income, on to the balance sheet and then along the results chain, as expenditure.

Box 19.1   Trustees and their responsibilities

Charity trustees are the people who serve on the governing body of a charity. They may be known as trustees, directors, board members, governors or committee members. The principles and main duties are the same in all cases.

Trustees have and must accept ultimate responsibility for directing the affairs of a charity, and ensuring that it is solvent, well-run, and meeting the needs for which it has been set up.

Duty of prudence – Trustees must:

- *Ensure that the charity is and will remain solvent.*
- *Use charitable funds and assets reasonably, and only in furtherance of the charity's objects.*
- *Avoid undertaking activities that might place the charity's endowment, funds, assets or reputation at undue risk.*
- *Take special care when investing the funds of the charity, or borrowing funds for the charity to use.*

Charity Commission 2008a, pp. 6–7

Argenti (1993, p. 214) argues that the task of trustees is one of acting as 'internal watchdogs on behalf of the intended beneficiaries'. Translate that in terms of financial stewardship, and the role of trustees becomes one of ensuring that the five principles on which this book is focused (see the financial stewardship map: fig. 1.2 on p. 8) are understood and exhibited in the behaviour and performance of the organisation.

Argenti's focus on the beneficiary promotes the task of trusteeship as being one of acting in the interests of the beneficiary, not the organisation – and rightly so. In terms of financial stewardship, this means that the trustee body has a duty to ensure that the financial decisions taken within the organisation enable it to maximise its impact over time. Without the focus on impact, there is the risk that the trustees, inadvertently or otherwise, will see their first duty as being to the organisation, not the beneficiary. If so, they will invest in institutional protection, not in beneficiary impact.

Distinguishing between executive and trustee roles

In practice, the distinction between the roles of the senior executive and the trustees is rarely as clear-cut as Argenti would encourage it to be. The Association of Chief Executives of Voluntary Organisations (ACEVO) (Blackmore *et al*, 1998) conducted research to try to determine what distinct responsibilities distinguished governance from management. The model of governance–management interface that emerged from the research was that three distinct roles had to be played (Blackmore *et al*, 1998, p. 32):

*If **management** is about 'putting strategic policy and practices into action' and **governance** is about 'ensuring that the organisation is held to account', **leadership** is about 'establishing strategic policies and priorities'.*

The responsibility for governance rests squarely with the trustees, and the responsibility for management rests squarely with the management... Leadership on the other hand cannot be exercised without the chair and chief executive actively working together to establish the future direction of the organisation.

This useful distinction suggests that trustees and senior executives would jointly determine the strategic direction of the organisation (principle 1, see p. 7) and define the expected attributes of the intended financial framework (principle 2, see p. 7). For example, it would be a shared obligation to agree the financial KPI targets and parameters discussed in chapter 16.

Governance role of the trustees

So, the governance role rests squarely with the trustees. It is for the trustee body to reassure itself that the financial resources of the organisation are being used wisely, and that the organisation accounts publicly for how the funds placed in its trust for public benefit have been used. It can only do this if it concerns itself with the overall purpose of the organisation, its strategic direction and its operational performance, as well as monitoring the financial performance and state of play. So, the trustee role becomes fivefold in relation to financial stewardship (see box 19.2).

Box 19.2   Financial stewardship role of trustees
■ To determine jointly with the executive the purpose, values and strategic direction of the organisation
■ To ensure that the organisation remains financially viable over time, using a robust financial framework
■ To ensure that the finances, work programme and strategies are appropriately aligned with the organisational purpose
■ To monitor overall organisational performance
■ To account publicly for the management of funds placed in their trust.

Executing trustee responsibility for financial stewardship

All trustees on the board – not just the treasurer – must assume responsibility for financial stewardship, and the treasurer may need to remind them of this periodically. By focusing the trustees' finance agenda on the five roles defined above, it should be possible to actively involve all trustees in matters of financial stewardship, and to help them appreciate the contribution that they can make in this field.

The responsibility demands far more than merely rubber-stamping the approval of a set of statutory accounts once a year, and indeed it may well be the case that trustees other than the treasurer are best placed to recognise what financial issues the board needs to address. Simply re-reading all the key stewardship questions at the end of each chapter should make it apparent to any trustee that they can bring value to the discussions pertinent to financial stewardship. For example, they may be the ones with their fingers on the pulse of likely funding changes or future areas of risk, able to make informed judgements on which expenditure profiles should be adopted, and therefore on how to allocate funds.

To execute the five financial stewardship responsibilities, trustee bodies have to include finance on each of their agendas. They must reflect continually on the financial matters that the organisation has to sort out, and on the financial performance and position that they wish the organisation to reach. However, all of these discussions should remain strategic in nature, rather than operational. To exercise their governance role of holding the executive to account, at each meeting trustees must monitor actual performance, consider latest-forecast operational and financial results, and reach judgements on the adequacy of those results.

The precise financial information they need to receive at trustee meetings will depend on the key stewardship issues, but all of them will relate in some way to the primary financial statements. However, a useful rule of thumb is that they need to receive actual and forecast financial results expressed on three pages – the SOFA, balance sheet and cash flow statement described in part 2. If the reports also identify what the actual and forecast results mean in terms of the organisation's financial KPIs, then the trustees have all the financial information they need to steward the organisation's finances from a governance perspective. More information may detract from the quality of governance rather than enhance it, encouraging trustees to worry about operational detail.

Delegating board responsibilities

Nothing concentrates the minds of trustees better than a reminder of how much time the board has to conduct its business. Typically, in the case of non-executive boards, it will be under 25 hours each year. This sounds frighteningly inadequate – especially after acknowledging the obligation to deal with formal duties (for example, complying with constitutional requirements such as approving the statutory accounts). So, as well as being tightly disciplined about which issues reach the board agenda in the first place, it is worth considering whether some of the duties of the board can be formally delegated. The governing document of the organisation may permit the board to use committees with limited powers to undertake particular tasks on its behalf, although the general rule is that trustees act together (see box 19.3).

Box 19.3 Delegating trustee responsibilities

Trustees always have the ultimate responsibility for running their charity. But they generally have the power to delegate certain powers to agents, subject to their governing document, and any relevant legislation.

All decisions by the trustees concerning a charity are taken by all the trustees, acting collectively and as a team.

Trustees can always invite some of their number to look into particular matters and make recommendations. The decision whether or not to act on the recommendations is for the trustees to take together. In some cases the governing document of a charity may permit the trustees to set up committees with delegated powers to carry out particular functions.

Charity Commission, 2008a, p. 10

Where committees are used, they can be established either with terms of reference and with decision-making authority to act on behalf of the board, or as an advisory body without decision-making authority, whose role is to sift the detail and present the full board with a much more focused agenda. It must be clear which of these two roles any committee is to play if it is to be effective. It is common for organisations to establish a committee to carry out many of its financial stewardship functions – especially where the subject is technically specialist and complex.

Types of committee that will be responsible for some of the financial stewardship responsibilities typically include the following:

- **Finance committee:** This committee has a general remit to undertake some of the detailed preparatory work related to the five stewardship tasks (listed in box 19.2) that face the board. Typically, this is the committee that would advise the full board on the financial framework, targets and parameters that are appropriate for the organisation. Often, it would also review the financial implications of strategies and plans and conduct the thorough review of the financial performance and state with the executive, ensuring that appropriate internal and statutory accounts are prepared. It would then report back to the full trustee body. It is also a suitable body to help the executive determine policies such as risk management, treasury management (including investments and currency management) and reserves.
- **Audit committee:** This committee has terms of reference to define and hold to account an internal audit function. This can also include responsibility for reviewing the satisfactoriness of the statutory accounts process on behalf of the full board, and for receiving the external auditor's post-audit report with

observations and recommendations. It can bring key points to the full board's attention. Guided by the audit committee, the external auditors can also prepare a presentation on their findings to the full board.

- **Investment committee:** This committee is charged with determining the board's investment objectives and its position on issues such as socially responsible investment. It also oversees the relationship with the investment managers, including monitoring their performance. Typically, it will account annually to the full board on investment matters. As with any other stewardship matter, uncertainty may warrant more frequent updates.
- **Remuneration committee:** This committee represents board members on issues relating to the terms and conditions of employment of staff. This might include overseeing the organisation's reward principles and policy or the terms and conditions of appointment of the chief executive, and acting as the final point of appeal on employment and other personnel matters.

There are opposing schools of thought about the appropriateness of using committees or subgroups. Opponents of committees argue that they disenfranchise the full governing body and generate more administration, while proponents point to the space that they create on the board's agenda to concentrate on other governance matters. What must be appreciated is that the existence of committees with decision-making authority does not remove the liability of the full trustee body for the actions of that committee, which box 19.3 confirms in the case of UK charities. So, like it or not, every trustee shares equal liability for the financial stewardship of the organisation.

Nevertheless, in the case of finance, much can be gained from well-defined delegation by the full trustee body to a committee, acknowledging that the key stewardship questions are not easy to answer or even perhaps to define. The quality of discussion, analysis and ultimate decision making can be significantly enhanced by a small, focused group whose understanding of the issues can be considerably greater than that of a diverse and larger trustee body. However good the organisation's professional development of its trustees, it is unrealistic to believe that all members of the board can or should bring equal expertise to each function – not least, finance.

However, it is worth raising two points of caution. First, ensuring that trustees understand their financial responsibilities, and have sufficient grasp of them to discharge them wisely, can become more difficult if the function is delegated to a committee. Even with a dedicated finance committee, time has to be devoted on the full board's agenda to enabling all trustees to undertake their financial stewardship duties adequately. Second, the very existence of a committee can reduce the discipline of focusing on matters of governance: with the luxury of more time, the committee can more readily meddle! Again, a useful rule of thumb is to insist that trustees – even in committees – concentrate only on the primary statements when reviewing financial information, whether for setting direction, targets and parameters or reviewing actual performance. This discipline forces the discussion to be high level and strategic (see box 19.4).

Box 19.4   Criteria for delegating to a committee

- The committee must offer governance, rather than management, on the matters falling within its remit.
- The board must find a way for the committee to be accountable to it, and for board members to be sufficiently informed on the matters that the committee presents to them to be able to make appropriate judgements and decisions.

Using committees to act on behalf of the trustee body, or advisory groups to guide it, does give the organisation scope to involve individuals who are happy to offer support without wishing to assume all the responsibilities and liabilities of trusteeship. This can prove particularly helpful with some of the more technical aspects of financial stewardship, such as investments and pensions.

The role of the treasurer

With or without committees, the role of the officers is crucial if the board is to undertake good financial stewardship. It is unrealistic to expect the board to carry out the stewardship roles expected of it (defined in box 19.2) without the committed time of officers and, in particular, the treasurer. Box 19.5 indicates the sort of skills and attributes that this jobholder must demonstrate in order to fulfil the stewardship role required of them. These include not just the traditional finance-based qualities but also, crucially, an ability to connect the finances to the business of the organisation and a willingness to hold themselves and others accountable for how the financial resources of the organisation are used.

Box 19.5   Honorary treasurer: role specification

- Good understanding of, and empathy with, the organisation's purpose, values and objectives
- Good understanding of the business model and strategy by which the organisation intends to deliver its purpose
- Ability to connect the finances of the organisation with its mission ('the results chain')
- Excellent knowledge of developing and implementing finance strategy suitable for uncertainty
- Strong capacity on technical financial matters
- Ability to analyse and assess the long-term financial consequences of strategic decisions
- Ability to communicate, orally and in writing, complex concepts in a clear and concise way to lay audiences
- Willingness and ability to challenge the board and senior executive
- Total integrity.

Key points relating to this role are as follows.

- The treasurer is the guardian and steward of the financial state of the organisation, above all others, and should be expected to guide the trustee body in how to exercise good financial stewardship.
- Fellow trustees must be able to look to the treasurer for advice on the kinds of stewardship questions that should be asked, and on which financial issues the trustee body should focus.
- The treasurer must lead the internal debate to determine which financial KPIs should be used and what targets and parameters should be set, and to direct the process of determining what information will be presented to enable the trustees to assess the efficacy with which the organisation has converted, or intends to convert, income into impact. The treasurer must also guide the trustees in interpreting that information, reaching conclusions, and understanding the financial implications of their decisions.
- The treasurer must act on behalf of the whole trustee body in accounting publicly for the financial performance and state of the organisation, explaining in published documents and at events such as annual general meetings how the finances have been managed, both to ensure the organisation's ongoing viability and to deliver its organisational purpose.

To play this role effectively, the treasurer has to spend time outside formal board meetings, working with fellow officers and senior management, to understand the organisation, how it works and how well it is performing, and to debate how it should move forward. As we have seen throughout this book, there will be competing demands on the resources of the organisation – not least as a result of the tension between impact today versus impact tomorrow. The treasurer must be able to guide the debate as to how the resources are applied – if necessary, encouraging the organisation to take unpopular decisions. Urging financial prudence in defence of long-term financial stability can seem widely at odds with the agenda of those internally whose principal concern is, understandably, one of service delivery to beneficiaries.

Building key relationships

Such is the importance of financial stewardship to the organisation that key relationships – for example, between the officers, and between the treasurer and the finance director – have to be built to enable disagreements to be dealt with constructively away from the full board. If these players are openly disagreeing with each other on matters of financial stewardship, this generates little confidence among trustees, and no guidance. So, as in other fields, the key finance relationships have to be robust and founded on trust and respect.

This requires investment of time and energy on the part of all the participants. They need to meet regularly, understand each other's point of view, hold frank discussions, and agree a party line – if necessary, by using external advice (for example, from advisers such as auditors, bankers and investment managers) to reach consensus. There is no substitute for spending time together. At the board meeting, these parties need to present an agreed approach in the form either of a single, firm recommendation, or as two or more options for the board to consider, with pros and cons articulated.

However, there is a fine line between guiding the trustees on financial stewardship and presenting them with *fait accompli* decisions that cannot be opposed. So, there must be genuine opportunity – either at the board meeting or outside it – for trustees to challenge and understand fully what is presented to them. The degree to which that will happen depends ultimately on the culture that has been developed among the trustee body. One of the chair's particular responsibilities is to nurture an appropriate culture. There are many ways in which the treasurer and other officers can help to develop a culture that encourages involvement, understanding, challenge and ownership of the key financial issues of the organisation (see box 19.6). Some of these techniques may be particularly helpful – for example, in the task of approving the statutory accounts.

Box 19.6 Ways to build a culture of inclusive financial stewardship

- Include financial stewardship in trustee induction programmes.
- Use plain words in place of jargon wherever possible.
- Present financial information in consistent, easy-to-read formats.
- Distribute information on stewardship issues (such as strategies, work programmes, performance information, financial reports and analyses) in writing in advance of meetings, in order to free up the latter for discussion and debate rather than information exchange.
- Hold pre-meeting briefings and surgeries for board members at which they can learn about the key issues at an appropriate pace.
- Invite external advisers, such as auditors, to speak to trustees directly.

Trustee accountability

If the trustees have a key role to play in holding the executive to account on behalf of the beneficiaries and the donors, then who holds the trustees to account? In other words, who governs the governors? Adopting transparent practices and accounting in the public domain is an important start, and the onus on governing bodies to be transparent and accountable is growing, as we saw in the opening paragraphs of chapter 10. Guidance for boards on the principles of good governance continues to evolve, evidenced by the UK Charity Commission's efforts to improve the readability and applicability of *Good Governance: a Code for the Voluntary and Community Sector* (National Hub of Expertise in Governance, 2005). 'Being open and accountable' is one of six 'refashioned' principles (see box 19.7).

Box 19.7 Principle of good governance: being open and accountable

The board will lead the organisation in being open and accountable, both internally and externally. This will include:

- *open communications, informing people about the organisation and its work*
- *appropriate consultation on significant changes to the organisation's services or policies*
- *listening and responding to the views of supporters, funders, beneficiaries, service users and others with an interest in the organisation's work*
- *handling complaints constructively and effectively*
- *considering the organisation's responsibilities to the wider community, for example its environmental impact.*

Charity Commission, 2010b, n.p.

The trustees' report

The trustees certainly exhibit public accountability – their fifth stewardship role – through the preparation of the statutory annual report and accounts, which includes a trustees' report. For example, UK charity accounting requirements, as defined by the SORP (Charity Commission, 2005), has placed increasing emphasis on the need for trustees to explain how the charity has gone about meeting its objectives, and the trustees' report is designed to offer a place to do this. Its purpose is 'to discharge the charity trustees' duty of public accountability and stewardship' (Charity Commission, 2005, p. 1) and it provides a ready-made channel for answering, in the public domain, the question that was posed right at the start of chapter 1: 'Is your organisation having as much beneficial impact on those it exists to serve as it should be, given the financial resources available to it?'

Of course, the report must highlight the key messages that can be drawn from the financial statements – commenting both on the financial performance during the year and the financial state of the organisation at the end of it – and alert the reader to any financial issues that will affect future performance and position. In addition, though, the trustees must provide a commentary on what has happened further up the results chain, drawing attention to issues that may affect future effectiveness (see box 19.8). Only this will give confidence that the trustees are truly stewarding the organisation's funds placed in their trust, rather than simply monitoring them. So, the report needs to provide 'a fair review of the charity's structure, aims, objectives, activities and performance' (Charity Commission, 2005, p. 6).

The annual review

Each year, in addition to the annual report and accounts, most organisations produce an annual review in which they outline in an eye-catching, emotive way what impact the organisation has had over the previous year, with a summary of the financial statements. While relevant legislation and best practice (such as the

SORP 2005 for UK charities) largely prescribes the format of the statutory accounts, the trustees have no such constraints about how they choose to account publicly in an annual review. Apart from a statement from the auditors confirming that any financial information included in the document represents a fair extract from the statutory accounts, trustees are able to present the financial information as they wish.

The focus of the annual review is not finance – it is impact – but through the stories and evidence of impact, the review is unquestionably an appeal to prospective donors and supporters. It is a presentation of 'value for money': an opportunity to showcase what return an investor in the organisation gets, whether that investment is of income or of non-monetary resources, such as time.

Box 19.8   The trustees' annual report

Charity accounts alone do not meet all of the information needs of users who will usually have to supplement the information they obtain from the accounts with information from other sources. Accounts also have inherent limitations in terms of their ability to reflect the full impact of transactions or activities undertaken and do not provide information on matters such as structures, governance and management arrangements adopted by a charity. The accounts of a charity cannot alone easily portray what the charity has done (its outputs) or achieved (its outcomes) or what difference it has made (its impact). This is mainly because many of these areas cannot be measured in monetary terms: indeed some areas are difficult to measure with any numbers at all. The Trustees' Annual Report provides the opportunity for charity trustees to explain the areas that the accounts do not explain.

Charity Commission, 2005, p. 5

Public meetings

In the spirit of accountability and transparency, some bodies open their doors so that the proceedings of meetings can be observed. An obvious example of this would be a public sector body that is making decisions using the public purse on behalf of the general public. The public can observe the debates and decision making, from the House of Commons to the local planning committee.

This accessibility is less common in not-for-profit organisations. Nevertheless there are examples – albeit of a more restrictive nature. An organisation that receives government funding might invite a senior official from the relevant government department to attend meetings of its board, in recognition of the importance of the partnership between the two organisations.

However, this is by no means straightforward. While a government department might be a major funder of the recipient organisation's work, often it is also the architect of the legislative framework within which the same recipient organisation has to operate to support its beneficiaries. Predictably, in these circumstances, the donor can be the object of the recipient's criticism.

The advent of the age of contracts, in which not-for-profit organisations have to compete against other possible service providers for government funds, has brought into sharp focus the potential dilemma of having the funder at the table – particularly in the run-up to a re-tendering process. Few would expect an organisation to be wholly transparent about impending negotiations in front of the other negotiating party.

THE ROLE OF THE SENIOR EXECUTIVE

There is probably not one senior manager or trustee of a not-for-profit organisation who has not wondered at some time – perhaps in frustration – whether their respective roles are sufficiently clear. Often, it is difficult to see the line in the sand where responsibility passes from one party to the other. The line of accountability from the executive to the governing body is rarely in dispute: here, it is the definition of who does what that causes the anxiety. Recent literature, research and practice seem to be united in distinguishing between management and governance in the way that the ACEVO research concluded (see p. 296). Hudson (2009, pp. 52–55), for one, reaches very similar conclusions (see fig. 19.1). So, the consensus is that the role of senior management of the executive is one of joint leadership with trustees in terms of setting direction, and of sole responsibility for its implementation – in other words, for delivery. The executive is responsible for 'doing': for converting income into impact and maintaining the organisation as viable, while the board for 'ensuring that it is done'. Both must satisfy themselves that it is done effectively.

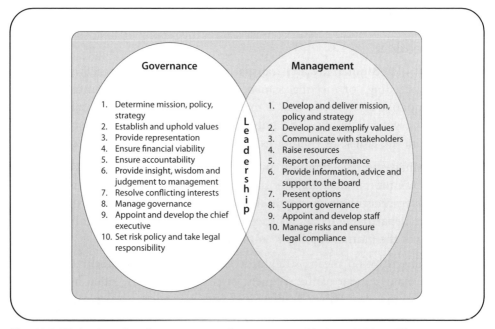

Fig. 19.1 Distinctive roles of governance and management (Hudson, 2009, p. 52)

In relation to financial stewardship, this means that it is the senior executive's role to:

- put the robust financial framework that is needed in place
- align resources and distribute them when needed
- react to changing circumstances and take appropriate action that ensures effective delivery
- to create and then nurture the right organisational environment that supports success (see box 19.9).

Box 19.9   Financial stewardship role of the senior executive

- To determine – jointly with the governing board – the purpose, values and strategic direction of the organisation
- To develop, implement and maintain a robust financial framework so that the organisation remains financially viable over time
- To make resources available as needed over the medium term, to support a work programme and strategies that are aligned with the organisational purpose
- To deliver effective day-to-day work programmes, using dynamic financial processes
- To create and sustain an enabling environment through appropriate structures, capabilities and systems.

So, the executive has to ensure that the board is sufficiently informed on the key financial and operational issues to be able to reach sensible decisions jointly – for example, about what financial KPIs should be used, and what targets and parameters should be set for those KPIs. It must then manage the financial resources dynamically, using tools such as the 'monitor, forecast, aim, plan, act' continuous financial stewardship model described in part 4.

The role of the finance director

Just as with the governing body, decisions have to be made about the staffing structure that will be used to play the financial stewardship role of the executive defined above. This is an issue at all levels in an organisation, and Hudson (2009, chapter 11, pp. 234–67) provides excellent advice on how to create the kind of flexible management structures needed for the organisation to thrive in conditions of uncertainty. Whatever structure is adopted, the executive's financial stewardship responsibilities are of such importance to the overall delivery of the organisation's objectives (having impact on beneficiaries) that the most senior management team must be directly responsible for their discharge.

No chief executive can avoid taking a strong personal interest in financial stewardship – an interest often stimulated by anxieties about income generation. However, organisations tend (wisely) to place the lead responsibility for this area in the hands of a chief financial officer or finance director: a senior manager with the ability to ensure that the tasks defined in box 19.9 are fulfilled effectively.

The role of the finance director is increasingly broad, extending well beyond the narrow confines of traditional accountancy and right into the heart of the organisation, driving performance. Typically, the position assumes responsibility for some or all of the support functions, such as IT, facilities, company secretarial duties and, sometimes, HR too, as part of a wide span of control under a generic banner of corporate or support services. This raises the question of the size of the senior management team. All of these functions are of strategic importance – and yet a leadership team in which all have dedicated representation would either result in an over-emphasis on administrative functions (rather than on programmes or income generation), or would require an excessively large team in order to maintain a sensible balance.

More importantly, the task of financial stewardship, as defined in this book, demands that the finance director has the authority and capability to contribute fully to the strategic leadership of the organisation. Hence Hudson's observation (2009, p. 242) that while 'everyone wants a seat at the top table ... the only department that seldom has to argue its corner is finance'. However, for that seat to add most value, traditional functional boundaries need to be less rigid. To fulfil the role now required, the finance director must be able to connect with the complete results chain and be able and permitted to discuss any part of the business of the organisation. As a result, this is one of the few roles that must retain an organisation-wide perspective at all times. The explicit and visible backing of the chief executive to play this role is crucial.

However, the role is tough to play well. Financial stewardship in not-for-profit and public sector organisations is highly political, and the finance director must enable delivery while simultaneously serving as one of the chief executive's principal guardians of good alignment and high performance. In particular, the finance director must advise on the difficult choices that have to be made – for example on:

- when to save rather than spend
- how best to allocate the available financial resources between competing demands
- when to withdraw funding from programmes that either are not generating sufficient return in terms of impact, or that have become lower priorities than other, new programmes which are ready to run but need financing.

To do this, the finance director has to earn the confidence and trust of senior management peers to become, in their eyes, a trusted business partner rather than a policing controller. However, this can be difficult. Fellow directors can quickly regard the finance director as an impediment to programme delivery rather than an aid, as a result of their apparent unwillingness or reluctance to make sufficient funds available when needed, and the seemingly intrusive nature of enquiries into how effectively funds have been spent. So, it is not surprising that Bryson (2004, p. 248) counsels that 'there is really no substitute for having a savvy insider who can both prepare and critique budgets effectively'. He continues: 'Make sure you have good analysts and wily and seasoned veterans of budgetary politics on your side.'

Hope (2006) characterises what is needed of the senior finance executive in terms of seven roles (see box 19.10). The descriptions of these roles offer telling insights about how the finance director can earn the accolade of 'trusted business partner' in order to truly lead the organisation's financial stewardship in line with the five principles espoused in this book. Not that the tension that the finance director role often creates in the senior management team by will disappear completely – and neither should it. If the organisation is going to face squarely up to the reality of varying performance standards and make the tough choices between alternative possible actions, then a certain level of tension must be continually injected into management deliberations.

Box 19.10   Reinventing the central finance officer: the seven roles

1. *Freedom Fighter*, liberating both finance and business managers from huge amounts of detail and the proliferation of complex systems that increase their workload and deny them time for reflection and analysis.
2. *Analyst and Adviser*, becoming a trusted and indispensable member of the business development team, who can add real value through incisive analysis and experienced interpretation of historic and emerging knowledge.
3. *Architect of Adaptive Management*, who can release managers from the detailed annual planning cycle and replace targets and budgets with more effective steering mechanisms, including continuous planning reviews and rolling forecasts, that enable them to sense and respond more rapidly to unpredictable events and to changing markets and customers.
4. *Warrior against Waste*, eliminating huge swathes of costs that have remained unchallenged for years ... eradicating non-value-adding work from all processes.
5. *Master of Measurement*, able to bring measurement back under control and provide clear guidance about its meaning – used to enable managers to learn and improve.
6. *Regulator of Risk*, providing an effective framework for good governance and risk management ... so that the right balance of risk can be effectively managed.
7. *Champion of Change*, capable of transforming the finance operation and performance management practices.

Hope, 2006, pp. 15–17, 53 and 211

The role of the manager

At the level of manager, further decisions have to be made about who does what in relation to financial stewardship. The financial management methodology set out in part 4 places responsibility for day-to-day financial stewardship at an activity level firmly in the hands of the operating units undertaking or supervising those activities. Once resources have been allocated to managers – whether from the corporate centre to the relevant director, or within a director's span of control – it is they who must ensure that the funds have the maximum impact.

Assuming financial stewardship of activities requires programme and operations management to adopt the continuous methodology described in part 4. They must continually assess financial commitments made, along with intended and expected outcomes, and any future events that may affect those outcomes. The manager must steward the funds to maximise the impact and keep the organisation informed of the expected outcomes for the beneficiaries and the associated financial consequences. To do this, the organisation needs to make relevant information readily accessible to the managers, to enable them to generate information such as results to date, findings of 'what if?' sensitivity tests, feed in forecasts, and interpret results, in order to reach conclusions about performance to date and to inform action planning for the future.

The organisation must be structured to enable operating units to assume responsibility for financial management of their activities, and be able to manage up the whole results chain. As a result, the finance function becomes significantly devolved – and the relative headcount and, more importantly, the decision-making authority, must reflect that. The need for a large central finance function diminishes. The role of the finance team running the central finance function becomes one of supporting operational managers to undertake their financial stewardship responsibilities competently, and of providing those services that are best provided centrally (see box 19.11).

Box 19.11   The financial stewardship role of the central finance function

- To design and maintain the organisation's financial infrastructure, such as policies, accounting systems architecture and business processes
- To support determination of the finance strategy and oversee its implementation
- To support decision making through the provision of high-quality analytics and assessments of results, trends and outlooks, both financial and operational
- To provide financial accounting services such as transactions administration, payroll, treasury and statutory accounting
- To design and maintain appropriate risk controls
- To improve constantly the financial stewardship capabilities of the organisation's people.

The finance team designs and maintains the finance 'infrastructure' that supports effective decision making, statutory reporting and risk control. It monitors income, expenditure and cash flows and their impact on the balance sheet. It carries out KPI measurement, and fulfils the organisation's statutory accounting and taxation requirements. It can support decision making about how to best climb the results chain by consolidating financial and operational results and plans. In addition, the team is well placed to undertake or commission reviews to assess the efficiency and/or effectiveness of expenditure, and to guide the organisation in ways to create fiscal space (see p. 272). It is also best placed to guide the organisation's development and use of risk controls. Finally, but equally importantly, members of the team play a key internal role in guiding the continuous development of organisational competence in financial stewardship.

Key stewardship questions

1. Do the organisation's board members, senior executive and managers have clear financial stewardship roles?

2. Does the organisation have effective structures to enable board members and the executive to play their respective roles?

3. How are the joint responsibilities of trustees and executive handled?

4. How is each party held accountable for playing its particular role effectively?

5. How can the finance director and his or her team become more effective business partners?

20 Capabilities: employing the requisite financial skills

Good financial stewardship by trustees, senior executives or managers requires that roles are not only well defined but are carried out by individuals with the appropriate financial capabilities. Ensuring that the requisite skills, knowledge and attributes are available in-house demands the continuous improvement and development of individuals. This is not about reaching an absolute level and then stopping: as an organisation's workforce ages,

> **Box 20.1   Definition of capability**
>
> The capacity to act resulting from the application of appropriate knowledge, skills and attributes.

and its business environment changes over time, it must continually invest in developing and sustaining its capability to deliver.

THE ENGAGEMENT CYCLE

The organisation must consider the need to develop and maintain appropriate financial capability throughout each individual's association with the organisation, whatever stewardship role they play – from the conception of the job to their succession. This is best considered in terms of the various stages of the employment lifecycle over which an organisation's relationship with an individual can be defined (see fig. 20.1). From the organisation's point of view, consideration of the financial stewardship requirements begins long before a specific individual is attracted to join. The organisational effectiveness stage of the cycle is concerned with macro-issues that must be determined before individuals are appointed. These include organisational design, employment principles, competencies and workforce planning. Similarly, the reward stage requires critical thinking about compensation, benefits, other forms of recognition and issues such as work–life balance to have been completed before recruitment activity begins. Reward will be a crucial component of the overall employment proposition by which the organisation intends to attract high-calibre individuals.

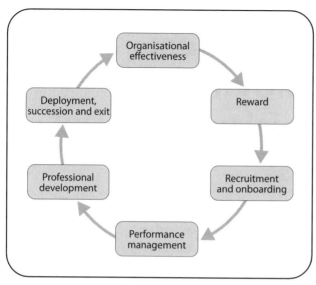

Fig. 20.1 The engagement cycle

The organisation must then manage the engagement with specific individuals – first, through effective recruitment practices that result in appropriately talented financial stewards being brought on board, and then through high-quality performance management and well-designed professional development support that motivates and retains the right personnel. The final engagement stage – deployment, succession and exit – is equally important, concerned with managing the movement of talent within and, ultimately, out of the organisation. The cycle as a whole offers an integrated approach to managing talent in any organisation.

DEFINING THE ESSENTIAL STEWARDSHIP COMPETENCIES

Competencies sit among the essential ingredients that underpin organisational effectiveness and the remaining stages of the engagement cycle. The term refers to those measurable capabilities (listed in box 20.1) that enable individuals to perform jobs successfully. At the institutional level, they enable the organisation to undertake effective workforce planning such as succession planning, which relies on having an overall view of the readiness of existing talent to assume more senior roles.

If well defined, competencies also support the recruitment, onboarding, performance management, professional development and redeployment of individual employees. For example, take the following tasks, all of which benefit from using a common language and definitional framework across the institution to articulate what is needed by the organisation and expected from jobholders:

- assessing skills shortages and staffing gaps
- designing organisational structures
- writing job definitions and person specifications
- devising recruitment and selection strategies
- defining organisation-wide learning requirements and designing solutions
- supporting individual assessments of current and future development needs
- recognising performance successes and addressing performance concerns
- coordinating the redeployment of employees into new positions.

So, what are the competencies needed of an organisation's financial stewards? Chapter 1 provided some early clues, with its reference to the broad remit encompassed by today's senior finance roles. Chapter 19 gave greater definition to the roles that need to be played by those in senior financial positions – both trustee and executive. More helpful still, perhaps, are the perspectives of the relevant professional institutes. Take the UK-based Chartered Institute of Management Accountants (CIMA). Its 2010 syllabus offers a good flavour of the types of competencies that its students must demonstrate in order to obtain full membership (see fig. 20.2). They are consistent with the definition of financial stewardship that this book embraces: one that requires capability right up the results chain.

	Enterprise pillar	Performance pillar	Finance pillar
Strategic level	• Interacting with the competitive environment • Change management • Evaluation of strategic options • Implementation of strategic plans	• Management control systems • Risk and internal control • Review and audit of control systems • Management of financial risk • Risk and control in information systems	• Formulation of financial strategy • Financial decisions • Investment decisions and project control
Management level	• Strategic management and assessing the competitive environment • Project management • Management of relationships	• Pricing and product decisions • Cost planning and analysis for competitive advantage • Budgeting and management control • Control and performance measurement of responsibility centres	• Group financial statements • Issues in recognition and measurement • Analysis and interpretation of financial accounts • Developments in external reporting
Operational level	• The global business environment • Information systems • Operations management • Marketing • Managing human capital	• Costing accounting systems • Forecasting and budgeting techniques • Project appraisal • Dealing with uncertainty in analysis • Managing short-term finance	• Principles of business taxation • Regulation and ethics of financial reporting • Financial accounting and reporting

Fig. 20.2 Chartered Institute of Management Accountants, n.d., n.p.

Note that finance forms only one of three pillars of the syllabus, which also covers enterprise and performance, with subjects that extend from change management, risk and controls to managing human capital.

One possible classification of the technical competencies that financial stewards must demonstrate is as follows (derived from competencies used in relation to finance-based positions at the World Bank). Within each competency, different levels – ranging from basic awareness to expert or mastery – can be used to distinguish between positions.

- **Financial accounting:** the tendency to understand accounting flows, properly record transactions and produce financial statements and reports required by external stakeholders such as shareholders, lenders, donors, partners and regulatory agencies.
- **Governance, risk and compliance:** the tendency to identify and evaluate strategic, operational and financial risks and effect appropriate risk management strategies and/or internal controls.
- **Planning and decision support:** the tendency to assist management at all levels to make better choices, design systems to generate decision-relevant information, set clear strategic direction and goals, align strategies, work programmes and financial resources, and evaluate the organisation's effectiveness in implementing its strategy to achieve these targets.
- **Financial management:** the tendency to understand and identify the organisation's funding needs and sources, contribute to the management of assets and liabilities, and manage the risks associated with maintaining the organisation as a viable entity.

In addition to technical competencies that are likely to be specific to financial stewardship roles, the organisation needs to develop and use a set of generic core competencies that are relevant to all positions internally. The following is one possible set of core competencies that would be relevant to an international organisation such as the World Bank. It is quickly apparent that the competencies selected by an organisation convey powerful signals about what sort of workplace its leaders wish to create:

- **Business acumen:** the tendency to connect with the organisation's mission, business model and markets
- **Client orientation:** the tendency to focus on client needs and concerns
- **Judgement and quality focus:** the tendency to gather and analyse information and effectively incorporate to improve quality
- **Innovation:** the tendency to introduce new concepts or ideas that result in enhanced solutions
- **Learning and knowledge-sharing:** the tendency to be open to learning, share own knowledge, and apply knowledge in daily work

- **Listening and communication:** the tendency to listen and speak respectfully and effectively, including varying points of view, across cultures
- **Results orientation/impact focus:** the tendency to make things happen and show drive for closure, impact and sustainable results
- **Teamwork and inclusion:** the tendency to collaborate with others and strive for a truly inclusive organisational culture.

Defining the stewardship needs of the organisation

Before embarking on a recruitment process to find a financial steward, the organisation needs to consider and determine what responsibilities the jobholder will carry out, and the attributes that they must have in order to be able to fulfil those responsibilities (in other words, to draw up a definition of employer need).

The most useful approach to defining a job is to identify what results the organisation requires that it cannot obtain from the existing resources. In this way, the added value of a job – its unique contribution – should be made apparent. Documentation such as job descriptions should enable the reader to understand what impact would not occur if the job was not undertaken. So, the focus is on outcomes or results, not processes or tasks, since it is the achievement of outcomes that must stimulate the need for additional resource. The influence of uncertainty on the roles, skills and attributes needed for financial stewardship cannot be overestimated. The greater the uncertainty, the more this is true.

Recall the frames of reference defined by Stacey (1993) as suitable for chaos management (see fig. 3.4, p. 49). Other observers of organisations, such as Haeckel (1999, p. 93 and p. 112), confirm this:

> One effect of operating a business in an environment of discontinuous change is that leaders can no longer know as well as followers how to get things done. A leader's role cannot therefore be one of devising battle plans and issuing orders down a chain of command to co-ordinate their execution ... Leadership has responsibility for creating, adapting and governing a viable organizational context, and for populating, with the right talent, the roles defined in it.

In terms of financial stewardship, this means adopting the roles defined in chapter 19 by which the five principles of this book can be applied: setting clear strategic direction, maintaining a robust financial framework, aligning resources to results, managing finances dynamically to ensure delivery, and nurturing an enabling environment. A useful discipline is to ensure that any prospective recruitment process is preceded by a written justification for the creation or continuation of the role. Some straightforward questions can be asked to stimulate careful consideration before the job is approved (see box 20.2). It may be, on reflection, that the cost–benefit of the job is inadequate, even if the assessment considers only the direct costs.

Box 20.2 Justifying a position

- What is the purpose of the position?
- What are the objectives of the position in the first 24 months?
- What alternative ways of achieving the objectives have been considered other than recruiting to the proposed position?
- What will be the consequences of not recruiting to this position?
- What are the direct costs associated with the position (for example, payroll costs, training or equipment)?
- What are the risks associated with creating this position?

Tools such as job evaluation schemes, which help assess a job against pre-defined factors, can help by providing a systematic way of understanding what prospective jobs are really about – as long as they are used properly. Job evaluation is often misunderstood as being a determinant of reward through the attribution of points to factors, thereby enabling each job to be scored, ranked and graded.

In organisations that have internally focused reward policies, pay structures are commonly built around grading structures. However, once it is recognised that different jobs have different marketplaces, the link between internal grade and reward is invalidated, thereby raising questions about the need for grading at all. For example, Sightsavers International has operated since 1999 without any grading structure at all.

Box 20.3 Person specification: inputs

Knowledge – *theoretical or practical understanding of some branch of science, art, learning, or other area involving study, research, or practice and the acquisition of skills*

Skill – *the ability to use one's knowledge effectively and readily in execution or performance: technical expertness*

Attribute – *quality, character, or characteristic*

Merriam-Webster, 2002, n.p.

However, in orientating job definition towards outcomes rather than processes, it is important to pay attention not only to results, but also behaviours. Technical competence has to be accompanied by inter-personal skills, and this can easily be forgotten – particularly in the more functionally specialist, analytical positions. So, outcomes can usefully be subcategorised into results and behaviours: the former needing to be achieved, and the latter exhibited. The highest performers offer both. The more senior the financial stewardship position, the more important it is that the jobholder demonstrates behaviours that promote and influence an appropriate corporate culture, and stimulate competent action in staff and volunteers.

If the job definition, or description, identifies what results and behaviours a jobholder should deliver, then the person specification identifies what inputs the jobholder must apply to the job in order to discharge their responsibilities effectively. These inputs can best be considered within three categories: knowledge, skills and attributes (see box 20.3).

Increasingly, recruitment practice is taking into account that while knowledge and skills can be acquired (the former through both education and experience), the personal attributes of jobholders are more difficult to change or develop. This means that it is of key importance to understand the attributes of good financial stewards. The precise knowledge, skills and attributes that are required will depend on the particular role in question (whether trustee, senior executive or manager) but, in an uncertain operating environment, they are likely to include many from the list given in box 20.4.

Box 20.4 Financial stewardship person specification: possible inputs

Knowledge of:
- Developing and promoting corporate visions and strategies
- Setting and using goals and targets
- Establishing and using corporate performance management tools
- The fundamentals of SOFAs, balance sheets and cash flow statements
- Fund management disciplines
- Applying and maintaining effective risk controls
- Adopting alternative resource allocation methodologies
- Designing and sustaining effective accountability mechanisms and processes
- Implementing good governance structures
- Developing and maintaining best-practice HR strategies
- Enabling IT to increase productivity and effectiveness.

Skills – ability to:
- Contribute to the determination of corporate direction and strategy
- Define and promote the organisation's results chain from income to impact
- Articulate the organisation's business model and key drivers of success
- Define and promote financial strategy and disciplines
- Communicate complex financial concepts, both orally and in writing
- Make trade-offs
- Influence without the formal authority to decide
- Provide objective analysis to support decision making
- Assess and report on performance up the results chain.

Attributes – must be:
- Focused on delivery of intended impact to beneficiary
- Strategic – able to see the big (medium to long-term) picture
- Courageous – willing and able to take difficult decisions
- Able to lead the organisation in adapting to uncertainty
- Challenging of assumptions, policies and strategies
- Systematic, logical and objective
- An advocate of transparency
- A champion of building financial stewardship competencies and capabilities
- Insistent on constant improvement in efficiency and effectiveness.

CREATING A COHERENT REWARD STRATEGY

The term 'reward', rather than 'pay' is used deliberately here (see box 20.5). While most of the attention directed at reward focuses on pay, it is worth bearing in mind that this is by no means the only component of an effective reward policy. Organisations competing in the employment market to retain existing people and recruit new ones, have much to offer actual and prospective employees other than pay. This is particularly important when considering the employment of financial stewards, whose skills are equally in demand in any of the sectors, and the more specialist of whom may be able to command larger compensation packages in the private sector than those typically available in not-for-profit and public sector organisations.

Box 20.5   Definition of reward

The return for services provided, given in the form of job satisfaction, working conditions, professional development, pay and other financial benefits, such as pension contributions.

A recent definition of the World Bank's employment value proposition illustrates the point (see box 20.6). The power of the first component – the mission – cannot be underestimated for any public or not-for-profit organisation. This is a hugely significant element of what attracts individuals to an organisation, and what enables the latter to retain them. No private sector employer can compete on that criterion.

Box 20.6   Components of the World Bank's employment value proposition

- *its compelling mission and cause;*
- *its standing in the international development community;*
- *competitive compensation and benefits;*
- *challenging and rewarding work;*
- *the range of experiences provided by the breadth of its client base, products and services;*
- *a diverse workforce;*
- *an intellectually dynamic environment; and*
- *opportunities for learning and development, career guidance, and potential to maintain marketability.*

World Bank, 2009a, pp. 4–5

Nevertheless, compensation and other financial benefits are likely to be central components of any organisation's reward strategy. Given the almost universal financial constraints faced, setting these at a level that enables the organisation to compete in the marketplace poses significant challenges. Arguably, the public accountability that is rightly demanded of public sector and not-for-profit organisations places undue attention on staff-related costs, which often represent a significant proportion of total expenditure. Organisations often find themselves on the defensive, trying to counter the erroneous conclusion that expenditure on salaries and benefits is an unnecessary 'cost' equating to administrative overhead, rather than an 'investment' in the organisation's capacity to deliver.

Keeping tight control of staff-related costs while rewarding staff appropriately is a difficult juggling act. Pay levels are often tied to historic public sector-originated reward schemes that guarantee not only cost-of-living adjustments but also increments, with staff rewarded for longevity of service. Consequently, staff costs rise faster than the index-linked funding agreements by which they are often financed and that typically cater only for inflationary increases in costs – not real ones. Organisations have to find other sources of income to cover the shortfall.

As a result, rewarding those jobholders in whom responsibility for financial stewardship, among other things, is vested, is not always an easy task. The position that an organisation adopts will be influenced by the following opposing tensions.

- **The external employment marketplace.** Organisations compete directly with employers in all sectors for relevant financial skills. Given the public and not-for-profit sectors' tendency to pay lower than the private sector, this creates upward pressure on reward.
- **Internal reward values.** Often, an organisation's pay structure – if not its total reward policy – is related to a ranking of jobs and/or a grading structure. On a comparable level internally, those jobs receive the same or similar pay and/or reward, irrespective of the external market. For many in the public and not-for-profit sectors, this best represents an organisation's values: its sense of fairness. This tends to deflate the level of pay of those jobs with higher marketability externally.
- **Donor values.** The level of financial rewards can be constrained, or occasionally inflated, by the funder's implicit or explicit expectations.

The importance of defensible principles

If an organisation wants to attract and retain individuals with the appropriate financial stewardship skills, it is crucial that it has a coherent reward strategy, underpinned by robust, defensible principles. These principles enshrine the organisation's attitude to reward, and they are sufficiently important to justify trustee attention and approval. They must articulate the organisation's stance towards the tension between external market versus internal values, and must outline where the employer intends to position itself within the relevant reward range. The first requirement is to decide which is the relevant range, before determining where within that range it intends to be positioned. For example, does the employer intend to be in the upper quartile, or to pitch around the median?

Two principles, above all others, are crucial (see box 20.7). First, any decision about reward must pass the test of being sufficient but no more than necessary. Note, too, the explicit acknowledgement in the first principle of the role of reward in retaining appropriate calibre people as well as recruiting them.

The second principle articulates more precisely the implications of the first one, by making two fundamental points. First, that the determination of reward requires the organisation to be externally focused. The organisation has to understand that it is competing in marketplaces against other employers requiring similarly skilled and experienced staff, and that the market's values will probably not align with its own. Second, that different jobs have different marketplaces.

Accommodating external markets and internal values

There is no one single employment market for individuals who wish to work in the public and not-for-profit sectors. There is not even one single employment market for a particular organisation. Each of the marketplaces for skills and experience in functions such as income generation, overseas development, IT and finance (to name but four) are different, with their own reward norms.

There are at least three obvious marketplaces in which organisations compete for talent, and competition can be intense once the difficulty individuals have in crossing from one marketplace to another is recognised. It is not unusual for the employability of individuals to be constrained by all three.

- **Sector.** Employers within one sector compete for specialist knowledge and skills that are difficult to acquire from other sectors.
- **Function.** Employers compete across sectors for individuals who offer relevant skills, knowledge and experience in one function, such as finance.
- **Geography.** Employers compete across sectors and functions for individuals in marketplaces that are defined in relation to the geographic proximity to the organisation.

The implication of this is a stark one that must be acknowledged. Two jobs within the organisation that might be regarded internally as being at the same level, or of the same worth, cannot be assumed to command the same reward externally. Competing in the marketplace may mean that the organisation has to offer differing levels of reward to jobholders at the same internal level – which of course risks conflicting with internal values.

If this is the case, then something has to give. Either the organisation holds the reward level of some positions below their market level in order to retain internal comparabilities cross-functionally, or the internal values have to be redefined. The former option is feasible to the extent that the organisation can compete with other sectors on non-pay grounds – on the sort of elements of the employment value proposition listed in box 20.6. But if the organisation expects to be able to attract and retain the right calibre staff while offering reward levels below market norms, then it must understand on what grounds it will be able to do so. What compelling proposition does it offer actual and prospective employees that will persuade them to sacrifice financial reward that they can command elsewhere?

Through careful design and implementation, it is possible for an organisation to maintain a reward policy that honours internal values but that also acknowledges the reality of the external marketplace. Sightsavers International offers one example. In effect, while Sightsavers sets each job within the context of the international non-governmental organisation (INGO) employment marketplace, the charity gives itself room in its reward policy to reflect other marketplaces in its positioning within the sector. Key elements of that policy (extracts of which are shown in box 20.8) reflect its efforts to accommodate both internal values and the external realities, as follows.

- A definition of what is meant by 'reward', and a rationale for it. The measure of success is the organisation's ability to attract and retain motivated, high-calibre individuals.
- An explicit statement that the charity does not reward performance or longevity of service with additional pay, while acknowledging that in exceptional circumstances poor performance may result in withholding a cost-of-living increase.
- A definition of the marketplace in which the organisation believes it is competing (the INGO market) while recognising that other markets may be relevant in benchmarking positions.
- A positioning statement that, as an employer, Sightsavers expects to set pay around the median as determined by its benchmark data, while acknowledging that pay might be set above or below the median.
- An explicit statement that pay increases might not be awarded to individuals whose pay level already exceed the relevant median.

> ### Box 20.8   Extracts from Sightsavers International's reward policy
>
> - *Reward forms a key part of Sightsavers' employment offer that should enable us to attract, develop, motivate and retain high calibre people with the appropriate skills and knowledge.*
> - *Pay is determined by the job, not the individual (therefore we do not differentiate pay for individual performance or for length of service).*
> - *Our Reward Policy applies to all our employees globally.*
> - *Reward levels should be targeted at the 'median' level within the relevant local marketplace.*
> - *Reward includes both pay and associated benefits (e.g. pension, holiday entitlement).*
> - *We will benchmark each job, based on the current job description, against comparable jobs in other INGOs (and where appropriate the non-INGO sector market) within the relevant country.*
> - *Each year the pay levels for each employee will be adjusted by a cost of living increase, determined for each country by reference to the relevant cost of living data. This percentage increase will generally be applied consistently to all Sightsavers employees within the country, although we may award a smaller or no increase to someone who is paid over the benchmark pay level. Exceptionally, in the case of demonstrated unsatisfactory performance of an individual, an annual pay review will not be awarded.*
> - *Exceptionally the pay level for an individual may be set below or above the median, if appropriate. For example for a new jobholder who is expected to grow into the job, but who is not yet at a fully competent level.*
>
> Sightsavers International, 2006, pp. 1–2

Reward for jobs with high marketability

By positioning reward for all jobs in terms of one sector range, such as the INGO sector, the employer can ensure that there is some constraint on the pay levels of those jobs with high marketability. By determining the position within the range, with reference to the relevant marketplace (whether that is the INGO market or not), the employer can meet its need to be competitive. In practice, this means that some jobs are positioned above the organisation's normal reward positioning, while others are below it. Sightsavers International recognises this. The 'sufficient and necessary test' should apply in all cases.

Benchmarking is not a scientific exercise. Crucial judgements have to be made – especially when determining what jobs offer a fair comparison. Often data about such jobs is scant, and job titles, descriptions and advertisements can be misleading. Procedures need to be in place internally to prevent jobs being 'talked up' in order to be benchmarked against more senior positions elsewhere. Similarly, the extent to which functional specialisms do truly have cross-sector appeal must be carefully considered. For example, with regard to senior finance positions, organisations certainly do have to compete with other sectors to attract individuals with appropriate skills, but typically the longer an individual spends within one sector, the less marketability they have outside it. So, attraction may impose greater upward pressure on pay levels than retention.

The risk of adopting practices that are at odds with the stated reward policy is always present, as in the following circumstances.

- **Where reward levels are driven by recruitment needs rather than retention strategies** – even though the costs of recruitment (in terms of direct recruitment and onboarding costs, plus the disruption to continuity from lost skills and knowledge) greatly exceed the costs of retention. This might occur where the pay for a vacant position is set at a level higher than received by its previous occupant, even though the responsibilities of the job are unchanged.
- **Where reward policies reflect a strategy of cost containment rather than genuine reward** – in such circumstances, the focus is one of minimising the costs of inputs (employees) rather than maximising the cost-effectiveness of outcomes (employee impact).
- **Where recruitment practice does not match the reward principle** – in other words, where the organisation seeks to attract 'the best' alongside a reward principle that positions the organisation at the median or below within the relevant marketplace.

These raise important lessons to learn, as shown in box 20.9.

Box 20.9   Lessons for determining reward
■ Understand the role of reward in the overall employment proposition. What is the organisation offering that will attract, develop, motivate and retain the appropriate calibre individuals? How important is reward? ■ Determine in which marketplaces the organisation is competing for talent. ■ Establish where the organisation wishes to position itself on the reward range within the relevant marketplaces. ■ Obtain good data about the reward commanded by other positions in other organisations that are genuinely comparable. ■ Decide whether to determine reward in relation to the job or the jobholder. Two individuals will bring different knowledge, skills and attributes to the same job.

RECRUITING THE RIGHT TALENT

As we have seen earlier in this chapter, attracting the right talent begins well before the recruitment process to fill a specific position is undertaken. Workforce planning and determination of the overall employment proposition are crucial prerequisites in order to ensure that the strategic task of growing and sustaining a high-calibre workforce over time is successful. For example, effective workforce planning maintains a constant overview of the changing business needs of the organisation, and translates this understanding into future workforce needs. It considers the gap between the people capability of the organisation today and what is needed going forward, and determines an action plan to close that gap, aware of what staff movements can be expected as a result of retirements, promotions and reassignments.

Uncertainly plays a huge role in influencing such planning, forcing leaders to think hard about how the organisation can maintain agility to respond as needed: about the respective need both for technical specialists and generalists with broad business skills.

It would be an eye-opening exercise in any organisation to see how much consensus there is about what talent is needed. Often, there is no clarity or agreement internally. The use of competencies will significantly aid that assessment. What is not in contention is the belief that the competition to recruit the best individuals is hotting up – the so-called 'war on talent'. That is most certainly true in the case of financial stewards. The knowledge, skills and attributes listed in box 20.4 are in short supply.

Two aspects of the recruitment process warrant attention here. First, how can the organisation attract the individuals of the appropriate calibre (sourcing), and second, what sort of recruitment process best enables candidates to be assessed effectively so that an appropriate selection can be made (screening)?

The traditional recruitment process operates by interviewing individuals who have responded to an advertisement inviting applications for a specific position, against a pre-defined job description and person specification. It is easy to see why this approach is popular. The hiring organisation acts when a vacancy arises. It solicits applications, targeting its audience through the choice of advertisement and/or media, and it selects the candidate that best matches the profile prescribed through an assessment following one or more interviews. However, this approach may not be optimal in terms of either sourcing or screening.

To effectively source talent of suitable calibre, organisations need to do more than place an advertisement and collect applications from those interested individuals who happen to notice it, and who are looking for a new position. They must maintain a pipeline of suitable individuals whether there is a current vacancy to fill or not. More proactive, targeted and aggressive approaches are often needed – ones that are undertaken systematically and continuously. These approaches include the following, defined by the ORC Worldwide consulting firm (ORC, 2006, n.p.) (cited in an internal World Bank report and presented in an adapted form here).

- Mining internet-based sources such as professional associations, affinity groups and niche job boards.
- Building relationships with potential sources of talent such as universities, professional societies and government entities.

- Maintaining partnerships *within* the organisation, for example between the recruiting function and local representatives to establish an ongoing understanding of the latter's interests.
- Maintaining and nurturing a list of personal contacts for different job categories that can be reached out to when needed.
- Maintaining a database of talent for future reference.
- Engaging *all* individuals in the organisation to undertake the above, so that there is shared ownership of the importance of recruiting talent and maximum networking and outreach to potentially interested and high-quality candidates. This can be formalised in an employee referral programme.
- Aggressively marketing the brand of the organisation, highlighting the features of the employment value proposition.

Effective screening makes use of a range of assessment techniques to provide as complete a picture as possible of the knowledge, skills and attributes of candidates, within a limited period of time. The process must establish with evidence whether an individual has what is needed. This is rarely possible simply through reviewing a written application and conducting a one-hour interview. It is worth thinking hard about what process will provide the evidence – for example, of the financial stewardship knowledge, skills and attributes listed in box 20.4. Asking candidates to complete written exercises and/or prepare and deliver oral presentations on relevant topics can be illuminating. Box 20.10 offers some sample topics.

Box 20.10 Exercises to assess for financial stewardship knowledge, skills and attributes

1. Outline what strategic direction the organisation should take, and why.
2. Describe what the organisation should be held accountable for, and how its performance should be measured.
3. Describe how an organisation might ensure alignment of its spending with its mission.
4. Outline a governance process that would reassure an organisation's stakeholders of its efficacy and effectiveness.
5. Write a brief report for the board outlining what key financial issues it should address in light of the latest published accounts (either the organisation's accounts or those of another organisation).
6. Describe the components of a robust financial framework.
7. Describe what you would expect an organisation's finance strategy to tell you.
8. Describe what effective risk control looks like.
9. Outline how an organisation should best equip itself to handle uncertainty.
10. Discuss the limitations of traditional budgeting and how these might be overcome.
11. Design a process to enable trade-offs to be made between competing demands on finite resources.
12. Define the respective financial stewardship roles of the board, senior executive and managers.

MANAGING FOR HIGH PERFORMANCE

The focus of this book has been on organisational performance (the conversion of income into impact up the results chain) and the role of financial stewardship in supporting and driving that performance. Achieving high levels of organisational performance depends on effective performance management of individuals within the organisation (see box 20.11). The two must align. Recall Scott's definition of strategic alignment (see box 11.2, p. 161). The objectives, work programmes, results and behaviours of individuals and units within an organisation must align with those of the organisation as a whole.

> **Box 20.11   Definition of performance management**
>
> *Performance management is the systematic process by which an agency involves its employees, as individuals and members of a group, in improving organizational effectiveness in the accomplishment of agency mission and goals.*
>
> *U.S. Office of Personnel Management, n.d., n.p.*

The relationship between the two may not be measurable in a strict, quantifiable way: the causal relationship between what an individual does and the impact on the organisation's overall performance is unlikely to be that direct. Nevertheless, it is reasonable to aim for a standard where each staff member has clear goals, responsibilities and authority, where the staff member and his/her manager are clear about where the individual's efforts will contribute to the results of the team(s) and unit(s) to which they belong, and where there is clarity about how the unit contributes to overall divisional or organisational performance against strategic objectives.

Maintaining a clear line of sight is one of seven conditions (drawing on internal review of performance management practice in the World Bank (World Bank, 2007) and information from the US Office of Personnel Management website (www.opm.gov)), on which achieving high-quality performance management depends.

- **A culture of excellence:** An organisational culture that expects performance management excellence enables staff and managers to work side-by-side, to continually improve the effectiveness of work undertaken at the individual and team level.
- **A clear line of sight:** Each individual should have a clear view of how their work contributes to the teams of which they are part, and ultimately to the organisation's overall objectives and performance. Individual goals and plans are channelled towards achieving organisational objectives. Performance monitoring links organisational results to unit and individual achievements.
- **Capable staff and managers:** Sustaining institutional performance capability requires an organisation to maintain a viable pipeline of individuals capable of succeeding today's employees, managers and leaders. It also requires

continuous adaptation to the changing operating environment through the development of new knowledge and skills.

- **Continuous and forward-looking performance management:** Performance management is a continuous forward-looking discipline, not a once-a-year backward-looking event. Monitoring and evaluation takes place all the time, plans get revised as necessary, and feedback to staff is ongoing.
- **Appropriate consequences:** Successful organisations have a strong culture of accountability. Individuals have clear responsibilities, decisions and results are communicated transparently, and there are clear consequences, whatever the level of performance, from excellent to poor.
- **Transparency:** This is a crucial attribute of well-run organisations. Where information is widely disseminated and where dialogue, discussion and feedback are promoted, the quality of decision making and other management practices is enhanced.
- **Enabling tools and processes:** The processes and tools with which performance management is exercised must support excellence. Too often, they are bureaucratic and insufficiently integrated into the day-to-day work of individuals, leading to frustration and cynicism. Instead, they must enable easy capture and aggregation of information and provide easy opportunities for dialogue and feedback.

In line with the financial stewardship model propounded in this book, plans and performance assessments of individuals should be expressed in terms of the five principles outlined in chapter 1: setting strategic direction, maintaining a robust financial framework, aligning resources to results, managing finances dynamically to ensure delivery, and nurturing an enabling environment. These must be aligned with the equivalent organisational plans and results. Managing for high performance within this model – which assumes uncertainty – has a number of important implications for each individual, just as it does for the organisation as a whole, as follows.

- Uncertainty means unpredictability: expectations, plans and targets may prove to be inappropriate measures of actual performance.
- Performance must ultimately be measured with hindsight in relation to the circumstances in which it was achieved. In the end, targets have to be separated from the performance management process.
- Planning must reflect the nature of the organisation's activities (and therefore individual staff members' work programmes) – not the accounting timetable. Plans need to roll forward across financial year ends, and be updated to reflect changing circumstances.
- Performance targets, if used at all, need to be outcome-orientated, measured by results and behaviours.
- Where available, relative performance measures (which are self-regulating) will be more effective than absolute ones.

329

MAINTAINING CAPABILITY EXCELLENCE THROUGH PROFESSIONAL DEVELOPMENT

Good financial stewardship demands that an organisation sustains its capacity to perform over time as business needs change. The culture that is needed is one in which learning – and the needs of staff to develop knowledge and skills – are valued, planned and supported. There are many ways for the organisation to demonstrate its commitment to professional development (see box 20.12), and through such approaches the organisation must help its people to understand and own its mission, strategy, values and culture, as well as mastering its processes and procedures. Staff must also maintain leading-edge technical skills, have access to external knowledge and networks, and learn from practice. Above all, they must take responsibility for defining and undertaking the ongoing professional development that they need in order to sustain performance excellence over time.

Box 20.12   Signs of organisational commitment to professional development

- Demonstrable investment of time by the organisation's leaders to champion professional development
- Staff policy committing the organisation to investing in staff development, e.g. expecting staff to spend x days in training and/or development each month, quarter or year
- An extensive onboarding programme (plus refresher programmes for established staff), during which training and development needs are recognised and addressed
- Explicit recognition of the responsibility of staff for their own professional development, and of managers for supporting staff
- Active management of training and development in line with external quality standards and accreditation
- Provision of an extensive range of training/learning opportunities, such as:
  - support from in-house specialists (for example, surgeries run by finance staff)
  - development of and coaching from in-house user experts (more experienced peers)
  - participation in specialist membership bodies
  - knowledge-sharing in external networks of peers
  - access to relevant external knowledge
  - workshops.
- Commitment to provide support (including funding, coaching and study time) to enable individuals to undertake training
- Performance management disciplines that focus on assessing and meeting future professional development needs
- Committed use of practical techniques of evaluation that assess the effectiveness of learning undertaken
- A learning culture that promotes knowledge capture and dissemination
- Incentives that support the values and actions needed for effective professional development.

Financial stewardship is so important to the eventual impact of the organisation that it must be one of the core tenets of its professional development strategy. It has to define what financial stewardship knowledge, skills and attributes it requires, in which jobs, and to ensure that the relevant jobholders have those competencies. Training strategies can be designed that offer alternative methods to enable jobholders to acquire and maintain the different levels of competency demanded of different positions.

Attention also needs to be paid to the overall governance of professional development in the organisation. For example:

- an overall framework is needed to articulate the goals of staff learning and to define the methods available to achieve those goals
- guidelines and standards for quality of training, together with advice on how to approach learning, will guide implementation plans. On-the-job learning, mentoring and e-based learning may well be more effective than traditional classroom-based learning
- financial resources must be protected for investment in professional development
- crucially, the incentives for individuals to invest in professional development must be appropriate – the organisation must reward those who invest in their capability and translate that into performance.

Investing in the professional development of the organisation's people is a must. If the organisation is going to climb the results chain successfully over time, then the cost implications (for example, the financial cost or opportunity cost) are precisely that – the consequences of an essential investment. Without it, productivity and motivation will quickly slide. So, professional development is an essential component both of the employment proposition (as box 20.6 illustrates) and the organisation's performance management.

DEPLOYMENT, SUCCESSION AND EXIT

Sustaining the financial stewardship, knowledge and skills needed over time requires an organisation to manage actively the career progression and eventual departure of its current financial stewards. It must also be willing and able to deploy the financial stewardship knowledge and skills to the prevailing business requirements as they are defined and evolve. In addition, it needs to nurture a pipeline of talent that can, in time, succeed the current technical, managerial and leadership incumbents. These tasks cannot be left to chance. Instead, there are essential HR practices to adopt in order to get the right people in the right place at the right time – but varying opinions about the most appropriate sequence of action by which to achieve this (see box 20.13).

Box 20.13   Which comes first – who or what?

First who, then what

The good-to-great leaders began the transformation by first getting the right people on the bus (and the wrong people off the bus) and then figured out where to drive it ... The key point is that 'who' questions come before 'what' decisions – before vision, before strategy, before organization structure, before tactics. **First** *who,* **then** *what – as a rigorous discipline, consistently applied.*

Collins, 2001, p. 63[1]

First what, then who

In the nonprofit world, it's actually 'first what, then who'. All the organisations we studied are guided first and foremost by their **mission***, and this purpose is the primary reason a person will take the job. These groups look for new hires with a passion for their mission, and a strong cultural fit. In other words, they already know where the bus is headed; they're looking for good people who are going in the same direction. Although the strategy or tactics may change over time, their overall cause is unlikely to change.*

Crutchfield and McLeod Grant, 2008, p. 187

Workforce planning

The organisation must look forward and translate its business outlook into an assessment of future financial stewardship knowledge and skills needs. It must then determine how it intends to source that knowledge and those skills (including whether in-house or through outsourcing), thereby defining its future workforce requirements. Technological advances are transforming how organisations think about workforce planning. Brand new sources of knowledge and skills are now available, bringing both opportunities about how work gets done and threats from new competitors offering more cost-effective alternative solutions.

Talent reviews

The organisation must maintain a constant understanding of its current capability, as reflected in the breadth and depth of knowledge and skills and the current deployment of relevant individuals. It must be clear who the best and worst performers are, which individuals are ready for promotion or reassignment, and who is likely to be leaving – whether voluntarily or involuntarily (for example, as a result of a mandatory retirement policy). Similarly, the organisation must be clear about which positions are most critical and are therefore most in need of having one or more ready-made successors in the pipeline.

---

[1] *Good to Great*, Copyright © 2001 by Jim Collins. Reprinted with permission from Jim Collins

Managed deployments

Relying exclusively on openly competitive recruitment practices to fill all positions as they become vacant is unlikely to ensure that an organisation's people will acquire the knowledge and skills necessary to grow and, in some cases, to become its future leaders. An understandable desire to subscribe to equal opportunities principles must be balanced by a responsibility both to deploy today's knowledge and skills, where needed, and to ensure that there is sufficient mobility internally for the talent pipeline to develop as needed.

There is a role both for competitive selection and for managed deployments. For example, the latter may be necessary in order to ensure that critical, difficult, hard-to-fill assignments are handled by high-calibre individuals. Meanwhile, incentives and strong support may be necessary to ensure that appropriately qualified individuals are willing and able to take on such assignments.

Employment modalities

Uncertainty, coupled with changing business needs, is forcing organisations to review the employment contract modalities that best suit its staffing strategy. There is increasing awareness of the need to complement long-term, often open-ended contracts (which enable organisations to retain vital knowledge and skills and offer career opportunities and job security to employees) with shorter-term contractual arrangements (which enable managers to vary the deployment of capacity as business needs change). The renewable fixed-term contract offers one potential solution to the awkward challenge of attracting and retaining high-calibre individuals while simultaneously maintaining the staffing flexibility needed by agile organisations.

Ending employment practices

As mentioned above, departures from organisations can be voluntary or involuntary. Organisations must seek to minimise the loss of high performers through voluntary exit. All other losses are either desirable or can be managed – or both. Managing separations is not easy, requiring both sensitivity and disciplined adherence to clear policy and processes, but it is a critical task if a public sector or not-for-profit organisation is to sustain the people capability it needs to maximise its impact over time on those it exists to serve.

Key stewardship questions

1. What financial stewardship knowledge, skills and attributes does the organisation require going forward?

2. What is the current level and distribution of financial stewardship capability?

3. How does the organisation intend to close the gap between the capability needed and the current capability?

4. What is the organisation's employment value proposition for current and prospective financial stewards?

5. How well is the organisation able to attract and retain high-calibre financial stewards?

6. How can the organisation better nurture sustainable financial stewardship capability?

21 Managing information with technology

THE INFORMATION NEEDS OF ORGANISATIONS

The final piece to place in the enabling environment is the information management system. Capable people operating with well-defined roles within an appropriate structure need excellent information systems if they are to make the financial stewardship decisions that enable the organisation to climb the results chain effectively. Peters (1992, p. 110) once described organisations as 'pure information processing machines – nothing less, nothing more: organizational structures, including hierarchies, capture, massage, and channel information. Period'. More recent texts such as Bill Gates's *Business @ the Speed of Thought* (1999) expound even more fervently on how critical good information management is to organisational success (see box 21.1).

The nature of financial stewardship that this book promotes, and the uncertain environment in which it assumes that organisations now have to operate, all place heavy demands on the quality of the information systems. Successful financial stewardship requires up-to-date information about the organisation's current position and latest thinking about the future in the context of defined direction and goals. The efficiency with which an

> ### Box 21.1 The importance of information
>
> *How you gather, manage, and use information will determine whether you win or lose* ... *The winners will be the ones who develop a world-class digital nervous system so that information can easily flow through their companies for maximum and constant learning.*
>
> Gates, 1999, p. 3

organisation can understand where it is now and what is ahead of it, and can make appropriate decisions that contribute to furthering its objectives, depends on the quality of information – which, in turn, depends on the quality of the systems that generate the information.

There needs to be urgency and dynamism associated with managing information in an uncertain operating environment. That is certain. All five principles of financial stewardship detailed in this book – setting strategic direction, maintaining the financial framework, aligning resources, managing finances dynamically, and nurturing an enabling environment – rely on the quality and timing of information. The whole methodology of part 4 in particular (designed to enable organisations to manage resources dynamically in response to emerging circumstances as they move and focus forward), relies on a capacity to digest information quickly in support of business decision making.

This information will be continually changing. We discussed the importance of measurement (in chapter 2) and identified the eight characteristics that the financial information required by organisations must exhibit in order to be of value (in chapter 14). Timeliness, accuracy and the other 'fit for purpose' characteristics of the management accounting information provide the criteria for judging the adequacy of the financial information systems.

THE POWER OF TECHNOLOGY

Increasingly, technology has the power to enable organisations to deliver impact, transforming how data is handled and how information can be generated and managed. Haeckel (1999, p. 163) calls it 'managing by wire' and Bill Gates (1999, p. xvii) 'a digital nervous system' (see box 21.2). Irrespective of the label given, there is universal acceptance that organisations now have the technical capacity through IT to generate and exchange appropriate information between appropriate parties at the appropriate time. While non-IT systems will continue to play a part in the provision of the information required, even the smallest and least-resourced organisation is placing increasing reliance on IT. Technology offers the possibility to deliver the right information to the right people, at the right time and place, and to thereby influence the decisions that will achieve the organisation's mission. The enticing reality for any organisation is 'any data on any desk', whether local, regional, national or international. In an IBM study (IBM, 2009)[1] of more than 2,500 chief information officers (CIOs), 18 per cent of whom came from the public sector, 83 per cent identified 'business intelligence and analytics' (p. 15) as among their visionary plans for enhancing organisational competitiveness: the top answer.

> ### Box 21.2   A digital nervous system
>
> *You know you have built an excellent digital nervous system when information flows through your organization as quickly and naturally as thought in a human being and when you use technology to marshal and coordinate teams of people as quickly as you can focus an individual on an issue. It's business at the speed of thought.*
>
> *Gates, 1999, p. 37*

In uncertain environments where organisations have to adapt, the influence of technology in supporting decision making increases tenfold. To master adaptation,

---

[1] Reprint Courtesy of International Business Machines Corporation, © 2009 International Business Machines Corporation

organisations must listen, experiment, innovate, evaluate, learn what works, and modify programmes and plans appropriately (Crutchfield and McLeod Grant, 2008, p. 131). Technology offers the capacity to do this at the required speed – to be able to capture, absorb, digest, interpret and respond to external data and noise and convert it rapidly into meaningful information that is relayed to the relevant people quickly and thereby enable appropriate decisions to be made and implemented.

Technology has the power to improve an organisation's reaction time inordinately. Haeckel (1999, p. 166) writes persuasively of organisations' need for 'electronic augmentation of our ability to sense "what's going on out there" and an electronic representation of our knowledge about "how we do things around here" '. In this way, technology can help an organisation's stewards maintain an effective radar screen and reach decisions about appropriate next steps in given circumstances. Stewards must 'proactively craft data into actionable information' (IBM, 2009, p. 22).[2]

THE CHALLENGE OF USING TECHNOLOGY WELL

The potential of technology to enhance organisational performance is clear. However, when it is used poorly, organisations find themselves disabled rather than enabled. Failure rates on IT development projects are high, and often the investment in IT fails to deliver the intended reform as organisations leap from 'technology bandwagon to technology bandwagon' (Axson, 2003, p. 218). The symptoms are not difficult to find (see box 21.3). The warning signs include: a flood of data, duplicated systems, excessive reliance on spreadsheet modelling, a plethora of local systems that cannot be easily aggregated, fragmented budgets and coding structures, frequent data re-entry, and endless reports that recipients do not use. Impatience and frustration quickly surface. 'Systems must deliver the right information, not just more information,' warns Axson (2003, p. 224).

Box 21.3　Too much detail and complexity

The technology 'bandwidth' is widening every year, and the resulting data flow throughout the organization is overwhelming managers' ability to make sense of it. 'Can't see the forest for the trees', 'swamped with information', and 'drowning in detail and thirsting for knowledge' are all regularly heard comments.

The average large organization wrestles with ten different ledger systems, twelve different budgeting systems and thirteen different reporting systems – in comparison, best-practice companies have standardized on a single platform.

Hope, 2006, p. 7

---

[2] Reprint Courtesy of International Business Machines Corporation, © 2009 International Business Machines Corporation

TECHNOLOGY AS A STRATEGIC RESOURCE

Bill Gates (1999, p. 317) is among many to recognise the importance of treating IT as a strategic resource, to the extent – in his opinion – that chief executives and other senior executives 'should become as engaged in IT as in any other important business function'. IBM's 2009 study suggests that organisations are increasingly recognising this, concluding that 'CIOs are increasingly recognised as fully-fledged members of the senior executive team. Successful CIOs are much more actively engaged in setting strategy, enabling flexibility and change, and solving business problems, not just IT problems' (IBM, 2009, p. 8).[3]

Box 21.4   The new voice of the CIO: actions to maximise the value of technology

- **Push business and technology integration** – offer solutions for colleagues' business dilemmas, even when the answer is not directly IT-related
- **Champion innovation** – explain how new processes and technologies can deliver more value to both internal and external customers
- **Enable the corporate vision** – increase the flexibility and efficiency of infrastructure and applications to support ongoing business changes
- **Make working together easy** – provide better partnering and collaboration technologies so internal and external customers stay connected and relationships are more productive
- **Concentrate on core competencies** – improve business agility by accessing business services, speciality technologies or IT services through third parties
- **Make the data 'sing'** – surprise the business with unexpected ways to meet customer needs and otherwise profit from enterprise data
- **Reach customers in new ways** – keep looking for more profitable paths to the end customer
- **Enhance integration and transparency** – address growing end-customer demands by proposing leading-edge technologies to create 'one version of the truth'
- **Standardise to economise** – simplify, then standardise those business processes that are deemed necessary – also work to standardise and reuse IT components, such as servers and databases
- **Centralise the infrastructure** – consolidate and use third-party services whenever it makes financial and business sense, particularly to gain economies of scale
- **Keep cost reduction a top priority** – remain diligent and creative in discovering new ways to lower enterprise costs related to technology
- **Present and measure IT in business terms** – engender shared responsibility for business success through joint performance metrics based on business outcomes
- **Cultivate truly extraordinary IT talent** – identify and grow savvy technologists into thought leaders who can expand the impact of IT
- **Enhance the data** – devote as much attention to data accuracy, availability and integration as to data security.

IBM, 2009, pp. 19, 27 and 35[3]

---

[3] Reprint Courtesy of International Business Machines Corporation, © 2009 International Business Machines Corporation

The IBM survey offers a thought-provoking set of recommended actions that organisations wishing to maximise the contribution of technology to performance should take (see box 21.4). All are relevant to conditions of uncertainty, with the survey noting that 'many industries face unknown and currently immeasurable changes ahead'. IBM reports: 'Across our sample, CIOs agree there will be an ongoing need for adaptability to unplanned changes and events' (IBM, 2009, p. 38).[4]

Given the potential power of technology to help organisations climb the results chain, and the seemingly high risk of generating low returns on investment, it becomes crucial for any public sector or not-for-profit organisation to establish a clear position and philosophy with regard to IT. It must be clear how committed it is to investment in information management systems – not least given the limited financial resources at its disposal. It is a question of risk assessment – of understanding the relationship between the quality of information management (generation and communication) and IT investment. Pressure to upgrade the quality of IT must be accompanied by the business case for doing so, and tempered by an acknowledgement that good enough is, indeed, good enough. It is worth asking how close to the crest of the technology wave the organisation needs to be. 'Just behind it' is often the most appropriate strategy.

HARNESSING TECHNOLOGY SUCCESSFULLY

Maximising the potential of technology to support organisational performance means addressing a host of issues that can be regarded as critical success factors. They can be usefully divided into those factors relating to the organisational environment within which the technology is used, and those relating to the technology itself (see fig. 21.1).

Organisation	Technology
■ Leadership ownership of technology ■ Integration of technology in business ■ Collaboration ■ Clear return on investment ■ Transparency	■ Selecting technology ■ Applying technology ■ Extracting inefficiencies ■ Simplifying and standardising design

Fig. 21.1 Effective use of technology: critical success factors

---

[4] Reprint Courtesy of International Business Machines Corporation, © 2009 International Business Machines Corporation

Organisational success factors

The organisational success factors highlighted in figure 21.1 are as follows.

Leadership ownership of technology

The organisation's leadership must embrace technology, understand its role and potential, and include it on its strategic agenda.

Integration of technology in business

The organisation can demonstrate corporate ownership of technology that is needed by successfully integrating thinking and decision making about technology into its operational planning and implementation processes. By assessing continually both how best to apply technology (for example, by questioning how business decisions can be better supported by high-quality, relevant data) and the adequacy of the return on investment, stewards can ensure that technology helps drive the organisation in the intended direction.

Collaboration

Ownership of information management systems from users comes from adopting a collaborative approach to their design, implementation and use. Axson (2003), Hope (2006), and IBM (2009) are just three sources that stress the importance of involving teams, breaking down functional barriers, and using collaboration and partnering technologies, including with external parties.

Hope (2006, p. 64) argues that:

> the reason most new tools and systems fail to live up to their hype is that they are implemented from the center and are therefore seen by frontline troops as just another control weapon in battle between head office staffers and frontline teams.

Also, integrating proposed IT developments within the plans of those business units whose information management needs the technology is intended to serve can greatly boost their ownership and commitment to the development's success.

Williams *et al* (1999, p. 20) encourage organisations to establish a staff and systems development group to support the chief executive and senior management in taking into account the needs of the whole organisation in managing technology developments (see box 21.5). Even with high levels of in-house collaboration across the organisation, there will be benefits from maintaining strong links with external knowledge and thinking. Such expertise can be accessed in various ways: from specialists on the governing body, from external technology networks, as members of technology user groups, by establishing an informal group of advisers serving on an IT panel, or in a more formal relationship with external IT advisers. It is worth noting the clear trend identified in the IBM survey that high-performing organisations are making greater use of third-party business or IT services, and seeking explicitly to develop relationships with external partners.

Box 21.5   Staff and systems development group responsibilities

- *Steering the organisation's use of technology*
- *Identifying and prioritising critical business issues*
- *Ensuring that these issues are linked to the organisation's objectives*
- *Prioritising projects to form a credible one-year development plan*
- *Initiating activities that will increase the organisation's ability to support new systems once approved and working.*

Williams et al, 1999, p. 20

A steering group of the kind described above offers the opportunity for the organisation to ensure that there is a common understanding of the overall business context and challenges, to hear the perspective of staff in the line about how technology can best support programme delivery, and to incorporate such feedback in developing a clear technology strategy, with a clear short to medium-term programme of IT priorities. This collaborative approach to managing technology also enables the organisation to establish a common set of corporate expectations on issues such as IT policy, risks, vendor relationships, staff development and learning and financial management.

The financial stewards of the organisation must have a keen interest in all of these issues – not least the latter, given the potential for investment in technology to affect expenditure materially over a number of years.

Clear return on investment

It must be clear how technology will support the successful provision of intended outcomes to the beneficiaries of the organisation. It must also be clear how information management and technology will enhance the capacity of the organisation to deliver, providing solutions to business dilemmas. Increasingly, this requires assessment using a broad set of criteria that enables the investment decision to made on the basis of total costs and ultimate impact, rather than being based solely or unduly on the seductive appeal of new technology (see box 21.6).

Box 21.6   How should IT investments be evaluated?
The pervasive impact of technology now means that, in many cases, information technology is so inextricably intertwined with people and processes that the identification of specific technology-related benefit streams is of marginal value. Only the combination of the judicious use of technology, optimized business processes, and suitably trained and motivated people can realize the true value of a technology investment.
One must abandon the idea that there are IT projects; there are no such things anymore. There are only projects targeted at improving business processes, developing new products or services, delivering more efficient customer service, or improving some other aspect of business performance. The ROI [return on investment] evaluation must match the total investments with the total returns regardless of the source of each. Doing this leads to the utilization of broader investment criteria than traditionally used for IT projects.
Axson, 2003, p. 222

Transparency

Information transparency is a hot topic, driven in part by the recent explosion of interest in organisational governance issues (see chapter 10) but also by increasing recognition of the corporate benefits resulting from shared, accessible and timely use of 'one version of the truth' information to support decision making and performance assessments. Climbing the results chain effectively – in an ethical, accountable way – is enhanced where information is widely disseminated, and where open dialogue, discussion and feedback are promoted. The organisation needs to be explicit in defining its philosophy towards information access. It has to promote transparency.

Technology success factors

The technology success factors highlighted in figure 21.1 are as follows.

Selecting technology

Collins (2001, p. 148) promotes the importance of 'pioneering [the] *application of carefully selected* technologies'. Successful organisations are ahead of the IT game – not necessarily in terms of choosing the latest technology, but in terms of how they apply technologies that have been rigorously assessed for their suitability prior to selection. Both Collins (2001, chapter 7, pp. 144–63) and Axson (2003, chapter 9, pp. 207–24) highlight the risk of responding to the latest technological fad, and the importance of staying balanced rather than reactionary: 'Instead of simply succumbing to the lure of every new technology, an effective IT organization rigorously assesses each new advance regarding its potential to deliver value to the organization', says Axson (2003, p. 213). 'You cannot make good use of technology until you know which technologies are relevant', says Collins (2001, pp. 152–53).[5]

In some cases, technology may not be the appropriate solution to a business need. In others, organisational agility may be enhanced by accessing IT services or speciality technologies through third parties (IBM, 2009, p. 19).[6]

Applying technology

Note Collins's emphasis on the *application* of technology. This is what the most successful organisations do best, he says. They are pioneers in application: 'Once they understand which technologies are relevant, they become fanatical and creative in the application of those technologies' (Collins, 2001, p. 153).[6] It is a common error to see organisations invest significantly more energy and time on the selection of technology rather than on the application of the selected technology. More effort is expended on deciding which technology to use than on ensuring that the chosen technology is used well. That cannot make sense.

Focusing on the use of technology includes ensuring the competency of users. Increasingly, decision makers have fast and direct access to the information they need through technology. In many circumstances, technology is influencing who the decision maker is, enabling decision-making authority to be decentralised, mandated to those closest to the beneficiary, donor or other stakeholder. The spread of responsibility through technology increases the importance of training in the use of the relevant systems.

Technology competency must extend beyond being able to generate or access essential information relevant to the results chain, including financial information. Users must be able, in addition, to analyse data, track trends, conduct sensitivity testing, and 'drill down' to pursue the audit trail of data. The better the design – including its simplicity and degree of standardisation – the more intuitive the system, and the more users will be able to help themselves and each other, rather than relying on experts. The sources of expertise, when required, could include knowledgeable users, the system's designers and external helpdesk facilities.

Extracting inefficiencies

In most organisations, there is scope to reduce the costs of technology and thereby drive up efficiencies. IBM reports that CIOs of successful businesses are eliminating expenses by maintaining a highly centralised infrastructure, by

---

[5] *Good to Great*, Copyright © 2001 by Jim Collins. Reprinted with permission from Jim Collins
[6] Reprint Courtesy of International Business Machines Corporation, © 2009 International Business Machines Corporation

standardising and, where appropriate, by automating business processes. There is a strong appetite for 'completely standardized, low-cost business processes' and for delivering services using simple processes that can be repeated (IBM, 2009, p. 25).[7]

Simplifying and standardising design

As the efficiency issue above implies, complexity and customisation come at a high price. The design of information systems and management processes must focus on simplification and standardisation – on creating one easy-to-use, unified system for the whole organisation. Financial stewards have a particularly important role to play in preventing the spread of fragmented and disconnected systems that result in reporting delays and high error rates (Hope, 2006, p. 66). The essential requirement of organisational agility is also served by developing and maintaining straightforward information systems that can easily accommodate changes in, for example, organisational structure or services. Simplify transaction processing, simplify (or even abandon) the budgeting process, simplify the general ledger, and simplify reporting systems, says Hope (2006, pp. 23–51).

The design phase must also address head on the issue of standardisation. Tackling this is crucial before automation is attempted – particularly for finance-related information systems where aggregation and benchmarking of data is necessary. The design and subsequent maintenance of coding structures, accounting policies and transaction processing disciplines must become part of the centralised infrastructure. Allowing decentralised units the freedom to determine these matters independently will lead quickly to inefficiencies and ineffective business support.

MANAGING SYSTEMS DEVELOPMENTS

Williams *et al* (1999, pp. 21–29) propose one framework that can be used for any systems development (see fig. 21.2). Formal project management disciplines are unquestionably necessary to manage the process of design and implementation of major systems developments, and financial stewards are particularly well placed to contribute to the overview of such developments, given their role and capacity to understand both costs and benefits. The framework reinforces the messages given earlier in the chapter – in particular, the sequencing of the design of systems only after there is clarity about a number of key business issues:

- the business drivers
- the expected return on investment

---

[7] Reprint Courtesy of International Business Machines Corporation, © 2009 International Business Machines Corporation

- the optimal organisational design (including structure) and business processes that technology should support
- roles and responsibilities.

Data gathering and analysis must precede technology design.

Data gathering	Analysis	Information and communication systems	Implementation
1. Identify the **critical business issues** 2. Be clear about the related **business objectives** 3. Set down in detail the **current process** for undertaking this work	1. **Redesign** the way work is done to address the identified shortcomings 2. Explore whether changes will be required at the **organisational level** in light of the redesigned process and established goals 3. Explore whether changes will be required to **individual(s) roles and responsibilities** in the light of the above	1. Determine the **information needs and IT solutions** that are now required as a result of the Analysis phase 2. Determine the **communications needs and communications technology solutions** that are now required as a result of the Analysis phase 3. Compare solutions in 1 and 2 to existing systems and equipment	1. Identify and record **benefits** of implementing the Information and Communications solutions arrived at in the previous phase. This will be used to measure achievements 2. Establish the **cost** of implementing the Information and Communications solutions arrived at in the previous phase. This will become the project's budget 3. **Installation** 4. **Evaluate** performance improvements by measuring benefits achieved and costs incurred against what was planned

Fig. 21.2 Framework for managing technology developments, Williams *et al*, 1999

The framework also usefully distinguishes between, and stresses the importance of, information and communication systems alike. Crucially, if information is to reach the decision makers that will use it, it must not only be generated but communicated. Most business processes cross organisational structures, involving multiple units. The handover points between units are particularly susceptible to communication breakdowns, with information losses and distortions. These points also provide most scope for efficiency improvements – for example, through avoiding data re-entry. Finally, note the inclusion of review at the end of the process: a crucial last step that enables the organisation to assess the cost-effectiveness of the development, and to plan action accordingly.

PROCUREMENT RISKS

One step in the systems development process that is not explicit in the Williams *et al* framework is that of procurement. The need to maintain a close overview of the procurement process by which outside vendors or consultants and technology solutions are selected increases with the size, complexity and anticipated impact of the proposed systems development. The larger or more complex the project (or the greater its likely impact), the greater the risks associated with the procurement process.

A formal request for proposals (RFP) process can help. The RFP process, in which an organisation outlines its business and technology requirements and then evaluates detailed proposals submitted by alternative vendors, imposes discipline, and thereby some enhanced control, to the selection. The process forces the organisation to define transparently what it is trying to achieve in the project, to link those objectives to wider organisational goals, and to articulate its proposed timeline for the development.

In addition, by issuing one set of requirements – one statement of proposed work – the organisation facilitates the receipt of comparable solutions offered by alternative vendors, enabling it to be more objective, thorough and ultimately effective in its selection process. The RFP process also provides scope for broad participation from within the organisation in preparing the RFP document and contributing to the selection process. All of the organisational critical success factors described earlier in the chapter can be supported through the process.

Nevertheless, the RFP process itself cannot eliminate the risks inherent in large, complex technology-based projects that can be multi-year in duration, and whose scope of work and timing can be difficult to define accurately up front. In fact, as we saw in chapter 10 (see pp. 153–54), the seeming discipline of the typical procurement process can disguise the real risks facing the organisation and the prospective vendor. There are several risks, including the following (Mawji, 2004, pp. 18–19, text adapted):

- Inadequate definition of scope and specification.
- Poor-quality relationship with vendor. Deterioration can start soon after the completion of the RFP process if the relationship is not well grounded in trust.
- Scope 'creep' coupled with inadequate controls, such as documentation of changes. This risk is particularly prevalent, leading to frequent design changes, time inefficiencies and bureaucratic approval processes.

- Poor terms and conditions which can quickly lead to a build up of costs without adequate return.
- Technical risks including reliance on sub-contractors, untested facilities and unproven technology.
- Poor project planning, including incomplete plans and ambiguous roles and responsibilities.

Many risk mitigation approaches can be introduced, adopting the disciplines explored in chapter 10. For the financial steward keen to climb the results chain cost-effectively in spite of uncertainty, key risk controls include the following (Mawji, 2004, text adapted):

- Establishing a relationship of trust with the vendor.
- Defining a clear statement of needs. A formal definition of needs is crucial noting that there may be hidden needs as well as explicit ones; constraints; and requirements for interfacing with other systems and processes.
- Negotiating an appropriate contract. Different contract types – including cost-reimbursable, fixed-price and incentivized contracts – can all be appropriate in different circumstances, depending on the degree of certainty present, the availability of competitive benchmarks and the degree of clarify about the work requirements.
- Using formal project management disciplines, including a performance measurement system that tracks which tasks have been completed and which have not.

Financial stewards can play several key roles on behalf of the organisation.

- They must remain objective, focused on the ultimate objective and the requirements of stakeholders, and insistent on tracking progress in a timely manner. Maintaining a neutral – perhaps sceptical – perspective can help the assessment of claims and promises made by vendors under considerable pressure to win the contract.
- They must lead the negotiation of the financial terms under which the contract is issued and settled, ensuring that the contracted deliverables are truly delivered before full settlement is made.
- They can help ensure that appropriate accountability of the relevant parties is upheld.
- They can promote and guide the kind of adaptive procurement process outlined in chapter 10, recognising all the uncertainties that face the organisation and the vendor at the start of the process. Ignoring those uncertainties defies reality, and indicates failure to build in the controls that will become necessary further along the system development process.

MANAGING IT-RELATED COSTS

IT solutions to business requirements such as financial stewardship absorb sizeable financial resources. For this reason, organisations need to manage expectations internally, from the board downwards. IT-related costs are likely to be an increasingly important form of expenditure, and to remain consistently high. So, culturally, it is important that such expenditure is recognised as an essential component of the organisational enablers: an investment of resources selected by organisational leaders as a priority in order to contribute to the achievement of mission, rather than as undesirable administrative costs.

Crutchfield and McLeod Grant (2008, pp. 185–86) identify infrastructure as one of three critical elements that are needed by organisations 'in order to maintain and deepen their impact over time: *people, capital* and *infrastructure*'. 'Invest in overhead', they urge, 'despite the pressure to look lean.'

The scale of the cultural shift that is required cannot be overstated. Despite a widespread recognition of the importance and value of building and maintaining a robust organisational infrastructure (including IT systems), there continues to be deep-rooted reluctance to incur expenditure that will be classified and regarded as 'overhead'. This is the challenge of covering core costs, referred to in chapter 6.

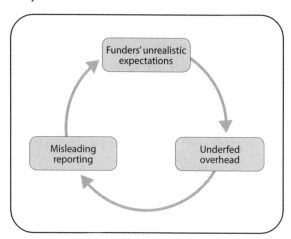

Fig. 21.3 The not-for-profit starvation cycle (adapted from Goggins Gregory and Howard, 2009)

Goggins Gregory and Howard (2009) conclude that 'a vicious cycle is leaving nonprofits so hungry for decent infrastructure that they can barely function as organizations – let alone serve their beneficiaries' (p. 49). They call it 'the nonprofit starvation cycle' (p. 49, see fig. 21.3), which starts with funders' unrealistic expectations about what it costs to run an organisation. This, in turn, creates pressure for the recipient organisation to conform to those expectations, which it does by 'settl[ing] into a "low pay, make do, and do without" culture' (p. 51). It reduces expenditure on overhead and misrepresents actual overhead costs, reporting artificially low expenditure of this type: behaviour that fuels the very donor expectations that generate the pressure, and so on.

Goggins Gregory and Howard (2009, p. 52, text adapted) offer several solutions. For funders, they recommend the following solutions.

- Shift the focus from costs to outcomes – an endorsement of the outcome funding approach described in chapter 6.
- Make general operating support grants that can be used to meet infrastructure needs.
- Encourage open, candid discussions about what the recipient organisations need in order to be effective.
- Commit to pay a greater share of administrative and income-generation costs.
- Encourage the development of a standard definition of the term 'overhead'.

Similarly, for the executive leadership of recipient organisations, Goggins Gregory and Howard offer a number of recommended actions.

- Commit to understanding the real overhead costs and the organisation's real infrastructure needs, and recognise the risks of failing to meet these needs.
- Share the real numbers with the governing body and engage them in the task of communicating a realistic picture with funders.
- Focus on how investment in infrastructure will benefit the organisation's beneficiaries, rather than reduce costs.
- Educate donors.

Even with the support of these solutions, generating the finance needed is burdensome – but it can be done. Recall from chapter 6 the alternative funding models that are promoted in order to finance core costs – full project funding, development funding and strategic funding (see p. 87). Crutchfield and McLeod Grant's study of 12 high-impact not-for-profit organisations confirms the potential of the second of these models: development funding. It observes that:

almost all of the groups ... needed to raise substantial capital, above and beyond their annual operating costs, to invest in the development of their organizations ... Many ran 'growth campaigns' to invest in the critical systems and teams they needed to keep up with program growth. They often structured campaigns as one-time events rather than folding them into annual operating costs, which helped to keep their overhead ratio low as well as generate momentum and excitement among funders.

Crutchfield and McLeod Grant, 2008, p. 200

Key stewardship questions

1. How much ownership of technology does the organisation's leadership assume?

2. How well are considerations of technology integrated with the business of the organisation?

3. How collaborative is the management of technology?

4. How satisfactory has the return on recent investments in technology been?

5. How can the organisation increase the return in the future?

6. How committed is the organisation to information transparency?

7. What is the relative attention paid to applying technology versus selecting it?

8. How can the organisation reduce the costs of technology and drive up efficiencies?

9. What scope is there within the organisation to simplify and standardise business processes?

10. Is the organisation investing sufficiently in infrastructure such as technology?

Bibliography

ACEVO (n.d.), 'Full Cost Recovery' [web page], www.fullcostrecovery.org.uk, ACEVO, accessed 30 January 2009

APQC (n.d.), 'About Benchmarking' [web page], www.apqc.org, APQC, accessed 22 November 2009

Aldrich, Tobin (2007), *A Fresh Approach to Using Lifetime Analysis as a Donor Recruitment Tool* [online document], www.tobinaldrich.com, Tobin Aldrich, accessed 15 March 2009

Argenti, John (1993), *Your Organization: What is it for?*, London, McGraw Hill

Australian Securities Exchange Corporate Governance Council (2007), *Corporate Governance Principles and Recommendations*, Sydney, ASX Corporate Governance Council

Axson, David (n.d.), 'Rolling Forecasts' [web page], www.davidaxson.com, David Axson, accessed 14 March 2006

Axson, David (2003), *Best Practices in Planning and Management Reporting*, Hoboken NJ, Wiley

Barber, Michael (2007), *Instruction to Deliver*, London, Politico's

Blackmore, Becky, Richard Hardy and Christina Hogg (1998), *Partners in Leadership*, London, ACEVO

Bond (2006), *Statement of Principles*, London, Bond

Bryson, John (2004), *Strategic Planning for Public and Non-profit Organizations*, 3rd edn, San Francisco, Jossey-Bass

Caulkin, Simon (2003), 'Break out of the Budget Cycle', *The Observer*, Guardian News and Media Limited, 20 July

Charity Commission (2005), *Accounting and Reporting by Charities: Statement of Recommended Practice*, rev. 2005, London, HMSO

Charity Commission (2008a), *The Essential Trustee: What You Need to Know*, CC03, London, HMSO

Charity Commission (2008b), *Charities' Reserves*, CC19, London, HMSO

Charity Commission (2010a), *Charities and Reserves*, CC19, London, HMSO

Charity Commission (2010b), 'Key Principles of Good Governance' [web page], www.charity-commission.gov.uk, HMSO, accessed 12 July 2010

Chartered Institute of Management Accountants (2000), 'Management Accounting Official Terminology', London, CIMA

Chartered Institute of Management Accountants (2007), *Introduction to Managing Risk*, rev. 2008 [online publication,], www.CIMAglobal.com, CIMA, accessed 26 July 2009

Chartered Institute of Management Accountants (n.d.), 'Professional Qualification' [web page], www.CIMAglobal.com, CIMA, accessed 12 October 2009

Collins, Jim (2001), *Good to Great*, New York, HarperCollins

Collins, Jim (2005), *Good to Great and the Social Sectors*, New York, HarperCollins

COSO (1994), *Internal Control: Integrated Framework*, New York, COSO

COSO (2004), *Enterprise Risk Management: Integrated Framework, Executive Summary*, New York, COSO

The Commission for the Compact, Compact Voice, Local Government Association and the Office of the Third Sector (2008), *Joint Compact Action Plan 2008–2009*, London, HMSO

Crutchfield, Leslie R., and Heather McLeod Grant (2008), *Forces for Good*, San Francisco, Jossey-Bass

Danninger, Stephan (2005), *Revenue Forecasts as Performance Targets* [International Monetary Fund Working Paper], Washington, International Monetary Fund

Denning, Stephen (2005), *The Leader's Guide to Storytelling*, San Francisco, Jossey-Bass

Department for International Development (n.d.), 'International Aid Transparency Initiative, Working to make Global Aid More Effective' [archived web page], www.dfid.gov.uk, DfID, accessed 23 July 2009

Dorotinsky, Bill (2004), 'Developing a Medium-Term Expenditure Framework', *Reforming the Public Expenditure Management System*, Séoul, The World Bank and Korea Development Institute Conference Proceedings, chapter 1, pp. 37–52

Dougherty, John R. (n.d.), 'Your Bias May Be Limiting Your Forecast Accuracy' [web page], www.partnersforexcellence.com, John R Dougherty, accessed 30 May 2009

Dyer, Peter (2008), *The Good Trustee Guide*, London, NCVO

Epstein, Marc J., and Adriana Rejc (2005), *Identifying, Measuring, and Managing Organizational Risks for Improved Performance*, Mississauga ON, CMA Canada and AICPA

Financial Reporting Council (2005), *Internal Control: Revised Guidance for Directors on the Combined Code*, London, Financial Reporting Council

Financial Reporting Council (2008), *The Combined Code on Corporate Governance*, London, Financial Reporting Council

Gates, Bill (1999), *Business @ the Speed of Thought*, London, Penguin

Gillingham, Shirley, and John Tame (1997), *Not Just for a Rainy Day?*, London, NCVO

Goggins Gregory, Ann, and Don Howard (2009), 'The Nonprofit Starvation Cycle', *Stanford Social Innovation Review*, Stanford, Stanford Graduate School of Business, Fall issue

Haeckel, Stephan H. (1999), *Adaptive Enterprise*, Boston, Harvard Business School Press

Hayek, Friedrich August von (1974), 'The Pretence of Knowledge' [lecture], Oslo, The Nobel Foundation

Herzlinger, Regina, and Denise Nitterhouse (1994), *Financial Accounting and Managerial Control for Nonprofit Organizations*, Cincinnati OH, South-Western Publishing Co.

Hind, Andrew (1995), *The Governance and Management of Charities*, London, Voluntary Sector Press

HM Treasury (2004), *The Orange Book: Management of Risk: Principles and Concepts*, www.hm-treasury.gov.uk, HMSO, accessed 26 July 2009

HM Treasury (2005), *Corporate Governance in Central Government Departments: Code of Good Practice*, London, HMSO

HM Treasury (2006), *Improving Financial Relationships with the Third Sector: Guidance to Funders and Purchasers*, London, HMSO

HM Treasury (2007a), *2007 Pre-Budget Report and Comprehensive Spending Review*, London, HMSO

HM Treasury (2007b), *The Future Role of the Third Sector in Social and Economic Regeneration: Final Report*, London, HMSO

HM Treasury (2007c), *Managing Public Money*, London, HMSO

HM Treasury (2008), 'Spending Reviews' [webpage – archived 5 March 2008], www.hm-treasury.gov.uk, HMSO, accessed 17 January 2009

HM Treasury (2009), *Compact on Relations between Government and the Third Sector in England*, London, HMSO

HM Treasury (2010), 'Public Expenditure Planning and Control in the UK', *Spending Review* [web pages – updated 22 March 2010], www.hm-treasury.gov.uk, HMSO, originally accessed 24 January 2009

Hope, Jeremy (2006), *Reinventing the CFO*, Boston, Harvard Business School Press

Hope, Jeremy, and Robin Fraser (1999), *The BBRT Guide to Managing Without Budgets*, release v3.01, n.d., Poole, CAM-I

Hope, Jeremy, and Robin Fraser (2001a), *Beyond Budgeting*, Boston, Harvard Business School Press

Hope, Jeremy, and Robin Fraser (2001b), letter to *Financial Management* in September, London, CIMA

Hudson, Mike (2009), *Managing Without Profit*, 3rd edn, London, Directory of Social Change

IBM Institute for Business Value (2009), *The New Voice of the CIO: Insights from the Global Chief Information Officer Study*, Somers NY, IBM

International Finance Corporation (2008), *Results Measurement for Advisory Services*, Washington, International Finance Corporation

Johnson, H. Thomas (1998), 'Reflections of a Recovering Management Accountant' [online article, 14 January], www.solonline.org, Society for Organizational Learning, accessed 15 February 2006

Johnson, H. Thomas, and Anders Bröms (2000), *Profit Beyond Measure*, New York, The Free Press

Kaplan, Robert, and David Norton (1996), *The Balanced Scorecard: Translating Strategy into Action*, Boston, Harvard Business School Press

Kaplan, Robert, and David Norton (2001), *The Strategy-Focused Organization*, Boston, Harvard Business School Press

Kaplan, Robert, and David Norton (2004), *Strategy Maps*, Boston, Harvard Business School Publishing Corporation

Kelman, Steven (2006), 'Improving Service Delivery Performance in the United Kingdom: Organization Theory Perspectives on Central Intervention Strategies' [working paper version], *Journal of Comparative Policy Analysis*, Routledge, vol. 8, no. 4, pp. 393–419

Kranen, Hay (n.d.), 'The Long Tail' [illustration on web page], www.wikipedia.com, Wikipedia, accessed 10 June 2009

Leitch, Matthew (2006), 'How to Embed Risk Management into Performance Management and Strategy Making' [online article], www.internalcontrolsdesign.co.uk, Matthew Leitch Associates Limited, 6 December

Leitch, Matthew (2008), *Intelligent Internal Control and Risk Management*, London, Gower

Leitch, Matthew (2010), 'Making Sense of Risk Appetite, Tolerance, and Acceptance' [online article], www.internalcontrolsdesign.co.uk, Matthew Leitch Associates Limited

Liker, Jeffrey (2004), *The Toyota Way*, New York, McGraw Hill

Lindsay, R. Murray, and Ken Mark (2005), Sightsavers International case: 9B05B018, Richard Ivey School of Business, London ON, The University of Western Ontario

Loungani, Prakash, and Jair Rodriguez (2008), 'Economic Forecasts: Too Smooth by Far?', *World Economics Journal*, International Monetary Fund, April–June, vol. 9, no. 2

Lynch, David (1994), *Quality in the Finance Function*, London, CIMA/Kogan Page

Managing for Development Results (2006), *Emerging Good Practice in Managing for Development Results: Sourcebook* [online publication], 1st edn, www.mfdr.org, OECD/DAC, accessed 23 July 2009

Managing for Development Results (2008), *Emerging Good Practice in Managing for Development Results: Sourcebook* [online publication], 3rd edn, www.mfdr.org, OECD/DAC, accessed 23 July 2009

Mawji, Amin (2004), *Programmed for Control*, London, Ernst & Young

Merriam-Webster (2002), *Webster's Third New International Dictionary*, unabridged, http://unabridged.merriam-webster.com, Merriam-Webster, accessed 12 July 2010

Moore, Mark H. (1995), *Creating Public Value: Strategic Management in Government*, Cambridge, Harvard University Press

Morlidge, Steve and Steve Player (2009), *Future Ready: How to Master Business Forecasting*, London, John Wiley & Sons

National Audit Office/Audit Commission (2006), *Delivering Efficiently: Strengthening the Links in Public Service Delivery Chains*, London, HMSO

National Audit Office (2007), *Implementation of Full Cost Recovery*, London, National Audit Office

National Hub of Expertise in Governance (2005), *Good Governance: A Code for the Voluntary and Community Sector*, London, NCVO

National Partnership for Reinventing Government (1993), 'Mission Driven, Results Oriented Budgeting' [web page archive], http://govinfo.library.unt.edu, National Performance Review, accessed 07 December 2006

Nordhaus, W. (1987), 'Forecasting Efficiency: Concepts and Applications', *The Review of Economics and Statistics*, The MIT Press, vol. 69, no. 4, pp. 667–674

OECD (2007), Teresa Curristine (ed.), *Performance Budgeting in OECD Countries*, Paris, OECD

OECD (2008), 'Performance Budgeting in the United Kingdom', *Journal on Budgeting*, OECD, vol. 8, no. 1, pp. 1–16

Office of Management and Budget (n.d.), 'Assessing Program Performance' [web page], www.whitehouse.gov, Executive Office of the President of the United States/The White House, accessed 12 July 2010

Office of Management and Budget (1993) 'Government Performance Results Act of 1993', Washington, The White House

ORC Worldwide (2006), *World Bank: A Study of the HRS Recruitment Function* [internal report], Washington, The World Bank

Paton, Rob (2003), *Managing and Measuring Social Enterprises*, London, Sage

Peters, Tom (1992), *Liberation Management*, London, Macmillan

Pfeffer, Jeffrey, and Robert I. Sutton (2006), *Hard Facts, Dangerous Half-Truths and Total Nonsense: Profiting from Evidence-Based Management*, Boston, Harvard Business School Press

Poffley, Adrian (1997), 'Power Tools: How to Build Better Management Accounts', *NGO Finance*, Plaza Publishing, January/February, pp. 32–3

Poffley, Adrian (1997), 'Super Structures: How to Engineer a Better Blueprint', *NGO Finance*, Plaza Publishing, March/April, pp. 32–4

Poffley, Adrian (1997), 'Shall I Compare Thee to the Best in the Business: or to the Budget?' *NGO Finance*, Plaza Publishing, May/June, pp. 26–7

Poffley, Adrian (1997), 'Preaching the Gospel: Spreading the Word about Management Accounts', *NGO Finance*, Plaza Publishing, July/August, pp. 34–5

Poffley, Adrian (1999), 'An Effort Worthy of Development', *NGO Finance*, Plaza Publishing, October, p. 58

Poffley, Adrian (2000), 'Global Concerns: Aid in Uncertainty', *NGO Finance*, Plaza Publishing, June, pp. 44–7

Poffley, Adrian (2002), *Financial Stewardship of Charities*, London, Directory of Social Change

Porter, Michael (1996), 'What is Strategy?', *Harvard Business Review*, Harvard Business Review Press, November/December, pp. 61–78

Powell, Mike (1999), *Information Management for Development Organisations*, Oxford, Oxfam

Purves, Libby (2006), 'Why Targets Miss the Point', *The Times*, News International, 2 May

Roche, Chris (1999), *Impact Assessment for Development Agencies*, Oxford, Oxfam

Rosenberg, Deborah (1998), 'Methods for Analyzing Trend Data', in *Analytic Methods in Maternal and Child Health*, Handler, A., Rosenberg, D., Monahan, C., and Kennelly, J. (eds.), Rockville MD, Maternal and Child Health Bureau, HRSA, DHHS

Sargeant, Adrian, and Elaine Jay (2004), *Fundraising Management: Analysis, Planning and Practice*, London, Routledge

Sayer Vincent (2006), *Achieving a Balanced Framework of Controls* [online publication], www.sayervincent.co.uk, Sayer Vincent, accessed 9 August 2009

Sayer Vincent (2009), *Adaptive Procurement*, unpublished draft discussion paper, London, Sayer Vincent

Scott, Graham (2001), *Public Sector Management in New Zealand*, Canberra, Centre for Law and Economics, Australia National University

Seddon, John (2003), *Written Submission to Public Administration's Select Committee's Inquiry into Public Sector Performance Targets*, www.systemsthinking.co.uk, John Seddon, accessed 29 November 2008

Seddon, John (2006), *Open Letter to Ruth Kelly, MP, Minister of Communities and Local Government* (8 May), www.systemsthinking.co.uk, John Seddon, accessed 30 May 2010

Seddon, John (2008), *Systems Thinking in the Public Sector*, Axminster, Triarchy Press

Sightsavers International (2005), *Overseas Programmes Department Manual* [internal document], Haywards Heath, Sightsavers International

Sightsavers International (2006), *Reward Policy* [internal document], Haywards Heath, Sightsavers International

Sightsavers International (2008), *Sightsavers International Annual Report and Financial Statements 2008*, Haywards Heath, Sightsavers International

Sightsavers International (2009), *Strategic Framework 2009–2013: Making the Connections* [online report], www.sightsavers.org, Sightsavers International, accessed 17 April 2010

Stacey, Ralph (1993), 'Strategy as Order Emerging from Chaos', *Long Range Planning*, International Journal of Strategic Management, vol. 26, no. 1, pp. 10–17

Taleb, Nassim Nicholas (2004), *Fooled by Randomness*, London, Penguin

UK Charity Awards (2001), 'International aid and development' [web page], www.charityawards.co.uk, Civil Society, accessed 29 May 2010

United Nations (n.d.), 'Background' [web page], *Millennium Development Goals*, www.un.org/millenniumgoals, United Nations, accessed 11 April 2009

United States General Accounting Office (1999), *Standards for Internal Control in the Federal Government*, Washington, United States General Accounting Office

Unwin, Julia (2001), *Funding our Future: Core Costs Revisited*, London, ACEVO

U.S. Office of Personnel Management (n.d.), 'Performance Management – Overview' [web page], Washington, www.opm.gov, U.S. Office of Personnel Management, accessed 24 October 2009

Wallander, Jan (2003), *Decentralisation: Why and How to Make it Work*, Stockholm, SNS Förlag

Warnes, Brian (1984), *The Genghis Khan Guide to Business*, London, Osmosis Publications

Warnes, Brian (1985), *The Genghis Khan Guide to Business: Cash Flow Handbook*, London, Osmosis Publications

Wheatley, Margaret, and Myron Kellner-Rogers (1999), 'What Do We Measure and Why? Questions about the Uses of Measurement', *Journal for Strategic Performance Measurement* June issue [accessed 27 November 2009 from www.margaretwheatley.com]

Williams, Clyde, Chris Nunn, Tasleem Chaudary and Terry Mitchell (1999), *Computers can be Managed: A CEO's Guide*, London, Sho-Net Systems Ltd

Williams, Harold S., Arthur Y. Webb and William J. Phillips (1996), *Outcome Funding*, New York, The Rensselaerville Institute

World Bank (2005), *2004 Annual Report on Operations Evaluation*, Washington, The World Bank

World Bank (2007a), *A Vision for Excellence in Performance Management* [internal document], Washington, The World Bank

World Bank (2007b), IDA 15 Fact Sheet [internal document], www.worldbank.org, The World Bank

World Bank (2008), *FY08 Trust Fund Portfolio Review: Raising Awareness of Trust Fund Complexities*, Washington, The World Bank

World Bank (2009a), *HR Strategy Update* [internal document], Washington, The World Bank

World Bank (2009b), *HRS FY09 Performance Memo* [internal document], Washington, The World Bank

World Bank (2009c), *The World Bank Annual Report 2009*, Washington, The World Bank

World Bank (2010), 'Evaluation Tools' [web page], www.worldbank.org, The World Bank, accessed 20 July 2009

Zanini, Michele (2009), 'Power curves': What Natural and Economic Disasters have in Common', June issue, *The McKinsey Quarterly*, www.mckinseyquarterly.com, McKinsey & Company, accessed 10 June 2009

Index

accountability
  goals-setting 22–27
  handling trust funds 90
  input-oriented 26–27
  outcomes-based 25–27
  public and not-for-profit
    organisations 1
  trustee 303–306
accounting
  accruals 219–220
  cash 218
  commitment 220–221
  SORP 2005 *Accounting and Reporting
    by Charities* 75, 100, 130
  see also fund accounting; Statement
    of Financial Activities (SOFA)
accruals accounting 219–220
ACEVO (Association of Chief
  Executives of Voluntary
  Organisations) 86, 296
activities
  classification of costs 130, 208–209
  determining fund priorities 267–270
  general 104–105, 237, 268–270
  matching funds 110–113, 210–211
  specific projects 236–237, 267–268
  support service functions 237,
    268–270
activity-based costing 87, 111
actuals
  interpreting accounts 218–221
administration costs 261–262
Aldrich, Tobin 234
allocation of resources *see* funds
  allocation
American Productivity and Quality
  Center (APQC) 206
annual accounts *see* financial
  statements

annual review
  trustees' 304–305
appeals
  auditors' role in determining
    design 94
  fundraising determination
    process 93–94
Argenti, John 39, 134, 135, 296
asset management 122–124
  see also fixed assets
asset turnover 123
Association of Chief Executives of
  Voluntary Organisations
  (ACEVO) 86, 296
audit committee 299–300
auditors
  independence 155
  role in determining design of
    fundraising appeal 94
  see also internal audit
Axson, David 207, 229–230, 337, 340,
  342

balance sheet 76
  cash flow illustration 118–121
  interpretation 80–81, 201
  relationship with Statement of
    Financial Activities (SOFA) 79
Balanced Scorecard 31, 253–254
  Sightsavers International 60–62
Barber, Michael 18, 22, 25, 43, 53, 282,
  285
benchmarking 206–207
Blackmore, Becky *et al* 296
the board
  delegating responsibilities 298–301
Bond 93
Bröms, Anders 19–20, 30, 31, 150

Bryson, John 32, 39, 41–42, 43, 45–47, 163, 244, 263, 309
budgets
  carry-over facilities 174–175
  contingency funds 177–178
  definition 173–174
  limited carry-over 175–176
  multi-year framework 180–181
  overspending 176–177
  resource allocation 162–164, 165–172
  rolling concept 179–180
  spending ranges 178–179
  unlimited carry-over 176
business processes
  review 274
business review 279–288
  communication 284
  discussion 282–284
  incorporating financial
    implications 288–289
  information 281–282
  preparation 280
  re-forecasting 289–290
  World Bank HR case study 286–288
  World Bank report formats 281

case studies
  OECD member governments 64–68
  Sightsavers International 58–64
  UK government performance
    management 69–71
  World Bank HR business review
    process 286–288
cash 115
cash accounting 218
cash flow 116, 117
  illustration of primary
    statements 119–121
  monitoring and forecasting 122, 228
cash flow statement 121
cash management 118–122, 228
chaos management 48–50
charity appeals *see* appeals

Charity Commission
  Accounting and Reporting by Charities
    (SORP 2005) 75, 100, 130
  reserves 100–103, 107
charity trustees *see* trustees
Chartered Institute of Management
  Accountants (CIMA) 145, 146, 202,
  315
chief financial officer *see* finance
  director
Collins, Jim 27–28, 332, 342–343
Combined Code 139
commitment accounting 220–221
commitments
  expenditure 104–105, 235–240
  future expenditure 238–240
  specific projects 236–237
  support service functions 237
Committee of Sponsoring
  Organizations of the Treadway
  Commissions (COSO) 140, 141
communication
  business review 284
  face-to-face presentations 217
  management accounts 211–218
compensation
  financial stewards 320–325
contingency funds 177–178
core costs 85–88, 348–349
corporate governance 139–140
  compliance burden 140–141
COSO (Committee of Sponsoring
  Organizations of the Treadway
  Commissions) 140, 141
cost recovery 85–88
cost-income ratio 85
costs
  activity classification 130, 208–209
  core 85–88, 348–349
  full cost recovery 86–88
  income generation 84–85
  information technology 348–349
  see also expenditure
creditor control 123–124

Crutchfield, Leslie R. 96–97, 332, 337, 348, 349

Danninger, Stephan 224
data
  evidence-based 27–31
debtor control 123
Deming, W. Edwards 18, 30
Denning, Stephen 281–282
designated funds
  impact on reserves policy 102, 103
Dorotinsky, Bill 196, 226, 232, 233, 264, 272
Dougherty, John R. 240
Dyer, Peter 295

employment
  financial stewards 313–331
endowment funds
  burden 91
  impact on reserves policy 102–103
Epstein, Mark J 145
evidence-based management 27–31
expenditure
  classification 130, 208–209
  commitments 104–105, 235–240
  desired profile 132–133
  direction 129–133
  distribution 130–132
  effectiveness 133–137
  future commitments 238–240
  level 128–129

finance committee 299, 300–301
finance director
  financial stewardship role 307–309
finance strategy 10–11
  assets 115–125
  purpose 75–76
  using financial statements 80–81
  see also expenditure; funds; income
financial forecasting see forecasting

financial statements
  cash flow illustration 118–121
  comparison with management accounts 209–210
  interpretation 80–81, 201
  public relations aspect 228
  trustees' report 304
financial stewards
  competencies 314–317
  deployment 331–333
  engagement cycle 313–314
  exit 331–333
  job definition 317–319
  performance management 328–329
  professional development 330–331
  recruitment 325–327
  reward strategy 320–325
  role 5–7, 76–77, 138, 295–311
  succession 331–333
financial stewardship
  5 step methodology 190–199, 291–292
  act (step 5) 190, 192, 279–292
  aim (step 3) 190, 191, 243–256
  delegating responsibilities 298–301
  finance director's role 307–309
  forecast (step 2) 190, 191, 223–241
  governing body role 295–306
  manager's role 310–311
  map 8
  meaning 5–7
  monitor (step 1) 190, 191, 201–221
  plan (step 4) 190, 191–192, 257–276
  principles 7–14
  risks 144–145
  senior executive's role 306–311
  treasurer's role 301–303
  trustee accountability 303–306
  trustees' governance role 297
fixed assets 110
forecasting
  cash flow 122, 228
  definition 223

forecasting—*continued*
  eliminating bias 225–226, 240
  expendable reserves 235
  future resource availability 232–235
  income 233–235
  legacy income 234–235
  level of detail 231
  purpose 223–225
  quality 240–241
  re-forecasting 289–290
  rolling 229–230
  timeframes 227–230
  updating 230
Fraser, Robin 34, 164, 223
fund accounting 77–81
  activities 110–113, 210–211
  distinct from private sector
    accounting 77–78
  restricted funds/income 91–92
  retrospective income 92
  see also Statement of Financial
    Activities (SOFA)
fundraising
  appeal determination process 93–94
  auditors' role in determining
    design 94
funds
  definition 99
  fixed assets 110
  form held 108–110
  management 99–113
  matching with activities 110–113,
    210–211
  reserves management 100–108, 260
  restricted income 89–92, 100
  unrestricted income 89, 100
  see also costs; income
funds allocation 161–172
  accountability trap 170–171
  activities furthering the
    organisation's objectives 262
  aligning allocations with policy
    choices 263–265

funds allocation—*continued*
  budgets 162–172
  carry-over facilities 174–175
  cash flow management 228
  committing allocated resources as
    needed 265–267
  contingency funds 177–178
  creating fiscal space 272–276
  decision-making cycle 270–271
  determining priorities 267–270
  draw-down expenditure direction
    approach 181–184
  ensuring optimal use of
    resources 267–270
  entitlement trap 170
  general activities 268–270
  income-generating activities 260–261
  lead times for multi-year
    allocations 263
  limited carry-over 175–176
  management and
    administration 261–262
  medium-term expenditure
    frameworks 196–197
  multi-year framework 180–181
  overspending the budget 176–177
  reserves 260
  rolling concept 179–180
  specific projects 267–268
  spending ranges 178–179
  spending target trap 165–170
  top-level medium term
    allocations 258–263
  trade-offs 276
  traps 164–172, 174
  unlimited carry-over 176

Gates, Bill 335, 336, 338
general activity *see under* activities
Gillingham, Shirley 103
goals *see* target setting
Goggins Gregory, Ann 348–349

governance
  key performance indicators
    (KPIs) 250–252
  public meetings 305–306
  trustee accountability 303–306
  trustees' role 297
  see also corporate governance
Greenpeace 7

Haeckel, Stephan H. 43, 50, 149, 164,
  189, 317, 336, 337
Hayek, Friedrich August von 30
Herzlinger, Regina 78, 129, 246
HM Treasury
  corporate governance 140
Hind, Andrew 42, 44–45, 80
Hope, Jeremy 34, 164, 206, 223, 250,
  309, 337, 340, 344
Howard, Don 348–349
Hudson, Mike 32, 306, 308

IBM 336, 337, 338–339, 340, 343
impact
  evaluation 135–136
  maximisation 1–2
  measurement 133–134
income
  corporate not-for-profit
    alliances 96–97
  cost-income ratio 85
  forecasting 233–235
  generating 84–85
  government source 95–96
  legacy 234–235
  levels 83–88
  restricted 89–92, 100
  sources 94–97
  strategy 83
  types 89–94
  unrestricted 89, 100
  see also funds

information systems *see* management
  information systems
information technology (IT) 336–344
  application 343
  collaborative approach to
    management 340–341
  critical success factors in effective use
    of 339–344
  efficiency drive 343–344
  managing costs 348–349
  procurement risks 346–347
  return on investment 341–343
  selection 342–343
  strategic resource 338–339
information transparency 342
internal audit 150, 154–157
  etiquette 156–157
  relationship with
    management 154–156
internal control 139–144
  compliance burden 140–141
  corporate governance 139–140
  definition 141
  see also risk management
international development sector
  expenditure effectiveness 136–137
  impact measurement 134
investment committee 300
investment management 124–125
IT *see* information technology

Jay, Elaine 234
Johnson, H. Thomas 18–20, 30, 31,
  150

Kaplan, Robert 31, 39, 41, 60–62,
  253–254
Kellner-Rogers, Myron 30–31
Kelman, Steven 20–21
key performance indicators
  (KPIs) 31–34
  definition 32

key performance indicators (KPIs)—
continued
    governance 250–252
    reporting 252–253
    selection 251
    setting 244–250

legacy income 234–235
Leitch, Matthew 141, 143, 149,
    150–152
Liker, Jeffrey 22
liquidity 115–116, 117
Loungani, Prakash 225
Lynch, David 219

McLeod Grant, Heather 96–97, 332,
    337, 348, 349
management
    relationship with internal
        audit 154–156
management accounting
    characteristics 201–207
    definition 202
    role 201–202
management accounts
    access 205, 217–218
    accuracy 204
    benchmarking 206–207
    by fund and activity 210–211
    comparison with statutory
        accounts 209–210
    face-to-face presentations 217
    format and structure 207–209
    graphic representation 215–217
    intelligible 204–205
    interpreting actuals 218–221
    presentation 211–218
    relevance 202–203
    timeliness 203–204
    trend analyses 212–214
management costs 261–262

management information systems 335,
    339
    collaborative approach 340–341
    development 344–346
    procurement risks 346–347
    simplification 344
    standardisation 344
manager
    financial stewardship role 310–311
Mawji, Amin 346–347
meetings 305–306
Merriam-Webster 318
mission statement 320
Moore, Mark H. 47–48

National Hub of Expertise in
    Governance 140, 303
Nitterhouse, Denise 78, 129, 246
Norton, David 31, 39, 41, 60–62,
    253–254
not-for-profit organisations
    accountability 1
    corporate alliances 96–97
    see also third sector

OECD 6, 18, 71, 128
    performance management case
        study 64–68
ORC Worldwide 326–327

Paton, Rob 33, 35, 36, 254–255, 275
pay
    financial stewards 320–325
performance management
    case study of OECD member
        governments 64–68
    cycle 40
    evidence-based 27–31
    financial stewards 328–329
    target setting risk 22
    UK government case study 69–71

performance measurement
  approaches 35, 36
  benchmarking 206–207
  key performance indicators
    (KPIs) 31–34, 244–256
performance review *see* business review
Peters, Tom 335
Pfeffer, Jeffrey 28–30, 39, 41, 42, 43, 52
political dimension
  strategic planning 45–48
Porter, Michael 39, 268
pricing policy
  internal pricing 274
procurement risks 153–154
  information technology 346–347
professional development
  financial stewards 330–331
public meetings 305–306
public relations
  financial statements 228
published accounts *see* financial
  statements
Purves, Libby 19

recruitment
  financial stewards 325–327
Rejc, Adriana 145
remuneration
  financial stewards 320–325
remuneration committee 300
reserves
  allocation 260
  definition 102–103
  designated funds, impact of 102, 103
  forecasting expendable reserves 235
  reasons for holding 100–102
  size, determining
    appropriate 103–106
  written policy 107–108
resource allocation *see* funds allocation
restricted funds/income 89–92
  accounting implications 91–92
  burden 91

restricted funds/income—*continued*
  management of level of balances 100
review *see* annual review; business
  review
reward strategy
  Sightsavers International 323–324
  World Bank 320
risk
  handling trust funds 90
risk management 139–144
  compliance burden 140–141
  definition 141
  effective risk control 148–154
  example risk controls 152
  financial stewardship risk 144–145
  procurement 153–154, 346–347
  risk-control processes 141–144
  Toyota Production System 150
  traditional process 145–148
Roche, Chris 133, 135
Rodriguez, Jair 225
Rosenberg, Deborah 213
running costs
  identifying 104–105, 237

salaries
  financial stewards 320–325
Sargeant, Adrian 234
Sayer Vincent 142, 153
Scott, Graham 5, 24–25, 26, 161, 328
Scottish Enterprise
  role of chief financial officer 6–7
Seddon, John 19, 20, 30–31
senior executive
  financial stewardship role 306–311
  role distinct from trustee 296–297,
    306
Sightsavers International
  expenditure distribution 130–132
  internal audit 157
  management accounts 209–210
  reserves policy 108
  reward policy 323–324

Sightsavers International—*continued*
  strategic framework case study 58–64
  tracking key performance indicators
    (KPIs) 253
solvency 116–118
SORP 2005 *Accounting and Reporting by Charities* 75, 100, 130
Stacey, Ralph 43, 48–50, 317
stakeholders
  political commitment 46
Statement of Financial Activities
  (SOFA) 78–81
  cash flow illustration 118–121
  interpretation 80–81
  relationship with balance sheet 79
statutory accounts *see* financial
  statements
strategic alliances
  corporate not-for-profit alliances 97
strategic planning 41–50
  chaos management model 48–50
  determining priorities 50–53
  development process 44–50
  political decision-making
    model 45–48
  rational model 44–45
  trade-offs 53
strategy
  definitions 39
  implementing 54–55
  Sightsavers International case
    study 58–64
  see also finance strategy
strategy map
  Sightsavers International 60–62
Sutton, Robert I. 28–30, 39, 41, 52

Taleb, Nassim Nicholas 143
Tame, John 103
target setting 17–22
  criticism 18–21, 248–249
  implications for accountability 22–27
  performance management, risk to 22

target setting—*continued*
  using key performance indicators
    (KPIs) 31–34, 244–250
third sector
  UK government funding relationship
    with 87–88
  see also not-for-profit organisations
Toyota
  embedded risk management 150
trading
  not-for-profit enterprises 97
transparency 249–250
  information access 342
treasurer
  role 301–303
treasury management 228
trustees
  accountability 140, 303–306
  annual review 304–305
  delegating responsibilities 299
  financial stewardship governance
    role 297
  responsibilities for financial
    stewardship 296, 297–298
  role 295–296
  role distinct from senior
    executive 296–297, 306
trustees' report 140, 304, 305

UK government
  departmental expenditure
    limits 180–181
  full cost recovery endorsement 87–88
  performance management case
    study 69–71
United Nations
  Millennium Development Goals 23,
    194–195
unrestricted funds/income 89
  management of level of balances 100
Unwin, Julia 85–88, 94, 110

value for money 127–128

Warnes, Brian 84, 115, 118, 124
Wheatley, Margaret 30–31
Williams, Clyde *et al* 340, 341, 344
Williams, Harold S. *et al* 24, 42–43,
   95–96, 168
World Bank 2, 328
   business review report formats 281
   employment value proposition 320
   funds allocation 179
   funds handling 89–90
   HR business review process 286–288
   impact evaluation 135–136
   impact measurement 134

Zanini, Michele 143–144